HOW TO MAKE MONEY WRITING ABOUT FITNESS AND HEALTH

*Celia G. Scully and
Thomas J. Scully, M.D.*

Writer's
Digest
Books
CINCINNATI, OHIO

How to Make Money Writing About Fitness and Health. Copyright ©1986 by Celia G. Scully and Thomas J. Scully, M.D. Printed and bound in the United States of America. All rights reserved. No part of this book may be reproduced in any form or by any electronic or mechanical means including information storage and retrieval systems without permission in writing from the publisher, except by a reviewer, who may quote brief passages in a review. Published by Writer's Digest Books, 9933 Alliance Road, Cincinnati, Ohio 45242. First edition.

Library of Congress Cataloging-in-Publication Data

Scully, Celia G. 1932-
   How to make money writing about fitness and health.
   Bibliography: p.
   Includes index.
   1. Health—Authorship. 2. Physical fitness—
   Authorship. I. Scully, Thomas J., 1932-
   II. Title.
RA773.6.S38   1986   808'.066613   86-11021
ISBN 0-89879-237-1

Design by Joan Ann Jacobus

The following four pages are an extension of this copyright page.

PERMISSIONS ACKNOWLEDGMENTS

To C.B.G.
With love and appreciation

CONTENTS

ACKNOWLEDGMENTS

This book would never have come into being without the help, advice, morale boosting, and midwifery of many friends, health-care professionals, writers, editors, word-processing instructors, and reference librarians who came to our rescue time and time again. To all who shared with us their time, ideas, experience, and expertise, we say thank you.

However, there are some who have been so generous in assisting us that they deserve a special word of appreciation here: fellow writers Mike Land and Alice Fleming for their suggestions and encouragement; Connie Emerson, whose editorial advice and unfailing good sense are always right on target; research assistants Bill Chau and Derek Newman; Jeff Vind and Tammy Anderson, who graciously helped us through all word-processing disasters; librarians at the University of Nevada-Reno Getchell Library, especially Jack Ritenhouse, Judy Sokol, and Susan Conway; Chuck Manley and his research staff at Washoe County Library; Joan Zenon, Laurie Conway, and other staff members of the University of Nevada School of Medicine's Savitt Library.

No book is born without the special support of many people behind the scenes. We wish to thank Carol Cartaino and Nancy Dibble of Writer's Digest Books for their editorial direction, as well as Leon Mandel, who introduced us to his literary agent—and now ours—Jacques de Spoelberch. Finally, we owe much to our children, whose love, patience, and encouragement meant most—especially when dinners were do-it-yourself affairs night after night and every chair in the house was piled high with papers, research materials, and book chapters in the making.

□ PROLOGUE FROM HIPPOCRATES TO ANN LANDERS AND BEYOND

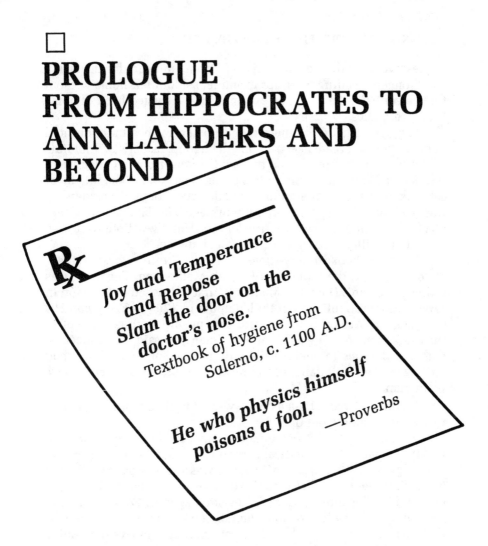

℞

Joy and Temperance
and Repose
Slam the door on the
doctor's nose.

Textbook of hygiene from
Salerno, c. 1100 A.D.

He who physics himself
poisons a fool.
—Proverbs

Some things never change.

No one wants to get sick while traveling. Busy men and women can't afford to lose a day's work because of illness. Every mother and father finds a guidebook handy in raising little ones and coping with high fevers or croup at 3 A.M. An apple a day still has its merits. Writers find a market ever ready for the latest on psyche, soma, sex, making sense of self, achieving fitness and good health. And the pendulum continues to swing from traditional to unorthodox, from scientific medicine to medicine *without* doctors.

The history of health and medical writing for the general public is a fascinating story of turf wars; conflicting idealogies, fads, frauds and phonies, and health pioneers—lay people as well as doctors, nurses, ministers, and others who firmly believed people should know how to preserve their own health, raise children, and care for the sick.

Pioneers heading west, for example, seldom left home without three essentials: the Bible, an almanac, and a trusted book of home health remedies.

The colonists before them relied on several health guides and publicly posted broadsheets, among them John Tacher's *A Brief Rule to Guide the Common People of New England How to Order Themselves and Theirs in the Small Pox or Measels* (1677). The first medical book published in the colonies and designed for public readership was Nicholas Culpepper's ninety-four-page *The English Physician* (1708). Culpepper also wrote *Directory for Midwives*. Both were easy to read and filled with practical medical advice.

Two other books deserve note. One was *Primitive Physick* (1747) by John Wesley, the founder of English Methodism. The other was William Buchan's *Domestic Medicine*, first published in Scotland in 1769, and later published in Philadelphia in 1795 as *Everyman His Own Doctor*. Wesley believed ordinary people were competent to treat sickness, and he was blunt. Physicians, he said, had concocted complex theories to confuse the ordinary person and "filled their writing with an abundance of technical terms utterly unintelligible to plain man."

Technical jargon, then as now, was a bugaboo to understanding that writers capitalized on.

As early as 1690, the Boston newspaper *Publick Occurrences* carried two paragraphs of medical news on smallpox in the area and epidemic fevers. In 1708, a Nicholas Boone was advertising in the *Boston Newsletter* that he sold Daffy's Elixir Salutis, Turlington's Balsam of Life, and Dr. Benjamin Godfrey's Cordial. Begun in 1704, the *Boston Newsletter* was the first of 200 colonial newspapers that for the most part carried items of medical interest, including essays on treating and preventing disease.

John Tennant's *Everyman His Own Doctor* or *The Poor Planter's Physician* was published in Williamsburg, Virginia, in 1734, and eventually went through four printings.

Poor Richard's Almanack and *Pennsylvania Gazette*, both published by Benjamin Franklin, frequently carried health aphorisms such as the familiar "Early to bed, early to rise/Makes a man healthy, wealthy and wise." *The Almanack* also carried excerpts from medical books, such as Lobb's *Directions for the Management of Children in Health and with an Account of the Distempers Common to Them* (1763).

By 1783, 1,700 almanacs had been printed in the colonies; 500 of these contained health information. Magazines as a source of health information began in 1741 with publication of *The American Maga-*

zine. A collection of letters, published in 1772 by the English physician Hugh Smith, found widespread acceptance under the title, *Letters to Married Women on Nursing and the Management of Children.*

By the early 1800s, health writing was flourishing. For example, Sir John Sinclair listed 1,878 books on health and hygiene in the bibliography to his four-volume work, *Code of Health and Longevity.* Within the next thirty years, hundreds of self-help and domestic health guides were published; among the best known were *The American Medical Guide for Use of Families* (1810) by Thomas W. Ruble, M.D.; *The Treasure of Health* (1819) by Lewis Merlien; *New Guide to Health or Authentic Family Physician* (1822) by Samuel Thompson, a New England farmer and proponent of herbal medicine; *Treatise of Domestic Medicine* (1824) by Thomas Cooper. In 1839, William A. Alcott's book *The Young Mother* acknowledged the father's extended absence from home and recognized mothers as having primary responsibility for child rearing.

However, it was a *mother* of eight children who, in 1811, wrote the first American book on child care and feeding of infants, *The Maternal Physician.* "Every mother," the anonymous author said, "ought to have a general knowledge of them (botanical remedies) so that she may prescribe them for slight complaints with ease to herself and infinite benefit to her little family."

These guides were written directly for the public, encouraging readers to treat themselves and their families when physicians were unavailable or those who called themselves doctors posed a danger to one's health. Many doctors, for instance, relied on harsh treatments, including purging and bloodletting. This was the Jacksonian period of American history, with its egalitarian spirit, strong anti-intellectualism, suspicion of "experts," and deep-seated belief in individual rights and self-reliance.

By mid-nineteenth century, the health reform movement was in full swing. Spiritualism was sweeping the country, and there was an explosion of interest in sports and exercise. All were part of a general movement toward social reform. Health advisors cautioned against the dangers of sedentary life in the workplace and urged balance between physical and mental labor.

Titles of new health guides flooded the market—books like Dr. A. Rogers's *The Annual Family Receipt Book or Every Body's Book* (1854); George Beard's *Our Home Physician—a New and Popular Guide to the Art of Preserving Health and Treating Disease* (1879); and Frederick Castle's *Woods Household Practice of Medicine, Hygiene and Surgery* (1880).

One of the best sellers of its time, Gunn's *New Domestic Physician, or Home Book of Health,* was first published in 1830 as *Domes-*

tic *Medicine* or *Poor Man's Friend*. By 1870 under its new title, it reached its one hundredth printing with no signs of slowing down. Gunn, a physician, claimed the book was written "In Plain Language Free from Doctor's Terms . . . intended expressly for the benefit of families."

Many Americans, distrustful of traditional medicine, turned to herbalists, hydropaths, homeopaths, naturopaths, lay healers, and spiritualists—each with a different set of theories, books, pamphlets, and guides. For example, *Water-Cure Journal* editor Russel T. Trall stated that "Nature Cures."

In 1873, Lydia Estes Pinkham built a multimillion-dollar business around a patent medicine for female complaints; contributing to this success were the compound's 18 percent alcohol content and her shrewd philsophy that "only a woman understands a woman's ills." In advertising her Vegetable Compound, Pinkham encouraged women to write her for advice about intimate health problems. Thousands of women responded to her selling point *and* promise that "no male eye would see the letters."

This need to communicate about fundamental health concerns hasn't changed in the last 100 years. Witness Ann Landers's 1985 sex survey in which more than 90,000 American women responded to her one question: "Would you be content to be held close and treated tenderly, and forget about 'the act'?" (Sex researchers are still trying to explain why more than two-thirds of the respondents said they prefer cuddling to "the act.")

Women's health issues began to appear in popular magazines at the turn of the century. In 1913, for instance, *The Ladies' Home Journal* published one of the first articles for the general public on cancer and the importance of early detection and treatment. However, seven years earlier, in 1906, the *Journal* had lost 75,000 subscribers when it published an editorial titled "Frankness with Children," which dealt with venereal disease.

Other pioneering articles in *The Ladies' Home Journal* accelerated the attack on the patent-medicine industry. (In 1892, editor Curtis Bok had closed the pages of the *Journal* to such advertising, stating, "Our first consideration is the protection and welfare of our readers").

In October 1905, *Collier's Weekly* launched the first of two series on medical quacks and patent medicines in one of American history's most famous investigations of the drug industry. That same year, the American Medical Association closed its own *Journal* to patent-medicine advertisements, and over the next five years the AMA distributed 150,000 copies of *Collier's* "The Great American Fraud."

Change was in the wind. In the 1919 edition of *The People's Com-*

mon *Sense Medical Advisor*, Dr. R. V. Pierce (one target of the *Collier's* series) urged readers to consult a physician at once in serious illness, admitting he was not so "presumptuous" as to hold that his book could make "every man his own physician."

SELF-HELP LITERATURE

Popular self-help literature was not strictly an American or British phenomenon. It was well developed in the fourteenth century when the Black Death was ravaging Europe.

At that time, Guy de Chauliac of France and other physicians wrote more than 280 *Plague Tracts* which not only described the Black Death but gave advice on how to prevent and treat the dread disease. Many were written in common language for the public. In 1348, Jaom d'Agramont of Lerida, Spain, wrote such a tract for "the common good." These tracts marked the beginnings of public health writing en *masse*. For example, on presenting his work to the city fathers, d'Agramont asked that it be given "to anybody who wishes to make a copy of it."

Before that, nearly all medical writing was designed to inform and guide the professional healer, medical student, physician, and surgeon.

Earliest how-to's on record are two Egyptian papyruses. The *Papyrus Ebers* (known as the "Book of Wounds") is a kind of medical textbook written around 1550 B.C. An even earlier work, the *Edwin Smith Papryus*, is a sixteenth century B.C. copy of an original probably written between 3000 and 2500 B.C. This manuscript records forty-two medical cases with recommended treatment, plus another sixteen the author deemed fatal and thus "an ailment not to be treated."

Hippocrates' *On Ancient Medicine* may well be the first known attempt to write about medicine for the *general public*. One of about seventy documents collected by his followers, it's found in the *Corpus Hippocratum*, which also contains the famous "oath" and the dictum "First, do no harm."

Before his time, medicine in the Greek world was closely linked to philosophy. Greek philosophers were, by definition, both teacher and physician. Many traveled the countryside dispensing advice and treating the sick—early versions of Dear Abby, Dr. Spock, and Jack LaLanne. (Greek medicine had a strong gymnastic element as well.)

During the Middle Ages, traveling healers attached parchment pages to their belts. Called *Ready Reckoners*, they were distant cousins of today's *Merck Manual*, an internationally recognized summary of up-to-date diagnosis and treatment. An eleventh-century general text on medical practice contained sixty-three chapters on women's diseases and childbirth written by a *woman* from Salerno known only as Trotula. The following century, Hildegaard of Bingen, a Benedictine abbess, wrote several works on nursing care. But it was Louise Bourgeois, midwife to the French court and Marie de'Medici, who, in the late fourteenth and early fifteenth centuries, wrote several texts on childbirth "to advise any woman interested in midwifery" and used pictures to make it easier.

In 1558, Luigi Cornaro wrote *Discourses on a Sober and Temperate Life*. Destined to become one of the most popular health guides of all time, Cornaro's book linked health and longevity to moderation of one's personal habits.

About this time, peasant women healers in Europe (in France, they were called *Les Sages Femmes*, or "wise women") began compiling guides to home-brew folk remedies and herbal cures. These "Herbals" and so-called Books of Secrets were storehouses of medical and pharmaceutical knowledge used extensively during the sixteenth and seventeenth centuries by successful do-it-yourself healers.

Such books were forerunners of home cookbooks which, well into the 1920s, still held recipes for poultices, mustard plasters, chamomile tea, and other home remedies. For instance, *The Home Cookbook* (1877) offered this advice in the "Medicinal Receipts" section: "To Restore From Stroke of Lightning: shower with cold water for two hours; if the patient does not show signs of life, put salt in the water, and shower an hour longer." Not all folk remedies were winners; but many were.

THE AGE OF CLEANLINESS

By the end of the nineteenth century, people had become aware of germs as a cause of infectious disease. In 1885, for example, a *Popular Science Monthly* article attributed a large part of the expanding interest in medicine to the public's acceptance of the germ theory, thanks to the pioneering work of Koch and Pasteur. Cleanliness, which John Wesley had proclaimed two centuries earlier as being "next to godliness," was now the order of the day.

Harvey Green, in his book *Our Homes and How to Make Them Healthy* (1883), extolled the virtues of the well-ordered house and the influence of a clean physical environment—including clean air and pure water. Beginning in 1897, the Sears catalogs became a major source of information for many housewives about soaps, laundering, toileting, and disinfectants.

But sex was still taboo. Not until 1929 did a newspaper dare to print the word *syphilis.* (In 1934, The National Broadcasting Company would not allow Dr. J. L. Rice to use that word on the air in a speech on public health.) However, an important turning point in the banning of all books on sex had come a few years earlier when federal judge Woolsey in 1927 lifted the federal ban on books about sex "published in good faith and with serious purpose." *Married Love,* by a Mrs. Stoop, was judged not to be obscene literature.

The modern era of health writing for the general public began in earnest with the first appearance in 1935 of *Modern Home Medical Advisor,* edited by Morris Fishbein, M.D. Currently marketed by the American Medical Association as *The Handy Home Medical Advisor,* the book has sold more than 1 million copies.

But that pales in comparison with *Baby and Child Care* by Dr. Benjamin Spock, which has sold more than 30 million copies since 1945. Coincidentally, in 1946, the Grolier Club of America listed *The Care and Feeding of Children* by L. Emmett Holt, M.D., first published in 1895, as one of the 100 books that most influenced the life and culture of the American people.

While Holt was giving advice to parents, the January 16, 1896, front page of *The New York Times* carried the news of the discovery of X rays in Germany. According to the lead paragraph, "Men of science in this city are awaiting with the utmost impatience arrival of European technical journals which will give them the full particulars of Professor Roentgen's great discovery. . . ." Then as now, the public often had medical news before physicians had an opportunity to learn the details through their professional journals and medical conferences.

But it was not until the early 1930s that science and medical writing emerged as a specialty within journalism. In 1934, the National Association of Science Writers was formed, followed by the American Medical Writers Association six years later.

No prologue, of course, can do justice to the whole story of medical advice and self-help literature. Limited space allows only the highlights in the saga of getting the health word out to the public in countless ways that have included books, magazines, newspapers, pamphlets, catalogs, cookbooks, almanacs, religious texts, advertisements, package inserts, children's primers, novels, poems, and proverbs.

One thing, however, is clear. Writing about health and medical matters has been, and continues to be, one of the most popular nonfiction topics of all times.

Across the centuries, people have had a love-hate relationship with medicine. And today, along with high-tech medicine, there's a growing emphasis on preventive medicine and self-help. *Megatrends* author John Naisbitt stated at a 1985 American Medical Association leadership conference, "the emphasis on taking care of one's own medical well-being is here to stay."

As a writer, you have a special role in promoting health and well-being. You also are writing at one of the most exciting and challenging periods of history. Over the centuries, human beings have evolved in one g of gravity. The *zero-gravity* environment of space opens up new vistas for medical and scientific research and manufacturing—and with it, new hope for medical advances.

Meanwhile, on planet earth, men and women—as they have for centuries—still look to writers to help them in raising their children, living healthier lives, and protecting the environment for future generations. Your work is cut out for you.

Enjoy it in good health.

1 □ HEALTH BEAT: THE CHANGING MEDICAL SCENE

He who has health has hope, and he who has hope has everything.
—Arabian Proverb

There are only two great roles—that of the doctor and that of the patient, quips Woody Allen in his film *Zelig*. What he doesn't say is that often these two aren't speaking the same language. While this may be bad for the patient, it's good news for writers who can come up with the kind of news, information, and stories patients need, readers want, and editors buy.

I didn't realize this until one of my first health-related articles, "How to Talk to Your Child's Doctor," was bought by *Ladycom*, a publication circulated to nearly a half million wives of military men living in the United States and overseas. At the time, I was primarily a travel writer. Though married to a pediatrician, up to that point I hadn't been thinking of medicine as a popular topic or myself as a health writer.

Yet once I linked health and travel, two other sales followed quickly to *Odyssey*. One covered traveling with sick children—something I had done all too many times as an Air Force wife moving with five youngsters. The other dealt with health considerations in traveling with grandparents. (My father had just had a total hip replacement and, feeling like a new man, wanted to make up for lost time in the sight-seeing department.)

Back home, I began checking our local newspaper for events which might trigger health-article ideas. When I spotted a feature in the arts section on a teenage drama group staging musicals in sign language, I worked it into a piece for *Grit* titled "Theater of Silence—Performing Teens Break 'Sound Barrier'."

STARTING OUT

A notice tacked to a campus bulletin board alerted me to one of the first talks given in America by controversial French obstetrician Frederick LeBoyer, an advocate of birth without violence. Arranging an interview through the university's public-information office, I was amazed to learn that the *only* other writer who had asked to cover the event was Caterine Millinaire on assignment from *People Weekly* in New York.

Given a controversial figure in medical circles and a fresh approach to easing a baby's first moments of life, the story potential seemed obvious to me. Where were the *other* free-lancers from my area?

Since then, in my hometown, I've interviewed people like F. Story Musgrave, M.D., America's first doctor-astronaut to walk in space, and Virginia Satir, famous the world over for her pioneering work in family therapy training. I've been asked to edit a 600-page psychiatric text on borderline personalities and an 80-page pictorial guide for those who work with disabled people. With a sports psychologist, I coauthored an article on elite athletes for *The Olympian* and now, we're expanding those same ideas into a book for recreational athletes. An audio cassette will follow.

Like everyone else, I've had my share of rejection slips and articles that needed reworking. I've learned from them. I've learned, too, from health experts—especially those who have asked me to consult on completed manuscripts they've sent out time and again to publishers and magazines to no avail. "What's wrong?" they ask. "This is as good as, if not better than, the stuff already out there. How do you go about getting published? Do I need an agent?"

There's no one answer to why a particular article won't sell or how you go about getting published. There are, however, a variety of ways that you as a *health-oriented* writer can increase your chances of success.

WHO IS A HEALTH WRITER?

If you've been thinking about writing and fall into one or more of the groups that follow, this book can help you meet your goals:

• *You are a health-care professional*—a nurse, physician, dentist, psychologist, nutritionist, administrator—who wants to write for the public and communicate your ideas, concerns, new and successful programs or practices.

• *You are a scholar, researcher, academician, or graduate student.* You'd like a wider audience for your findings, whether they're the result of years of clinical or laboratory studies, or slave labor on a thesis or dissertation.

• *You are a teacher, counselor, coach, trainer, health educator.* You've pinpointed a need for a new patient-information sheet, employee-training manual or guide, or textbook with study guide for elementary, high school, or college-level use.

• *You are a homemaker, office worker, athlete, parent, or patient* whose personal experience or special expertise has given you unusual insight into an area of health, healing, or heartbreak—but you're having trouble putting the words on paper or getting them published.

• *You are a writer* who wants to know how to break into the health and medical-writing field, what qualifications it takes and where to sell what you write.

If you've yet to publish your first piece, this book will alert you to the vast opportunities for publishing in this growing, well-paying, and rewarding field. It will peel away the mystique that surrounds the medical and allied health professions. And it will help you better understand the process from brainstorm to by-line as it relates to writing nonfiction for the popular or medical media.

No book, of course, can guarantee you a sale or a magic formula for cracking a particular market. But all writers agree that the things you care most about are the ones you'll write best about. They're also the ones you're most likely to sell. Writing about health and medical matters can give you the best of both worlds—a chance to write about what you care deeply about and on subjects that make a difference in readers' lives.

This was a point made often at a recent workshop on writing for the health and fitness markets, sponsored by the American Society of Journalists and Authors. Said one author with fourteen books to her credit: "Writing about health and medicine gives you an opportunity to be a do-gooder in a *constructive* way—and it's also financially profitable."

HEALTH—A HOT ITEM IN A GROWING MARKET

The fact is, if ever there was an exciting time to write about health and medical matters, it's now.

Revolutionary changes are sweeping the nation's health-care system. The stories are there. The market is expanding. Wellness is in; sickness is out. With a renewed sense of self-help, Americans are focusing on heathier life-styles and physical and emotional well-being.

Caught up in the trends, issues, breakthroughs, advances, and dilemmas of the health-care field, people want information. Editors want to provide it. So do health professionals who know the doctor-patient information gap has never been more critical or costly. In audiovisual companies, publishing houses, and editorial offices from coast to coast, the welcome mat is out for the writer who can bridge the gap with energy, enthusiasm, and know-how.

Can you write for this rewarding and growing market? You can if you're willing to discipline yourself, hone your writing and research skills, and learn more about the health and medical field.

Let's take a closer look at what's going on in this all-important area and what it takes to break into it.

The Well Body is "In"

Keeping it that way is fast becoming top priority as the realities of medical economics sink in and changing American life-styles focus on health and fitness. "Fitness isn't just a fad, it's a major life-style shift and it's here to stay," says best-selling author and motivational psychologist Denis E. Waitley. The evidence is clear.

Twenty years ago, only 24 percent of adults were exercising daily. A 1983 *Reader's Digest*/Gallup survey, however, showed that 77 percent of American adults engage in some kind of physical exercise or sport; nearly half (47 percent) do so daily.

A 1984 *Better Homes & Gardens* survey reported in *USA Today* revealed the following major health concerns. In looking at these statistics shaping our lives, it's important to remember that respondents could choose more than one answer.

Maintaining the right weight	81.4 percent
Getting the right exercise	77.5
Eating a balanced diet	74.9
Using less sugar	50.8
Getting enough sleep	49.9

Leading researcher Daniel Yankelovich, in an interview with *American Health* editor T. George Harris, confirmed that Americans are focusing on their physical well-being, energy levels, and healthy lifestyles. "As I read the polls," said Yankelovich, "the desire for physical well-being has been at the top of the list of American needs, except when it was topped by the need to *look* healthy."

For free-lancers, this means the celebrity interview and carefully researched how-to or service piece packed with information and quotes from health, fitness, diet, or dental experts have never had better chances of selling. If you happen to be an expert who can write well, you're way ahead of your competition. Look at Norman Cousins's *Anatomy of an Illness; Pulling Your Own Strings* by psychologist Wayne Dyer; *Second Opinion* by Isadore Rosenfeld, M.D.; and *The Jane Fonda Workout Book.*

Don't forget that Americans are among the most health-conscious people on earth. In a 1982 Gallup poll, they ranked being in good health second only to having a good family life. A survey by Louis Harris and Associates, Inc., for Playboy Enterprises found health *first* in the top eleven values of men eighteen to forty-nine years old.

While American men and women may not follow through on giving up smoking in twenty-four hours, losing ten pounds, cutting down on salt, or reducing corporate stress, they avidly soak up all the news, inspiration, information, and self-help that writers, editors, and cassette manufacturers come up with. And the incentives to work at health are growing.

Today, staying well is everybody's business—and *big* business. Insurance-premium breaks, for example, are being considered for thin nonsmokers. Thousands of companies operate health-promotion programs for employees and executives (and not infrequently a top executive's personal experience with bypass surgery, lung cancer, or high blood pressure played a major role in initiating such programs). According to a *New York Times* report, one consultant in the field says market data shows overall industry expenditures "in the area of $1 billion." And the market is ripe for more. For instance, market researchers at a Minneapolis company which develops computer software and other services for such programs have found "a multibillion-dollar potential" for such employee-health promotion products and services—good news for writers who can produce vital backup materials.

America's Love Affair with Medicine is Over.

Like any split when there's been a long and close relationship, there's disillusionment, anger, struggle for control, and poor communication between medicine and clients. Some say, too, there are broken promises—for everything from medicare payments to cures for cancer and, ultimately, for death itself.

How we've gotten to this point in medicine and where health care is heading in this country are elegantly analyzed by Paul Starr in his widely acclaimed book *The Social Transformation of Medicine*. The noted Harvard sociologist and Pulitzer Prize winner traces two hundred years of dramatic changes in American attitudes toward medicine—attitudes that allowed hospitals to become medical workshops while government programs subsidized and further enhanced the dominant role of doctors.

This alliance has been costly. In 1983, for example, Americans spent an estimated $355 billion on health care—making it the nation's number one industry. Predictions are that the country's health-care costs will double every six years until they reach $1.9 *trillion* by 1999.

The first wealth may be health, as Ralph Waldo Emerson claimed, but increasingly Congress, taxpayers, patients, and health-care professionals themselves are unhappy with the system and care it provides. The result? In record numbers, Americans are checking out other health-care options, therapies, and approaches to wellness such as holistic healing and Oriental medicine.

Congress is demanding accountability. Patients and their families are demanding greater *say* in decision making. Attorneys are fighting for and winning ever-larger awards in malpractice suits. At the same time, doctors are not only losing the traditional control they exerted over the system, they're being threatened by a new industry of health-care conglomerates that may well prove no more economical, humane, or responsive to the public's needs.

Market Growth

Each year *Writer's Market* lists more than 4,000 places to sell what you write. In the "Health and Fitness" category alone, twenty-four publications were listed in 1984, an increase of 30 percent from the year before. The 1985 edition describes thirty-one publications in the same category, representing a 29 percent jump in health and fitness markets over 1984. And that's only a sampling of statistics on this dramatic increase.

Virtually every publication (large or small circulation) is a potential market for the targeted, carefully researched, well-crafted health-related story. If in doubt, check the magazine cover lines at your nearest newsstand. Look in the city, regional, and in-flight publications next time you're traveling. Don't forget the Sunday newspaper magazine supplements like *USA Weekend* and *Parade*.

You may not find "health" per se, but you're sure to find articles on everything from acid rain and its effect on the food we eat to behavior and coping strategies for single parents; health spas and resorts featuring fitness facilities; the latest in microbe power and science; where we are in the battle against Alzheimer's disease, impotence, herpes, or AIDS (acquired immune deficiency syndrome); how diet can alter mood and behavior or affect cancer; what we're learning from space-age medicine, and why hospital treatment at home is a $7 billion industry that's just beginning to take off. The latter appeared in the August, 1984, issue of *Venture, the Magazine for Entrepreneurs* and points up the growing relationship between business and the for-profit sector of medicine.

"Health is an area that just snuck up on us," explains Reno-based free-lancer Joan Morrow. "First it was running, and everyone said, 'ha, ha.' Then it was stress and aerobics, and they said, 'just a passing fancy.' Then diet and vitamins. Now health is a topic that's become very important to people and the magazines are full of it—not just the specialty ones on running and fitness, but just about every magazine you pick up."

Not only that, editors like Kate Rand Lloyd of *Working Woman* feel a need to keep readers abreast of health issues. "I believe that all women's magazines have a responsibility in their own way to make women aware of health issues. Because as women . . . we have been too much the victim of the first-you-get-sick-syndrome, then call-the-doctor-pattern in matters of health. And we can't afford that—the time it takes to be ill, or the costs. We can't afford," she says, "the *damage* to our lives."

Nor is it only the mass media that has discovered the value of good medical writing.

"The relatively recent finding that it's important to *repeat* information to patients is beginning to penetrate medicine and health care," says University of Nevada—Reno professor Barbara C. Thornton, coauthor with Gary L. Kreps of a college textbook, *Health Communication*. "The challenge becomes particularly acute in instruction sheets where information needs to be condensed to one or two pages," she says. "Nowhere are content, organization and delivery such a challenge."

MEETING THE CHALLENGE

Writers who can take complex topics and produce accurate, clear, fair, and concise information not only provide a service—they earn anywhere from $25 to $75 an hour doing it. The full range of opportunities for free-lance writers is covered in chapters 3 and 14. Included are everything from writing for medical trade publications and creating audiovisual materials used in professional continuing education to producing weekly newspaper columns, self-help books, and salable magazine articles.

In every community, first-class stories are there for the digging. You see them in television documentaries; radio news features; newspaper op-ed (opposite editorial page) pieces; association newsletters; alternate care and holistic medicine publications; and in the press releases or announcements from medical societies, hospitals, professional schools, and state health-care agencies. You may have to read between the lines to find the story-behind-the-story, but top-flight medical writers know when to put their investigative skills to work.

Any writer who isn't cashing in on this rapidly expanding interest in keeping body, psyche, nation, and health-care industry running at top efficiency is missing a good bet. You don't have to have an M.D., R.N., Ph.D. or other impressive initials after your name to crack this wide-open market. What's important is knowing what to look for, who to ask, and how to evaluate the answers you get and communicate them to others.

SHOULD NONPROFESSIONALS WRITE ABOUT HEALTH?

At this point you may be asking yourself, as I used to, whether someone who doesn't have a scientific or medical background should be writing about health, medical research, or bioethical issues. I know physicians who state in no uncertain terms that no one but a trained health professional can understand complex medical issues and that no layperson should ever write about medicine. On the other hand, I've talked to editors who feel just as strongly that doctors write only for *other doctors.*

These editors know that all too often the message doesn't get to the public unless a professional writer has a hand in shaping the material. While reworking a manuscript is sometimes carried out in-house by a publication's staff members, just as often a ghostwriter, co-author or editorial consultant who can work with the expert is just what the doctor ordered.

Here's what *The New York Times* medical correspondent and columnist Lawrence K. Altman, M.D., said when I asked him if there's a danger in having a person without a medical degree reporting on medical and scientific news. "Degrees don't necessarily give competence in explaining things clearly."

"Non-medical-degreed persons writing and asking questions may be more akin to the patient's asking questions, so it may be a decided advantage," says Altman, one of the nation's few full-time physician-journalists. "What counts is how the answers to those questions are organized, interpreted, put in perspective as well as being able to assess whether those answers are on target or not. For example, just because an M.D. says black is white, doesn't make it true."

When it comes to the black-is-white syndrome, experienced writers and journalists know one of the best antidotes is checking out facts and getting information from several different sources. "You develop a sixth sense," one writer told me. "You *know* when something doesn't sound right—whether it's your own words or somebody else's."

In part, a sixth sense is intuition. But it's also the subconscious interplay between your hunches: what you already know about a subject; your experience in interviewing authorities in the field; and the degree of skill you have as a writer and researcher. The more experience and skill you have, the *sharper* that sixth sense becomes.

REAPING THE REWARDS

Whether you're writing the history of your local hospital, a patient brochure on a new medical procedure, a television script, a book, an article, or a health textbook and teacher's manual for grades four through six, you'll find health and medical writers can help narrow the information gap and make money, too.

But you'll also discover something else. While it's satisfying to bank incoming checks for your writing, some of your most rewarding stories will be those you don't make a dime on.

Your words, for example, may help a terminally ill child take that once-in-a-lifetime trip to Disney World; assist a disabled person in finding work in your community; put families of patients with rare or chronic diseases in contact with each other as well as with regional or national sources of help. Your writing may spur fund-raising efforts for a desperately needed transplant organ or an operation to improve the quality of life for someone you barely know.

It's these stories, which sometimes fall into the "freebie" category, that often enrich your own life far beyond dollars and cents.

In short, it's a rewarding time to be a health or medical writer. The market is expanding. The opportunities are numerous. And despite what some writers will tell you about an overcrowded field, there's always room at the top for the best writers.

If you are a layperson, don't let the technical nature of science and medical writing scare you off. Don't let yourself be intimidated by the medical or scientific community. Yes, there are some writing assignments that require basic-science or health-sciences degrees—particularly in full- or part-time positions in the pharmaceutical industry. For the most part, however, the right research, basic intelligence, a willingness to learn more about medical or scientific subjects, plus the ability to write well will enable you to tackle *any* subject.

A deaf and blind mother of four whom I once interviewed told me. "You're only handicapped if you let yourself *think* that way."

If you want to write about health and medical subjects but feel hesitant about starting, I can only say: Stop psyching yourself out. Don't let the way you think about science or medicine be your handicap. Make it instead, your entree to meeting some of the world's most responsible, exciting, truly humane people and writing about their work, ideas, and dreams for a healthier world for all of us.

How can you do this successfully is what this book is all about.

2 □ STARTING POINTS: WHAT'S REQUIRED?

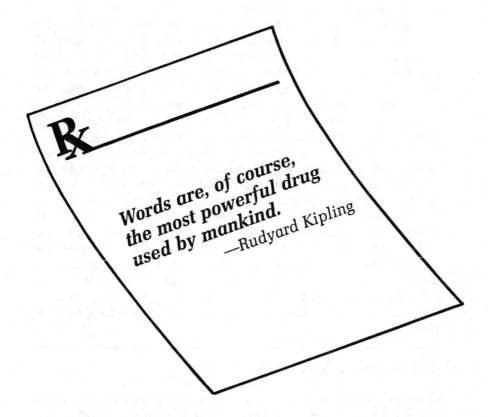

R℞

*Words are, of course,
the most powerful drug
used by mankind.*
—Rudyard Kipling

For the last 112 days of his life, Dr. Barney B. Clark was hero, celebrity, and front-page news worldwide. So, too, was Dr. William C. DeVries, the Salt Lake City surgeon (now at Humana Hospital Audubon in Louisville, Kentucky) who implanted the world's first permanent artificial heart in the courageous and hitherto unknown dentist.

It was, according to a *New York Times* headline, a story of modern marketing as well as modern medicine. "The merchandising of Barney Clark and his plastic heart," wrote *Times* reporter William J. Broad, "has to a large extent occurred as part of a growing, if indirect, tie-in between medical advances, communications and commerce."

Careful planning was the first step in telling the story to the world, says John Dwan, spokesman for the University of Utah Medical Center where the historic operation took place in 1982. More than two years before Dr. Clark had arrived on the scene, preparations for the heart transplant and plans for coping with every aspect of the surgery and recovery were set in motion. Included were plans for working with the media, plus ways to educate reporters about the project and limit factual errors by journalists.

In dealing with the media, Dwan said in a talk to Northern Nevada members of the International Association of Business Communicators, he and his staff developed a hard-and-fast rule: "If you don't hear it from us, you can't be sure it's true. Also, if you go around us to get a story—stalking nurses in the parking lot for example—then the next news you hear will be from your competitors."

Dwan's rule is a good one to follow in any situation. Get your information right from the source—and get it right.

In the Barney Clark case, Dwan told me, reporters received background and historical materials and photos, but only in the beginning. "Then we just gave daily briefings and let everyone write their own pieces." The briefings became news events in themselves.

"We had no restrictions on the media," he said. "We really had no interest in who they were . . . and trying to find out and issue them badges, etc., would have just taken time and served no purpose. We passed around a yellow legal pad at the end of each day and asked those who wanted to be called if a 'significant event' occurred during the night to put down their name and number. . . . It was very informal. Free-lancers were welcome to jump in and compete with the rest of them."

BECOMING AN ENTREPRENEUR

Competing for the hard news or breaking story is not easy for the free-lancer who's up against the wire services, local and regional journalists, and special medical-news agencies. But competing for your share of the public's attention—whether in the medical media or popular print, broadcast or audiovisual media—is the name of the game in free-lancing.

What this means is that the successful free-lancer is an entrepreneur at heart. He's a risk taker who can take rejection as being editorial, not personal. She's a go-getter who's determined to make her work and ideas the editor's first choice when another equally good idea or article is lying right beside it on the editor's desk. For the health and medical free-lancer, it means keeping abreast of trends in the field, knowing your strengths, and building on them—as either a specialist or a generalist. It's not easy, but it's not as hard as you may think. After all, no one is born a medical writer.

Generally speaking, you'll find two major kinds of free-lancers who specialize in writing about medicine and the allied health fields. There are those who write for the popular print and broadcast media and those who work in the medical media reporting on medical meetings for professional journals, for example, or writing drug-package inserts for pharmaceutical companies and continuing education materials for health professionals. Many of these writers regularly cross over from the medical to the popular media.

"The way I've been able to be so successful," explains free-lancer Mark L. Fuerst, "is to have *two* markets. When I write a story about clinical medicine, I always try to spin off into a story for a consumer publication." For example, says the former *Medical World News* editor, a story he wrote about surgeons who have fewer than ten fingers appeared in *Surgical Practice News* in August, 1982. He then took the same idea and wrote it for United Features newspaper syndicate. That article appeared in October. Next he was able to sell a spin-off feature to *Medical World News* about one of the surgeons included in the original article. Published in November and headlined, "Dextrous Despite Hand Loss at 17, Eye Surgeon Operates with Prosthesis," this article was a profile of Abilene, Texas surgeon James L. Tucker, Jr., who is missing a hand.

This is one time, Fuerst says, he wasn't able to sell a spin-off story to a consumer publication, but it wasn't a total loss either.

"I tried to sell the story," he says, "to a major consumer magazine, but both *Reader's Digest* and *Parade* turned me down. However, the query to *Reader's Digest* did lead to a working relationship with an editor there and I have since sold the magazine a story about sleep problems."

Another free-lancer with expertise in forensic medicine always tries to get double duty out of each article idea—with the same research, she slants one piece to physicians and a second to attorneys. One appears in a publication for doctors; the other, in a legal journal.

NO TYPICAL HEALTH WRITER

How do you get into health and medical writing if you haven't done it before? Ask 100 free-lancers what served as their springboard to either full- or part-time careers in the field, and you'll receive 100 different answers. There is no one route, no single educational background or professional expertise that serves all writers equally well. However, talk to enough writers and some general patterns begin to emerge. Among the most common are:

Journalistic/Publishing Route.

It makes sense that reporting, editing, and research skills used every day in the publishing industry or newspaper and magazine business would serve any free-lancer well. Jody Gaylin, whose by-line appears regularly in *Family Weekly* and major women's magazines, started out as a fact checker for *Psychology Today*. Cynthia Bell, a New York writer whose by-line has appeared in *Seventeen*, *Parade*, and the Gannett Westchester newspaper supplement, *Suburbia Today*, was an editorial assistant at Doubleday before striking out on her own.

After thirty years as science/medical writer for the Associated Press in Chicago, Charles-Gene McDaniel began second and third careers—one as free-lancer and the other, journalism professor and director of the journalism program at Chicago's Roosevelt University. David R. Zimmerman, an award-winning free-lancer, was trained in English and history, worked on college and local newspapers, came to New York, and started up the newspaper ladder at the *News* and *Post*, where he says he "never went anywhere."

Zimmerman, whose by-line appears often in major women's publications, says his start in medical writing came with an introduction to a medical publisher who had a manuscript called *Pitfalls of Gynecology* that had "lots of pitfalls in common English." He repaired those, he says, got into book doctoring, and eventually went to work— first for the New York Academy of Medicine and then for *Medical World News*. Later he had a chance to do the *Ladies' Home Journal's* medical column, which he did for almost thirteen years before quitting to write a book on the Rh factor.

Academic/Professional Route

It's not necessary to have graduate or professional degrees in the medical or scientific field to be a successful writer. But if you have the highly valued R.N., M.D., D.D.S., or other credentials *and* a way with words, you can't lose. Many of today's best-known editors and writers combine communication skills with academic degrees or professional expertise.

Among them are Lawrence K. Altman, M.D., staff medical correspondent for *The New York Times*, who also holds a teaching appointment at the New York University School of Medicine; Earl Ubell, health editor of *Parade* (degree in physics); Dianne Partie, R.N., health director of *Self* magazine, who worked as a hospital staff nurse and for a New York dermatologist before starting as a researcher in *Vogue's* beauty department; and Dr. Lewis Berman, one of the nation's most prominent veterinarians whose monthly column "The Pet Dr." appears in *Family Weekly*.

Best known of all is Dr. Benjamin Spock. It's estimated that his classic guidebook, *Baby and Child Care*, first published in 1945, has been translated into thirty-eight languages in thirty-one countries and has sold 32 million copies.

Independent Route

Writers who have come this route are some of the best entrepreneurs in the medical writing, fitness, and health-marketing or advertising fields.

Greg Nielsen, for example, is a University of Minnesota humanities major who found he had a knack for explaining science to non-scientists. Coauthor of *Pyramid Power*, he has also self-published several self-help books. In 1982, Nielsen founded his own company, now called Wordsmith Worldwide, and promptly secured the exclusive writing contract to provide all health-related writing and advertising copy for Vierling Associates International, a Reno-based health-care cost-containment marketing firm.

"I also do a lot of writing for other clients," says Nielsen. "Everything from corporate profiles to newsletters, radio and TV scripts, newspaper columns and features. I'm developing a statewide campaign to educate legislators, decision makers and the public about advanced practitioners of nursing and have hired three other free-lancers to work on it with me."

Summing it all up, he adds: "I'm a total entrepreneur now—I think like a *businessman* first, a writer second, and I'm constantly looking for ways to extend my business even wider."

Look at Judi Sheppard Missett, a former professional dancer, whose name is synonymous with fitness and *Jazzercise*—a program that combines music and dance with exercise, is led by trained instructors, and energized all the way by "positive feedback." Jazzercise revenues in 1982 alone totaled more than $40 million, with about half that amount going back to the franchised instructor-owners.

Today Missett is not merely president of the Jazzercise empire, she's also a best-selling author, columnist, and talk-show guest whose drive for quality and perfection spills over into everything she does.

Another woman whose by-line spells quality is Dodi Schultz, who specializes in writing about medicine, children, and psychology. Her articles have appeared in major magazines including *Ladies' Home Journal*, *McCall's*, *Parents*, *Today's Health*, and *The New York Times Magazine*. She's also ghostwritten speeches for physicians and authored or coauthored more than a dozen books.

In *The Complete Guide to Writing Nonfiction*, she says that when she came up with an idea for her first in-depth treatise on a medical topic, the publisher liked her proposal but insisted that she find an

M.D. coauthor so "readers will know they're getting real expertise."
She "found" Virginia E. Pomeranz, M.D., and *The Mothers' Medical
Encyclopedia* was published in 1972. Five years later, a revised and
expanded edition came out, retitled *The Mothers' and Fathers' Medical Encyclopedia.*

Says Schultz, who's received several journalism awards, "I just
want you to know that there's more than one route to being a medical
writer. I was a college dropout—I don't even have a bachelor's degree."

"Free-lancers," agrees medical writer-editor Beth Allen, "are a
special kind of breed. We are independent types and the job we do is a
unique one. I don't know of any other job where you have to deal in
such detail." Citing editing examples, she comments, "Who else has
to worry about something so small as a diacritical (a mark that's attached to a letter to indicate its phonetic value) . . . or the number of
characters on a page or in a column line of type?"

SCHOOLING YOURSELF TO WRITE

One way to get started is to take a writing course. That's what Florence
Isaacs did years ago. "I was working as an advertising copywriter in
New York City," says Isaacs, "but my first love was journalism, so I
signed up for an evening, beginning-nonfiction class at the New
School for Social Research." She followed that up with a more ad-
vanced course.

Since then, Isaacs has made a name for herself writing magazine
articles on medicine, health, marriage, and related topics. Her by-line
has appeared in *Reader's Digest, Rx: Being Well, Off Hours, Family
Circle, Good Housekeeping,* and *Mademoiselle.* But, she says, it took
her about three years to crack these markets. Isaacs started out writing
health articles at $15 each for a small New York City weekly; her first
major sale was to the *New York News Sunday Magazine* for $700.

Another way to begin a medical writing career is to major in basic
or health sciences and take writing courses on the side, or specialize
in the relatively new area of study called biomedical communications. Specialists in this field are experts in the planning, production,
uses, and evaluation of audiovisual media. Among the media often
used in health education are television and videotapes, films, slides,
overhead transparencies, posters, manuals, pictures, programmed
texts, audiotapes, models, and computer-assisted learning packages.

For the most complete listing of science and health communication degrees and programs, consult the latest edition of *The College
Blue Book* (Macmillan), found in the reference section of most librar-

ies. For more detailed descriptions of health, medicine, and science communication courses and programs, check the *Directory of Science Communication*. This thirty-nine-page publication is not readily available in most libraries, but copies can be ordered directly from the Department of Chemistry, State University of New York at Binghamton, Binghamton, NY 13901 for about six dollars including postage.

Nearly seventy programs are listed, including one in Canada at Ottawa's Carleton University. For example, Philadelphia's Drexel University Department of Humanities and Communications grants a master's degree in Technical and Science Communication. Polytechnic Institute of New York offers a graduate program in Medical and Science Reporting within its Specialized Journalism master's program.

Still another highly targeted program is conducted by the University of Nebraska Medical Center in Omaha. Here students combine hands-on experience in the biomedical communications department with formal graduate courses in Instructional Media/Technology in Health Sciences, Biomedical Writing and Editing, Introduction to Research, and the Psychology of Adult Education, among others.

The journalism department at Oregon State University in Corvallis offers undergraduates a health sciences minor. According to Department Chairman Fred C. Zwahlen, Jr., "More students are pursuing a health sciences minor with the technical journalism degree than were previously. And we have offers of more journalism internships for the students at hospitals and nursing homes. The minor is thriving!"

Students at universities and colleges that do not offer such specialized courses should look into internships or volunteer work in hospitals, clinics, medical centers or schools, research institutes, or local chapters of the so-called disease organizations, such as the American Cancer Society or American Diabetes Association. This is an important way to obtain first-hand experience in writing news releases, features, publicity, or fund-raising materials and editing house organs or employee publications.

Constance A. Arkus, who now works for the American Society for Hospital Marketing and Public Relations, says she worked at one time for a Chicago agency that hired several free-lancers to help with public relations. "Best way to get a foot in the door," she suggests, "is to make yourself known. Do an internship with an agency that does health-related advertising, marketing, or public relations." Arkus has a degree in journalism and feels it's invaluable to anyone who plans to go into the field.

Don't underestimate the value of materials you produce in your courses, internship, or volunteer experience. Save copies of your best work. Samples of such work in your portfolio, clip-file notebook, or string-book are helpful in landing other assignments. Many professional writers find a bound vinyl folder large enough to hold about twenty-five plastic inserts (8½ by 11 inches) makes an attractive and flexible portfolio.

When you're job hunting or making free-lance proposals to clients with differing needs, it's important to be able to change the samples in your portfolio to show your best and current work—whether it's brochures, articles, fact sheets, or photographs. If you're interested in pursuing an audiovisual, television, or radio career in health and medical communication, keep copies of any videotapes, film clips, or on-the-air broadcasts you do. Be faithful in saving these and protecting them from wear and tear. You'll find your tapes and portfolio are among your most valuable tools in going after new business.

KEEPING CURRENT

While formal study of health communications and medical journalism is a good beginning, it's not feasible or appropriate for every would-be writer. What's important is knowing your craft and being up on medical news, topics, and trends.

Writers' conferences, such as the annual one sponsored by the American Society of Journalists and Authors, often feature workshops in writing on health, fitness, self-help, and medical topics. Here free-lancers, editors, and publishers share information on market needs and how to meet them. Especially helpful to pro and novice alike are the workshops and continuing education (CORE) program offered by the American Medical Writers Association (AMWA). More information on AMWA and other professional groups is contained in appendix F.

One way to keep up with what's happening in the medical field is to attend lectures and other public events at your nearest university, medical school, or hospital. For instance, over the last few years, on audit basis, I've taken university courses in the history of medicine, biomedical ethics, and contemporary issues in medicine. I've sat in on weekly grand rounds at the county medical center. These sessions, which are open to the public but not widely publicized, feature leading speakers and hospital staff members who present interesting clinical cases, research findings, and the latest methods in treating everything from alcoholism to Zenker's Degeneration (a necrosis of the intestinal diverticulum).

I've attended meetings and special seminars at the state university medical school. If there is a subject I need to know more about for a book or an article, I've been able to make special arrangements through the school's Public Information Office to sit in on an occasional lecture given to students, use the medical library facilities, and interview leading professors in a given field.

I also try to time my travel plans so that I can catch medical and writers' meetings in other cities as well. For instance, on a trip to New York City a few years ago, I attended Women's Health Day at the New York Hospital-Cornell Medical Center. I wrote ahead to two of the speakers, noted authors Isadore Rosenfeld, M.D. and Helen S. Kaplan, M.D., requesting interviews. Rosenfeld graciously agreed, even suggesting I call him at home on the weekend when he would have more time to talk. Kaplan, noted for her work in sex therapy, declined an interview but said I was free to quote from her presentation.

Topics discussed that day by these doctors and two other outstanding specialists included: brittle bones, women and coronary heart disease, physical examinations, and sex life and good health—a bonanza of salable psyche-, soma-, and sex-related article ideas plus quotes for the asking.

Nor was I the only writer taking notes. Sylvie Reice, a former editor of *McCall's* and *Family Health* who now free-lances, was completing research for an eight-page special section on women and beauty, health, and fitness. Titled "The Anti-Aging Lifestyle," it appeared in the September, 1984, issue of *Ladies' Home Journal*.

"It used to be that editors were looking for writers who were generalists," says Reice, "but today it's the specialists who are in demand; and if your specialty is health or medical writing, you are in the driver's seat since this is the top interest of women readers and, consequently, women's magazine editors."

When I asked *Good Housekeeping* articles editor Joan Thursh if she agreed that the specialist is more valued as a regular free-lancer for her publication, she replied, not necessarily.

"I think when you're dealing with something as special as health or doing an in-depth article about a particular health area or problem, a writer should specialize in health articles or, at least, have an experience *pool* to draw on. "But," she added, "if one is dealing basically with a personal experience story that is health-oriented, detailing a case history or the progress of an illness in somebody's life, you certainly do not have to specialize."

Thursh claims the same qualities that determine if you are an effective writer also determine whether you can do a story that requires some expertise and the ability to translate technical information for a layperson. Summing it up, she says: "The qualities that make a good writer capable of turning out a good story in *any* area are operative here, too—being able to write, being able to interview effectively, having the intelligence and the discrimination to know what is important and what isn't, and how to ask questions."

TO ENLIGHTEN, ENTERTAIN

Good medical writing follows the same rules and nonfiction guidelines you'd follow for any magazine article or newspaper feature. What you must always keep in mind is the makeup of your *audience*. Who's going to read this piece? Why are you writing for them, and what are you trying to accomplish?

If your answer is that you want to explain medicine or science to the general public, take a tip from medical/science journalist William A. Check, who holds a Ph.D. in microbiology. "Be careful about educating people who don't *want* to be educated," cautions the former staff writer for the medical news section of the *Journal of the American Medical Association (JAMA)*. "If you have a popular angle and can work in some scientific material as well, then good. I used to be a snob about that until I realized that I was working all day, and even when an interesting nature program came on TV, I was too tired to watch it—I just didn't want my mind to absorb any more information. Remember," he warns, "your readers are in that position, too."

J. Eugene White, coordinator of news and publications at Texas Tech University School of Medicine in Amarillo, agrees. "In writing for the general public, you're *dead* if you don't entertain while educating them."

"Lots of people don't get the story," he explains, "because we don't keep them long enough to get it. We can live day after day submerged in dramatic stuff all the time, [yet] we become anesthetized to it. We're looking for facts . . . to tell the story, and we pass over the drama. You don't need to embellish," says the former newspaper reporter and magazine editor. "If plain vanilla is all you've got, use it. Keep your integrity—because then people will believe you when you do use tension and drama."

Remember, your words are competing with thousands of others on radio, television, film, and paper for the attention of the health consumer. Your words are competing for the time of the health-care professional who's bombarded daily with new drug announcements, professional journals, drug-company pamphlets, pharmaceutical product books, manuals, continuing-education course offerings, and medical travel brochures plus an unending stream of requests for charitable donations and free lectures.

Don't let your words be the junk mail that gets tossed into the garbage sight unseen.

HIGH STAKES

Of course, if your audience is one of health-care professionals or scientists, your purpose is not to entertain, but to *inform*. Manuscript style either follows professional journal guidelines to a T—or it's rejected outright. Creative style is not a plus in the clinical or scientific manuscript, although it's highly prized in the laboratory and the right stuff when it comes to Nobel Prize winners.

I was thrilled, for example, when I learned that Rockefeller University biochemist R. Bruce Merrifield had been awarded the 1984 Nobel Prize in chemistry. During the mid-1950s before my husband and I were married, I did office work for two years at the Rockefeller Institute for Medical Research (as it was called then) for Merrifield's colleague and chief, Dr. D. W. Wooley.

Dr. Wooley was diabetic and blind. He expected each of us in his office and laboratory to be able to describe exactly what we saw—and not miss a thing. Instinctively, he knew when we missed and called us on it.

All manuscripts sent from his laboratory went through an elaborate checking process. First, they were read aloud in a group; then, corrected as needed, rewritten, and reread aloud several times before the final approval was given to mail the paper off to a journal. Always, we were checking for accuracy, clarity, conciseness, punctuation, and journal style.

For me, it was first-rate (if tedious) training in paying attention to detail. I learned, too, the value of reading a manuscript out loud to fine-tune it.

Nobel winner Merrifield, then in his mid-30s, was coauthor of many of these scientific papers. Little did we know that much of that time-consuming effort polishing manuscripts would go toward paving the way for the worldwide acclaim he's now received for his ingenious laboratory method of synthesizing peptides—complex protein substances important in genetic engineering and drug development. But the lesson is clear: on a day-to-day basis, you rarely see the big picture.

Though media headlines tout the "gee-whiz" and breakthrough aspects of science and medicine, scientific research moves ahead in increments—often minuscule ones. The results, however, are of great interest to those in the discipline and to the scientific community at large. But it's one thing to have original ideas and scientific results; it's quite another to write effectively, publish those ideas, and submit them to peer review in the scientific world.

What makes medical and scientific writing so intriguing is its potential to make a difference. And not on any small scale. University tenure and promotion policies are often linked to publication, as in the adage "publish or perish." As each success breeds another, professional reputations are secured; job offers become more tempting, research funds come more easily—and rivalries among competing scientists and doctors escalate.

Writers need to be aware of such competition in doing their own research.

"There's always the possibility that you can be misled," explains Lucy Kavaler, whose articles have appeared in Self, Good Housekeeping and Woman's Day. "There are many rivalries in science and in medicine. Many scientists and physicians have their research underwritten by an organization or a drug company. And sometimes, what you think is an exposé, really is not."

The point is, says Kavaler, that physicians and scientists can and do have biases just like anyone else. And it's particularly important to consider the source of such bias (rivalry is certainly one such) when a breakthrough or contradiction of a long-held theory is being described.

So it's important, she adds, "not to go right off and say, for example, that you have immediately discovered that the cholesterol theory is all wet, or that such-and-such drug has ghastly side effects and should be withdrawn from the market. It [the drug] may very well have them, but [the informant] may also be someone who's supported by the competitor."

Whether you are writing for the New England Journal of Medicine or popular publications like Self, Essence, Good Housekeeping, or Health, your work must meet four criteria: accuracy, clarity, fairness (or balance), and good taste. Statistics and facts can be put together in just about any way to make whatever point an author wants to make. But fairness requires that you as a writer do justice to whomever and whatever you're talking about.

THE (BIG) PICTURE OF HEALTH

Doctors have a saying that if you don't think of the disease, you won't make the diagnosis. Writers who aren't thinking "health" in its broadest context won't make the health connection that opens the door to some of today's best-paying, wide-open, and fastest-growing markets in the publishing business.

Yet I know excellent writers who would never even consider writing a health or medical piece. They've ruled themselves out of the market simply by telling themselves, "I'm not a health writer."

They've got tunnel vision when it comes to health.

Perhaps it's a throwback to high school or college, where introductory health courses imparted a narrow view of health along with a heavy dose of lectures on smoking, drinking, venereal disease, and personal hygiene. Be sure you're not limiting your chances of success by thinking of health in too *narrow* a framework. Don't forget, the health-care consumer is not only the patient but also the *well* person seeking to maintain his or her health and enhance the enjoyment of life.

Health is a word derived from an Old English translation of "wholeness." And while the term *health* continues to take on new connotations as society, the health professions, and publishers interpret illness, wellness, and related topics in various ways, we all have our *own* concept of what it means to be healthy, whole, and well.

In his poem "He Makes a House Call," emergency medicine specialist and poet John Stone, M.D., says, "Health is whatever works and for as long."

The World Health Organization has defined health as "a state of complete physical, mental, and social well-being, and not merely the absence of disease or infirmity."

And the American Hospital Association's "Policy and Statement on the Hospital's Responsibility for Health Promotion" gives this definition for health promotion:

> Health promotion (including health information and health education) is the process of fostering awareness, influencing attitudes, and identifying alternatives so that individuals can make informed choices and change their behavior in order to achieve an optimum level of physical and mental health and improve their physical and social environment.

While that's a tall order for society and the medical profession, it does open the door for a link between just about any topic and health. So make the most of it. Chapters 3 and 14 describe some of the dozens of free-lance opportunities. Chapter 4 shows you how to develop ideas and market them in ways editors find hard to resist.

MAKING THE TIME TO WRITE

Making a name for yourself so that when editors want a story they think of *you* first is, of course, every free-lancer's goal. Making that first sale is a big ego booster. That's why it's important for any writer just starting out to experience success as quickly as possible. How?

For starters, you may need to dump some mental baggage, clear the decks for work, hone your skills, and adopt some new attitudes and self-talk.

First, get rid of the myth that successful writers are supersmart, supertalented, superlucky, and not pressed for time the way you and I are. There may be a few to whom it all comes naturally, but most selling writers I've talked to are hard-working, self-disciplined, inner-directed men and women. If they don't have time to write, they squeeze writing into the time they have.

There are physicians, like E. Ted Chandler, an associate professor of medicine at the Bowman Gray School of Medicine, who write between 4:00 and 6:00 A.M. before heading off for early hospital rounds or clinic appointments. Young mothers, like professional writer Jody Gaylin, can find baby's naptime a quiet time to work on a manuscript or interview people over the telephone.

There are fathers, like Paul Levine, who works with mentally retarded persons as a rehabilitation counselor. "I try to write every day," says Levine, whose by-line appears often in *The New York Times.* "Since I work full-time, finding the time to write is quite difficult. I am sometimes too tired, or there is a good TV program on, or one of the kids (we have five) needs to be driven somewhere. But I don't let that stop me. I can't."

And there are counselors, like Patricia A. Halvorson, Ph.D., and Patricia A. Neuman, Ph.D., of North Dakota State University. While working full-time, they completed their first book on the eating disorders *anorexia nervosa* and *bulimia* in nine months. "We met weekly for one or two hours," explains Halvorson, "and each time we set a goal for the coming week for the writing we would do. The next week we would meet to see if we had met our goals and set a [new] goal. This worked very well and we found we got a great deal of work done in a short period of time."

Says one New Jersey free-lancer who formed her own editorial consulting company, "There are ways to do it if you're willing to put in *time* and *effort,* and don't need gold letters on the door."

ESTABLISH YOUR OWN WRITING SPACE

If your manuscript is spread across the kitchen table and your typewriter has to be set aside each time the family wants a meal, "gold letters on the door" is a luxury you might not want even if you could afford it. Don't make the mistake, however, of underestimating the importance of having some writing space, somewhere, that's yours alone. Every writer needs a place where typewriter, papers, and research materials can be left out overnight.

This isn't a luxury. It's crucial to the writing process to be able to add a word, a phrase, a couple of paragraphs or whatever when the creative juices are flowing. Often it's when you're doing the dishes, driving a car, shopping in the supermarket that the right word or idea pops up unexpectedly.

When the muses strike, you've got to be prepared with notepad and pen or pencil wherever you are. But it's not enough to have your pockets stuffed with notes. They need to be added to your manuscript as soon as can be, to see if they fit and, if not, *why* not. It's much easier to do this if you don't have to haul everything out first from closet or corner.

Also, there can be tax advantages as well as psychological ones in having your own office or space used *solely* for writing. It serves as evidence to the Internal Revenue Service that you are seriously pursuing writing—not just as a hobby but as a business. Psychologically, you're telling yourself your work is important. It deserves attention. It merits room in your life, your day's schedule, your thinking time.

Develop the habit of looking at everything you do, read, or hear, or experience as potential writing material. Ask yourself: Is there a story in it? If so, what's my angle? Is there a need for information that I can meet in some way that's *fresh* or new?

To earn top free-lance dollars, you have to know how to market your material and yourself as a professional writer. The truth is, editors tend to assign articles to certain writers they've worked with successfully before.

If your goal is to become one of these regular contributors, remember this: In the long run, the free-lancer who can produce an article by deadline, in the style and length the publication requires, is much more likely to get these assignments than the writer who is brilliant—but who must have an editor working hand in hand with him for ten days of solid rewriting just to make the manuscript work.

RX FOR SUCCESS

What does it take to become a successful free-lance writer in the health and medical field? I asked that question of hundreds of writers I interviewed in researching this book. Here in brief is their advice:

● *Love what you're doing.* You'll be working at it five days a week plus Saturdays, Sundays, and holidays.

● *Know what you're doing.* Know your craft, and be accurate. There's no room for error. Inaccuracies in medical reporting not only cause pain to the author and his or her sources, but in many cases, can cause distress or raise false hope in patients and their families as well.

● *Pick an area of interest.* Learn all you can about it. Tease out different story ideas and write them up from various angles. Sell several on step-families, autoimmune diseases, health-care financing, or whatever your specialty is, and next thing you know, you are the writer editors call *first* when they need a story in this area.

● *Be patient.* Some medical and scientific stories take *time* to research and develop properly; others must be waited out. When accuracy and ethics are at stake, don't be pressured into rushing the story before it's ready to be told.

● *Keep records.* Don't settle for a verbal work agreement; get it in writing. "Always submit a confirming letter restating the nature of the product, the fee, and the number of drafts to be expected for that fee," advises Cathryn D. Evans, president of Chandos Communications, a Palo Alto, California, free-lance and consulting firm. For a magazine article, send a brief letter to the editor confirming your understanding of the assignment, fee, and terms.

● *Never promise more than you can deliver.* Meet deadlines.

● *Invest in yourself.* Set high standards for your work; then join professional groups which assist you in meeting your goals. Make contacts. Take courses; go to medical meetings; attend writers' workshops. Learn the new technology—it's the wave of the future.

● *Don't let age scare you off.* With ideas on paper the selling point between you and an editor, late bloomers have as much to offer as the youngest free-lancer right out of school—and often, more to offer in information, life experience, and good grammar, spelling, research skills, and "stick-to-it-iveness."

● *Plan ahead.* Learn how to market yourself so you can sell your work. Think twice before making the leap from steady job to full-time free-lancing unless you've got a few regular referrals or backup clients you can depend on—and steady fiscal nerves.

"You need a certain kind of whacky personality to be a free-lancer, in that you must accept ambiguity and insecurity," explains Jean McCann of Cleveland Heights, Ohio, president of her own company, Medical News, Inc. "If you're addicted to a set paycheck every Friday, don't be a free-lancer—you may have zero in the bank one day and $5,000 the next."

Finally, if you're going to free-lance in the health and medical field, think of yourself as a *professional* from the start. From query to final copy, send out only your best words. Keep faith in yourself. It's not always easy when your manuscripts bounce back attached to form rejection slips.

Learn from them. Learn what you *don't* want to do the next time around. Then move on. Remember Kipling: "Words are the most powerful drug used by mankind." Use them wisely. But never forget that recycling rejects, and rewriting, revising, and rethinking ideas have always been signs of a *real* pro.

3 □ FREE-LANCE OPPORTUNITIES: MAKING THE HEALTH CONNECTION

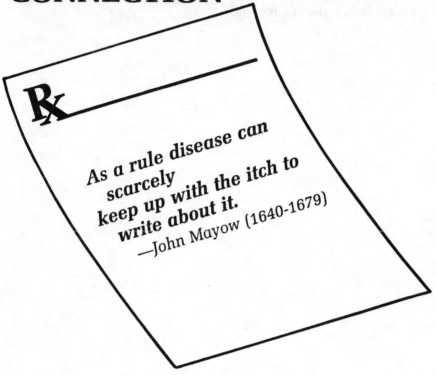

As a rule disease can scarcely keep up with the itch to write about it.
—John Mayow (1640-1679)

Join any group of independent writers and sooner or later the talk turns to who's buying what and what's the going rate. Newspapers, of course, are notoriously low paying. Payment at magazines can range from a few cents a word in small-circulation publications to $3,000 or more for major assignments from the so-called slicks such as *Woman's Day*, *Reader's Digest*, and *Playboy*. In between are hundreds of special-interest and trade publications which pay anywhere from $150 to $750 on acceptance of your manuscript or, all too often, only after it's been published.

It's the rare free-lancer who makes a living writing solely for these markets. Most independent writers make ends meet with the help of a working spouse, other jobs, or writing for a combination of several markets and clients. It's estimated that only about 5 percent of free-lance authors earn more than $5,000 a year. But that's the down side. A 1981 Columbia University survey of contemporary American authors (defined as those with at least one published book) revealed that there are also writers in the top 10 percent of all the nation's wage earners, making $45,000 or more each year. Still others are in the top 5 percent of all wage earners—those whose incomes are $80,000 and beyond.

In short, there's always room at the top for the best.

What makes it all worthwhile on the way up? Obviously, it's a buyer's market. What makes it worth the effort, in addition to being your own boss and whatever you're paid, is the by-line. Visibility. Your ideas and your name in print. Not only that, it's *seductive*. Sell one piece, and you want to sell more.

GOING INTO (MARKET) ANALYSIS

Before you put your first words on paper, take time to evaluate your potential markets. This can be a time-consuming task, as markets that accept free-lance material are varied, distinct, *and* numerous. Bear in mind that just because several publications fall into the same category, such as health or fitness or women's magazines, that doesn't mean they're all the same.

"Each magazine is different and has very special attributes," says *Good Housekeeping* editor-in-chief John Mack Carter. "Different magazines have different images that people come to expect."

Editors are unanimous in saying that one of the major reasons rejected manuscripts miss the mark is that the writer hasn't taken time to study the publication before submitting material to it.

"Read and study the magazine," advises *50 plus* editor Bard Lindeman, who's also a syndicated columnist for the Associated Press. "It's not some arcane science—what goes into the magazine. Every editor goes for the same kind of story, the kind of article he believes right for his magazine. Spend two or three solid hours looking through six issues." Standard fee after a free-lancer has written once for the publication is $1,000 to $1,500. "Health and finance," Lindeman says, "are very important to the over-fifty population."

Ann Caputo, editor of *Today's OR Nurse*, receives about thirty manuscripts and queries each month. She accepts only ten to twelve a year. What's wrong with the rest? "Inappropriate topic, inappropriate format, and lack of depth for a professional audience," she explains.

Patient education is the aim of *Rx: Being Well*, a bimonthly consumer-health magazine distributed through physicians' waiting rooms. Editor Mark Deitch pays $250-$750 for articles written by doctors or by knowledgeable health writers working with recognized medical authorities in a given field. "But we have a particular approach and style of presenting health information," he says, adding, "Most unsolicited manuscripts are way off the mark. Writers must read our magazine carefully."

Free-lance writers who want to avoid rejection slips and earn top dollars make it their business to know how each magazine differs and what starts an editor's adrenaline running when it comes to good article ideas.

Here are some steps for getting started:

Know the Markets

Marketing, for both beginner and pro, is an on-going process that starts with knowing not just the obvious markets but the *hidden* ones as well. Read or scan every publication you come across that uses health or medically related material. Check the masthead, which lists the editors and contributors. Cross-check these names with the bylines appearing on the contents page. This will give you a good idea of who's writing what and how many of these writers are free-lancers. Do the same with your own subscriptions.

Take advantage of time you spend in doctors' or dentists' waiting rooms to skim all the magazines and health literature you can put your hands on. If a publication looks promising, copy the title, editor's name, and the address of the editorial office. (In some cases, this address will be different from the advertising and subscription service addresses listed on the masthead.) Do the same with magazines and journals you find in medical centers, clinics, hospitals, friends' homes, libraries, newsstands, bookstores, health-food stores, drug counters, and supermarket checkout stands.

Often, when I'm not rushed for time, I deliberately stand in slow-moving checkout lines so I can look over the latest news magazines and consumer publications I don't receive at home. When I buy a magazine, I write the name of the publication on the sales slip or receipt and circle the price. Then I file the receipt with our other writing expenses so it will be easy to find later when we're making out our income tax.

Don't forget that there are also overseas markets. And educate yourself about the less-visible world of *trade* publications. "I started out thinking that eventually I wanted to write for popular magazines," says William A. Check, Ph.D., an Atlanta-based free-lance writer specializing in scientific and medical topics.

"But there's a whole hidden world sponsored by drug companies," he explains. "These are *trade publications* at all different levels—and I've built 70 or 80 percent of my business around scientific and technical publications. It's a wonderful field I've found [to be] less crowded, and I would advise you to think seriously about it," says Check, whose by-line appears often in *Health*, *Self*, and other consumer magazines.

Zero in on Your Best Bets

Once you've got the overall picture, focus your efforts on those markets that interest you most. Review writers' publications and newsletters for market listings and pointers on what editors are looking for.

Study several back issues of the publications you want to write for. Analyze the style. Check on the kinds of articles the editors run. If, for example, the magazine you're hoping will buy your humorous piece on aid and comfort to the tall woman or New Year's resolutions gone astray runs mostly scientific articles by-lined by M.D.'s and Ph.D.'s, you'd be wise to query another editor. If you notice a publication consistently uses *upbeat* stories, and you want to write about sudden infant death syndrome (SIDS) or what happens to airline passengers emotionally just before a crash, save your postage.

Do your homework first so you can determine which markets offer you the greatest chance of success. Don't forget, you not only want to be in sync with the type of articles editors prefer, you also want to be able to write in a personal style that's consistent with the publication's—be it humorous, informative, chatty, or scientific. "As you analyze markets and article types, don't neglect to analyze your own writing strengths and interests. Those will determine what kinds of articles you will write best," says Connie Emerson in *Write on Target* (Writer's Digest Books). This is a highly readable book which guides you through market analysis and helps you take stock of your writing self.

Health/medical market information, for instance, can be found in each November issue of *The Writer* magazine. Tips on "hot markets" and regular listing of publications using health and medical material appear often in the monthly *Writer's Digest*. *Writer's Market*, published by Writer's Digest Books and updated yearly, contains listings of many, though not all, consumer, trade, and special publications that use free-lance material. Listings are classified by both subject and age/interest divisions.

To find out more about trade journals, house organs, and company publications, check the current *Ayer Directory of Publications*. One of the most comprehensive references of print media, it lists both

American and Canadian newspapers and magazines; consumer, business, technical, professional, trade, and farm publications, with alphabetical index; addresses, names of key editors, and type of material carried. If you have an article to sell with newspaper as well as magazine appeal, you can find a complete list of daily and weekly papers nationwide in the annual *Editor & Publisher International Yearbook*.

Two other excellent reference guides are the *Standard Rate & Data* service directories (one for consumer, another for business, and a third for farm publications) and the Gebbie Press *All-in-One Directory*. This spiral-bound market guide includes daily and weekly newspapers and news syndicates; television and radio stations; general, consumer, and trade publications as well as business papers.

For instance, under the heading *Medical-Surgical*, you'll find 149 publications plus another 37 medical-society journals, ranging from *Medical World News* to the *Ear/Nose/Throat Journal* and *Diversion*, a magazine circulated to 185,000 doctors with an interest in travel, recreation, sports, and entertainment. Other health-oriented categories include psychology, with ten publications; drug-pharmaceutical, twenty-two; hospitals-nursing, thirty-five; optical, eighteen; dental, twenty-eight, and safety with eight publications, among them *Hygiene News*, *Industrial Safety*, and *Occupational Health Nursing*.

Don't forget the possibility of foreign trade-journal sales. Many of those publications are listed in *Ulrich's International Periodicals Directory; International Literary Market Place* and *The Europa Year Book*. This world survey, in two volumes, includes under each country a section on the press and specialized publications, ranging from science and medicine to general-interest and women's publications.

Most libraries keep these guides and directories at the reference desk. Many writers, however, have obtained copies of the *Standard Rate & Data* directories, which are updated monthly, simply by asking a local advertising agency for last month's copy.

Develop Your Own Files

Keep track of what's happening at the companies and publications you want to reach. A three-by-five-inch card for each magazine, newspaper, or trade journal with title, key editor's name, address, and phone number is a good beginning.

Even more helpful in tailoring article ideas and query letters is a folder of additional information clipped from writers' newsletters, publications, or other sources; a sample copy or two, and current *Guidelines for Writers*. You can obtain publisher's guidelines by putting your request in writing and sending the letter to one of the editors listed on the publication's masthead. Be sure to enclose a self-addressed stamped envelope (SASE) for a prompt response.

Go to a university health-sciences library or one in a hospital, medical, dental, or nursing school near you. Skim the professional journals for ideas. These reference materials cannot be removed from the premises. But often, you can make arrangements with the librarian to use the library's copy machine for any materials you want to add to your own files.

In my card file are hundreds of entries divided into categories as follows:

Professional and trade journals

Syndicates

Audiovisual producers

House organs/company publications

Newspaper and Sunday supplements

General-interest magazines

Children's/teens' publications

Men's/women's magazines

Fraternal/association publications

Travel/in-flight magazines

Business journals

Health and fitness magazines

Sports/sports medicine publications

Religious periodicals

Body/beauty magazines

Diet/nutrition publications

Child care/parenting magazines

Science magazines

Over-50/retirement magazines

Regional/city magazines

Mental health/psychology magazines

Reprint markets

Needless to say, I haven't written for all these markets. But I do keep track of them. When the right idea hits me for a behavior, nutrition, medical news, or health-care products piece, for example, I want to be up-to-date with the most recent marketing information on all potential buyers.

The key word in developing your files is current. Editors change, editorial needs shift, inventories can (and do) pile up. Relying on an old copy of the magazine masthead or writers' guidelines that are three years old is about as foolhardy as taking medication whose potency expired three months ago.

Spot (or Create) a Need and Fill It

The corollary, of course, is: Play up your strengths. Are these in copy editing, abstracting, translating, indexing, researching? What about writing fund-raising materials, advertising copy, doctors' brochures, speeches, patient-information booklets, monographs, film scripts, training manuals? Basically, these are *low-visibility* opportunities for free-lancers, but they often *pay better* than those that carry your by-line.

"Think about what you do best, what you're most comfortable doing, then persevere in your goal," advises Bernice Heller, a Philadelphia-based consultant to authors and publishers. After twenty-five years' experience as a senior editor with W. B. Saunders Company, McGraw-Hill Book Company, and J. B. Lippincott Company, she decided it was time to "free-lance at the work I knew best and enjoyed most."

These days, Heller, whose professional service is called Write It Right®, is not only called upon to write, but also to act as indexing consultant, development editor on difficult projects, and project coordinator of large publishing projects. Occasionally, she also critiques original manuscripts.

Fluency in a foreign language is another asset free-lancers parlay into steady assignments. One writer translates abstracts of articles and research protocols from French to English for an American pharmaceutical company. (A protocol is a document that specifies in detail exactly how patients will be selected for research projects and how the procedure[s] will be carried out.)

For many Spanish physicians who have problems writing in English, Marta Pulido, M.D., of Barcelona, Spain, is the key to publishing research and clinical papers in the English-language medical journals such as the *New England Journal of Medicine, ACTA Medic Scandinavica,* or *The Lancet,* a leading British medical journal.

Every year, Dr. Pulido, a full-time free-lancer who also gives medical-writing workshops throughout Spain, spends a week or more in the publications office of the Mayo Clinic in Rochester, Minnesota, where she brushes up on new professional journals as well as her writing, rewriting, and editing skills.

Creating a medical journal from scratch is a big project. Publishing it yourself is an even riskier one. But that's what versatile free-lance writer/editor Sheila Nauman-Todd of St. Paul, Minnesota, did when she needed more information on health care in a particular area—and couldn't find it easily.

"I had been researching things for physicians," she explains "and they'd say, 'Let me know what's new in such and such area.' I found there were either *no* reviews, or else they were hard to find, and I was really frustrated at that. I know the book market well and I believe in the patient's right to know. I believe physicians need to know what their patients are reading, too."

As a result, in October, 1983, she started her own publication,

Health Literature Review. The bimonthly contains medical news, fillers, briefs, and 150-500-word reviews of current and contemporary health literature. One of the problems in putting out such a journal, says publisher Nauman-Todd, is that "it's hard to define the health market and get statistics on it because it falls into so many areas like self-help, psychology, fitness, beauty. There's such diversity that you have to go to many different categories."

Sell Yourself—If You Don't, Who Will?

Every successful free-lancer has to be a good *self-marketer.* This means anticipating the needs of editors, publishers, or clients and proving to them that you can do the job. It means thinking like an entrepreneur and acting like one. It helps to be alert to the trends, to stay on top of topics, and come up with creative solutions to the age-old dilemma: What do I write about next and for *how much?*

Selling yourself *doesn't* mean prostituting your values, your integrity, or your workmanship to make a quick dollar.

The truth is, most free-lancers tend to undersell themselves: Either they don't know what their skills are worth, or they're afraid if they ask a realistic fee, they won't get the job. Some independent writers also fall into the trap of putting value on credentials the media don't necessarily value at the *same* monetary rate.

I recall a writers' conference at which an irate scientist argued with other free-lancers whose background was journalism or the humanities, that he should be paid *more* for his words since he qualified as an expert in genetic engineering. It can come as a shock to find out that the media marketplace doesn't always think the same way. Having a graduate or professional degree certainly is a respected union card in the scientific and health-care field. But don't count on it to boost what editors will pay you for your words.

Nor is this discrepancy in pay limited just to free-lancers. It's true even at *The New York Times,* where award-winning staff correspondent Lawrence K. Altman, M.D., says one of the disadvantages of being a physician-journalist is *less income.* "You're paid as a reporter," he says, "not as a physician."

Don't be discouraged, but do be a realist. You can make money as a free-lancer. How much will depend on your abilities, your contacts, your ingenuity, how hard you want to work—and yes, a little luck. "I'm a great believer in luck," Thomas Jefferson wrote nearly two centuries ago, "and the harder I work, the more luck I have."

Despite what you may have heard about picking up an assignment through a lucky phone call to an editor, the *best* way to sell your idea—whether for a book, article, or audiovisual—is still the query letter or proposal. "Don't tell me," say most editors, "show me in writing what you can do."

Chapter 4 shows you how to write queries an editor finds hard to refuse. Writing book proposals is covered in chapter 13. If you're in a hurry to know what to charge for a free-lance job or how to get an assignment, skip ahead to chapter 15, "Rx for a healthier bank account."

MAJOR FREE-LANCE OPPORTUNITIES

It's not possible in one chapter to fully describe all the markets that buy health, science, and medical material from free-lancers. But the overview of major opportunities that follows will give you a head start and help you better your odds in selling what you write.

NEWSPAPERS AND SYNDICATES

According to the most recent edition of the *Guide to U.S. Medical and Science News Correspondents and Contacts*, few newspapers with circulation of *less* than 50,000 designate any specific correspondent to cover health or scientific subjects. Of larger circulation papers surveyed nationwide, more than 300 dailies have editors or reporters whose assignment includes (or, in the case of several dozen of the largest papers, is *limited to*) medical and scientific subjects.

These full-time journalists, whose beat is health/medicine/science, are called upon to cover everything from the latest transplant technique to accidents at nuclear plant facilities, surgery on presidential polyps, announcements on the newest vaccines, or chilling evidence of drug tampering.

In addition, newspapers carry syndicated features and columns by fitness experts, nutritionists, psychologists, dentists, veterinarians, and physicians. (Times have changed from the early 1970s, when such columns by *practicing* physicians would have been considered an unethical form of advertising for patients.)

To get an idea of the *amount* of outside material in the health/science/medical field used by nineteen newspapers, see the chart below taken from an excellent overview, "Science Sections: Gee-whiz vs. Issues" by Fred Jerome of the Scientists' Institute for Public Information. The article, which appeared in the November, 1984, issue of *The Quill*, makes the point that from Memphis to San Jose, newspapers have followed the 1978 lead of *The New York Times* and started their own weekly science sections. On the other hand, the networks, with only 13 million viewers, have junked theirs. Concludes Jerome: "While debate continues over the role and goals of the new (science/health/medicine) sections, there can be little doubt that the general public is hungry for science and technology."

NEWSPAPERS WITH WEEKLY SCIENCE SECTIONS

Newspaper	Section Title	Day of Week	Date Started	% Own News*	% Other Sources*	Circulation**
The Boston Globe	Sci-Tech	Monday	4/83	98%	2%	514,817
Chicago Tribune	Tomorrow	Sunday	4/10/83	33%	67%	116,403
The Cincinnati Post	Newscience	Friday	9/23/83	50%	50%	135,585
Columbus Citizen-Journal	Medic one	Monday	8/1/83	75%	25%	121,676
The Columbus Dispatch	Discovery	Sunday	9/4/83	50%	50%	352,842
The Commercial Appeal [Memphis, TN]	Future Currents	Sunday	11/28/82	33%	67%	280,880
The Dallas Morning News	Discoveries	Monday	8/1/83	70%	30%	328,332
Detroit Free Press	Science/New Tech	Tuesday	5/4/82	50%	50%	635,114
The Detroit News	Science/Computers	Thursday	5/83	95%	5%	650,683
The Evening Gazette [Worcester, MA]	Today/Science-Health	Thursday	9/83	60%	40%	85,273
The Globe and Mail [Toronto, ONT]	Science/Medicine	Monday	6/84			310,689
The Journal-News [Rockland County, NY]	Discovery	Thursday	10/82	25-30%	70-75%	43,772

Newspaper	Section Title	Day of Week	Date Started	% Own News*	% Other Sources*	Circulation**
The Miami Herald	Science/Medicine	Wednesday	1981	40%	60%	424,939
The New York Times	Science Times	Tuesday	1978	99%	1%	910,538
Newsday [Long Island, NY]	Discovery	Tuesday	10/2/84			525,216
The Oregonian [Portland, OR]	Science	Thursday	11/3/83	Over 50%	Under 50%	289,600
The Plain Dealer [Cleveland, OH]	Science-Health	Tuesday	9/83	60%	40%	493,329
San Jose Mercury News	Science & Medicine	Tuesday	11/16/82	33%	67%	290,109
The Washington Post	Health	Wednesday	1/2/85			718,842

* Figures are estimates supplied by editors.
** Figures are daily averages from 1984 Editor & Publisher Yearbook. Sections appearing on Sundays list Sunday circulation.

From an article by Fred Jerome, of the Scientists' Institute for Public Information, printed in the November, 1984, issue of The Quill.

If you're competing for space in newspapers, your words are coming up against copy, features, fillers, and columns supplied by staff reporters, feature writers, supplement editors, wire services, newspaper syndicates, medical-news agencies, independent news brokers, and other free-lancers who syndicate their own columns on medicine, fitness, self-help, and nutrition. Not only that, many independent writers "string" for newspapers and news agencies that lack coverage in certain subject areas or regions of the country.

In brief, it's a tight market for free-lancers and one that pays little. However, that's only one side of the story. The other, as many free-lancers know, is that a newspaper by-line can be the key to opening new editorial doors for your work and ideas.

"If getting your ideas across is important to you, then newspapers can offer a first-rate forum," says Arthur L. Caplan, Ph.D., of the Hastings Center, a New York research institute that examines ethical issues in medicine and science. Caplan's by-line appears often in major papers, including the *Los Angeles Times*, *The New York Times*, *Newsday*, and *USA Today*, which asked him to submit articles.

"I had published some editorials and op-ed pieces in newspapers such as *Newsday*, and someone from *USA Today* saw one of those and got in touch with me—*they* found me, actually," he says. "On the ones sent in to *Newsday*, I took a chance. I knew *Newsday* was running op-ed pieces on different topics, some of which had run over into health care. Given the fact they had covered things like Barney Clark and Baby Jane Doe, [I thought] they would be open to topics on medical ethics. So I called them first, and asked them. They said yes and so I tried."

And the good news is newspaper readers want more health, medical, and science information. As reported in *Editor & Publisher*, a 1984 study on reader needs and tastes prepared by researcher Ruth Clark for the American Society of Newspaper Editors (ASNE) revealed that readers are hungry for "facts" about health, diet, nutrition, science, technology, and child rearing.

Odds are that newspaper editors will follow up on Clark's findings. They did it before, says *Editor & Publisher*, when her 1978 landmark reader-needs survey showed a demand for more local news, useful information, and articles on "how to cope," as well as for newspapers that were generally easier to read, less time-demanding, and more personal in tone.

As a free-lancer, your best bets in selling your work to large-circulation newspapers include opinion pieces, articles, an occasional feature, or stringing as an out-of-town correspondent to cover a breaking story, medical meeting, or convention that staff reporters cannot cover themselves.

On hometown or small-circulation papers, you may be able to sell editors on your providing *all* the health-news coverage in your area, plus regular features, interviews, and even a fitness, health, or psychologically oriented weekly column.

To the uninitiated, writing a column of about 750 words can look easier than it is. For one thing, you have to keep coming up with fresh ideas on a regular basis. For another, writing in newspaper style, if you're not used to it, can add to the chore. Before you work up six to eight sample columns to show an editor, check to make sure no one else is covering the same topic in the newspaper you're interested in.

Don't be surprised if an editor offers you little more than thirty-five cents a column inch, or between five and eighteen dollars for the total column. The only way free-lancers make money writing a column is to sell it to more than one *noncompeting* newspaper or have it syndicated.

NEWSPAPER UPDATES

Editor & Publisher, the weekly trade publication that covers the newspaper business, is an excellent resource for anyone who wants to keep up-to-date on news, trends, personnel changes and issues plus information on the syndicates. Check the library or write for subscription data (575 Lexington Avenue, New York, NY 10022).

Editor & Publisher's annual *International Yearbook* is an all-in-one, global newspaper guide divided into seven sections, including American, Canadian, and foreign newspapers, and news and syndicate services. Free-lancers will find the *Special Editions/Sections* listed under individual newspapers particularly helpful in selling stories targeted to newspaper supplements.

For example, the *Colorado Springs Sun* each January publishes a special section called "Let's Get Physical." A telephone call to Special Sections Editor Elizabeth W. Lewis confirmed that she does buy free-lance work for the annual section, which covers sports, recreation, nutrition, skin care, and other health-related topics.

Lewis says she buys copy from a variety of news services, such as Associated Press and Copley News; writes at least two stories per edition herself, and also uses part-time staff writers who get paid for free-lance work. Whether she uses other free-lance writers depends on how much copy she needs—but the door is *always* open to a good free-lance idea.

A good market for both original and reprinted articles is *Sunday Woman Plus*, currently in the process of changing from its present title to just *Plus*. This reflects the weekly supplement's change in slant from women-only to a broader range of family topics. *Sunday Woman Plus*, distributed by King Features Syndicate, runs in more than 80 markets in the United States and Canada, with an estimated circulation of over 4 million. Editor Merry Clark needs solid reportorial articles of 1,000-1,500 words on topics affecting families, life-styles, relationships, careers, health, money, and business. Clark comments that although she's not interested in rehashes of the same stale topics, she's always looking for new, fresh ideas and approaches. She's also happy to consider previously published material, but write a query, don't telephone her. If you're submitting story ideas for the first time, include samples of your writing with an SASE.

SYNDICATES

Writer's Market lists more than sixty syndicates. Among those that market health, medical, science, and fitness material are Los Angeles Times Syndicate; Amersand Communications; Stonewall Features Syndicate; Erwin Lynn Advertising Features; Dave Goodwin & Associates; Authenticated News International; Intercontinental Media Services, Ltd.; International Medical Tribune Syndicate, and Curious Facts Features, which is especially interested in "strange anomalies of medicine."

Remember, new syndicates keep coming along, and it doesn't hurt to get in on the first round of authors accepted. For example, Science, News & Publications Syndicate is a new market for columnists, cartoonists, feature writers, and editorial artists. "We are looking for standard newspaper features written in a better or different way," says syndicate president Richard B. Diehl. "A professional attitude and some experience at the local level is helpful, but you need not be a professional writer to apply to be a success. Often an area of special interest may be your key to syndication, [and] innovative ideas not yet appearing in newspapers are encouraged."

How to Syndicate Your Own Newspaper Column by successful Chicago-based free-lancers W. P. Williams and Joseph H. Van Zandt shows you how to develop a column idea or concept, how to market it to newspaper or syndicate, and what to do if no one seems interested—syndicate yourself.

Before you go the self-syndication route, however, take a second look at what you're offering in the column. It's not enough, as one clinical psychologist found out, to rehash in laymen's terms the results of research already published in professional journals.

To be successful, a column must be broad-based and appeal to a cross-section of readers who are daily becoming more sophisticated about their body, health, nutrition, fitness, and emotional well-being. Being a columnist is demanding—but it does give you the enviable right to pick your own topics, say what you want, and get paid for it.

MAGAZINES

The most dramatic change in magazines in recent years has been the decline of general-appeal periodicals and the rise of hundreds of highly specialized publications. During the late 1970s and into the 1980s, new magazines oriented toward health, fitness, and popular science burst on the scene in the wake of the do-it-yourself and wellness movements.

A look at seventeen of the top circulation leaders that accept freelance submissions shows that only five magazines were on the market at the half-century mark. Another three saw light of publication during the 1960s.

CIRCULATION LEADERS THAT ACCEPT FREE-LANCE SUBMISSIONS

Monthly	Est.	Circ.*	Payment**
1. Prevention	1950	3,034,503	N/A
2. Popular Science Monthly	1872	1,802,726	$200/pg. min.
3. Self	1979	1,089,640	$700-$1,500
4. Health	1969	974,469	$400-$1,100
5. Psychology Today	1967	856,405	$1,000
6. Weight Watchers Magazine	1968	847,463	$200-$600
7. Omni	1978	832,282	$1,500-$1,750
8. American Health	1982	750,000	$600,$2,000
9. Science 84	1979	719,282	$400
10. Science Digest	1936	575,365	N/A
11. Shape, Merging Mind & Fitness	1981	462,081	negotiable fee
12. Today's Living	1970	440,000	N/A
13. Muscle & Fitness	1940	408,662	$150-negotiable
14. Bestways Magazine	1973	300,000	10 cents/word
15. Total Fitness	1972	200,000	$75-$300
16. Vegetarian Times	1973	150,000	5 cents/word min.
17. Let's Live	1933	135,000	$50-$150

* Figures from 1985 Ayer Directory of Publications
** Figures from 1985 Writer's Market

CIRCULATION LEADERS

Basically, there are three types of magazines: house organs, trade publications, and consumer magazines. (Professional journals make up a separate category of publications.)

Consumer Magazines
Consumer magazines are those written for the general public. You see them all the time—publications like *Esquire, Ladies' Home Journal, Reader's Digest, Atlantic Monthly,* and many of the health and science publications listed on the chart. Within that mass of men, women, and children who make up the general public are *target* audiences that the specialty publications try to reach. For example, *Seventeen, Parents Magazine, Weight Watchers Magazine,* or *Black Family Magazine* have obvious constituencies.

Consumer publications depend heavily on advertising revenues to stay in the black. To attract advertisers, the magazines must be able to deliver a "market segment" of readers. It may be the eighteen- to thirty-four-year-old women *Redbook* aims at or the twenty-five- to thirty-nine-year-old group of men with high discretionary income that *Gentlemen's Quarterly* is designed to attract. But the only way an editor *holds* this readership is to come up with a mix of topics, month after month, appealing to that magazine's particular readership.

Health, fitness, and medical topics appear regularly on the contents page for one main reason—readers want such information and are willing to buy the magazine to get it. Subscription renewals play a big part in determining just how successful a publication is in meeting reader needs. But according to one New York editor, "The best barometer of how well we're doing is what happens with our sales figures month after month. This is what everybody in the business watches—your *newsstand* sales figures, more than anything else."

Look at it this way. Subscribers may like some issues of the magazine better than others, but they receive *all* of them in the subscription package they've already paid for. Impulse buyers, on the other hand, are free to skim the contents and cover of a magazine *before* they buy it. Newsstand sales figures tell editors in terms of dollars and cents whether they're right on target in meeting the needs of the casual reader as well.

If you want to sell what you write to these consumer publications, study the covers. "The pictures tell a lot," says free-lancer Connie Emerson, who's sold more than 250 magazine articles, "but the words say even more—both in terms of the audience the editor wants to reach and the kinds of articles he or she is eager to buy."

Keep in mind that even though you think the public should know more about a certain medical topic, you can only educate people in the areas they are *receptive* to. As one self-help writer puts it: "It's no good dishing up tofu, no matter how nutritious it is, if all the readership's interested in is new uses for Hamburger Helper—they just won't buy it." No one knows better than the editor what his or her readers will buy, and you have to *sell* the editor first.

Subspecialty Publications

Within the health field, there are also what I call subspecialty publications—those aimed at the general public, but a public that's hospitalized, recuperating, learning to cope with their disease or disability, or helping others do so.

Some but not all of these magazines fall into a category known as *house* magazines. These are publications often distributed without charge to a "controlled" list of readers who purchase the products or services of the sponsoring company, hospital, or organizations. These publications are truly a hidden market for free-lancers who may not even know they exist unless their work, a family member's health—or their own—has put them in a position to see such magazines.

For example, the quarterly *Diabetes Self Management* pays $500-$800 for up to 2,000 words on new product, new treatment, how-to, and diet articles related to diabetic self-care. Circulation: 250,000. Another publication oriented toward a single disease is *Alcoholism, The National Magazine*. Pay here is $100 per printed page for articles on alcoholism, its treatment, and "the adventure of recovery." Editors want writers who know about alcoholism in depth and who can make tough material readable and palatable for a popular and professional audience of 30,000.

Still another quarterly that has recently opened up to free-lancers is *Ostomy Journal*. Edited by Kathryn Pape, the magazine is the official publication of the United Ostomy Association, Inc., an information and support group for those who have undergone abdominal ostomy—a surgical procedure in which the intestinal tract is brought to the surface of the abdomen to bypass an obstructed or diseased portion of the bowel. Editorial priority goes to articles on living with ostomies and new medical, surgical, and technological advances in this area, but Pape doesn't rule out pieces on life-styles, artistic activities, new products, and humor.

Listen, a quarterly with circulation of 150,000, specializes in drug prevention and positive alternatives to drug dependencies of all kinds. Audience: high school students and those who work with them, including teachers, counselors, health professionals, and law-enforcement officers. Crucial to making a sale here is a *teenage* point of view. Recent article examples: "Inhalants—High Way to a Big Fall" and "How to Face a Crisis."

Some of these magazines may not pay much for first rights, but they are good markets for *reprint* sales (second rights). One of these is *Accent on Living,* a quarterly aimed at physically disabled persons and rehabilitation professionals.

Another is *TLC, the Magazine for Recuperation and Relaxation,* a bimonthly that reaches 250,000 hospital patients who receive it free during hospital overnight stays. Although editor Rebecca Stefoff isn't interested in health-related materials as such, this is a good reprint market for any articles you've written on topics that entertain and divert readers—e.g., personality profiles, games, humor, sports, food, travel, personal finance, grooming—many of which play a big part in fostering the enjoyment of life and a sense of well-being. Payment is negotiated on an individual basis.

Trade Publications

Subspecialty magazines differ from *trade* publications, which report on an industry, business, or profession as a whole and are dependent on subscription fees and advertising. Among the "trades" are publications like *Podiatry Management, Private Practice, Medical Economics, Genetic Engineering News, Health Industry Today,* and *Modern Healthcare.* The latter, for example, carries features on management, finance, building design, construction, and new technology for hospitals, nursing homes, and other health-care institutions.

Chapter 14, "Specialized Health Communications," examines free-lance opportunities in writing and editing for the trades and other print or audiovisual media. Selling what you write to consumer publications is covered in depth in several other chapters throughout this book.

BOOKS

Each day, Americans publish 125 new books, claims Tom Parker in his book *In One Day.* Of these 15 are new works of fiction, 8 are new children's books, 20 are books on sociology and economics, and 6 deal with history. There are 5 new reference books, 8 or 9 on medicine, 9 on philosophy or psychology, 15 on science and technology, and 6 on religion. Americans, he says, buy almost 5 million books a day.

Most of these books, however, have a short lifespan on the shelf. Says one bookseller with a major chain, "The big chains will tell you one thing; small bookstores, another. It's an individual judgment call, but normally, with us, it's about four months for psychology/medical topics/self-help books. If we don't sell enough copies of a book to merit reordering and ongoing shelf space in four months, that's it."

While this doesn't daunt the hundreds of established and would-be authors who seek publishers for book-length manuscripts, it does point up the need to do your homework first.

The big questions are always, *Who* will buy this book and are there *enough* of these potential buyers to warrant publication? Without a clearly identifiable market for your manuscript, the best idea, the finest research, and the most intriguing case histories will not be enough to land a publisher. (This doesn't rule out self-publishing, but it should make you think twice about your potential market.)

As Jane Adams points out in her book *How to Sell What You Write*, matching your idea to the market is easier to do with magazines than with books. However, "If a glance at a buyer's catalog indicates that he never publishes the kind of material you've written," she says, "it would be pointless to try to sell your product to him."

The bright side of the picture is that your chances of selling a nonfiction book are nine times greater than they are for fiction. Publishers know health, fitness, diet, and self-help are steady sellers. And some publishers, like Prentice-Hall, aren't sitting back waiting for book proposals to come in. They're actively seeking them out.

At a recent American Medical Writers Association meeting, Prentice-Hall acquisitions editor David Wright placed this notice on a conference message board:

> Rapidly expanding line of popular health books, and looking for new authors interested in, and experts in nutrition, preventive medicine, natural healing, health improvement, even traditional and folk medicine and remedies, for practical books for the public.

Finding a Publisher

Writer's Market lists more than 160 publishers of books in the health and medical field, including scholarly and reference works, how-to and self-help, and textbooks. For a more complete listing of publishers, consult your library copy of *Literary Market Place*. One of the most comprehensive resources, it lists American and Canadian book publishers, book clubs, literary agents, and associations.

Another good source of information on publishers is *The Publishers' Trade List Annual*. This buying and reference guide to books and related products includes a complete publishers' list with addresses, catalogs in alphabetical order, and a subject index.

For example, under the subject heading "Health Science/Health

Service," you'll find 138 publishers ranging from Boy Scouts of America and Rodale Press to New American Library and Howard University Press. Although there's some overlapping of publishers listed in certain subject areas, 99 publishers are listed under "Medicine and Dentistry," 165 under "Science and Technology," 22 under "Programmed Learning and Multimedia," and 147 under "Psychiatry and Psychology"—among them, Random House, Doubleday, Crown Publishers, and several university presses.

What does it take to write a successful book for the public on a health or medical topic? Isadore Rosenfeld, M.D., who has written two popular consumer books on medicine, says, "First of all, you've got to have a message—you can't just want to write a book because you want to write, you've got to have something to say. And it should be unique."

Unique is a word editors abhor. But the truth is, you do need an *original* message, *new* information or an *update* on what's already known, a *fresh approach* to the subject, and a *passion* for the topic that doesn't blind you—but rather, *fuels you* for the long haul of writing a book about it.

Subject Guide to Books in Print, an annual found in all libraries and most bookstores, lists more than 270,000 book titles now available from U.S. publishers, indexed under 42,500 headings. *Paperbound Books in Print* lists thousands of paperbacks by title, author, and subject. Looking over these titles can give you an idea of which companies have published books on the same topics you're interested in. It can also show you quickly whether or not somebody else has already written the book you have in mind.

Subject Guide to Forthcoming Books is issued bimonthly and lists books to be published during the next five months. If no other author seems to have hit on your idea, you know where to send your book proposal or manuscript.

You may think that because a publisher already has one or more books on child-rearing or female sexuality or dieting, there's no point in sending a similar book idea to that house. Not so. Book publishers tend to stay with popular topics they've already invested in—and your book could be just what they need for next year's spring or fall list.

For the inside scoop on publishing trends, plus the most up-to-date information on the industry itself, take a look at *Publishers Weekly*. Read by almost everyone in the trade, its influence is without parallel. Health or medically oriented titles are reviewed in a monthly column that includes other books as well. You can keep abreast of upcoming books and topics by skimming *PW's* spring and fall announcement issues, which include annotated lists of forthcoming titles. And if you can pick up a pattern or sense a trend, take a second look at your book idea. If you can shape your proposal along these new lines, you're onto something hot that should be ready to sell just as your book rolls off the presses.

If you're interested in writing for young people, check the latest edition of *Children's Media Market Place*, edited by Carol A. Emmens. Here you'll find everything from periodicals for children to audio-visual producers and book publishers, classified by format, subject, and special interest.

Under the subject heading "Health," for instance, 146 book publishers are listed, including scholastic presses. Under special interests, such as "Reading Disabled," there are 62 publishers; "Blind," 16; "Deaf," 23, and "Mentally Handicapped," 45 publishers. Of course, these categories are only a sample of the diversity of topics available to those writing for children or teenagers. Publishers are now more willing to tackle subjects once considered taboo—subjects such as sexual abuse, venereal disease, teenage pregnancy—although in some cities the distribution of such books is limited because of restrictions imposed by parents, schools, or libraries.

Other Publishing Options

Selling your book to a major trade publisher is not only an ego booster, it has certain advantages in terms of marketing, advertising budget, national distribution, and getting the book reviewed.

However, it's not always possible to go this route—even when you have an idea an editor thinks is a *winner*. For example, what if a major publisher tells you your book deals with an important topic, but the marketing/trade committee doubts there's a big enough audience willing to plunk down money for it at the bookstore?

This happens all the time. If it happens to you, keep trying. However, if you receive rejection slips from several publishers, you may want to consider some other possibilities.

Your options at this point are to drop the project, self-publish, find a sponsor, work with a vanity press (not advised), or submit your proposal, outline, and sample chapters to a small-press publisher or book packager.

Relatively new on the publishing scene, book packagers operate as both editors and publishers—taking ideas, working with writers, editing manuscripts, raising money to bring the work to the camera-ready or bound-book stage. Then they sell the package to an established publishing company and may even deliver the books to the publisher's warehouse. However, the packager does not market or distribute the book; instead, it licenses the publisher to sell the book.

Some packagers offer authors a percentage of the royalties as they come in from the publisher; other packagers pay the writer a flat fee.

In her book, Jane Adams notes that some packagers rival major publishers in scope of titles and quality of work. *The Joy of Sex*, she says, and the *Handbook of Separation Techniques for Chemical Engineers* both began as package books. So obviously, there's a wide range of topics and audiences that can be approached this way successfully.

For more information on small presses, consult the latest edition of *The International Directory of Little Magazines and Small Presses*. One of the most comprehensive and detailed listings, with more than 4,000 nonestablishment markets for writers, this reference work has been called "the bible of the business" by the *Wall Street Journal*. Included are regional, subject, and distributors indexes with about 100 publishers and publications ranging from *Medical Self-Care* to *Sunshine and Health, The Nudist Magazine*. If your library doesn't have a copy, you can order one for about $20 from Dustbooks, P.O. Box 100, Paradise, CA 95969.

And if you're tired of stuffing manuscripts into manila folders and rejection slips into desk drawers, Judith Appelbaum and Nancy Evans's *How to Get Happily Published* may be just the tonic you need for your publishing blahs.

You may have trouble finding a publisher at first, but that can be overcome. The one thing you don't want to do is write a book nobody wants to read. And unfortunately, all too many health-care professionals find themselves with just such a manuscript (or two) on hand. Usually what they've done, says one best-selling physician-author, "is mix apples and oranges. They've tried to straddle the fence between writing for the public and writing for their colleagues—and it just doesn't work."

For pointers on putting together an effective book proposal or outline and tips on promoting yourself as an author the way the pros do, see chapter 13, "Proposing and Promoting Your Book," which takes you through the steps in putting together an effective book proposal or outline. Also covered are tips on working successfully with a ghostwriter or creative collaborator, plus pointers on how the pros work to promote their books.

4 □ PAGING AND PACKAGING BRIGHT IDEAS

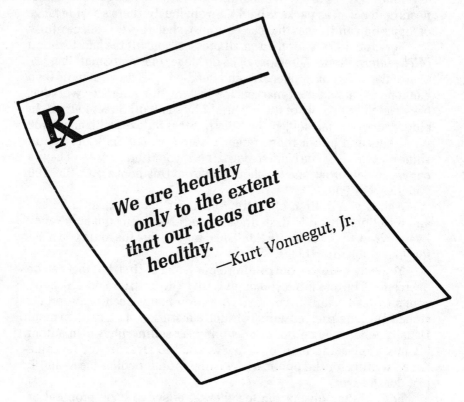

We are healthy only to the extent that our ideas are healthy.

—Kurt Vonnegut, Jr.

On the 449th of the famed Arabian Nights, the dazzling Scheherazade "began to speak of medicine."

By the time she had finished—six nights later—she had covered everything from human anatomy and how to treat or diagnose disease to beauty hints for reddening the cheeks or deferring grey hair and tips on personal hygiene, diet, and sex. Sex, she said, "hath in it many and exceeding virtues and praiseworthy qualities, amongst which are that it calmeth the heat of love and induceth affection and dilateth the heart and dispelleth the sadness of solitude," to say nothing of how it "lighteneth the body."

Scheherazade had the right idea.

Making the health connection paid off then, as it's paying off now for hundreds of successful free-lancers and medical writers. They know, as she did, that for human interest, news value, consumer appeal, and drama in real life, there's no beating stories about what's at stake in living, looking, feeling better or how to come up with the wherewithal to pay for it.

"Of all the subjects readers are interested in, health ranks number one every single time," Hara Estroff Marano, executive editor of *American Health*, said at a writers' conference. "So any article you do is bound to get the attention of readers. The only problem—*first* you have to get the editor's attention. How? With a terrific proposal."

Terrific proposals start with salable ideas. And salable ideas are those that are timely, well honed, carefully thought out, and sharply focused. Where do they come from?

The fact is, there's no secret to finding ideas in the health category when almost every aspect of our lives, jobs, leisure activities, and interpersonal relationships has a health component.

"Thinking up ideas is a talent you can learn," says free-lancer Jody Gaylin. "It's not something you're just born with. I find I get ideas from the newspaper, from things that I'm thinking about with my own children, conversations with friends . . . but the important thing is to make sure the magazine you're submitting to hasn't just run the same article."

WHO'S ALREADY RUN WHAT?

If you've collected several recent copies of the publication you want to write for, it's fairly easy to check: Have they or haven't they already come up with your idea? But no writer can keep up with *all* the magazines. That's where three indexes found in almost every library come in handy.

- Reader's Guide to Periodical Literature *covers about 180 general-interest periodicals. Here's the place to see if* Reader's Digest, McCall's, Atlantic Monthly, *or several other major publications have already run a story along the same lines you're considering. If they haven't, go for it.*

- Access: The Supplementary Index to Periodicals *complements other general periodical indexes in that it includes such city/regional magazines and special-interest publications as* Village Voice, TV Guide, Omni, Discover, American Lawyer, *and* Early American Life.

- Magazine Index *is a microfilm index of 370 magazines from 1976 to the present. It includes graded reviews of movies, plays, restaurants, books. Especially helpful in rethinking ideas is a three-ring binder it produces with monthly inserts of "Hot Topics" in the news—beginning, as you might expect, with abortion.*

An easy way to take the pulse of the nation's general-interest article ideas is to write *Reader's Digest* and ask to be put on the mailing list for a free copy of its annual index.

TAKING TITLE

Read the magazines you want to write for—not only for style but for ideas. Good ideas don't lose their appeal—they're perennially interesting. If an idea has sold once, it can easily be sold again with a slight twist, a different angle, new data. Skimming the titles in any of these indexes is often all that's needed to trigger new ideas.

For example, try creative free-wheeling with titles in subject areas that interest you. For the moment, ignore label titles (those with no verb, e.g., "Premenstrual Tension" or "Dental Caries"). Concentrate on titles with nouns *and* verbs. Titles that ask a question, give a command, or deal with a negative are natural idea sources. (For more on titles, see chapter 7).

Wordplay starts when you take a key word and substitute your own. If, for example, the word *winter* appears in the title, try *summer.* If the title reads, "What You Want Your Doctor to Know," try substituting *Dentist* or perhaps, *Stepfather.* (A piece on stepfathers, for instance, would work well for a Father's Day Sunday-supplement feature or teenage magazine.)

See what happens when you turn negative titles into positive ones, and vice versa. Think in terms of opposites, e.g., *hot* and *cold,* or *mad* and *glad.* Consider complements: *yin* and *yang, fall* and *spring.* Don't forget holidays, rituals, anniversaries—or the weather. One intriguing title I've seen asks, "Storms—Are They Sexier than Sunshine?" (The answer, just in case you're interested, links barometer readings of 29.90 or lower, usually associated with some sort of storm center or frontal system, with increased sexual activity in married couples.)

IDEA TURN-ONS

Train yourself to think like a writer. Develop the ability to filter everything you do, see, experience, hear—or overhear—through your own idea-screening system. Ask yourself: Is there an article idea here?

Next, look beneath the most obvious facets of what you're doing, reading, experiencing, etc. Run through the newswriter's trusty five W's (who, what, where, when, why), and don't forget how and how much.

Ask yourself: What's behind all this? What's ahead? Is there a new twist to an old medical tale, fact, belief, or therapy? Lastly, turn detective. Ask around—discreetly, if you must. Maybe the real story idea is in what somebody else or some government agency is doing, or not doing.

That's what Detroit Free Press medical reporter Dolly Katz turned up in her award-winning series "Bad Doctors," which documented that governmental licensing does not ensure that the public is safeguarded from inept or unethical doctors. In researching her story, Katz obtained access to many records not generally open to the public—then went well beyond the records to talk to the people behind them to get their stories.

An idea, Robert Frost once said, "is a feat of association." All it takes is practice in making the association with health and knowing where to start.

NEWSPAPERS—HEALTH WRITER'S GOLD MINE

New York free-lancer Diane Ouding, whose by-line has appeared in Cosmopolitan, Viva, Working Woman and The New York Times, says one of her best idea sources is her mother, who lives in the Midwest and sends newspaper clippings back east. For instance, her Times story on fear of flying, says Ouding, began with a Sunday magazine supplement clipping from a Michigan paper which told of famous people who suffer from that phobia—one she shares. The idea jelled, she says, with an "episode from the 'Bob Newhart' show. I figured if both Bob and I were scared, there must be a story in it."

Reading the Sunday papers, particularly the feature sections, advises Ouding, is a good way to find ideas. Of course, many other free-lancers are doing it, too, which helps to explain the certain circularity to free-lance writing. "An idea will catch on," Ouding says, "and then every magazine will want a story about it. If you find an idea, sometimes you can ride the crest of a trend. And there are lots of little trendlets going on at any given time."

Remember, however, that most editors read many of the same newspapers, especially The New York Times and other major dailies. An idea spawned by an out-of-town paper editors aren't likely to see has a much greater chance of success. To convert a hometown story to one of regional or national interest, give it a geographic spread through the experts you quote, the statistics or anecdotes you select.

That way, the information in the piece doesn't relate only to your state—unless you're writing for a state or regional publication.

RADIO, TELEVISION, AND OTHER MEDIA

One evening while driving, Joyce Bermel heard a newscast on her car radio that not only triggered an article idea but gave her the lead as well. Bermel is managing editor of the *Hastings Center Report*, a journal devoted to ethical issues in science and medicine. Here's what she wrote in "Is the Media the Last Resort in Donor Cases?" which appeared in *Medica*, a publication for women practicing medicine:

> One evening, as I was driving my son to a music lesson, I heard a familiar message on the radio. An 11-year-old girl with a fatal liver disease needed an organ transplant. If a liver donor didn't come forward quickly, the girl would die. The following week, my evening paper reported the end of that story. A liver donor was not found for Michelle Heckard. She died the same day in Children's Hospital of Philadelphia.
>
> When I read that account, I couldn't help wondering whether we are entering a new phase in the relationship between the media and the public over the issue of organ transplants. It could be pure chance that no donor turned up for Michelle. But media appeals may also be losing their effectiveness with the public.

COMMERCIALS AND ADVERTISING

Anyone who watches the CBS evening news knows the agony of prime-time advertising's five H's—halitosis, hemorrhoids, hair loss, heartburn, and headaches. But don't discount commercials as an idea source.

A Sperry Corporation TV commercial pointing up the company's commitment to "listening" and its importance in our lives triggered free-lancer Cynthia Bell's idea alert. She called Sperry's public-relations department and learned that an ongoing employee-education program included a lecture on the art of listening by an expert in the field.

Bell explained that she was writing an article and asked to attend a lecture, which turned out to be extremely interesting and a source of good quotes for the piece. The public-relations director also supplied her with a packet of materials related to listening and what Sperry was trying to accomplish. Her article appeared in 1982 in *Family Weekly*. It was later picked up by CBS Educational and Professional Publishing and purchased for a microcomputer program designed to teach adults speed-reading techniques in ten lessons. Bell's query for this highly successful commercial-inspired piece appears on pages 77-78.

OTHER IDEA SOURCES

No writing specialty, whether it's sports, medical, religious, or outdoor writing, has a monopoly on idea sources. All writers' guidebooks cover the same ground—ranging from capitalizing on your own and your friends' experiences to culling the *Yellow Pages* for trade journal ideas. Here are eleven major idea sources reported by successful health and medical writers.

Congressional Record

"Read the *Congressional Record*," Chicago-based free-lancer Bonnie Remsberg suggested at a writers' conference. Remsberg, who received a prestigious award for her *Family Circle* piece on nuclear testing in Nevada during the 1950s and 1960s and its effect on a small Utah town, says she has plumbed this record of America's tax money at work "because congressmen are entering into it all sorts of material from around the country that won't be seen anywhere else."

Medical Journals

"It's in the medical journals that go to doctors that you can spot trends before they occur," says New York free-lancer Lucy Kavaler, author of *A Matter of Degree: Heat, Life and Death* and fourteen other books. "A number of years ago, for example, I sold an article to *Good Housekeeping* on the heart drugs—this was just before everybody was talking about heart drugs, but I knew that information. More recently, I sold an article to *Self* magazine in which it was necessary to know about the endorphins and substances that act like morphine.

"In other words," she says, "you really need to stay a little bit ahead of the topic. You not only read to have knowledge about health topics, you read to convince an editor, too."

Don't forget, many editors are also perusing these professional journals. When the idea a writer proposes is weak, off base, or lacking in credibility or backup authority, they can spot these problems or check them out with one of the magazine's health-care consultants or contributors—people who are experts in the field.

Health Newsletters, Reports, Medical Information Services

"I subscribe to a number of medical periodicals such as the *Harvard Medical School Health Letter*," reports California research writer

Diane Monahan, who specializes in investigative reporting on medical topics. Other widely circulated health newsletters/reports include: *Mayo Clinic Health Letter; University of California, Berkeley, Wellness Letter; Executive Health; Taking Care,* published by the Center for Consumer Education, and *Morbidity and Mortality Weekly Report (MMWR).* This concise, easy-to-read bulletin from the Centers for Disease Control alerts you to new diseases and national and international epidemics as well as what's happening in public health.

New on the idea-sparking scene is *Newsearch,* edited by free-lance medical writer Joseph H. Bloom. Billed as "A Medical Writer's Information Service," the quarterly is mailed free to free-lance medical writers, newspaper science writers and editors, and broadcasters dealing with health-related issues. "The idea behind *Newsearch,*" says Bloom, "is to provide you with possible starting points for a story that you might want to bring to the attention of the general public."

A recent issue, for instance, contained sixteen idea leads, with medical journal citations ranging from *Lancet* and *British Journal of Dermatology* to *Journal of the American Medical Association (JAMA), Journal of Gerontology,* and *Canadian Family Physician.* Among topics covered: "Backache Ahead? Computers to the Rescue," "The Role of Zinc in Human Health and Disease," "Decoding Body Organ Talk," and "A New Malady: 'Dermatitis Simulata'." To be put on the mailing list for a complimentary copy, write to Bloom at Box 95, Spring House, PA 19477.

Trade, Association, and Medical News Publications

There are hundreds of these health news tabloids and trade and association publications, including *Medical News & International Report* and *American Medical News,* the weekly published by the American Medical Association. More information on trade journals and writing for them is found in chapter 14.

Free-lancer Alice Lake, whose by-line has appeared in *Reader's Digest* and all major women's magazines, told writers at a New York conference that in addition to reading *The New York Times* and *Pyschology Today,* she regularly reads the *New England Journal of Medicine* and two other news/trade publications, *Medical World News* and *Medical Economics.*

Titles in a recent issue of *Medical Economics* point up the fact that you don't need to have a science or medical background to write many of the articles that appear in such publications. Some examples: "Is Your Broker Your Biggest Investment Risk?" "How Many Doctors Are Cheating Their Way into Practice?" and "Doctors and Handguns: The Arming of American Medicine."

Meetings, Workshops, Seminars

Many of my best article ideas have been triggered by titles of talks listed in conference and workshop brochures or programs. Coupled with information from the "bio" beneath the speaker's name, I've been able to write an effective query letter with minimum time and effort.

For example, *Ladycom* bought an interview I did with Joan Gillette Tannebaum, one of the nation's first woman athletic trainers and a recognized authority on women's sports injuries. Seeing her name and the title of her talk listed in a program for a Sports Medicine Conference program held weeks before in Reno, I called the meeting chairperson and explained why I wanted to contact Gillette. Once I had her address, a phone call to Gillette and her agreement to be interviewed at a later date provided all the initial information I needed to query an editor.

Hospital Hot Lines

What's the *big question* now? Know that and you're certainly in tune with major health concerns of hundreds of Americans around the country. "Many hospitals will provide a printout of questions most frequently asked via the hot line," says William A. Check, who worked three years for a prestigious medical publication before deciding to free-lance full-time. Another good source of information on patient concerns is the National Council on Patient Information in Washington, D.C.

Need for Information

The book *How Do I Feel—What Do I Need?* was designed by Jean Roberts to meet a specific need in *both* the arts and the rehabilitation field. An arts enthusiast and registered occupational therapist, Roberts is convinced that people with physical handicaps are often at a disadvantage in museums, theaters, and arts centers because ushers, volunteers, and staff aren't trained to assist the disabled person in that setting.

Teaming up with Sierra Arts Foundation in Reno, she put together a pictorial guide for those who work with handicapped persons. Published by the nonprofit foundation, the soft-cover book is now in its third printing, and proceeds from its sale go toward improving accessibility to the arts for disabled people and for special arts programs and workshops.

Need of another sort prompted Dr. Harry C. Huneycutt, a Reno obstetrician and gynecologist, to write *All About Hysterectomy* with the late Judith Davis as coauthor in 1977. A forerunner of books to come,

All About Hysterectomy offered women—and the men in their lives—the opportunity to educate themselves about the female body and the risks and benefits of surgery to remove the uterus, so that they could make decisions based on facts, not folklore.

Talking to People

"I think a lot comes from talking to other people, especially people out of your own age [range] or your particular socioeconomic group," says New York City free-lancer Alice Fleming, who has written hundreds of magazine articles and twenty-three books.

"I find in talking to younger women I can often get a fix on the problems bothering them. Or when we go to the country, I talk to people up there and they have a different orientation than we do here in the city. Even traveling or visiting friends in another city. I don't know if it's just because I'm an outsider and I look at it differently, but I get a lot of ideas that way." For a detailed look at how she sells articles *before* she writes them, see her article proposal on page 80.

Personal Experience and Observation

"In the pharmacy one day, I looked at all the things we can treat ourselves at home with and the next thing I asked myself was, We can do all this at home, but *should* we?" says Barbara Chapman, media director for the National Center for Missing & Exploited Children in Washington, D.C. That question became the focus of a free-lance article on home-medicine-cabinet remedies which appeared in the October, 1984, issue of *Better Homes & Gardens.*

When a routine examination by Jody Gaylin's gynecologist turned up a click and a murmur between the "lub" and "dub" of her heartbeat, he insisted she see a cardiologist as soon as possible. Suspected diagnosis: a mitral valve prolapse.

Gaylin was scared. Her fears escalated when she was told that before the heart specialist would see her, she would have to complete three tests, one of which included wearing a Holter Monitor for twenty-four hours to obtain a continuous recording of her heartbeat. Furthermore, the doctor urged her to act quickly. Yet no one had explained what a mitral valve prolapse was—or reassured her that the essentially benign condition is so common it's sometimes called the "cardiac disease of the decade."

After the diagnosis was confirmed, Gaylin set out to learn more about her condition. She consulted medical experts, wrote up her experience supplemented with facts on mitral valve prolapse, then submitted an article proposal to *Woman's Day.* Her story, "Something Is Wrong With My Heart," appeared in the November, 1983, issue.

Professional Practice and Contacts

Doctors, nurses, psychologists find contact with patients and fellow professionals a steady source of salable book and article ideas.

William Southmayd, M.D., for example, teamed up with Marshall Hoffman to write *Sports Health: the Complete Book of Athletic Injuries*. Southmayd, who is medical director of Sports Medicine Resource, Inc. (the largest sports-medicine clinic in New England) and a consulting physician for the Boston Red Sox, acknowledges he's always asked two basic questions: What are the safest sports? and How can I prevent injuries? The book provides those answers.

Jacqueline Hornor Plumez, Ph.D., is a clinical psychologist who has written three books. One, yet to be published, deals with the psychological reasons why people have money problems; another, *Successful Adoption: A Guide to Finding a Child and Raising a Family* is currently being revised for a new paperback edition. Her third book, *Divorcing a Corporation: How to Know When . . . and If . . . a Job Change Is Right for You* speaks for itself. All of these ideas, says Plumez, grew out of her private practice in psychotherapy and career counseling—but entailed extensive research thereafter.

Spinoffs from Other Projects

British neuropsychologist Jonathan Miller is best known to American audiences for his popular PBS series "The Body in Question," in which the fast-talking Miller delivered an engagingly contentious history of medical science.

As a result of that series, Miller and graphic designer David Pelham came up with an idea for *The Human Body*. The entertaining and informative children's book of pop-up illustrations with moving parts became an international best seller. And since one good idea leads naturally to another, this creative duo has now produced its second pop-up book, *The Facts of Life*.

Ideas from Editors

Following a spate of her articles in major women's magazines, which all came out in spring, 1985, *Ladies' Home Journal* editors suggested several ideas to free-lancer Jody Gaylin, who picked the ones she liked best. (However, even when the idea originates with an editor, writers are still expected to submit a query letter or article proposal showing how they will approach the subject.)

In *The Youngest Science*, Lewis Thomas, M.D., credits former *New England Journal of Medicine* editor Franz Ingelfinger with inviting him to write some essays for the *Journal* in the early 1970s. He also says it was Elisabeth Sifton, an editor at the Viking Press, who sold him on the idea of collecting the essays into a book. Other publishers had approached him about the project, he explains, but they wanted new essays ("connective pieces") plus rewriting of some of the originals. Sifton thought otherwise and in 1974 brought out Thomas's first book, *The Lives of a Cell.* Since then, he's written three others.

At some larger publishing houses, explains Gene E. Malott, a partner in GEM Publishing Group, "editors get together and decide pretty much what they want on the book list—a certain number from this category, certain number from another and so on. If you're in the stable of writers, you may get the assignment; getting *in,* however, is the hard part."

Sometimes, all it takes is *visibility.* A clinical psychologist I know was quoted in a *New York Times Magazine* article one month and invited by Prentice-Hall sports editor Tom Power to submit an idea for a book the next.

Author Feedback
Following publication of her article in *Family Weekly* on the disease systemic lupus erythematosus, Montana-based free-lancer Kathy Crump received a call from a New York public-relations firm asking if she'd be interested in doing an article on a new surgical technique for a form of bowel surgery developed by one of the company's clients. The PR person said one of the reasons they wanted *her* to write the piece was because after the lupus article had appeared, the Lupus Foundation of America, which was mentioned in the piece, had received a record 2,000 inquiries in one week.

Letters to the Editor
I hit the letters-to-the-editor jackpot last year while visiting relatives in Westchester County, New York. While reading a local newspaper, I spotted a letter supporting a recent court ruling on grandparent visitation rights. The writer included not only his address but background information on his family situation which deprived him of the right to see two young grandchildren. I looked up his telephone number, called, explained my interest in writing about grandparent rights, and set up a time for an interview.

When I left his house two hours later, I had photocopies of all the *New York Times* and local newspaper articles on grandparent rights he had collected; copies of poignant family letters to and from his own grandchildren; names of other grandparents suffering the same plight; plus names and addresses of members of Congress working on grandparent-rights legislation. Since he had videotaped congressional hearings on the proposed bill, I watched these as well as television talk show interviews with grandparents, family-relations experts, and others supportive of their rights.

Dissertations, Theses, Professional Papers

San Francisco dream expert Patricia Garfield, Ph.D., was able to turn her dream research and other data gathered for her doctoral dissertation into a highly readable book for the public titled *Creative Dreaming*. But this editorial feat generally eludes most would-be graduate-student authors.

The problem, says Elaine Silverstein, acquisitions and development editor in the National League of Nursing's Communication Division, "is that neither journals nor publishers want dissertations because they are not written for a lay market. They are not written for any market but the person's committee." And anyone who's ever dealt with academic committees knows writing for that audience is *deadly*—even when the ideas and data are fascinating.

Silverstein, who gives writers' workshops for nurses, says dissertations are publishable, but "not in their original form. In some cases, the research done has implications for a lay market, but it requires a vast amount of rethinking and rewriting." In her workshops, she asks nurses to tell her what the topic was and then the group works on how different strands can be teased out of the subject and what audience would be interested in such information. "Very often," she says, "we come up with five or ten different papers out of one topic."

Idea Files

Now's the time to capitalize on the fact that the human brain records everything a person experiences. Functioning much like a fantastic computer, it can come up with new combinations of stored data and fresh associations between paper files and mental files. The problem, more often than not, is finding *time* to do it.

Wading through a mass of unsorted clippings, articles, reports, or scribbled notes can be either a chore or a treasure hunt—especially when what seemed important a month ago may be a throwaway four weeks later. But that's a small price to pay for finding an idea whose timing is ripe for further development. Some writers, like Sheila Nauman-Todd, set aside time each week to look over the idea pile and cull the most promising.

IDEAS—TESTING THE BEST, WEEDING OUT THE REST

It's said that writers should be sitting at a typewriter with a catcher's mitt because life hurls so many experiences and ideas our way. But the key to success isn't merely latching onto an idea—it's recognizing a *salable* one.

First of all, it's important to realize that a subject *isn't* an idea; neither is a category. *An idea is a topic combined with an approach.* I once overheard a woman at a writers' conference approach *Parade* health editor Earl Ubell with an idea for a story on mental illness. "It's so important for people to know more about it," she said with urgency in her voice. "What about mental illness?" Ubell asked as gently as he could. "That's an enormous topic—you have to take a particular aspect of it."

You can expect the same answer from any editor worth a blue pencil if you propose articles on topics like job stress, teenage emotional disorders, or health-care financing. *What about them?* What any editor wants to know when you propose an article idea is:

- *What approach will you take to the subject?*
- *How are you going to break it down into appropriate and manageable article size?*
- *Where will you get your information?*
- *Are you an expert? Will you have a coauthor who is an authority on the subject?*
- *Why should the magazine run this article now? Is there something new people should know about—perhaps new research, a new treatment, a news peg that makes it important for people to understand more about the subject at this time?*
- *What's significant in the idea, and why should I care?*

Without convincing answers, you won't sell an editor on your idea. So take the initiative. Save yourself postage and rejection blues. Weed out the ideas that are weaklings before you've invested much time in research or writing—before an editor sees your idea and says "no-go."

A good article idea has one strong concept behind it plus a message for readers. A salable article idea must be informative and/or entertaining. And most important, it must speak to the needs or interests of a sizable group of readers.

FIVE NEWS VALUES TO JUDGE BY

When in doubt about market appeal, you can't go wrong checking your idea against five time-honored news values. You may object that your idea doesn't deal with news per se. But these qualities, which journalists consider (consciously or unconsciously) in deciding what to put into a news story or broadcast, can help you pinpoint the strength or weakness of almost any idea.

Timeliness

Today—now and *at this moment*—can't be upstaged for timeliness. Is yours a breaking news item? A story in which the "when" factor is significant? Daily news and broadcast journalists are the ones most likely to answer yes in the short haul. But book authors and magazine freelancers often take the "now factor" and spin it out in an article, for example, on "Latest Developments in the Orphan Embryo Battle" or a book, *Heart Transplant Surgery Today.*

Proximity

A toxic-waste spill or preschool sexual-abuse case in your community is top news not only in your local newspaper but in regional and often national ones as well. However, the "nearness factor" is not only in *geographical closeness* to such events but also in *relevance of an issue* to readers. Editors respond to a story that hits close to home—whether in physical, fiscal, political, or emotional terms.

Prominence

Names make news, and none more so than those of celebrities, experts, outlaws, and ordinary citizens caught up in windfalls, disasters, medical anomalies, miracles, or ethical dilemmas. The more prominent or notable the person, the more significant the story's impact.

Foremost, of course, is the president of the United States. When President Eisenhower suffered a heart attack in 1955, the value of stocks on the New York Stock Exchange dropped $14 billion. When President Reagan donned a hearing aid, business in hearing aids soared. Following his surgery for cancer of the colon, callers swamped medical hot lines, cancer societies, many doctors, and clinics with colon queries and, once again, the dollar's value dropped in foreign trading following a false rumor he was in a coma.

When First Lady Betty Ford was operated on for breast cancer, millions of other women hastily examined their breasts for lumps. Several books followed, among them, Betty Rollin's *First, You Cry*, and breast cancer updates still are a mainstay of women's publications. A name that makes news can give you an unbeatable "news peg" on which to hang a query and even your lead.

Consequence

Think *cause and effect, fallout, aftereffects,* and *ripples as a result of,* and you're on the right track in judging whether a story will have significant reader or viewer impact.

In Washington, D.C., for example, when Surgeon General C. Everett Koop set up newborn-nursery hot lines for the anonymous reporting of alleged medical neglect of handicapped infants, the immediate effects were felt in every hospital across the country. But that was only the beginning, as physicians, nurses, attorneys, parents, and groups like the American Academy of Pediatrics felt the aftereffects of what some termed "Big Brother in the Nursery" and others, a protection of the right to life.

Each group affected had its story to tell. While the *Washington Post* and *New York Times* dealt with national consequences, hometown papers covered what was happening in the community hospital, how the hot line was affecting the way area doctors were treating newborns at risk, and stories of local parents coping with infants born with serious birth defects.

Of course, the more significant the ruling, event, or meeting, the more newsworthy its impact. Forty-five years after the dropping of the first atomic bomb, for instance, we are still examining the tragic effects. But life is lived in small, pleasurable ways, too—picnics, a day at the beach, skiing on the slopes. Editors find a ready audience each season for basic safety and coping articles such as those that deal with consequences of too much sun, too much snow, or too much family at traditional holiday get-togethers that should be fun but aren't.

Human Interest

"Don't pooh-pooh human interest stories," *American Health* executive editor Hara Estroff Marano said at a national writers' conference. "They are very difficult to do. And shared experiences are at the root of human connectedness and (not incidentally) of high readership as well."

People stories give us a glimpse into how others live, work, play, and sometimes, how they die. We learn what makes them tick, what tickles them, and what gets them ticked off. All of this is deliberately intended to strike a chord in the reader's feelings or sensibilities in some manner. Written with a high ratio of "personal" words to total words, these stories often have a feeling of warmth that factual articles do not. We can *identify* with these people and events.

Life's basic themes—love, hate, pity, compassion, suffering, empathy, curiosity, anger, and grief—lie at the heart of these tales. But the bigger picture includes *surprises, drama, conflict, suspense, novelty,* and people's somewhat *gossipy* or *nosy* nature. (The word *gazette* which adorns the masthead of so many newspapers, may in fact have its roots in the Italian word for "gossip.")

In evaluating whether an idea or story lead will suit a human-interest approach, writers should ask themselves, How can I present the story so readers can identify with it? What is the basic human theme that could be emphasized? (When *Parade* health editor Earl Ubell, for example, reported little Vicki Wright's desperate need for a liver transplant, he focused the story on what it's like to have to *wait for more than a year* for a donor organ. Anyone—with or without liver disease—could relate to the agony of such an enforced wait.)

Often, the human interest lies in the natural *drama* of the situation. Other times, the writer must tease out the *common threads of personality,* for example, which might link people who survive cancer against all odds. Woven into the story, but in a subordinated role, is the medical background or information on a certain disease, for instance, or the relationship between mind and body.

In further testing an article or book idea, I suggest my writing students ask themselves these questions:

1. *Is there a market?*
2. *Can I list at least three publications or publishers that might buy it?*
3. *What format or type of article would be most suitable and salable? What do I want readers to get from this?*
4. *Can I get the research, photos, and quotes I need? Can I get a coauthor I can work with?*
5. *How enthusiastic am I about writing up this idea? Am I interested enough to stick with it if I get a go-ahead?*
6. *Is the idea sufficiently intriguing so that I won't mind the time it takes to develop it?*

Science sections often make it seem as though breakthrough stories occur every few days. But medical science reveals itself in bits and pieces, with fanfare and without, through tedious testing and experimentation—and sometimes, serendipity. A good medical writer must not only know how to wait, but what *else* to write about while waiting.

TREATMENT—DECIDING FACTORS

Once you've decided your idea is viable and has potential, the next stop is to decide how you will treat it. There are two main considerations: what can you do within the *marketing realities*, and what can you do within your own *skills* as a researcher and writer.

If you've kept up with markets you want to write for, you know what kind of publications to approach. (For a quick review, see chapter 3.) Now's the time to tailor a list of your best bets—newspaper supplements, for example, or trade and specialty magazines that use similar material—complete with the editor's name and publication address.

The *approach* you take in selling and writing up your idea depends on what you want to show or prove or what you want the reader to experience in the article. The slant or focus of your piece will then determine the kind of data gathering you need to do. In short, What is your message?

Try to write your main idea in one sentence. Include what you want to show or prove, why it's important readers know about it, and what your approach will be. (This is the basis of every successful query and a must if you're trying to sell nonfiction.) Don't forget there are at least fifteen different article types to choose from:

Informative/factual article	*Exposé*
How-to/self help article	*Review/critique*
Interview	*Historical sketch*
Opinion piece/essay	*Biographical essay*
Investigative piece	*Nostalgia piece*
Personality profile/sketch	*Humor*
Adventure/drama-in-real-life	*Quiz*
Inspirational/religious piece	

In fact, you may find you can write several different articles from the same idea and research. One way to define the direction your idea can take is to come up with a working title for one or more articles. Put "How-to" in front of your basic idea; try "What's behind such and such," "A new look at . . . ," or "What you should know about. . . ."

The title alone won't make a sale, but it helps to focus your thinking and keep you from getting sidetracked as you uncover interesting tidbits of information in your research.

TAKING THE QUERY ROUTE TO MARKET

Coming up with ideas may be the easiest part, but marketing those ideas is a different story. Scheherazade had a captive audience for her ideas; today's writers don't. Not surprisingly, at most writers' conferences, the standing-room-only workshops are those dealing with how to sell what you write and how to promote yourself as a writer.

Novice free-lancers often write articles first, then try to sell them; experienced writers know it's the other way around. These professionals take an idea, do some initial thinking and research, then "sell" it to an editor—usually by query letter or article proposal (sometimes called an article memo).

Most editors want to see your idea in writing. They don't want to hear it over the phone. However, if you have an idea for a local newspaper or one on a hot item or breaking news story, then a telephone call is all right. (Don't cry wolf, though; you'll lose not only your credibility but your chances of selling another story as well.)

In other words, the idea is the starting point. How you *package* that idea is the *selling* point. Good writers make it look easy. But any writer can learn to write effective query letters and proposals that sell an editor and result in a go-ahead.

Whether you write a query or proposal, the purposes are the same: (1) to showcase your idea, (2) to allow you to audition before an editor, and (3) to find out if an editor is interested in your idea *before* you've written about it. A good query or proposal saves you time, energy, and money—in postage, telephone bills, gasoline, and cost of photographs, supplies, and other research fees. If no one wants to publish your article, you'll know it early on.

But that's not all. A query or proposal allows an editor some *input* in shaping the idea before it's written.

For example, when I first queried *Ladycom's* editor about the Joan Gillette Tannebaum story mentioned earlier, I suggested a personal interview centered around preventing sports injuries. After some discussion, however, the editor assigned me to do a round-table discussion in question-and-answer form, with five military wives asking questions of the noted sports trainer—a refinement that certainly makes sense for a magazine that goes to half a million military wives around the globe.

QUERIES AND PROPOSALS

A query is simply a marketing tool in the form of a letter to an editor. As such, it shows you're familiar with the publication's editorial needs and tells about your article idea plus what you plan to do with it in word length and slant.

Good query letters are generally no more than a page or two in length, (preferably only one page, one side, and single-spaced). I use the same basic format that most other professional writers do. In four or five tightly written paragraphs packed with information, I try to convey the excitement of the idea, what the article will be about, and what my qualifications are for writing it.

As in business letters, a query letter contains the writer's address and the date in one corner. For a more professional look, purchase your own business cards and stationery printed with your address and telephone number. (See "The Business of Business Cards" in chapter 15.) Drop down four or five lines and type the editor's name and title, the name of the publication, and the address.

The first paragraph has one purpose—to hook editors so they're willing to read on. Never underestimate the value of these first hundred words. If an editor hasn't worked with you before, she has no way of telling whether you can make summer safety tips, penile implants, or DRGs (diagnosis related groups) sound like must reading—unless you provide a preview of your most intriguing prose in the query.

Start off with a strong lead sentence—one that wastes no time in letting the editor know what's on your mind. Then build on that with significant facts, a pertinent quote, or even a question if warranted. Don't play games, and don't rely on gimmicks. Here's where previous analysis of the publication comes in handy.

Next comes a descriptive paragraph or two telling briefly which aspects of the topic you'll cover and what information you'll include. Give the approximate length of the piece (check *Writer's Market* or magazine guidelines for desired word count), and give the proposed article a catchy working title. Even though the editor may change it later, it helps you define your idea and zero in on your slant.

In the third paragraph, you can expand a bit. Highlight additional facts you've uncovered. Tell where you'll go for information and which experts you'll consult or interview. Mention availability of photos or other art work if it's appropriate to your article.

The final paragraph lists your relevant published credits and lists your qualifications for writing the piece. A whole resume of your career isn't called for, but you should state something about your professional background or expertise, personal experience, or interest in the topic that makes you qualified to write about it. The same applies to any coauthor you may be working with.

Pay attention to details, and double-check the spelling of the editor's name. Says one editor, "If a query is written accurately and interestingly by someone who *reads* our magazine, it's a pleasure to deal with that writer. But if I get a query with my name misspelled, it's *curtains* for that writer no matter what follows."

Query Letter

Cynthia Bell's by-line has appeared in major publications including *Seventeen, Parade,* and *The New York Times.* Here, with her permission, is her query letter of January 4, 1982, that sold Kate White, then a *Family Weekly* editor, on Bell's idea for a piece on the art of listening.

Kate White
Family Weekly
641 Lexington Avenue
New York, NY 10022

Dear Ms. White:

At the suggestion of Linda Konner at Weight Watchers, I am writing to propose an article, "Listening—It's More than Hearing."

Ours is a society of voices. As Harvard professor Dwight Bolinger observed in a recent article, "Over a period of slightly more than 100 years, we have gone from voice to print and back again." If we used the energy we now spend ignoring or silencing voices, and instead actively participated in the listening process, our improved relationships with our families, friends and colleagues would enrich our lives. Listening, like the tango, takes two.

I can prepare an article that will explain what good listening is, how we often set out to listen but defeat ourselves and why, how to accomplish good listening, what cathartic communications are and how to deal with them, what part silence plays in listening, and why true listening has been called a way to be behaviorally loving.

I have taken a six-month course given on listening and have attended workshops directed by Dr. Paul Donoghue, founder and director of Touchstone, which teaches communications skills across the country. I also attended a Sperry corporation-sponsored session given by Dr. Lyman K. Steil, professor of rhetoric at the University of Minnesota and head of his own consulting firm.

I am a free-lance writer with articles published in *Seventeen*, *Yachting*, *Westchester Magazine* and more than a dozen pieces in the *N.Y. Times.*

As the quantity of time spent within today's family becomes increasingly short, is *Family Weekly* interested in improving the quality of that time with an article on how to improve good listening habits?

Bell closed with "sincerely" and included a self-addressed stamped envelope. She received a go-ahead three months later on April 1 and on April 19 returned to White a signed contract for first North American serial rights and an article of approximately 700 words. Before filing her photocopy of the query, however, she added a few notes at the bottom as follows:

4/1/82 go ahead

600-750 words—$300

at least 2-3 experts' quotes

standard service format

light & factual

not too woman's mag. type—have a dual audience

Commenting on these notes, Bell says she uses the query letter as a memo pad when she makes a follow-up phone call to the editor. "That way," she explains, "I have it right in front of me so I can answer any questions they might raise on the article's focus, scope, etc. Then I have notes for the follow-up letter mentioning our (oral) agreement for the article."

Bell had written something else at the top of her letter—"also queried *McCall's*, *Ms.*, *Redbook*, *Woman's Day*"—all of which rejected the idea. But she didn't give up.

"I went ahead with it," she says, "because I was personally involved in the subject and originally wanted to emphasize listening as an activity on the hearer's part as well as the stages of empathetic listening (à la Carl Rogers). But even in the cut-down version, it elicited audience response, so I was gratified it was published at all." (Editors changed Bell's title, however, to "Five Steps to Better Listening.")

Article Memo/Proposal

Many writers present editors with a more detailed query, known as an article proposal or memo. For example, John Grossman, a contributing editor of *Health*, submitted this article memo to *American Way*.

Query

NEW WAYS TO TAKE MEDICINE

For Many Patients, Pills May Soon Be Passe
and Tablets Timeworn

*Predicting medical breakthroughs and advances is often
risk business. One area, though, seems poised for considerable activity, namely, new drug delivery systems that should
in many cases do away with swallowing pills and tablets
and receiving injections. Besides convenience, the new delivery systems promise more controlled doses of medication
and more effective uptake into the bloodstream. The big drug
companies are competing furiously to reach the marketplace
first with intriguing new technological and pharmaceutical
advances, many of which have an almost Buck Rogers cast
to them. A few are already in use, some are recently pa-
tented, many are quickly heading through R&D (research and
development), testing, and the necessary federal approval
processes. In no special order, here's a quick rundown:*

Grossman then listed and briefly described five of the most
intriguing and promising of the new drug-delivery methods (ranging
from drug delivery triggered by a magnetic field to the dispensing of
drugs electronically) and wound up the memo with this summary
paragraph:

*The story, then, would try to sketch the bounds and some of
the likely specifics of an important new trend in medicine.
At the same time, these new delivery systems raise some
safety questions and one need also ask if the projected benefits will equal the increased costs.*

American Way ran the piece in May, 1984, retitling it "A Better
Pill to Swallow." Even though editors often change titles suggested by
writers in their queries, Grossman says, "I've found a good title and
two- or three-line subhead helpful in selling stories—a kind of 'one-
two punch' that grabs an editor even before line one." And *selling* is
what queries are all about.

Alice Fleming casts her queries in article proposals that begin
(double-spaced) with the actual opening paragraphs of the article itself—a second type of article memo.

Writers using this format usually shift to single-spacing for the re-
mainder of the proposal which, like the query letter, includes a synop-

sis of what the article will cover, approximate word length, sources of information, interviewees, and other data relevant to the subject.

A final paragraph gives the writer's credentials or experience and published credits. Of course, if you are a frequent contributor to the publication, you can skip the credentials and credits since editors already know your work.

To see how closely the lead of the article proposal resembles the final product, compare Alice Fleming's proposal with the opening paragraphs of the *Reader's Digest* version titled "How to Direct Your Dreams."

ARE YOUR DREAMS ON RE-RUNS?

An article proposal by Alice Fleming

A young man I know has a recurring bad dream: on the day he is to receive his college degree, he discovers that he cannot graduate because he has forgotten to take a required course.

Ironically, the young man graduated from college, with honors, four years ago. What is even more interesting, however, is that in discussing the dream with friends, he learned that several of them have the same dream and that the father of one of them—a man in his fifties—has been having it for over thirty years.

Remarkable as this story may seem, dream researchers note that a high percentage of people, both adults and children, have repetitive dreams and that the scripts of these dreams, while not always identical, often show surprising similarities in both content and theme.

HOW TO DIRECT YOUR DREAMS

by Alice Fleming

A young man I know has a recurring bad dream: on the day he is to receive his college degree, he discovers that he cannot graduate because he has forgotten to take a required course. Yet he *did* graduate, with honors, four years ago. Interestingly, in discussing this with friends, he learned that several of them have the same dream—and the father of one has been having it for over 30 years!

Remarkable as this story may seem, dream researchers note that a high percentage of both adults and children have repetitive dreams that, while not always identical, often show surprising similarities in both content and theme.

Though it looks easy, few writers are able to dash off this kind of lead in a few minutes. But it's worth the time it takes for two reasons: you've got the lead for your article when the assignment comes through *and* you know it's one the editor likes.

"Do whatever it takes to make the editor care about your subject and you as a writer," advises Fleming. "What you're trying to do in a proposal is to give a very complete picture to get the editor turned on."

Fleming submits her proposals with a brief covering letter on her stationery, which is white with blue lettering. Occasionally, she will send out article suggestions—one page with three or four ideas, complete with working title and brief two- or three-sentence description. In the covering letter, she says something like, "I wonder if you'd be interested in any of the enclosed ideas. If so, I'd be happy to send along a more detailed proposal."

While most editors say they don't appreciate such "fishing expeditions," they sometimes work. For example, Fleming once submitted three ideas: "Celebrating Christmas: The New vs. the Tried and True"; "How to Survive the Holiday Hassle"; and "Are You in a Job Rut?" *Woman's Day* assigned the Christmas piece after seeing a detailed three-and-a-half-page proposal.

Keeping Track of Query Submissions

Once you enter the query business, it's important you don't lose track of which ideas are where, who's rejected what, and which editors have requested additional ideas or information or more detailed proposals.

I've yet to computerize my query files, still relying on three-by-five-inch cards filed in a metal recipe box to keep track of query traffic flow. Even if your current rate of query submissions doesn't seem to warrant a filing system, resist the temptation to be casual about your writing business. The simple method I use may work for you, too.

For each query, I complete a file-card history as follows:

WORKING TITLE: _____

BYLINE/CO-AUTHORS: _____

PUBLICATION	DATE SENT	RESPONSE	DATE

EDITOR'S COMMENTS: _____

DEADLINE: _____

DATE MANUSCRIPT SENT: _____

DATE PAYMENT/KILL FEE RECEIVED: ____ AMOUNT: $ ____

PUBLISHED IN: _____ ISSUE/DATE: _____

RIGHTS SOLD: _____

Since my recipe box has file dividers labeled BOOK PROPOS-ALS; QUERY LETTERS; ARTICLES TO WRITE; MISCELLANEOUS; MANUSCRIPTS SENT, and MANUSCRIPTS SOLD!, it's a simple mat-ter to put the card of a query that results in an assignment into the "Ar-ticles to Write" file, or to check the card of an accepted piece to see if I've been paid for it yet.

By the same token, if I receive a kill fee (a percentage of the agreed-upon price for an assigned article that later was cancelled), I then transfer that card back to the QUERY LETTERS file to send out again. Keeping track of who's bought reprint rights is important in get-ting all the extra mileage possible from your writing output. (The term *reprint rights* refers to the right to reprint an article, story, or poem that originally appeared in another publication. Though sometimes used interchangeably with reprint rights, *second serial rights* generally re-fers to the sale of a portion of a book to a newspaper or magazine after, or about the time a book is published, regardless of whether there was any first serial publication elsewhere.)

As you start mailing out queries and proposals, you'll find editors respond to your ideas with terms like "go-ahead," "on speculation," or "on assignment." You can learn them easily by checking the glossa-ry in any edition of *Writer's Market*, which also contains more infor-mation on writing queries.

WHY EDITORS SAY NO

Successful writers learn to deal early on with rejection slips, letters, telephone calls, and any other way in which the editorial "no-go" is delivered. It's the only way they can survive in the free-lance business. But the question behind each rejection never changes: Why?

At many publications, the decision to accept or reject an article proposal or manuscript is made by an *editorial board* consisting of the editor-in-chief and various department editors. An article may be rejected because a similar article has already been assigned or is in inventory, the topic is inappropriate, or the format is not right for that magazine—among other reasons.

Journalism professor and author Myrick E. Land, who teaches nonfiction article writing, asked twenty-five editors why they say no to the manuscripts they receive. The following reasons, he says, were reported over and over:

- *The article idea is trite, vague, or too general. The writer offers the magazine half a dozen ideas, rather than one or two fully developed ones. The article ideas are all right—but no more than that.*

- *The writer hasn't bothered to analyze the magazine, and careless errors (like misspelling the editor's name in the query) cast doubts about the writer's general ability to do the job.*

- *The writing is weak; the article limps along with no apparent logical structure.*

- *The article lacks* authority.

You need to convince the editor that you know exactly what you're talking about, and this is especially true in writing scientific and medical articles. You need facts and quotes—not merely from your family doctor, but from one or more recognized experts in the field as well. Editors need to know that information in the piece will be accurate, authoritative, and helpful to readers. That doesn't mean the writing has to be heavy-handed.

The most eloquent and memorable language is the *simplest* (not simplistic) and most direct.

A QUERY A DAY KEEPS THE BLUES AT BAY

The most successful free-lancer I know plays the numbers game. In any given week, she has from thirty to fifty different queries in the mails. Her theory: the more article ideas she has circulating among editors, the better her odds of selling. She also knows that the more queries a writer has out, the less it hurts if five or six are rejected.

"The act of writing," says actor Spalding Gray, "is like having a child—it's something to leave behind." Yet any writer will tell you that having that "child" rejected by an editor or publisher hurts, no matter how strong the writer's constitution or makeup.

"At this stage of my career, I don't know if I can take the editorial roller-coaster ride," one psychologist told me after getting back a rejected magazine article. "I'm used to success in my field and I'm not sure I can live with the elation you feel one day when they ask to see your manuscript and dejection the next, when it bounces back."

Rejection of your material usually takes one of three forms. You may receive a printed slip of paper that reads something like this: "We are sorry your material does not meet our editorial needs and we wish you success in placing it elsewhere." Or you may be sent a standard shopping list of reasons why—ranging from "We already have a similar article assigned" to "We are no longer accepting free-lance submissions."

It's the third type—the personal note or letter from an editor—that causes both joy and confusion. On the one hand, the editor was sufficiently gracious and/or impressed with your idea or writing to take time to write—perhaps to encourage you to keep trying or invite you to submit other article ideas. That's a plus worth following up.

On the other hand, I've known writers who spent enormous effort submitting dozens of ideas following such encouragement, but who never did succeed in making a sale to the publication. I think there comes a point in such situations where common sense must prevail. For whatever reason, you and the editor are simply not on the same wavelength—and you'd do better to submit your ideas elsewhere.

You might say as much in a letter. While you're at it, tell the editor you'd hoped that one or two of your suggestions might have worked for her publication, and ask if she can tell you why so many of your ideas missed the mark. But don't expect much. Most editors can tell why material misses the mark by a wide margin, but few can pinpoint why an almost-made-it idea wasn't quite good enough. Not only that, answering is time consuming. Editors are paid to edit, not to conduct private tutorials for free-lancers.

The important thing to remember is that the rejection is editorial—not personal. "The worst thing you can do if you've had a manuscript rejected is to put it in a drawer and let yourself get stuck with feeling depressed," warns Los Angeles psychologist Thomas Backer, who specializes in career consulting with creative people.

"Don't make it [rejection] into a global self-criticism—I'm a bad person, my work is not good," says Backer, who emphasizes that such self-criticism often leads to creative blocks. "Self-criticism turns into a self-fulfilling prophecy, and the [negative] self-image suppresses your creative thinking—and the writing—that can take you from Square One to the printed page."

All professional writers agree that a healthy attitude toward rejections is crucial to selling your work. You've got to be able to accept honest criticism and to learn from it, or you won't survive or grow in your craft. If your query letter, book proposal, or manuscript has been rejected, Backer suggests you do a careful analysis of what went wrong with the piece. But also, he adds, "identify the specific things you did right and give yourself credit for them."

Don't give up with your first turndown. Look at the bright side— one editor's reject is often another editor's cover story.

5 □ BASIC RESEARCH

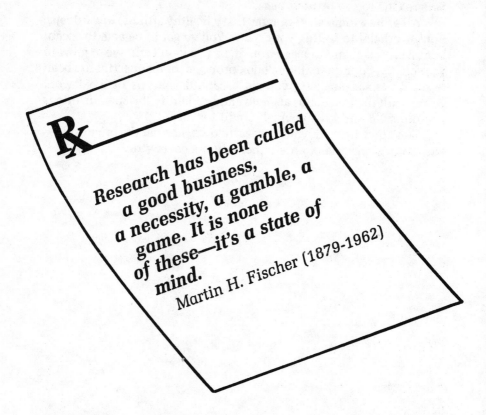

Research has been called a good business, a necessity, a gamble, a game. It is none of these—it's a state of mind.

Martin H. Fischer (1879-1962)

"Seek and you shall find," Matthew urges us in his no-frills gospel. But starting on that search—especially if it's the first time you've ever opened a medical journal, watched a surgical procedure, or stepped into a research laboratory—can leave you feeling less than sure of yourself and even a bit queasy. The purpose of this chapter is to help you take the *search* out of *research* and feel more confident while doing it.

Basically, you've got four methods to work with: *asking* others; *observing* a situation for yourself; *reasoning*—that is, putting two and two together and figuring out the answer isn't five; and *reading* or using broadcast and other audiovisual media to learn what information is already available on a subject. Mails, telephone, tape recorder, and camera are used by almost every researcher at some time or another, but as electronic equipment comes down in price, modem and VCR (video cassette recorder) are becoming more common as data-gathering tools.

Whether your reason for doing research is to find new markets for your work, restock your depleted idea file, or delve into a topic for a book or article, the starting point is always yourself. Here are five questions no researcher/writer can afford to ignore:

1. *What do I need?* This will depend on how much you know about the subject and what else you would like to know; what you think the reader wants to know; what the reader needs to know; and what angles the editor is eager to have you pursue.

2. *Where can I get the information fast? How?*

3. *What's it going to cost in time, dollars, emotional energy?* When Jody Gaylin agreed to write an article for *Parents Magazine* on parents whose children had died, she never realized the toll interviewing these parents would take on her personally. Pregnant with her third child at the time, she says this was one of the most difficult assignments she has ever had. "I'd never do it again," she says now.

4. *How can I best keep track of my research and where am I in the process now?*

5. *How do I keep from overresearching? How much do I really need?*

A rule of thumb that works for many writers is to have three times as much research as they *think* they need. This provides choices. If you've got six anecdotes, for example, you can pick the two best. If you've interviewed several experts, you've got extra quotes that will come in handy if you decide to write up the topic from another angle. Don't forget, professional writers always try to get more than one article out of the same research materials—and one thing editors easily spot is a certain "thinness" that's obvious when a piece has been underresearched.

Begin with the facts you can find. Go to the authorities in the field for answers and opinions. Ask these experts as well as your reference librarian to point you in new directions. And listen to those around you—family, neighbors, co-workers, fellow joggers, friends. Their questions and concerns are those readers will have, too.

FACTS AT YOUR FINGERTIPS, ALMOST

According to Alvin Toffler, "the shortest path between two facts may well be Alden Todd." I agree and keep Todd's book *Finding Facts Fast* close at hand when I'm in the midst of research. Not only does Todd

suggest practical research techniques in this guide, he helps you select the right reference index; locate specialized collections in libraries, businesses, and trade and professional associations; and tap into
information networks, such as congressional offices, alumni offices,
chambers of commerce, embassies, tourist offices, and public-relations sources.

The other general reference book I find invaluable in speeding up
research is *Writer's Resource Guide*. This one-volume directory contains 1,600 sources of free information for writers. Among resources
included are libraries, companies, and museums divided into thirty
subject areas, including health and medicine; family; human services;
science, engineering, technology; farming and food; environment and
earth; the workplace; information services, and many others.

The section on Health and Medicine, for example, includes
eighty listings, beginning with the Acupuncture Research Institute
and ending with Warner-Lambert, a New Jersey pharmaceutical company. In between, you'll find listings for professional societies like the
American Academy of Periodontology and the American Medical Association; for "disease" organizations such as the Cystic Fibrosis
Foundation and the Canadian Schizophrenia Foundation; and research centers like the Institute for Child Behavior Research and the
National Center for Health Services Research.

Each listing gives you the name, address, and telephone number
of the source, plus the person to contact, type of services or information offered, and tips on how to obtain data you need. Also covered
are photo sources and how to get on worthwhile mailing lists.

You can find many of the reference books and resource guides
discussed in this chapter in the reference section of the main branch
of your public library and in most college, university, or other educa-
tional-institution libraries. However, some highly specialized medical directories, guides, journals, or books can be found only in life-science, medical, or health-related libraries, usually located on major
university campuses and in hospitals, medical centers, research institutes, and the like.

Most of these major reference works are very costly. Medical journal subscriptions can also add up. Although established medical free-
lancers often subscribe to major professional journals, we don't recommend that you do so until you know exactly what you need and in
which areas of health and medicine. Remember, if you live in a metropolitan area or near a university, hospital, or medical center, you can
usually make arrangements to use reference materials, books, and
journals in the medical library. (You'll find pointers on making such
arrangements on page 91.)

If you're not familiar with the *Medical and Health Information*

Directory you're missing a bonanza of consolidated information—twelve thousand entries in thirty-two sections including state, national, and international organizations; government agencies; hospitals; health-care-delivery agencies; journals, newsletters, publishers; research centers and educational institutions; audiovisual services, libraries, and information centers.

Two other data-packed publications are *Health Statistics: A Guide to Information Sources* and *Health Services Directory*, which covers programs, centers, clinics, and services treating health and social problems. If your topic involves mental health, check the *National Directory of Mental Health*. For a directory of hospitals and health-related organizations, see the annual *American Hospital Association Guide to the Health Care Field*.

Gale Research Company publishes scores of helpful directories, as does the R. R. Bowker Company. In one chapter, however, it's possible to highlight only a few. To make short work of finding the right reference book, consider buying a copy of *Reference Books: A Brief Guide*, published by Enoch Pratt Free Library, 400 Cathedral St., Baltimore, MD 21201. A gem of a paperback costing around three dollars, this guide contains the best-edited and most-useful descriptions of reference books around. (If it's not available in your local bookstore, you can order a copy from Enoch Pratt Free Library.) For a more detailed (and massive) list of reference works, check your library's copy of *Guide to Reference Books*, edited by Eugene Sheehy. With more than 8,000 entries, it's the reference librarian's bible, but you're free to use it, too.

To locate magazine articles, check *Reader's Guide to Periodical Literature* and other magazine indexes listed in chapter 3. *Poole's Index to Periodical Literature* covers serials from 1802 to 1906.

Among major newspaper indexes are those to the *Christian Science Monitor, The New York Times*, the *Los Angeles Times*, the *Wall Street Journal*, and the *Times* of London. *NewsBank, Inc.* indexes articles from about 100 newspapers throughout the country (including those from all state capitals) and prints texts on microfiche. Topics include science, health, and medicine.

Books in Print lists more than 180,000 books under about 45,000 subjects. But, remember, these are only *American* listings. Other resources to check include publishers' catalogs, the spring and fall listings in *Publishers Weekly*, and the annual *National Library of Medicine Current Catalog*, which lists books acquired by and located in *NLM*. *Medical Books in Print* is a sub-set of *Books in Print* and includes monographs and serials indexed by subject, name, and title.

Through interlibrary loan, you can request a book or photocopied materials from a member library. However, postal or circulation problems are not uncommon in such loans, and this could be a problem if you're working on a tight deadline.

Chambers of commerce, governmental agencies, embassies, tourism bureaus, and congressional committees are all invaluable sources of information. So, too, are yearbooks, fact books, handbooks, encyclopedias, atlases, almanacs, and hundreds of other general reference works too numerous to mention in this chapter.

If, however, you have problems finding reference or other materials you need, don't hesitate to ask the reference librarian for help. Get to know this person well. He or she will become your most valued resource—if not your best friend. Librarians enjoy working with serious writers. As experts in sources of information stored in computers and in print, they expect to be approached for help. They'll go out of their way to help you find what you need or find it for you. Ultimately, your success is theirs, too.

SPECIAL LIBRARIES

As a writer on medical topics, you may need to do editorial research in one or more special information centers or libraries. For example, in *The Cinderella Complex*, a book about women's hidden fear of independence, author Colette Dowling writes:

> Early in the research I was exhilarated by my work in two particular libraries and decided that too often libraries get overlooked in writers' acknowledgements. Therefore, I want to express my thanks to the Princeton University Library and the New York Academy of Medicine Library. The Princeton University Library has open stacks (open even to the public), which is a joy to the serious researcher. While the stacks are not open to the public at the New York Academy of Medicine Library, its librarians are competent, fast, and unfailingly courteous to any and all who come to them for help.

When Martha Lee Hildreth was working on her doctoral dissertation titled "Doctors, Bureaucrats, and Public Health in France, 1888-1902," her research took her not only to the Bibliotheque Nationale and public health archives in Paris, but also to the Lane Medical Library at Stanford University. "Lane," explains Hildreth, now assistant professor of history at the University of Nevada—Reno, "has a tremendous collection of nineteenth-century medical journals and primary source materials in the history of medicine—not just from France, but the United States and other countries as well."

Three directories can ease your search for a special collection or library: the *Directory of Special Libraries and Information Centers;*

The American Library Directory, and Subject Collections: A Guide to Special Book Collections in Libraries, edited by Lee Ash. The latter is organized by subject—e.g., health education, medical care, biomedical engineering—and lists special collections within general libraries as well as libraries devoted to one subject.

Be sure to ask your reference librarian to show you the office copy of the special libraries directory of your city or metropolitan area. Few writers realize the quality and quantity of special-interest collections often available in their own backyards. For instance, the "Special Libraries Directory of Greater New York" (published by the New York chapter of the Special Libraries Association) lists 1,200 such resources.

Since Nevada is such a sparsely populated state, its equivalent publication is called the "Nevada Library Directory and Statistics." About forty facilities statewide are listed, among them special historical, law, and hospital libraries. Similar directories of Special Libraries Association members and their institutions are available for your area, too.

Health-science and medical libraries are vital resources in every university, hospital, research institute, and medical, dental, nursing, and veterinary school. Reference materials must be used on the premises, but generally you can make arrangements with the librarian to photocopy pages you need. Call before you visit, to see if there are special visitor's passes or other requirements for using the library. (Don't forget that if public tax monies are helping support the facility, it's hard for librarians to say users aren't welcome.)

Opening the door to a special or private collection may take more effort. Some background information on your reasons for needing to use the collection, plus a letter of introduction from your editor or referral from a medical school dean or professor can help.

Most librarians or special collectors are flattered when a serious researcher requests such privileges and will usually try to accommodate the request. Few can resist an appeal that begins, "I'm working on a study of such and such, and I'm told that yours is the outstanding collection on this topic in this city. I would really appreciate the opportunity to come in and see you."

FOUR SPECIAL RESOURCES

1. The National Library of Medicine (8600 Rockville Pike, Bethesday, MD 20209; [301] 496-6308) is the headquarters of the Regional Medical Library Networks. Open to the public, it houses the nation's largest collection on medicine, health sciences, dentistry, public health, nursing, and biomedical research, as well as a special collec-

tion on the history of medicine. The library will conduct literature searches and those available on request are listed in *Index Medicus*. Free *NLM* literature searches are done on "hot topics."

The library is also a source for black-and-white photos and color transparencies on the history of medicine (portraits, scenes, and pictures of institutions) but not for current personalities, events, or medical science. Minimum charge is six dollars per copy print (prices subject to change without notice). A credit line is required, and no pictures are sent on approval.

2. American Medical Association, Division of Library and Archival Services (535 N. Dearborn St., Chicago, IL 60610; [312] 751-6000). Special collections here include the Archive of the American Medical Association and of Organized Medicine; sociology and economics of medicine, with complete world coverage since 1962.

A few years ago when I was preparing the proposal for this book, I needed some statistics on what was important to Americans and where health fit into the picture. A phone call to Jane Larkin at the AMA produced all the statistics I needed on the spot. Within the week, she had sent me all the necessary backup materials—and the fee for photocopying was minimal.

3. American Dental Association—Bureau of Library Services (211 E. Chicago Ave., Chicago IL 60611; [312] 440-2553) covers all phases of dentistry. Special collections include photographs and association archives. Library use is a privilege of membership, but generally is open to all dental auxiliary personnel, physicians, nurses, graduate students, and to all others on an individual basis. The American Dental Association Library will help you find what you need or refer you to a dental library closer to home. A major West Coast dental collection, for example, is housed at the University of Southern California's Dental Library (Norris Dental Science Center, Los Angeles, CA 90007).

4. New York Academy of Medicine Library (2 E. 103 St., New York, NY 10029; [212] 876-8200). Probably the granddaddy of all medical-society libraries, this one has an outstanding collection in medical Americana and the history of medicine, plus extensive holdings in medical biography; rare books; health reports; food and cookery. The library is open to the public for reference use only.

"The important thing to remember," says University of Nevada School of Medicine reference librarian Laurie Conway, "is that there is a three-tiered nationwide information network called the Regional Medical Library Service and every medical library—from hospital-based on up to the National Library of Medicine—is aware of it, and participates in it. You can tap into the network at any level," explains Conway, who is also a registered nurse.

"If the library where you start your data gathering can't meet your information needs, you'll be referred to one that can. Don't be surprised if you're also referred to a public library—as the smaller, private facilities often do not have the capability for interlibrary loan or other special services."

INDEXES AND DATABASES

Since 1966, more than 4.3 million articles have appeared in some two thousand medical journals. The major source of current information, these publications are the primary channels for communicating the latest biomedical research and results of clinical studies. Without an index, finding a specific article among millions would be like looking for the proverbial needle in a haystack.

The National Library of Medicine puts out a "reader's guide" to medical literature called *Index Medicus*. It can be used either in print form or via computer. The computerized on-line equivalent of *Index Medicus* is called MEDLINE.

If you have a word-processing/communications system, the modem (a device that allows two computers to communicate with each other over telephone lines) will enable you to dial a vendor like DIALOG or the National Library of Medicine and immediately access MEDLINE, the Newspaper Index, Psychological Abstracts, or dozens of other databases right in your own home or office.

If not, a reference librarian will do a literature search for you, generally for a fee. The libraries absorb much of the cost of these services, but the user generally pays for on-line computer costs, telephone charges, each citation printed off-line, and each abstract. Since these charges can add up fast, determine in advance what your limit on spending will be. Then, target your research needs and be as specific as possible in stating what it is you're looking for. If you don't, you may end up with useless citations you pay for anyway.

But this isn't the time to be penny-wise and pound-foolish. Computers are becoming the research tool of the 1980s and, despite costs, many authors elect to have literature searches done for them because time, too, is costly and they'd rather spend it writing. Not only that, research librarians are trained in helping you define what you need. They can save you money, since they're able to dart in and out of databases and know just where to look for information. According to reference librarian Laurie Conway, "an average computer search on MEDLINE performed by a librarian skilled in searching techniques takes only about twenty minutes." And many times the cost is less than ten dollars.

Suppose, for example, you're doing an article on teenagers who feel helpless to change the direction their lives are taking. You decide to do a literature search to see if any studies have been done in this area. For bibliographic databases, each reference on the printout will contain author (AU), title (TI), and journal or paper source (SO). Other information, such as abstract or subject headings, may also be included. Here's a sample citation from *Psychological Abstracts*, plus the abstract or summary of the article:

Abstract #	AN 04215 72-2. 8502.
Author(s)	AU MOORE-TERRY-W. PAOLILLO-JOSEPH-G.
Title	TI DEPRESSION: INFLUENCE OF HOPELESSNESS, LOCUS OF CONTROL, HOSTILITY AND LENGTH OF TREATMENT.
Source	SO PSYCHOLOGICAL REPORTS. 1984 JUN VOL 54(3) 875-881.
Code #	CD PYRTAZ..
ISSN #	IS 0033-2941.
Language	LG EN..
Year	YR 84.. CC 3210. PT 10..
Major Descriptors	MJ DEPRESSION-EMOTION. PESSIMISM. INTERNAL-EXTERNAL-LOCUS-OF-CONTROL. HOSTILITY. TREATMENT. ADULTHOOD. SC 13650 38020 26150 23350 54190 01150.
Index Phrases	ID HOPELESSNESS & LOCUS OF CONTROL & HOSTILITY & LENGTH OF TREATMENT, DEPRESSION, OUTPATIENTS OF RURAL MENTAL HEALTH CENTER.
Check Tag	CT HUMAN.
Abstract	AB EXAMINED THE RELATIONSHIPS OF THE CRITERION VARIABLE, DEPRESSION, TO 7 PREDICTOR VARIABLES. FOR 317 OUTPATIENTS (AGED 19 + YRS). THE FINDINGS SUPPORT THE VIEWS OF DEPRESSION IN WHICH HOPELESSNESS AND COVERT HOSTILITY ARE REGARDED AS IMPORTANT CORRELATES OF DEPRESSION.

Such findings may be interesting, but are they really important? Editorially, only you can make that decision—because you know what your subject is and what angle you're pursuing. If in doubt from a medical point of view, check it out with an expert.

Other Health-Related Databases

MEDLINE consists of references to articles from more than 3,000 journals in all languages. About 70 percent of these references include an abstract. Subject scope includes human medicine and health, basic sciences, biomedical research, veterinary medicine, dentistry, nursing, and communications disorders. The database covers 1966 to the present. But there are more than 100 other health-related databases available today. (*The Computer Data and Database Sourcebook* lists nearly all databases and service offered.)

Here's a partial listing of selected databases available from the National Library of Medicine:

AVLINE	*audio-visual software*	1975+
BIOETHICS	*biomedical ethics*	1973+
CANCERLIT	*all published cancer literature*	1963+
CATLINE	*books at NLM*	1900+
HEALTH	*health administration/planning*	1975+
HISTLINE	*history of medicine*	1964+
POPLINE	*population*	1970+
TOXLINE	*toxicology*	1971+

Selected health science databases from other vendors are:

BIOSIS	*biological sciences*	1969+
NAHL	*nursing/allied health literature*	1983+
EXCERPTA MEDICA	*medicine*	1974+
FAMILY RESOURCES	*family-related literature*	1970+
IPA	*pharmaceutical sciences*	1970+
NARIC	*rehabilitation*	1956+
NIMH	*mental health*	1969+
PNI	*drug industry news*	1975+
MPP	*medical/psychological previews*	
PRE-MED	*clinical medicine*	current 3-4 mos.
PRE-PSYC	*psychology/behavior*	current 12 mos.
PSYCINFO	*psychology/behavior*	1967+
SCISEARCH	*life/physical sciences*	1974+
SOCIAL SCISEARCH	*social sciences*	1972+

Four other nonmedical databases often provide the missing link in relating health topics to public interests: ASI (American Statistics Index); CIS (Congressional Information); ERIC (Education Resources Information); and INFORM (Abstracted Business Information).

In addition, there are indexes to other specialized magazine and journal articles you may need to tap, depending on the focus of your research. "You may have to search a bit for these indexes because most of them are carried by special libraries rather than by general libraries," advises research expert Alden Todd. "But a cordial professional librarian can help you locate them."

The fourteen indexes that follow, for example, would be helpful in learning more about child development, the environment, hospital care, nursing, public health, or general health and science: *Abstracts of Health Care Management Studies; America: History and Life; Applied Science and Technology; Bibliographic Index of Health Education Periodicals; Biological & Agricultural Index; Child Development Abstracts and Bibliography, Completed Research in Health, Physical Education and Recreation; D.S.H. (Deafness, Speech and Hearing); Environment Index; General Science Index; Hospital Literature Index; Index to Legal Periodicals; Mental Retardation Abstracts;* and *Medical Socioeconomic Resource Source.* This last index includes public health and economics and is designed to integrate materials from the social sciences and health-care field.

At this point you may be saying to yourself, "But all I want is a clear, easy-to-read overview of a health topic." If so, check the *International Nursing Index.* Covered by MEDLINE as well, this index provides subject and author sections, with each topic indexed under at least three headings. "Nursing-journal articles," explains nurse-librarian Laurie Conway, "more often are overviews of a subject, whereas medical-journal articles usually cover new research and complex technologies."

MEDICAL JOURNALS THE FIRST TIME AROUND

The first American medical journal, *Medical Repository,* was published in New York in 1797. Its success led Dr. John Redman Coxe to publish the *Philadelphia Medical Museum* in 1804. Sixteen years later, *The Philadelphia Journal of the Medical and Physical Sciences* was created by Dr. Nathaniel Chapman to counter the superior Continental attitude that the world as yet owed nothing to American physicians or surgeons.

Although no one knows the exact number of journals edited today for physicians alone, one pharmaceutical company claims eight thousand is not farfetched. And that doesn't include the multitude of professional journals directed toward other health-related specialties. Nurses, dentists, nutritionists, chiropractors, osteopaths, dental hygienists, psychologists, and virtually every other group of health-care specialists all have their own professional journals. You will see hundreds of these journals lining the shelves of any medical library. Where do you start?

If you're just browsing, start anywhere your fancy takes you. Here's some advice from New York author Alice Fleming: "I've gotten a lot simply from reading medical and psychiatric journals. I've done that from time to time when I've had no [article] ideas. I go and rev up the motors by reading.

"I might read the *New England Journal of Medicine*. I would probably read a couple of nursing magazines. They have good stuff because nurses are doing a lot of psychiatric/social work. I might pick up the *American Journal of Psychiatry* or the *Journal of Psychology and Social Science*. I just wander around, pick them up and leaf through them, and see what they're writing about."

If something catches her eye, Fleming says, she might photocopy it or make a note of the date and volume, then go see what else she can find.

Medical journals, like popular magazines, often have an editor's page or corner with an overview of the contents or editorials on important issues covered in that issue. A quick reading of this page can alert you to significant articles in the journal and also make you aware of any controversy over their interpretation.

Among the most responsible journals in the medical field are the *New England Journal of Medicine, Annals of Internal Medicine*, the *Lancet, Pediatrics, American Journal of Psychology, American Journal of Psychiatry, American Journal of Nursing, Journal of Consulting and Clinical Psychology, Journal of the American Dental Association*, and the *Journal of the American Medical Association (JAMA)*.

Consult the "Brandon List" for additional journals that are highly recommended. This list of selected books and journals recommended for small medical libraries is compiled by medical-library consultant Alfred N. Brandon with Dorothy R. Hill, assistant professor of medical education and collection-development librarian at a New York medical school. The influential list appears in alternate years in the *Bulletin of the Medical Library Association*.

If you are a health-care professional, you already know how to read a journal in medicine or some other specialty. You're familiar with the style of scientific writing and the format for presenting clinical material to your peers and to the editors for publication.

If you are a free-lancer who feels professional journals are "over your head," here are a few pointers on what to expect, what to look for, and, possibly, how to become a better-informed health consumer yourself. (See chapter 14 for tips on writing for this specialized market.)

The typical professional journal article is made up of a title and six sections:

1. *An abstract or summary of the study*
2. *Introduction (usually includes a brief review of the literature to date)*

3. *Methods and materials (data sources, patients, or group[s] in study, etc.)*

4. *Findings or results (accompanied by charts, photos, etc.)*

5. *Conclusion and often, discussion or interpretation of the findings for the group under study, and sometimes, implications for other patients, groups, etc.*

6. *References and notes*

Articles also include the author's address, where requests for reprints can be sent. This also makes it easy to follow up for additional information or quotes later on.

The three most common types of journal articles you'll run across are the *retrospective* and *prospective* study (both of which are basically "observation" studies) and the *experimental* study, which relies on randomized clinical trials. In addition, most journals contain letters to the editor, opinion pieces, and preliminary communications.

But remember, just because something is published in a medical journal doesn't mean it's a profound truth.

"I think every journal makes mistakes—anyone can blow it," says Dr. David A. Bergman, assistant professor of pediatrics at the University of California—San Francisco School of Medicine. "What journals are getting better and better at is assuring that the methodology of the study is sound; questions posed by the study can be answered; analysis is correct and, to a lesser extent, the study's conclusions deserve consideration. What's *not* being considered is how the information presented is utilized by the clinician in practice."

Here's advice Bergman gives to medical students, but it serves writers as well:

● *First, scan the article.* Look at the title. Ask yourself, "Am I interested?" Time is your most precious asset, so you don't want to waste it. Even if the topic *isn't* interesting, is it useful to you?

● *Look at the author's track record.* This is easy to do if you're in academic medicine and research—academicians keep track of who's doing what. If you're not in academic medicine or the author's name is unfamiliar to you, check the references at the end of the article you're interested in. Is this one in a series of articles by the same author(s)? Consult the Author section of *Index Medicus*—what else has this person published during the last five years, and in which journals? Ask a local medical expert in the same field, "Have you ever heard of this person and his work?" Finally, if you decide to interview the author, call or write and ask for a copy of his C.V. (*curriculum vitae*) which will list his whole track record and more.

● *Read the abstract or summary of the article.* If the author's results are really true, will they be useful to you? Your research? Your patients? Your readers?

● *Where was the study done?* If it was carried out on tribespeople in Katmandu, it may not relate to your patients (or readers) back home.

● *Use your discrimination.* You can't read everything. Look for "seminal" articles in your particular field. Seminal articles, explains Bergman, are those that have become classics in a given field. (References to "classic" articles can often be found at the end of a chapter in medical textbooks.)

"No one," says Bergman, "can possibly keep up with the medical literature. To take just one example, in the field of internal medicine, to keep up a doctor would have to read 270 articles and editorials each month. Information is compounding at a rate of 67 percent a year. A lot of doctors and many practicing physicians don't read medical journals at all," he says, adding, "many doctors generally believe anyone who works in academic medicine has only a minimal grasp of reality."

Given that, is it likely you will need to do medical-journal research? Naturally, it depends on your subject. But don't underestimate the kind of information editors and readers want. In a *San Francisco Chronicle* article on women's magazines, *Vogue* editor Grace Mirabella was quoted as saying, "What they [our readers] want from us, and what they get, is the best in fashion, the perfect piece on the arts, the most *medical-journal* kind of advice." (Italics added.)

If you've got an assignment for a lengthy project or a deadline causing you sleepless nights, you may find it faster and less costly to hire a graduate student to do research. But choose your researcher carefully. I've had good *and* bad experiences.

Once when I needed an annotated bibliography for a book on grandparenting, I hired a doctoral candidate who was interested in the history of family relationships, had a car, and was willing to spend time in the library researching the subject. The finished product, however, was not only expensive but skimpy on annotation.

Your best bet in hiring a research assistant is to check references, be clear in directing the research, set fees in advance—and a *limit* on spending to be cleared with you if additional research costs turn up. Now, when I need a research assistant, I ask other writers who've done similar projects for names of people they'd recommend. If you need a professional researcher, consult the editorial services section of *Literary Market Place,* or ask a reference librarian for recommendations.

STOCKING UP ON READY REFERENCES

You may decide it's a time-saver to have some of your own reference materials on hand. Medical bookstores can usually be found on university campuses which house medical schools, or near medical centers and schools off-campus. Besides those books directly related to your project, you may find it helpful to have your own copy of certain basic reference works, such as the annual *Physicians' Desk Reference (PDR)*, a pharmacological reference with complete information on more than 2,500 drugs, the most recent edition of *The Merck Manual*, which covers major diseases and diagnostic tests and provides information on current drugs; the latest edition of *Current Therapy: Latest Approved Methods of Treatment for the Practicing Physician*; the *Manual for Authors & Editors: Editorial Style & Manuscript Preparation* (a stylebook prepared by the American Medical Association); and a medical dictionary.

In choosing the latter, your choices range from inexpensive paperback editions like the *New American Pocket Medical Dictionary* to the more expensive, but highly regarded, *Dorland's Illustrated Medical Dictionary*; *Taber's Cyclopedic Medical Dictionary*; or *Stedman's Medical Dictionary*. If you are doing extensive research in the mental-health field, you may need to consult *Psychiatric Dictionary*. For dentistry, see the *Illustrated Dictionary of Dentistry*.

Deciphering "medicalese" is easier when you know the abbreviations, notations, and symbols that make up professional jargon. You can take the drudgery out of learning medical vocabulary using Peggy C. Leonard's step-by-step method of programmed learning in *Building a Medical Vocabulary*.

The text is organized by body system. An index/glossary of more than 2,000 terms plus an extensive list of word parts make this an excellent reference tool from which most medical terminology can be derived. Leonard has included challenging crossword puzzles, clear illustrations, a guide to pronunciation, and appendices that include common medical abbreviations and pharmacological terms plus drugs and their use. Can you *really* teach yourself? Our twenty-year-old daughter, a premed student, has just taught herself medical vocabulary using this book—and I'm next on the list of borrowers.

Building your own reference library is highly personal. A book one writer refers to daily may be one another free-lancer would never use. If you're a casual health or medical writer, you won't need specialized style manuals, grant-writing guidelines, or the latest update on medical-journal information to authors.

For example, my husband's bookshelves are filled with books

and journals on pediatrics and ethics, including *The Encyclopedia of Bioethics* and copies of the *Hastings Center Report*. Published bimonthly by The Hastings Center (360 Broadway, Hastings-on-Hudson, NY 10706), this journal contains information on new regulations and discussions of controversial and legal cases involving biomedical ethics.

On my reference shelf, however, are Roget's *Thesaurus*; two dictionaries, John Brady's *The Craft of Interviewing*; several books of quotations, including *Peter's Quotations: Ideas for Our Time* and *Medical Quotations*, edited by Maurice R. Strauss; many books on medical history, English usage, and writing listed in the bibliography of this book, plus *Literature and Medicine: An Annotated Bibliography*, revised edition by Joanne Trautmann and Carol Pollard. Beginning with the classics, this book takes you through the dramas, novels, short stories, and poetry of medieval times, the Renaissance, and the eighteenth, nineteenth, and twentieth centuries with a "topic list" that starts with abortion and ends with women as patients.

Two books helpful to any researcher whose work covers alternative medicine are *Rodale's Encyclopedia of Natural Home Remedies* by Mark Bricklin and the *Encyclopedia of Alternative Medicine and Self-Help*, edited by Malcolm Hulke.

Adding to your personal library can be a good investment. But until your article sales (or personal interests) justify the cost, beware of investing in expensive specialty reference books you can just as easily consult at the library.

FIVE SENSES ON-SITE

Working tours, walkabouts, and taking part in workshops are but a few of the many opportunities for primary research, which run the gamut from examining the physical therapy equipment used by injured athletes (Cleveland Clinic Foundation provided this seminar for National Federation of Press Women) to standing on the street corner observing strangers make or not make eye contact. (Kate White did this for "Eye Power," a *Glamour* article which includes her "detailed diary of a week's worth of staring.")

Tours and open houses provide a chance to see firsthand the actual workings of a company or health-care facility. The planners, in turn, hope some type of third-party endorsement will follow—e.g., news, feature stories, and possibly broadcast-media coverage. To this end, there may be speeches, information kits, photos, displays, brochures, slide shows, videotapes, and even product samples, souvenirs, or mementos.

Event coordinators will arrange interviews, answer questions (from the company point of view, of course), and get extra photos if you need them. They appreciate your sending tear sheets or clippings of any stories you write later about the facility, its programs, or personnel. Be sure you ask to be put on the mailing list for publications, press releases, future events, etc.

Do-it-yourself on-site research projects require some advance planning and, depending on the circumstances, caution or stamina as well. For example, after Kate White decided to test the staring rules herself, she reported in the article based on her experiment: "I live in New York City, where staring at strangers could be considered a health risk, so I went about my experiment cautiously. I also decided not to complicate my staring with other body language, such as smiles, frowns, or raised eyebrows. I only stared."

When Jan Goodwin went to Calcutta, India, to spend a week working with Mother Teresa, Goodwin, who's executive editor of *Ladies' Home Journal*, got more than she bargained for. In her article, she describes what happened on the Sunday of her visit to Kalighat, where she was surprised to find *no* nuns. Apparently, without telling anyone, the nuns had decided to stay at the Mother House to celebrate a religious holiday. But without extra volunteers, it meant Goodwin and two others would have to feed, wash, and dispense medication for 107 patients. As fate (or Divine Providence) would have it, a busload of American tourists arriving on the scene was pressed into emergency nursing duty.

By being on-site, Goodwin captured a picture no other writer has given us of the "quirky casualness" that underlies the operation of Mother Teresa's homes and her distrust of "systems." Goodwin stresses that the care these patients receive is undoubtedly better than anything they've ever had before, but adds, ". . . it is equally true that without systems, large organizations do not always run as smoothly as they could, that medications and supplies do not always get moved to where they are needed."

The first-hand experience of that is what gives her writing a *depth* it wouldn't have had otherwise. That's the advantage of being on the scene—though one suspects the tourists might not agree.

Getting Hospital Clearance

In India, the busload of tourists could walk into Mother Teresa's facility without prior notice and be welcomed on the spot. However, if you plan to do some research in a hospital here, you must clear it first with hospital authorities. At issue is not only the patients' right to privacy but also getting clearance to be in certain areas of the hospital that are normally closed to the public.

For example, if your research takes you into the delivery room, operating room, or other area where sterile procedures are required, you will be asked to put on gown and gloves and mask your face after adequate surgical scrubbing. Even though you have received permission to be there from the hospital administrator, the public-relations or media coordinator, the operating surgeon or other specialist, you should clear your presence with the operating room nursing supervisor. It is this person who is responsible for infection control and the flow of traffic. She or a designated assistant would be the one to show you how to scrub and properly prepare yourself for admittance to these restricted areas.

Suppose, for instance, you're doing a story on heart surgery. You've already talked to a surgeon who's given you the green light to observe him at work. To get clearance to the operating room, call the public relations/media coordinator and explain the situation. "Look, I'm doing a story on heart surgery and I'd like to cover it from start to finish. I've talked to Dr. So-and-so, the surgeon, who says it's okay with him, but how do I get clearance to be in the operating room?"

If this is the first time you've watched a surgical procedure and you think you might be queasy, you might want to build up your tolerance to seeing blood, incisions, etc. Seeing a videotaped operation first or watching a few simpler procedures in the emergency room might help. Some people think skipping breakfast makes them less likely to feel light-headed or nauseated, but that's not necessarily true. The last thing nurses want is an observer keeling over in the O.R., so ask the surgeon—beforehand—what you should do if you feel you've seen enough.

FINDING THE EXPERTS

Whether it's background information you need or quotes from authorities in the scientific and medical world, identifying the experts is much simpler when you know where to look and whom to ask. Sometimes, the most effective way to start is close to home.

For his book *Talking Medicine: America's Doctors Tell Their Stories*, Peter MacGarr Rabinowitz began interviewing the five or six physicians he knew personally. Each in turn introduced him to ten or fifteen others and eventually, during two years of researching the book, he talked at length to more than seventy doctors around the United States.

In 1984, when June M. Reinisch, Ph.D., became director of the world-famous Alfred C. Kinsey Institute for Sex Research, she promptly changed its name (now it's the Kinsey Institute for Research in Sex, Gender, and Reproduction) to reflect her broad interest in the human condition. She also decided to write a question-and-answer column about sex to help put the Bloomington, Indiana, institute in the public eye. The column sells now to more than 100 domestic newspapers and 23 foreign papers, generating more than 200 letters each month. But to solicit questions for the first few columns, Reinisch not only enlisted the aid of a local gynecologist, she also interviewed students in Bloomington's Bear's Bar.

Finding authorities to quote is easy when a medical center, clinic, or research institute is devoted to study in a certain field. A letter or phone call to the public-information or media-relations officer is usually all that's needed to put you in touch with an expert.

If you are researching a specific disease, the major "disease" foundations, e.g., March of Dimes Birth Defect Foundation or National Genetics Foundation—and governmental institutes—such as the National Institute for Mental Health, the National Cancer Institute, or the Centers for Disease Control—all have public-information or media departments whose job it is to answer questions. Once they know exactly what information you need, they can put you in contact with experts whose research they fund—research carried out at most of the nation's major medical centers and research institutes. (To contact these foundations and the national clearinghouses mentioned below, check addresses and telephone numbers in standard directories or resource guides, such as Writer's Resource Guide, Medical and Health Information Directory, and American Hospital Association Guide to the Health Care Field, discussed earlier in this chapter.)

There are also national centers and clearinghouses for information, such as the National Center for Family Studies, National Clearinghouse for Alcohol Information (NCALI) and the National Clearinghouse for Drug Abuse Information (NCDAI). Manufacturers of health-care products band together in associations and societies, as do those who work in the health-care field.

You'll find groups as varied as the American Osteopathic Hospital Association, Contact Lens Manufacturers Association, American Dental Hygienists' Association, National Association of Health Underwriters, and National Association for Poetry Therapy. (Bear in mind, however, that these associations, like all other special-interest groups, have their own agendas and programs to promote.)

When requesting information, make it easy for the expert to help you. Be precise in asking for what you need. Enclose a self-addressed, stamped return envelope for the reply, or suggest he or she call you collect, if you can afford it. For tips on interviewing, see chapter 10.

Remember, an expert in one sense is anyone who has the information you want—whether layperson or health-care professional. That doesn't mean, however, that a quote from your family doctor is the same as one from a medical-school professor at Harvard, Stanford, or Johns Hopkins. Editors look for recognized names in the field and, prior to publication, verify that quotes attributed to these experts are accurate. Here are several ways to find the people in the know:

• *Encyclopedia of Associations* (annual) lists titles and addresses of hundreds of trade organizations and associations, professional societies and leagues, etc., with addresses and description of the group and/or services. Since Americans tend to be "joiners," finding the expert may first require identifying the professional association he or she has joined. Section 8 lists twenty-nine categories of health and medical organizations—starting with allergies and ending with veterinary science. Locate the group's headquarters, then call or write. If this book is not available, the *World Almanac* lists more than 1,000 associations and addresses.

• *American Medical Directory* lists physicians and pertinent information about them, such as the medical schools from which they graduated. (There are similar directories for medical specialists, dentists, psychiatrists, and women physicians.) This resource is helpful only when you already know the name of the physician. For example, if you were doing a story on former Olympic athletes practicing medicine today and knew that skating gold-medalist Tenley Albright had become a doctor, you could find her address in Boston where she has a surgical practice.

• *Current Biography; Who's Who; Who's Who in America; International Who's Who; Who's Who of American Women; American Men & Women of Science; World's Who's Who in Science;* plus *Directory of Medical Specialists* all contain brief background information on people of note. Regional editions of *Who's Who* cover the East, Midwest, West, South, and Southwest. (For short biographical sketches of those who have died, see *Who Was Who in Science and Technology.*) Technology Recognition Corporation publishes a *Who's Who in Technology Today.* Volume six includes important people in biomedicine.

• *The Address Book: How to Reach Anyone Who's Anyone* by Michael Levine gives names, addresses, occupations of more than 3,000 celebrities, corporate executives, and other VIPs.

• *Guide to U.S. Medical and Science News Correspondents and Contacts* lists key staff in selected media, independent and free-lance correspondents whose work centers on, or includes, medical and scientific subjects. *Editor and Publisher International Yearbook* covers *all* newspapers—great and small. If you're working on a story that requires a geographical spread of experts, often a call to a journalist in another city will result in a list of people called on for expertise by reporters in that area.

• Media Resource Service is a free referral service offered to journalists and authors by The Scientists' Institute for Public Information (SIPI) (355 Lexington Ave., New York, NY 10017; [212] 661-9110; toll-free number outside New York: [800] 223-1730). The MRS maintains a database of about fifteen thousand science, technology, and health experts who represent the full spectrum of positions on science/medical-related stories. You can call for names and telephone numbers of these experts who have agreed to speak with the media within their area of expertise. For a fast-breaking story, turnaround time for being in touch with an expert can be as short as twenty minutes. Callers range from local newspaper reporters to national programs such as ABC's "Nightline," NBC's "Today," and CBS's "Evening News."

• National Referral Center (NRC) of the Library of Congress (John Adams Bldg., R. 5228, Washington, DC 20540; [202] 287-5670). The center directs those with questions on any subject to organizations that can provide answers and maintains a special subject-indexed referral database for this purpose.

• National Science Foundation (1800 G St. NW, Washington, DC 20550; [202] 632-5728) and the Educational Foundation for Nuclear Science (5801 S. Kenwood Ave., Chicago, IL 60637; [312] 363-5225) both aid in arranging interviews, as does the National Bureau of Standards (Department of Commerce, Washington, DC 20234 [301] 921-3181). The NBS is the nation's central laboratory for measurement and advanced physical-science research.

• Gehrung Associates, University Relations Counselors, Inc. (222 Main St., Keene, NH 03431; [603] 352-5300). With a national clientele of universities and their medical centers, Gehrung Associates can put you in touch with professionals who qualify not only as foremost experts but also as articulate interviewees for electronic media.

However, says founder-president Gehrung, "if a press query ends up taking us to a university that is not a client in order to come up with the best authority for one subject, that's exactly what we'll do. We've all been media people, and we view the media as our actual client—so we do not flak it, which is why they keep turning to us."

Don't forget you can always eliminate the middleman by calling the public relations office of any college, university, medical school, or research institute and asking to talk to someone who's a specialist in the field you're writing about. You'll find many of these experts listed in the *Directory of American Scholars* or the *National Faculty Directory;* which provides an alphabetical listing of more than 495,000 names and addresses of college educators in the United States and Canada. Many universities maintain speakers' bureaus, listings of personnel and their areas of expertise, or a directory of official sources—faculty members who are experts on everything from exotic poisons to the common cold.

● PR Aids' Party Line, published by PR Aids' Periodicals, Inc. (330 West 34th St., New York, NY 10001; [212] 947-7733) is a weekly publication that reaches public-relations departments in major industries and corporations. Managing editor Betty Yarmon says writers on assignments in which PR-related material might be useful can drop her a note with all pertinent details, and she will include the request free in an upcoming issue.

Here, for example, is a recent notice (minus the author's address) which, says Yarmon, resulted in an excellent response:

> Represent *mental health professionals?* Marilyn Larkin, who writes relation-type stories for a wide variety of national publications—including *Vogue, Woman's World, Globe* and the new *Feeling Great*—needs access to mental health professionals who can be interviewed and quoted for a number of articles on which she is now working. This is a continuing need for her.

● Author query: Writers often place brief and explicit requests for information, along with their name and address, in major newspapers, specialty publications, and book reviews. For example, here's one placed in June, 1985, in the *New York Times Review of Books* by Allan M. Brandt of Harvard Medical School's Department of Social Medicine and Health Policy:

> For a collection of narratives by women who had an abortion before it became legal, I would appreciate hearing confidentially from anyone who has a narrative or is willing to be interviewed.

In a May, 1984, issue Seebert J. Goldowsky, M.D., placed this query:

> For a biography of Dr. Usher Parsons (1788-1868), the only surgeon at the Battle of Lake Erie and later a prominent Rhode Island surgeon, I would appreciate hearing from anyone who has information about the present whereabouts of his daybook of practice, which I understand was offered for sale about ten years ago, so I may either consult or procure it.

But authors have no guarantee their query will appear. The *Times* and other publications are swamped by such requests for information, documents, correspondence, etc., related to biographical subjects. Furthermore, the tendency is to publish the more literary ones.

• Classified advertising: For a few dollars, your message comes across exactly as you want it—and when. The trick here is to place your ad in the right spot to reach the target audience you need. If your story deals with cocaine users, *High Times* would be a good bet. For an article on the delayed effects of stress experienced by rescue workers at airline-crash sites, newspaper ads in cities where such disasters have occurred would be a logical starting point. University of Cincinnati social psychologists researching famous siblings and their families sought people to interview through ads in city newspapers *and* college alumni magazines.

Be sure you test the market first so that you don't blow your whole advertising budget. See what response you get, then follow up on the winners. Check on free classifieds. Does your area have a "shopper" or publication with free ads? Any special deals, like two insertions for the price of one?

A good ad is clear, strong, and to the point. You want to include enough information so respondents you *want* to have answer will; those you don't, won't. If you work out of your home, be cautious about putting your name and address in the ad. Use a post office box number, if you have one; consider getting one, if you don't.

Giving your telephone number may set you up for obscene or pesty calls, but nothing says you can't hang up at the first sign of "heavy breathing" or audible graffiti. If worse comes to worst, be as professional as you can, thank the caller, and say you've already filled your quota of original material or interviews for that project.

• Professional meetings. There's no problem finding experts at medical, scientific, and health-care meetings. However, if you haven't made prior arrangements for an interview—either through the media coordinator for the meeting or with the experts themselves—you may miss out.

Press passes are required for entry to most medical meetings and for access to the press room where conference staff members help in arranging personal or telephone interviews. The press room is also where complete programs and a catalog of abstracts are available—materials you won't want to leave behind after your interview.

If possible, telephone the conference coordinator ahead of time to make arrangements for an interview. Ask to have an advance copy of the program sent to you. Once you've seen it, you may discover other article ideas or additional experts to interview.

To find out when and where professional health-care groups are holding conferences or annual or regional meetings, consult January and other issues of the *Journal of the American Medical Association.* For instance, meetings in the United States were listed in the January 1, 1985, issue; foreign meetings, January 11; state association meetings, January 18. If you forget, however, the contents page of every *JAMA* issue refers you to other issues listing meeting dates. For pointers on covering medical meetings for the print media, see chapter 14.

PHOTOS AND GRAPHICS

A quick check with several professional free-lancers showed about a 50-50 split on supplying art. Those selling articles to large-budget consumer publications rarely, if ever, were asked to provide photos or art work. Writers working with professional journals or specialty, trade, and other small-budget publications often supplied not only copy but line drawings, photos, and graphics as well. Authors of books, on the whole, took an active role in suggesting artwork to editors—often going to great length (and some expense) to obtain pictures, photos, and graphic material.

For instance, when pathologist and medical historian William B. Ober needed illustrations for his book *Boswell's Clap and Other Essays,* his search took him to places like the British Library, where he found a facsimile of the first page of Swinburne's "The Flogging Block" as well as William Oldys's copy of Langbaine's "English Dramatick Poets" (1691) with his holograph annotation on Shadwell's death.

When Gary Kreps and Barbara Thornton wanted to illustrate certain points in their college textbook *Health Communication,* they did the pen-and-ink graphics themselves. "I thought they were pretty good," she says proudly, "but the publisher ended up doing a fancier job of them." For the artwork in her next book, which covers how to communicate with your doctor, Thornton says she's getting a computer with graphic capabilities.

When F. Donald Tibbitts, professor of biology at the University of Nevada—Reno, needed illustrations for a laboratory manual and another book he was working on, he turned to free-lance biological illustrator Christi Bonds, one of his undergraduate students, for the artwork, which was submitted to the publisher camera ready.

Illustrating the Point
Before you shell out dollars, photos, or graphics (or worse yet, spend hours with pen, ink, or camera in hand), check with your editor.

Large-budget consumer publications generally have art departments and prefer to use professional photographers and artists they've worked with before. Smaller publications with limited budgets often depend on writers to suggest sources of photographs and other artwork.

Some publications will accept only black-and-white glossies; others insist on 35mm color transparencies. Some editors want to see contact sheets only; others want all artwork camera ready. It pays to find out what's what *beforehand*, and if you'll be paid for photos and artwork used. *Writer's Market* and publication guidelines include such information.

If you need illustrations for your book or article, you can:

1. Try to interest a professional photographer or artist to work with you on speculation. This worked for me on an article on which I had a go-ahead from *Seventeen*. Professional photographer Jim Mildon, whose photo credits included *Life* and other major publications, but not *Seventeen*, was willing to shoot about four hundred color transparencies on spec.

2. Suggest to the editor the name of a competent photographer or artist whose work you're familiar with, then leave it up to editor and photographer to negotiate an assignment.

3. Hire your own medical photographer or illustrator to produce the art or photos you need, either collecting payment from the publication or footing the bill yourself.

4. Go to a professional or "disease" association in the field you're writing about and let the director know what type of illustrations you are looking for.

5. Go to the companies that manufacture the drugs or products your article covers. Many of these firms employ their own physicians and researchers who test the products, and have photos and other graphic materials on file.

6. Check credit lines on similar articles, books, and monographs and seek out the same photographers or artists. Often good medical librarians can point you in the right direction, as they know people working in the field.

7. Put together a package of already existing graphics and photographs which would be helpful in illustrating your article. Picture sources run the gamut from industrial and corporate offices to public-relations companies; pharmaceutical houses; university, medical-school and hospital public-information services; community, region-

al, and state agencies; professional societies and associations. In addition to these, individual doctors, dentists, researchers, and others are often willing to provide free quality photos or graphic art in exchange for a credit line.

One source often overlooked by writers is the stock photo agency. However, my experience is it's more economical to let the editor know stock pictures are available than to get the photos from the agency myself. Fees at many agencies can run as high as several hundred dollars for color photos and often begin around twenty-five dollars for one-time use of black-and-white shots.

However, Compu/Pix/Rental (C/P/R) (22231 Mulholland Highway, Suite 119, P.O. Box 4055, Woodland Hills, CA 91365; [818] 888-9270) is a division of Associated Photographers International. As such it provides a computerized stock photo service which gives writers, editors, researchers, and others free and instant phone access to the more than six million photographs registered in its photo bank.

"Simply tell us as specifically as possible what type photographs you are interested in renting—either by phone or mail," says assistant manager and photo librarian Dixie Thompson. "The computer operator then calls up records of photographers who have listed medicine or health or dentistry, for example, as a specialty plus a brief description of the kinds of photos for sale." Callers then receive the name, phone number, and information about the work of the photographer, who then can be contacted personally.

Price negotiations, she says, are strictly between you and the photographer. C/P/R receives a "small percentage" of the photo purchase price, but not the fifty-fifty split that most agencies demand, says Thompson, adding, "we function as a referral agency rather than a photo warehouse."

Unless payment from the publication will make it worthwhile, the writer is better off looking elsewhere for photos. Some stock photo agencies set fees in accord with publication rates or include additional charges for researching the pictures needed. Although the latter fees are deducted or refunded from the total bill after the publication chooses its photos, the writer conceivably could be stuck with payment if the magazine selected none.

Other good sources of illustrations are museums and libraries, both of which usually offer Photostat services. For a small fee, you can obtain copies of documents and pages from old books or prints. When I was researching an article on Nevada's first woman physician, Eliza Cook, I wrote to Stanford's Lane Medical Library because I knew she had graduated in the early 1880s from Cooper Medical College (now Stanford University School of Medicine).

For a modest fee, Lane Medical Library not only sent me photocopied materials but also checked the portrait file of the class of 1882 and discovered it contained individual pictures of each of the graduates. I had my photo—one that not even Dr. Cook's Nevada relatives knew existed.

One medical historian, whose books are noted for their meticulous research and apt illustrations, has found Princeton University's Index of Christian Art the perfect source of artwork. For his most recent book, he told me, "I drove over there, spent the morning in the library, made a list of about thirty pictures I wanted from scattered places around the world, then called my travel agent—all tax deductible."

The National Library of Medicine and Library of Congress, Prints and Photograph Division, also provide visual materials, as does the Bettmann Archive, Inc. (146 E. 57th St., New York, NY 10022; [212] 785-0362). Services here include analytical, bibliographical, historical, interpretive, and technical information in several areas, such as food, health/medicine, science, nature, technical data, and self-help. The archive also offers five million black-and-white photos, engravings, etc. and 150,000 color photos for a variety of rights, among them one-time and editorial rights. A minimum research fee of thirty-five dollars is required on most orders.

Medical Illustration

Medical illustrators are highly skilled artists, generally employed by medical schools; large research or medical centers; private, state, and federal hospitals, clinics, dental, and veterinary schools. Others work on a free-lance basis for medical publishers, pharmaceutical manufacturers, agencies, or media production units.

If your work requires such graphics, call the nearest medical school or large research institute, ask to speak to someone in the communications or medical-illustration department, and find out who does free-lance medical art in your area.

Accredited programs in medical illustration are currently offered in the Department of Medical Illustration at the Medical College of Georgia, Augusta; Department of Biocommunication Arts, College of Associated Health Professions, University of Illinois at the Medical Center in Chicago; Art as Applied to Medicine, The Johns Hopkins School of Medicine, Baltimore, Maryland; the School of Medical and Biological Illustration, The University of Michigan Medical Center, Ann Arbor; the Medical Illustration Division, School of Allied Medical Professions, Ohio State University, Columbus; Biomedical Illustration Program. Department of Biomedical Communications, the

University of Texas Health Science Center at Dallas; and the Graduate Program in Medical and Biological Illustration, University of California at San Francisco.

The Association of Medical Illustrators (Route 5, Box 311 F, Midlothian, VA 23113; [804] 794-2908) publishes a newsletter and directory of members which lists employment affiliations and those available for free-lance work. Independent artists usually base their charges on hourly rates.

If, however, you decide to create your own graphics and this is new territory for you, Jan V. White's *Using Charts and Graphs (1000 Ideas for Visual Persuasion)* explains the graphic design and production techniques of creating diagrams, charts, tables, frames, and boxes. Commentary along the way helps you select the right design and approach for presenting your data.

If you're not near a medical center and need anatomical artwork, Diane L. Abeloff's *Medical Art: Graphics for Use* may be the answer to your illustration prayers. Abeloff, an experienced medical illustrator, has put together a loose-leaf collection of uncluttered line drawings of the body, arranged according to the usual body-system divisions— e.g., skeletal system, muscular system, cardiovascular system. While there's broad coverage of all anatomical areas, there's no great detail (e.g., only two line drawings for the whole endocrine system).

All her drawings are printed on one side only of quality paper stock and suitable for labeling with felt pen or ink to suit the user. The big advantage, of course, is that you can use these pictures as camera-ready art—or cut them out, photograph, photocopy, or add to the drawing—all without worry of copyright infringement or the need to obtain permission to reproduce from the publisher.

For a "how-to" on photography in the life sciences, see *A Guide to Medical and Dental Photography* by Kenneth S. Tydings, SPE, usually available in camera shops. Such photography generally calls for special equipment and expertise. However, if you run into problems, the Technical Assistance Group at Polaroid maintains a free telephone hot line which handles all types of photography questions. Hours are 9 A.M. to 8 P.M. E.S.T., business days. Toll-free line (800) 225-1618; from Hawaii, Alaska, and Massachusetts, call (617) 547-5177.

FAST-TRACK RESEARCH

Some writers enjoy research; others find it a chore. Whether you're a writer who dreads getting started or one for whom the hours in the library are heaven, here's some advice to make your research life easier:

Be Realistic You can't cover the *whole* field, so try to pinpoint what it is you really need, the editor wants, and the reader will *read*. Editors will expect you to support your thesis with facts, quotes from experts, and perhaps, statistics or anecdotes. You're limited by the *length* of your article or book, and by the amount of money you or your editors are willing to spend on obtaining the necessary research.

Become a Collector Pick up all the free literature, fact sheets, resumes, business cards, medical-workshop programs, and whatever else you can get your hands on. When you ask experts for information, also request reprints or other printed material. You can always throw it away later, but a bird in the hand, remember, is worth many hours spent later trying to locate data that was easily available the week before.

Always *date* and include the source of articles; newspaper clippings; brochures; fact sheets; reports; notes you take at meetings, interviews, or the library; and any other materials you come across. Be sure you keep a detailed bibliography, complete with sources of all your facts. Include the library card-catalog number for the book. It will save time later if you need more data from the same source. Think ahead. If you won't remember a month from now why you thought this information or business card would be important, give yourself a *clue*—a slug line at the top of the page or a cross-reference in your idea file. Note where you met the person; the type or title of the meeting; date; and any important items discussed; then file, either in a card file or a plastic photo holder—the kind used to protect thirty-five-millimeter color transparencies. Group these in a three-ring binder alphabetically or by subject area, and you've got a ready-made information network and source of expertise to draw on.

Think Color White paper is the norm, so use color to flag important papers, facts, details you might otherwise miss. I don't like colored highlighters, but my husband swears by them. I find rainbow-colored three-by-five-inch note pads, file cards, and file labels a boon in locating materials I need. For instance, all the chapter files for this book have a blue label; for our bioethics book, a purple one; for a sports psychology book, a green one. With the same color label on the file drawer, it's easy to return folders to their respective slots.

As soon as you start piling up research materials, start a folder. Label it. Keep it with related materials. For years I used heavy cardboard boxes to hold files. When my husband and I went to New York for a sabbatical year in which he immersed himself in biomedical ethics, all our files were shipped and *kept* in packing boxes we then worked from. Metal files are neater, but don't kid yourself—you can work out of any space and files you can live with and keep track of.

Be Good to Yourself Fanny fatigue and eye strain are but a few of the occupational hazards that go hand in hand with research. Some libraries have good lighting, but I've found tinted glass on windows may cut down on glare but does nothing for my eye problems. Chairs, especially the more "comfortable" they're supposed to be, leave me with a backache.

Here's my solution. In my purse in plastic sandwich bags, I always carry a magnifying glass, supply of paper clips, small stapler, note pad, ball-point pen and extra filler (I hate to run out of ink at the crucial moment of copying important data).

I always take an extra sweater. If the air conditioning is too cold, I keep warm. If the heat is blazing, I fold it into a pillow to support my back. And just in case someone else has already found the table with the best reading light, I am prepared. My compact travelers' book light (the battery-powered kind) works just as well in dimly lit libraries as it does in low-watt overseas hotel rooms. (You might spend an extra minute or two passing through the security guard's domain, but so far, the go-ahead has always come through for me.) Once inside, nothing says you can't clip it to your briefcase or purse to light up your page.

Research, Albert Szent-Györgyi once said, "is to see what everybody else has seen, and to think what nobody else has thought." Resolve today to make your research environment conducive to *both* good health and good thinking.

6 □ WRITE TO BE READ

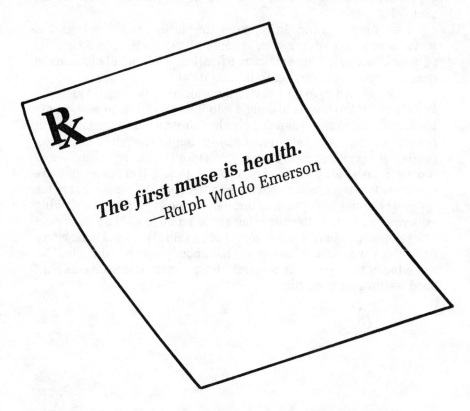

Rx

The first muse is health.
—Ralph Waldo Emerson

Supposedly, when Michelangelo was asked how he was able to breathe such life into his marble sculptures, he replied the block of stone *already* contained the life—his job was merely to let it out. So it is with writers. But the raw material isn't marble; it's the thousands of words collected in research, interviews, notes. And the job is letting life come to light in print.

THE PLATINUM RULE

Forget for the moment everything your mother ever taught you about the Golden Rule. When it comes to writing, your first task is to Do unto Others as *They* Would Have You Do unto Them—the so-called *Platinum Rule.* Shifting the focus of "doing" from your need to write to the reader's need to know or be entertained is the first step in writing to be read.

A similar situation exists when the paternalistic doctor tells a patient, "Do this; it's good for you." But the patient who values his or her autonomy resents this doctor-knows-best treatment. If there's no other doctor to go to, the patient may have to acquiesce. But readers *always* have other choices, and so do editors. Give them lively writing and stories with life, and you become the free-lancer they want to see more often in print.

For example, editors say: "Show me. Inform me. Interpret for me. Entertain me. Astonish me. Move me intellectually or emotionally so that I change my outlook in some way or care enough to act." This is the philosophy that rules magazines today because it rules so much of human activity. What counts for editor and reader alike is: Why should I read this? Why should I *care?*

The answer lies in your words. While no one can teach you to write if you don't have any "feel" for words, you can learn how to put them together in leads that hook readers, anecdotes that make the point for you, and quotes that not only break up blocks of print but also bring people to life.

OVERCOMING THE MEGO FACTOR

Certainly the way in which copy and photos are lined up on a page affects reader impact. But how words themselves are used can make all the difference between I-can't-put-down-the-article appeal and the deadly MEGO factor.

MEGO, according to publisher Truman M. Talley of E. P. Dutton, Inc., means "my eyes glaze over." In other words, the writing is too dull to bother with—and my eyes spot it right away.

Compare, for instance, these two pieces dealing with the same complex chemical analyzer which had been purchased and installed in the toxicology laboratory at Texas Tech University School of Medicine in Amarillo. Both were written by J. Eugene White, the school's coordinator of news and public relations, but one tells about the new machine while the other shows it in action. Which grabs your attention first?

The new gas chromatograph/ mass spectrometer at Texas Tech Medical School in Amarillo is a state-of-the-art computer-controlled chemical analyzer which can identify more than 7,000 chemicals, drugs, pesticides, and environmental pollutants and their metabolites.

Made possible by a grant for a portion of its cost from the Harrington Foundation, it will be used in the toxicology lab of Thomas W. Hale, Ph.D., assistant professor of pediatrics.

"It is the most sophisticated analytical instrument available for use in immediate identification of drugs and other chemicals," said Richard Palmer, president of the foundation.

A blood or urine sample (¹⁄₁₀₀th drop) can be analyzed for identity of drugs in 11 minutes. (Time often is critical in poison cases.) For instance, with acetaminophen (active ingredient in Tylenol), an antidote must be administered within four hours or the liver will be destroyed.

Currently no analytical instrument is available in the panhandle area (of Texas) for determining the identity of drugs in cases of poisoning. Last year Tech's Department of Pediatrics alone treated 7-10 cases in which the toxicant was never identified. (Even if the patient should recover without treatment, it is often important

One sweltering day last August, Thomas W. Hale, Ph.D., assistant professor of pediatrics, received an urgent phone call from a local physician. Could the Tech toxicologist test a urine sample to determine the possibility of poison in a young child's system, and if poison was present, could Dr. Hale identify it?

With a positive answer, the physician rushed a small urine sample to the medical school.

The specimen was from a 2-year-old boy who suddenly had been taken with seizures. The child had no history of seizures, and his physician could find no apparent cause. The suspicion grew that the youngster might have taken some household poison internally.

With a delicate and highly sophisticated piece of equipment, Dr. Hale discovered a carbamate insecticide somehow had entered the child's system. A quick check with the boy's parents revealed their lawn had been treated with Sevin, a trade name for the type of insecticide found.

Dr. Hale explained that the child probably had not ingested any of the insecticide. "He would have had to do nothing more than play on grass," says Dr. Hale. "Carbamates are easily absorbed right through the skin. Rolling in the grass could have presented opportunity enough to know the toxic damage. For instance, benzene is carcinogenic (cancer causing). If a person becomes poisoned with benzene, his physician will know to watch especially close for cancer for the rest of the patient's life. . . .

for the insecticide to enter the child's system."

It was a frightening experience for the parents, but they were relieved to learn the exact cause of their son's seizures.

But what if they had not discovered the cause? . . .

Both news release (on the left) and feature (on the right) eventually cover the same important facts. But which *approach* is best? Gene White, who wrote both, says of the feature: "This is a long way from being ideal copy. But is is so much better than the first [news release], I have no problem saying that this is the kind of writing you and I ought to be doing, or trying to do all the time.

"The information is conveyed, not in a statement of cold fact, but through actions and speech, thoughts and *feelings*. Because finally I put a kid in there, a person," he explains, "and while I was telling about the kid who was saved from 10 or 12 years of medication, whose parents were relieved in a matter of moments. . . . while I'm telling *this* story, I'm also telling *how* it happened and what it was done with—a piece of *machinery*."

Writing pros agree with White. If you can get your message across through *other* people's experiences, eyes, or feelings, you've got the makings of a story with strong reader (and editor) appeal.

EMOTIONAL APPEAL—GOOD OR BAD?

One thing medicine has never lacked is controversy. And White's news release and feature, which he discussed at a medical writers' workshop on using fiction techniques in nonfiction writing, stirred up a heated debate over the use of emotional appeal in medical writing.

The fact is many doctors and biomedical scientists still equate emotions with *irrationality*—which isn't the case at all.

One reason they're leery was expressed by an osteopathic physician who put it this way: "My concern is whether you're talking about truth or propaganda. And it seems to me that the reason scientists generally object to this is that emotion may rule reason, and emotion can get in the way of what might be in the patient's best interest."

Just to be on the safe side, before going any further, let's be clear on one thing. The kind of emotional appeal we're talking about in writing for the general public is *not* the sensational or voyeuristic appeal to the emotions which some supermarket celebrity/news tabloids flaunt in one-inch headlines.

You know the kind—unidentified hospital, unconfirmed report, major breakthrough in medicine. Unidentified doctors reveal the first brain transplant in a human, a newborn who sings and talks in the nursery (supposedly this feat took place in a Hong Kong maternity clinic), or the latest miracle cure for arthritis, cancer, gallstones, and whatever else ails you.

No serious health or medical writer wants any part of that kind of irresponsible journalism.

Good stories, award-winning articles start with facts that are accurate. "But unless you're Mr. Spock on *Star Trek*," says White, "your emotions are going to help guide whatever you do. I'm making a plea for a *positive* use of the emotions. Tell a story with accuracy, but also with drama. You've heard it so many times—show me, don't tell me. It's harder on you as the writer, but it's easier on the reader—easier to read, to remember, and to remember the *author's name*."

LEADING WITH A WINNER

The first step in putting together a compelling lead is to be aware of your choices. You have at least a dozen options, but only one goal: to hook the editor and your readers—and *keep* them reading on. There are no second chances in the "lead" business, which is why seasoned writers never underestimate the power of a lead. They may spend hours, a whole day, or several days, getting it right. They know that without a strong lead, there's no article to sell.

What makes a lead good? You'll find winning leads are:

- efficient. *Without using any unnecessary words, a good lead not only catches but holds the reader.*

- enticing. *The reader who's been skimming the book or magazine's contents is compelled to stop—this is worth reading. Interest is piqued by the lead.*

- clear. *An effective lead doesn't lose and confuse the reader, nor diffuse the topic. Prose is simple; verbs, active.*

- appropriate. *The lead fits the publication, the article, and the subject in style, tone, and pacing.*

- honest. *It doesn't make a big to-do about very little. Nor does the lead hold any false allure because it tells somewhere in the first few paragraphs exactly what the article is all about.*

Some writers call this a *billboard statement* and others, a *capsule sentence*. Most readers aren't even aware of them. But once you've learned to recognize this kernel sentence, you'll realize how integral it is to the lead.

Sometimes the billboard is right up front, as in this lead I wrote for an article in *The Olympian* on the U.S. Olympic Training Center Sports Psychology Program:

> Know thyself, the first of three maxims inscribed on the Temple of Apollo at Delphi, is also the goal of sports psychology—a relative newcomer in the official black bag of sports medicine.
>
> Though it sounds deceptively simple, the athlete who knows how stress affects his or her performance, how to relax and what incentives keep him going, has the key to a lifetime of success—whether it's a world class medal today or highly competitive job tomorrow.

The rest of the article elaborates on how sports psychology helps the athlete to "know" himself or herself and the various strategies used to accomplish this. The one-sentence second paragraph is the billboard. That, in a nutshell, is what the article is about.

At other times, the pace is more leisurely: The capsule statement doesn't appear until the fourth or fifth paragraph, as in "The Great American Penchant for Spreading around Disease" by Thomas Swick.

> On the whole we Americans are a hospitable people, and we good-naturedly share our diseases with others. There are major illnesses, like herpes and mononucleosis, and lesser things like colds and flu. I'd like to address the latter.
>
> How often do you hear, "Just about everybody's got the flu" or "There's a really bad bug going around"? Often enough, I suppose. For years I had heard them as inevitable consequences of the inclemency of climate. They, or rather the illnesses that they proclaimed, seemed the products of something unmanageable in the atmosphere. The very use of the word "bug" associated them in my mind with an untamed, indiscriminate targeting, against which there was no defense.
>
> For all this, the words had a soothing effect on those who had "come down with something," consoling them with the idea that they were not alone.
>
> My belief in man's inculpability in this whole business was shattered recently in a conversation with some foreign friends.
>
> Spending their first year in this country, they have been startled by Americans' habit of going to work sick. To their horror and amazement, in each of their offices, someone had come in ill and contaminated most of the other employees one by one. Where they come from, this happens only in the closest families.

Why people go to work *sick* is the gist of this *Los Angeles Times* First Person piece. And the lead, while not arresting, is suitable for a personal rumination on this dastardly American custom. (Having just picked up a flu "bug" from our son, who had caught it from a co-worker, I feel particularly adamant on the subject of taking fevers to the marketplace.)

Suppose, however, you had submitted this article. Your editor wants to buy it but says you'll have to cut the length from 1,500 words to about 850. (This is not an unusual cut; for example, many Sunday supplements and women's publications run short health-related pieces of 1,000 words or less.)

Where do you start? Take a look at the lead. As it stands, there are 227 words. The crucial billboard statement is in the final paragraph. This is the paragraph to save. But what can you eliminate?

By getting rid of nine sentences from the original lead, adding one brief question at the end, and inserting "some foreign friends of mine" for the pronoun "they" in the last paragraph, you can reduce the lead by 60 percent. Here's an eighty-four-word version of the same lead:

> Spending their first year in this country, some foreign friends of mine have been startled by Americans' habit of going to work while sick. To their horror and amazement, in each of their offices, someone had come in ill and contaminated most of the other employees one by one. On the whole, we Americans are a hospitable people, and we good-naturedly share our diseases with others. But where my friends come from, this happens only in the closest of families. Why the difference?

The moral of all this cutting is: In a pinch, *save the capsule sentence* and take it from there. The corollary is: Don't discount the value of a good billboard statement—it's the backbone of the lead, the article's whole *raison d'etre*.

Leads by the Dozen

Sometimes there's only one lead and it's obvious from the start. It may be a quote you've picked up in an interview, a fact from your research. It feels right, it looks right on paper; it works well with the rest of the article. Congratulations. You've bypassed a writer's biggest headache—finding the *right* lead.

But then there are the other days when you sweat blood searching for those pithy words that will grab reader and editor alike. At times like this, it helps to review your options. Well-known newspaperman and author Max Gunther used to tell students in his writing courses that there were three basic types of leads: the anecdotal, the statement, and "prose-poetry."

Prose-poetry is the type least often seen in nonfiction. But its rarity makes it all the more moving and memorable when well crafted.

This lead which William Hedgepeth wrote in 1971 for the *Look* Special Issue on Birth is one of the most beautiful examples of the prose-poetry lead I have ever read:

> Birth evokes something superbly primeval deep in our collective selves. Each borning becomes, at once, a culmination of man's entire past and glimpse of all his infinite potential. It is continuity. It is the entire inventory of human hopes. It is renewal of vision. It's a wrenching, a wince, a pain, a wild glittery yell—and suddenly, five new nailmoons rising over the sky of an infant hand.

Much more common are the anecdotal and statement leads. Most writing pros identify a dozen or more variations as follows:

● *Summary.* Seen often in news stories and certain kinds of how-to articles, the summary lead sums up in a sentence or two the important information and what the piece is about.

● *Factual.* Straightforward and crisp, the factual lead usually contains statistics, facts, or contrasting numbers. Jean E. Laird, for example, uses this type in "Driver Decisions that Could Save Your Life":

> Experts tell us the average driver must make 20 decisions per mile; he makes a mistake every two miles and has a near accident every 500 miles. Here are some frequent problems you should think about in advance.

● *Quotation.* It doesn't matter whether your quote comes from a book of familiar quotations or the person you've just interviewed. Good quotes make good leads. Superb quotes make *outstanding* leads.

● *Question.* This lead may be one question or a series. *Science Digest* editor Madeline Chinnici starts out with a question in "Understanding Male Infertility." Note that she wastes no time in giving her readers a head start toward that understanding.

> Are you one of the 12 million Americans who suffer from infertility? If you're a man, you may say no because you think infertility is a woman's problem, but it's now estimated that at least half of the infertile Americans are men.
>
> The possible causes are many and run the gamut from bacterial infections and exposure to environmental pollutants, such as the much-publicized pesticide EDB, to smoking marijuana and sitting in a hot tub.

● *Teaser.* Sometimes cast in a believe-it-or-not framework, sometimes in a question with a no-you're-not-right answer, this lead is effective if not overdone. Here's a good example from *Working Woman's* "New Findings about What Makes Workers Happy":

Most workers don't like their jobs, and in a high-tech, who-cares world, there's not much to be done about it, right?

Not necessarily, say the Conference Board and the General Electric Company. They have done surveys that challenge the standard assumption that technology produces alienated workers. The Conference Board has found that nearly four out of five Americans are satisfied with their jobs—especially older workers and those who earn $25,000 or more a year.

- *Shocker.* Frequently seen in tabloids, the shocker often contains a statistic that boggles the mind or a paradox. "The world's heaviest woman eats only 150 calories a day" may instantly catch our eye, but almost as quickly we discount its possibility and move on. A word to the wise: if you're going to shock—and there *are* times when the subject is indeed worthy of shock treatment—be sure you have *facts* to back up your statements, however outrageous they may seem.

- *Definition.* Appealing to authority—whether Webster, or your own favorite medical dictionary—is a good way to start this lead. However, some topics lend themselves to creative definitions. If you're clever, give it a try. Here's one case where you can *always* fall back on the experts and come out a winner. (But if you're writing a textbook, note the trend *away* from the definition as explained in the case history lead.)

In his article, "The Missing Link," for instance, nationally known psychiatrist and author Kenneth R. Pelletier effectively uses a definition lead to introduce us to a new field of medicine exploring the relation between emotions and disease:

> PNI stands for *Psychoneuroimmunology.* A real jawbreaker, but what it means is quite simple. *Psycho* means your thoughts and feelings, *neuro* your brain and nerves, *immunology* your body's immune response. Put them altogether and you get *PNI,* the field that looks at the ways thoughts and emotions influence the immune system. Recent studies suggest that PNI may be the missing link between psychological factors and disease.

- *Descriptive.* In this lead the author takes reader and adjectives in hand to present the story with high appeal to all five senses. In "Haute Goes Healthy," Carol Kramer tells us that when taste and nutrition join forces, eating well is the best revenge.

> To call it a revolution may be premature, but to think of it only as a guerilla movement is to underestimate its force and appeal. Not only is the army of keep-it-fresh-simple-and-nutritious rebels growing but it is also just possible that when the mesquite smoke clears, the firm, the fat-free, and the fit will have prevailed over the pile-it-on-the plate-and-smother-it-with-butter old guard.

Across the country, in fast-food emporiums and haute cuisine restaurants, menus are changing. Health consciousness may be the prime mover behind these changes, but no one—not a single soul—is calling this new cuisine "health food." This time around, the right stuff goes by the name of natural, light, fresh, nutritious, salt-free, low-fat, fat-free, fitness menu, Spa Cuisine, lite-and-fast, heart-healthy, or prudent. Its purveyors are working hard to reposition their image—away from that of bean-sprouty health food stores manned by aging hippies, and onward to the world of hanging plants and brick walls or further up the scale to chrome and glass, marble tile, fresh freesias, and three-figure expense-account lunches. And their work is paying off.

Who would have imagined a few years ago, for example, that New York's ultrachic Four Seasons restaurant would be offering its power-elite clientele "Spa Cuisine"—meals in which every calorie, every single gram of calcium, fiber, zinc, and iron has been checked out by a nutritionist? Or that one of the most elegantly appointed and popular restaurants in Houston, Chez Eddy, would be run by the Institute of Preventive Medicine of the Methodist Hospital?

● *Chronological/historical.* The march of time may start in the present and flash back to events which have led up to the event, incident, or situation, or simply begin at the beginning. That's the approach *San Francisco Chronicle* science editor David Perlman takes in the first article of a three-part series on chronic pain and the latest medical advances in its control.

Dr. Scribonius Largus, who practiced medicine in Rome more than 1,900 years ago, had a sure-fire treatment for pain.

He had his patients grip electric eels or torpedo fish underwater, and the sudden voltage through their bodies swiftly banished their pain—for a while at least.

Today's scientists know far more about the causes and treatment of pain than old Largus ever dreamed of.

These three paragraphs lead readers into a discussion of pain's electrical and chemical pathways through the body's nervous system and new ways of treating pain with more scientific precision.

The next four leads are "people" leads—those that give us a glimpse into someone else's life, problems, feelings, and character.

● *Case history.* The case history is a report of what happened in a given situation. Whether it's one history or a series of abbreviated histories, this lead is a natural for many health-related articles and textbooks. Here's how Gary L. Kreps and Barbara C. Thornton launch chapter 1 of their college textbook *Health Communication.*

The young woman needed four wisdom teeth extracted. The procedure was a routine one that could be performed in the dentist's office. Nitrous oxide was administered as an anesthetic. The woman's mother accompanied her but was directed to sit in the waiting room, with the promise that she would be called if needed. During the course of the treatment, the woman had a drug reaction. She began to experience terror and wanted her mother. She felt her mother could help her feel secure enough to relax, and perhaps even enjoy the novel drug experience. The client tried to ask for her mother, only to find that she was unable to talk. Feeling helpless only increased her terror.

At no time during the one-hour dental procedure did either the dentist or the dental assistant inquire into the client's comfort. After the procedure, the client had several psychological reactions, including nightmares which persisted for several months. Today, almost a year later, she continues to feel aversion toward dentists. The dentist and his assistants, questioned by the parent as to why they had not inquired into the client's comfort, explained that they typically become so involved in the procedure that they often do not inquire; also they felt at a loss as to how they should approach the client during a procedure.

Many similar stories can be recounted of inadequate communication with clients who are experiencing pain or fright. However, health professionals (with rare exceptions) perceive themselves to be helpful and altruistically motivated persons. How does the communication disparity between "intent" and "execution" occur?

Only after these three paragraphs do the authors give us their definition of health communication as "an area of study concerned with human interaction in the health care process." And by then, we've seen the lack of such communication *in action*.

● *Dialogue*. This lead builds up to story-line action through recounting a conversation. C. W. Smith in his *Esquire* piece on the pain of the divorced father tells us:

> Years ago I called a college buddy I hadn't heard from in a while. He had divorced his first wife but had remarried. I asked him how many kids he had now.
> "Just the one."
> "One? I thought you had two."
> "Aw hell!" he snorted. "You're thinking of the ones I had with Judy. They don't count."
> A silence several seconds wide dropped between us while I pictured those two fatherless children drifting into space without a tether. How could a man discount his children's existence with the indifference of a claims adjuster?

● *Example*. A quick series of examples is often an effective way to state a problem (or puzzle), as Scott Kraft demonstrates in this *Los*

Angeles Times article headlined "World Beating a Path to Door of Wichita Forensic Expert":

> In Hong Kong, a policeman dies of six gunshot wounds to the chest—behind a door locked from the inside. Is it suicide?
> A young Pennsylvania woman survives a fire in her home but dies two weeks later of a bad liver. Is there a connection?
> In North Dakota, two men die within a week of each other in the same hotel sauna. A coincidence?
> Stumped by those cases, pathologists called Dr. William Eckert, who runs a sort of forensic Interpol here from his house, his office, and occasionally, from pay telephones on the road. His International Reference Organization in Forensic Medicine, or INFORM, is the only forensic pathology research center in the world, a library of whodunit mysteries, each of which is true.

● *Biographical.* Birth, education, marriage, career, and death may be the chronology of a life, but where does one begin to tell the story? With what scene? "The business of deciding at what age the hero shall be introduced is vital, intrinsic indeed to a biography's entire structure and may well have been decided early in research. Or it can be determined by trial and error," writes Catherine Drinker Bowen in *Biography: The Craft and the Calling.* You don't need to be writing a book, however, to profit from the chapter titled "The Opening Scene."

● *Anecdotal.* This lead consists of a brief narrative—a ministory that dramatically portrays something about someone. There's action, tension, change, or resolution of one kind or another, as Carolyn Males and Julie Raskin demonstrate in this telling lead from "The Children Nobody Wants":

> Sixteen-year-old Liza* is a throwaway child. The small, thin redhead returned from her waitress job one night and found she no longer had a home. Earlier that evening, her mother, well into the Scotch, had started another of their stormy rows. As usual, Liza's father avoided it by fleeing the house for a while. Despite this constant turmoil, Liza had managed to keep up good grades at school and hold down her part-time job. But none of her efforts helped now, as she clutched the note she found on her pillow. "Please be out by tomorrow. Leave us your keys. Mom and Dad."
> The next morning, the nightmare continued. Her parents offered to help her pack. "You can't just throw me out," she protested. "Where will I go?"
> "I don't care!" shouted her father as he grabbed her arm, twisting it behind her back. As Liza squirmed to free herself, the harried man kicked her in the stomach.
> *Although cases are real, names have been changed.

Liza fled. The first night she slept in a graveyard; the next in a neighbor's back yard. From other street kids she heard about a runaway house. Counselors there helped her rent a room, and now she is finishing high school and continues waitressing. Each night she hitch-hikes back to her empty room. "I'd give a lot to come home to a nice warm kitchen and say 'Hi' to someone I love," she says, trying to hold back the tears. But the spunky teen-ager knows she will have to make it on her own.

PROTECTING PRIVACY

Leads based on real people and their experiences can pose some special problems for the health and medical writer in cases where invasion of a person's privacy is, or could be, at stake. Males and Raskin avoid that problem by placing an asterisk by Liza's name in the opening sentence. The asterisk refers to a note informing readers that cases are real but names have been changed.

Here are eight common methods authors use to disguise the identity of real people and situations:

● Initials. J.W., a victim of recent cuts in Medicaid; T.D., who suffers from agoraphobia. . . .

● Occupation/locale. A New York financier; a farmer from Georgia; a California schoolteacher. . . .

● Age/role. A thirty-five-year-old nun who contracted AIDS following a blood transfusion; a grandfather, sixty-three years of age. . . .

● First name only. Most famous was David, the child born with congenital immune deficiency, who became known as "the Bubble Boy" because he spent almost his entire life in a germ-free plastic world.

● Assigned name in quotes. "Robert," whose mother is schizophrenic; a secretary we'll call "Martha"; when "Janice" first discovered the lump. . . .

● The "Doe" group. Baby Doe, John and Jane Doe; closely related is Baby Fae, the anonymous infant who made medical history by living longer than anyone else to receive a heart transplant from an animal.

● Composite. "Elaine," a composite of several women interviewed, is a character based on several similar case histories; "Joe Harper," a composite of many men who work at the test site. . . .

● Disclaimer. Anne Jones (not her real name) thought her mothering days were behind her; Eric H., a pseudonym for a young car mechanic who lives near Philadelphia. . . .

Additional pointers on respecting the right to privacy are covered in chapter 10, which deals with interviewing. But you'll find, as New York writer Jody Gaylin has, that many people *want* you to use their names in the story.

"I prefer to use real names," says Gaylin, who's written for all the major women's publications, "because I think it sounds better. You can spot a fake name, somehow, but I'm just astonished at what people permit you to do. I did a piece on endometriosis, which is a very personal illness, and every woman said, 'Oh, go ahead and use my name. Don't worry about it'."

Gaylin's anecdotes are always true stories which she cuts down to fit the piece.

VITAL SIGNS OF THE ANECDOTE

Temperature, pulse, respiration, and blood pressure are vital signs checked in determining a patient's condition. Editors, too, check for certain vital elements in determining whether an anecdote survives the blue-pencil cut.

An anecdote, according to the dictionary, is a brief account of some incident; a short narrative of an interesting or entertaining nature. These short-short stories make easy reading, and writers use them to illustrate, amplify, or back up points they want to make. Some editors insist on anecdotes—the more "people stories" the better, they say; other editors don't place that much stock in them. Be sure to check whether the publication you're writing for uses anecdotes and if so, what kind.

Are they mini "slices of life" or capsule histories? Are they short? Some anecdotes are complete in only a few sentences; others take several paragraphs, and still others are split—the anecdote begins in the lead, is interrupted by other material, and continues to the end later on. Whatever the style of your anecdote, make sure you build into it the four vital signs editors look for:

1. *Credibility.* Is the anecdote believable? Is it real? Does it *sound* real? Some editors insist that the anecdote be *authentic*, i.e., based on real people in actual situations. Other editors say it is enough that the anecdote, though manufactured by the writer, seems real enough to make the point.

Writers are divided on this issue. Says Alice Fleming, whose byline regularly appears in major women's publications, "Some interviewees are very anecdote-oriented. They will tell you a story at the drop of a hat and all the stories will be good, but there are a lot who are not.

"What I usually do is *improvise* and do my own anecdote, either based on something they've told me or on a situation that accurately reflects what they've said. Because I've found it works very well to have an anecdote [ready] and then have a mental health expert comment on what the people are doing. They will give you the comments quite easily, but the anecdote doesn't come so easily. Either they don't think in those terms, or else they don't want to reveal a confidence if they have a specific patient."

2. *Impact.* To be successful, an anecdote must evoke feeling on the part of the reader—be it surprise, empathy, horror, or some other emotional reaction. Most often, such punch is achieved through selective use of detail, dialogue, or a quote which quickly enables readers to see, hear, feel, grasp what's important in the piece.

Suppose, for example, your story deals with various ways friends and neighbors help raise funds to buy needed equipment for disabled children. What impresses you most is the *spirit* behind these efforts—and you want readers to share your feeling.

One anecdote deals with a postal clerk who's turned his kitchen into an apple-pie assembly line on weekends and holidays. Proceeds from the sale of his pies have already provided a down payment on a $2,300 wheelchair for a child who has cerebral palsy. Since insurance companies are unwilling to continue coverage, additional pie-generated funds will go to a trust fund for the child's care. A quote sums up the postal clerk's enthusiasm and dedication and, at the same time, evokes in the reader a feeling of admiration for such generosity and zeal: "We've got pies up to the eyeballs," he says, "and this Christmas, we're sending out for dinner. There's no room in the kitchen for anything but pies and people to bake 'em."

3. *Relevance.* The anecdote must illustrate the *point* you want to make in the piece or relate to the *subject* being discussed.

4. *Economy of Words.* Tell your little story as directly and simply as you can. Exclude any information that's not germane. Don't waste words, but use enough of them to tell the story well. If your story calls for a *punch* line, rearrange words to achieve maximum impact. (For more on the beauty of brevity, consult *The Elements of Style*, Strunk and White's plain-speaking classic on usage and writing plain English. As White points out in his introduction, eliminating unnecessary words "requires not that the writer make all his sentences short, or that he avoid all detail and treat his subjects only in outline, but that every word tell.")

QUICK EXITS THAT SATISFY

A conclusion, according to Martin H. Fischer, "is the place where you got tired thinking." But tired thinking, like tired blood, isn't enough reason to take the easy way out—especially when you're so close to The End.

Good endings don't fade away; they exit with grace and style—leaving behind a sense of wholeness. Each article mandates its own closing. The ending is determined by the way you've organized your material and the purpose of your article. Whatever type of ending you choose, however, there's a rule you don't want to break. Make it satisfying—and make it *quick*.

"The best endings work because the narrative worked before them," explains Hal Higdon, senior writer for *The Runner.* "Some wise sage before me once said that a good article has a beginning, a middle, and an ending. If the first two are sub-par, no amount of editorial trickery will make the third work. More likely, the reader won't get that far."

The seven endings most often seen are: the summary statement; question; quotation plus booster; surprise or twist; full circle; anecdote or split anecdote; and the prose-poetry ending that picks up on the mood of the piece.

Remember, the difference between the news story and magazine article is that the former is written inverted-pyramid style (see chapter 8) and *stops.* The article, on the other hand, *closes.* And that closing strives to achieve a response, effect, reader action, or reaction. Let's see how the writer achieves this closure.

1. Summary statement. Summing up what has gone before, this ending recaps the development of the article and frequently restates the billboard statement of the lead in different words.

Essentially, in the lead you are saying, "Here's what I'm going to tell you in this article." Rephrased in the closing, it refreshes the reader's memory and leaves her feeling she got something out of the piece. That something may be where to go for further information, steps to take to solve a problem, a final word of advice, or the inspiration to carry on.

2. Question. Ending his article with a question can be highly effective, as Dr. Lewis Berman proves in one of his regular *Family Weekly* columns on pet care titled, "Keeping Your Animal and Yourself in Shape":

> When it comes to exercise, follow your pet's lead. Don't push the animal where he doesn't want to go. Forget about these trendy aero-

bics courses popping up for pets. They're ridiculous. Why ask your cat to do what it will surely find preposterous and beneath its dignity? Why subject your dog to push-ups, sit-ups, and deep knee bends? Why not let it retrieve a ball, or a Frisbee, and enjoy life instead?

3. Quotation plus booster. Often a quote is just what the doctor ordered for a snappy article windup. The booster reinforces the main message, as in this example from William E. Poole's article, "Playing Pain Away." In the piece, Adrianne Burton, child life coordinator at the University of California Medical Center in San Francisco, discusses the challenges of her job—namely, to find ways of decreasing the often traumatic impact of hospitalization on children. Many of these young patients must undergo repeated tests, chemotherapy, and other painful treatments. Play, of course, is important but it's play with a purpose and plan. Before she begins, Burton makes a diagnosis similar to a medical diagnosis of the kinds of play a child needs. The major point of such play is summed up in this final quote: ". . . Children haven't learned some of the grim lessons adults have taught themselves. They haven't learned, for example that they can't turn off painful sensations if they want to. An adult comes and says, 'You can do it,' and it doesn't occur to a child that he can't. That is the beauty of a child's psyche—all things are possible. Some of these kids have more belief in the process that I do, and I'm constantly renewed by knowing them."

4. Surprise or twist. Sometimes the final quote actually contradicts the point being made, but takes the reader so by surprise, he remembers the point of the article long after he would have with a more conventional ending. See how well this twist cum quote works for Cornelia Bowe who was reporting in *Press Woman* on "Working Tours—an Emphasis on Sports Medicine":

> Dr. Jack T. Andrish, head of orthopedic research, is investigating ways of improving recoverability, especially for the knee joint, which accounts for 50 percent of the clinic's [Cleveland Clinic Foundation] practice. His patient studies include gymnasts, ballet dancers, little leaguers, and others. He confirmed that each activity does appear to have a pattern of injuries. What about break dancing, he was asked.
> "No pattern yet, only one injury, a broken elbow. When the patient told me the injury was from break dancing, I asked 'What is break dancing?' The patient promptly dropped to the floor, spun on the elbow and rebroke it."

5. Full circle endings. Think of the popular film title *Back to the Future*, and you've got the working definition of full circle exits. Often called "echo" endings because they return to a theme or key word introduced in the lead, these closings then take it one step further with extra oomph.

Suppose you're writing an article debunking the myth that "real" men don't cry. Beginning with instances in which an American president, a military general, and a well-known television anchor "blubbered" long before women's liberation made it popular for men to weep, you build your case with quotes from experts and results of studies which show that crying is an important emotional release for men as well as women. An ending that would capture the theme of the piece and "echo" a key word from the lead might describe an instance in which a former astronaut wept and include a quote like, " 'Tears aren't just a luxury,' he said. 'They're a sign that we're vulnerable; we weep because we care.' "

6. Anecdotes—whole and split. For a satisfying exit, it's hard to beat the mini-story that sums up what the article is all about. Such a story brings real people, events, and ideas into sharp focus. Less common (because it's harder to find anecdotes which lend themselves to this technique) is the split anecdote, which allows you to develop the story in more detail, beginning the article with the first part, perhaps breaking off on a cliffhanger moment of suspense, and then ending the piece with the story's conclusion. It's an especially effective way to handle a complex health-related story.

For instance, an article on new medical techniques used in treating children in near-drowning accidents might open with a tense story about a four-year-old being pulled from icy lake waters and rushed to a hospital emergency room. After describing the methods and the seeming "miracles" they can produce, the article could conclude with the most recent accomplishment of that same child two years later—a first grader whose doctors and teachers say he's one of the most remarkable children they've ever met.

(Don't forget: a final quote from the child or someone who knows him can tell more about what makes a person "remarkable" than a dozen declarative sentences.)

7. Prose-Poetry. Difficult to pull off without becoming maudlin, this ending is most often used to elicit an emotional response from readers rather than to provide them with last-minute information or spur them to action. With this technique, award-winning author Richard Selzer, M.D., brought his article to a totally satisfying, uplifting close as shown in this excerpt titled "Encounter with a God." In this piece, a surgeon observes a young woman from whose cheek he has removed a tumor. In the process, a nerve—the one to the muscles of her mouth—has been cut, leaving her mouth twisted, clownish. Her husband is with her.

He stands on the opposite side of the bed, and together they seem to dwell in the evening lamplight, isolated from me, private. Who are they, I ask myself, he and this wry-mouth I have made, who gaze at and touch each other so generously, greedily? The young woman speaks.

"Will my mouth always be like this?" she asks.

"Yes," I say, "it will. It is because the nerve was cut."

She nods, and is silent. But the young man smiles.

"I like it," he says. "It is kind of cute."

All at once I *know* who he is. I understand, and I lower my gaze. One is not bold in an encounter with a god. Unmindful, he bends to kiss her crooked mouth, and I so close I can see how he twists his own lips to accommodate to hers, to show her that their kiss still works.

I remember that the gods appeared in ancient Greece as mortals, and I hold my breath and let the wonder in.

Letting the wonder *in* will always be a thrilling and humbling part of writing about health, medicine, science, and human beings. But equally important is being able to come up with new ideas, give form to them, write clearly and with accuracy, and (as Michelangelo would tell you) let the *life* trapped in your materials spill out in your words.

7 □ TLC FOR YOUR MSS.

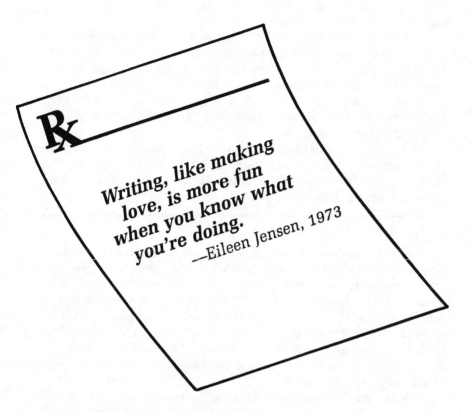

Writing, like making love, is more fun when you know what you're doing.
—Eileen Jensen, 1973

Health-care pros know that tender, loving care is worth the extra pa-tient-time it takes. TLC pays off for writer, too, when it comes to care-ful editing, polished writing, and attractive manuscript presentation and packaging. Tying the manuscript together are the title, transi-tions, and tone.

TITLES THAT TALK

In January, 1983, *The New York Times* best-seller list indicated it didn't hurt to have *life* or *living* in a book's title. Two fiction and three nonfiction books were at the top, including Leo Buscaglia's *Living, Loving, & Learning* in the sixth spot and *Life Extension* by Durk Pear-son and Sandy Shaw at number ten.

Two years later, Buscaglia's book was still there (in the number eight spot) but *life* and *living* as "in" title words were out, at least for the time being.

Just how important *is* a title in selling an article or book? And if an editor is going to change it anyway, how much effort should an author put into finding the right one?

"Never underestimate the selling power of a title," says New York literary agent Richard Pine. "The title's got to be a grabber so that when someone walks into a bookstore and sees the book, he says, 'I've got to know more about that for myself!' "

From the writer's point of view, a good title not only helps to catch the editor's eye initially, it also helps the writer remain *focused* on a particular theme or angle.

Although you'll discover many variations, basically there are only two classes of titles: those *with a verb* in one form or another, and those *without*. The latter, known as *label* titles, tend to show up more often in book publishing.

Labels

These titles are short, accurate descriptions of what an article or book is about. Labels typically contain only two or three words—usually a noun and an adjective or two. Good examples are *The Pill Book* by Dr. Harold Silverman and Dr. Gilbert I. Simon or *Creative Dreaming* by Patricia Garfield, Ph.D. In magazines, a label title is often followed by a blurb such as this one in *Gentlemen's Quarterly*: "The Desk Set: Working Out in Your Office Is—Surprise—No Hardship." (A blurb is basically a subhead title that helps to define the tone and tack of an article or book.)

If you are a "known commodity" as a writer, health professional, or celebrity, adding your name to the title can be a sales booster. Look at *The James Coco Diet*, written in collaboration with Marion Paone, or *Jane Brody's The New York Times Guide to Personal Health*.

Verb Titles

With a verb in the title, you can speak directly to the reader with a question, a command, or a telling quote from the piece. For these and other reasons, magazine editors generally prefer titles with verbs or verb forms.

American Health, for example, ran an article on a new diet theory titled "Taming the Hunger Hormone." Author Tim Page describes his feelings about his wife's pregnancy which ended in miscarriage in a *New York Times Magazine* opinion piece, "Life Miscarried." An article in *Cuisine* on gourmet nutrition was called "Haute Goes Healthy."

Variations

Here are ten title variations on the basic label/verb theme:

1. *How to.* Straight and simple, and ideally suited to the self-help article, these titles get right to the point, i.e., how to water ski safely, how to add spice to a saltless diet, how to know when you're in love. A cover story in *Vogue* was titled, "How to Interview Your Plastic Surgeon."

2. *Shockers.* The hook here is shock value—startling the reader into taking a second look at a subject he might otherwise pass over. For example, many readers might skip a story such as "Trash Can Babies" which appeared in the *San Francisco Chronicle*. Subtitled "What Kind of Person Would Throw Away His or Her Own Child?" the article piques the reader's curiosity so that he sticks with a story and statistics on the rising number of babies abandoned each year by their parents.

"World's Sex-Change Capital," a *Reno Gazette-Journal* story, isn't about Denmark or Sweden, but Trinidad, Colorado, of all places, where in the last fifteen years more than 1,000 "gender identification" operations have been performed. Surprised? Surprise of a different kind underlies philosophy professor Michael Levin's "My Turn" opinion piece in *Newsweek*, "The Case for Torture," in which he argues there are situations in which torture is not merely permissible but morally mandatory. Shocking?

3. *Superlatives.* Most, newest, fastest, least, worst, best. You'd better be *accurate* when you use these words in a title or you'll lose your reader, editor, *and* credibility fast.

4. *Questions.* You can't go wrong with who, what, where, why, when, how, and how much when writing about health and medical matters. "Can Heartbreak Bring Heartburn?" asks John E. Gibson in one of his *Family Weekly* people quizzes. Joyce Bermel questions the burden society places on parents who must plead for transplant organs for their critically ill children in her *Medica* article, "Is the Media the Last Resort in Donor Cases?"

5. *Numbers.* Bigger isn't necessarily better, but a title like "120 Best Doctors in America" *(Good Housekeeping)* certainly is an attention getter. Who can resist Susan Brownmiller's article in *New Woman*, "36-26-36: The Outrageous Idea of the Ideal Female Figure." Or this one in the *San Francisco Chronicle*, "How to stay two when baby makes three."

6. *Negatives.* I find titles with negatives a refreshing change of

pace—e.g., "I Didn't Go to Med School to Let Patients Play Doctor," the title of a *Medical Economics* article by Stephen M. Del Giudice, M.D.; "What TV Didn't Reveal about 'An American Family's' Pat Loud," in *Family Circle*; "Men Who Don't Have Heart Attacks," a chapter in *Sex Can Save Your Life*.

But be forewarned. Among positive thinkers and some psychologists, negatives (and even words with negative connotations) may provoke strong reactions. For example, one Ph.D. author I know refuses to *say* or even use the word *deadline*—calling it instead, an editorial timeline. I've worked with another psychologist who is uncomfortable writing titles or sentences with negatives. Negative statements, he believes, are extremely powerful and leave people with the wrong rather than the correct message.

7. *Commands. Do, don't, stop, start* succeed in arresting the reader—if only for a moment. But that's all it takes to hook the reader if the rest of the title appeals. For example, *"Floss* for a Flashing Smile," or *"Walk* Your Way to Happiness." Frank A. Oski, M.D., a nationally renowned pediatric hematologist and author, titled his book, *Don't Drink Your Milk!* The subtitle reads: "The Frightening New Medical Facts about the World's Most Overrated Nutrient."

8. *Quotations/Dialogue.* Newspaper editors often headline a news or feature story with a line of dialogue or a quote from the story. *Reader's Digest* frequently uses quotation titles in its Drama in Real Life series or in stories such as this one by Kenneth Y. Tomlinson about a young woman who wanted work as a waitress but found the union boss had other ideas. Title: "You'll be a Hooker—or Else!"

9. *Poetic Devices/Play on Words.* These titles are fun to work with. From clever reversals of famous sayings to puns, poetry, or biblical passages, you've got a wide range of sources to draw on in composing a title that catches the exact flavor, sense, or nuance of your manuscript.

Gannett Westchester Newspapers, for example, titled a story by Jack Smith "Experts Exercise Right to Be Wrong." An article by Paula Dranov in *Family Weekly* was called "Brace Yourself: Good News for Adults with Crooked Teeth," while one by Michael D'Antonio was headed, "Placebo Power: Pills That Are Easy to Swallow."

Rhyme makes the point in Dr. Richard Browning's piece in *Woman's World*, "Keep Your Summer Minus Sinus." A booklet jointly prepared by Scholl, Inc., and The American Podiatry Association is titled "Meet Your Feet." A television documentary spells it out in "Battered Wives, Shattered Lives."

Contrasting words point up the irony of fate in Rabbi Harold S.

Kushner's humane approach to suffering, *When Bad Things Happen to Good People*. Reversing the word order in a *Glamour* piece, Mimi Swartz comes up with a different dilemma, "When Good Things Happen to Bad People."

Alliteration (repeating the initial sound in words close to each other) is a playful ploy, as in "Feeling Fresh at Fifty," "Winter's Warmest Workouts," or "Tempting Taste Treats for Die-Hard Dieters." If you're using this device, remember a little goes a long way. The same applies to *onomatopoeia*—the imitation of natural sounds by words, e.g., "Whizzz! Swoosh! It's Future Bike!"

10. *False Lure.* I often wonder if people who write these titles think they're being clever or if they just aren't thinking at all. Guaranteed to annoy the reader, this kind of title has no relevance to the article or at best, a very slim link. Who would guess, for instance, that "Barking Made Easy," which appeared in the March, 1976, *Writer's Digest*, is all about writing *titles*? And the bigger question, what's barking got to do with writing them in the first place? Personally, I'd rather know up front what an article is about. My advice: Even in a title pinch, skip the false lure.

WRITING RIGHT-TRACK TITLES

Rarely do the muses strike with a full-blown title that's just right the first time around. Here are some guidelines for coming up with a title that sells an editor and hooks a reader.

Go with the Style of Your Magazine. Check two or three back issues. What kinds of titles appear most often? Does the editor use label titles followed by blurbs that elaborate on the topic? If so, follow suit. A good title is usually short and crisp. Rule of thumb: six words or less, but there are exceptions, such as *Cosmopolitan*, where eleven-word titles turn up more often than not.

Be Aware of a Publisher's Book List. You don't want to submit a title that's the same as one already on the market or, worse yet, one that's been published by the same house you're sending your manuscript to. *Publishers Weekly*, the most widely read trade journal in the publishing industry, is a good resource for title updates, as is the *New York Times Book Review*, published in the Sunday *Times* and available in most libraries and some bookstores. (*Books in Print* and *Reader's Guide to Periodical Literature* are not as up-to-the-minute, but they offer wider scope on what subjects have been recently published under which titles.)

Titles are not covered by copyright laws. In theory, you can use any title you want, including a best-selling one. But it's not advisable. Using a well-known title invites comparisons between your work and the original—and yours may suffer in the process. Also, the public is likely to find two books with the same title confusing—and maybe, not buy yours. Since it could appear that you are trying to capitalize on the popularity of an earlier work, a court might enjoin duplication of such a title. Better by far to come up with your own.

First, start with a working title. Make it a simple, accurate description of what the book or article is all about.

Keep your ears and eyes open for key words or phrases. As you do your research, interviews, and writing, listen for the catchy phrase, watch for attention-getting words. Write these on a separate title sheet in two or three columns. Then mix and match. Review the various types of titles and play with the words to make questions, commands, superlatives, or negatives. *New ways to* and *a fresh look at* are always potent attention grabbers.

Don't forget, a good title often has some *surprise* quality—an original touch that catches a reader off guard and begs to be read.

You're on the right track, says Richard Pine of Pine Literary Agency in New York City, "if you can get a nice two- to four-word title that sums up what the book's all about, has a little twist to it, or hits at a basic need."

IN TRANSITION, BUT NOT FOR LONG

In one of my favorite Charlie Brown cartoons, Snoopy sits on the roof of his doghouse typing a novel that ends on the brink of medical discovery:

> It was a dark and stormy night. Suddenly a shot rang out. A door slammed. The maid screamed. Suddenly a pirate ship appeared on the horizon.
>
> While millions of people were starving, the king lived in luxury. Meanwhile on a small farm in Kansas, a boy was growing up.
>
> End Part I
>
> Part II
>
> A light snow was falling, and the little girl with the tattered shawl had not sold a violet all day. At that very moment, a young intern at City Hospital was making an important discovery.

Snoopy ends with, "I may have written myself into a corner." But that's not the only thing he's done. Except for letting us know Part I has ended and Part II is about to begin, America's favorite beagle for the most part has ignored transitions—those workhorses of writing that ensure smooth reading. Without them, sentences pile up abruptly, and no apparent logic links one to the next.

Transitions ferry the reader between point A and point B. They serve as bridges, linking one part of the story to another. As bonding agents, they connect one thought, sentence, or paragraph to the next. When transitions work smoothly, the reader is carried along—oblivious to the mechanics of the transit system.

In general, the better the technique, the less obvious the transition is. Here are some pointers that should help you find the right bridge or bonding agent next time you're stuck in the business of moving readers along quickly:

Transitional Words. Webster's defines transition as "passage from one place, state, stage of development, time, type, subject, concept, etc. to another." Sometimes, the unity of the story is most easily ensured by a simple *linking word* such as *next* or *however* that visually conveys how what's gone before relates logically to what is about to follow. Overworked, awkward connectives, like "meanwhile, back at the ranch" or "and that brings us back to" generally reveal a lack, not only of effort but also of imagination. Some examples of commonly used transitional words are:

next	then	afterward	before
finally	and	but	besides
instead	earlier	later	also
hence	thus	however	moreover
another	first	last	while
furthermore	therefore	consequently	likewise
nevertheless	similarly	whereupon	meanwhile

Fast Forward/Speedy Reverse. Some of these linking words are useful in making time and spatial transitions; others, in linking one thought and paragraph logically to the next. Time transitions are the easiest but can become monotonous if the writer bogs down in "every" day, "each" hour, etc.

That's where words like *since, while, originally, ultimately, next* come in handy—allowing you to take giant steps in time, space, and thought, all the while conveying a sense of time, order, or priority. You can write "on her next birthday," for example, or "three weeks later," "every Saturday night," or "during the Gold Rush Years" and get on with the story. The same applies to spatial relationships, like "around the corner," "across the river," or "to the east."

Often sweeping generalities and aeons of evolution can be handled most adroitly in a phrase or clause, as *San Francisco Chronicle* television critic Terrence O'Flaherty proves in a review titled, "Hold Out for a Nice Doctor."

> Homosexuality is a subject that has fascinated human beings ever since the second crop of apples in the Garden of Eden. For this reason, tomorrow night's candid ABC Theater production, "Consenting Adult," is certain to be one of the most discussed television dramas of the season.

Repeating Key Words. A variation of this is to echo the last point made or sum it up in slightly different words as a bridge to the next point. I used the key word *pictures* to link paragraphs in this article on "Family Theater," a form of conjoint family therapy pioneered by the renowned Virginia Satir.

> "Now, take an expression and hold it," Virginia directs the family groups. The audience smiles appreciatively. Three generations in two families—posed and linked in a human portrait.
> It's a picture taken from everyone's family album.
> But pictures in an album only tell us people mated. Not how they met, how they communicated, what they learned, or what happened under stress.

Leading Questions. In her *Discover* piece on "Einstein's Brain," Gina Maranto makes a seemingly effortless transition from one paragraph to another with *two* leading questions—one looks back to the preceding paragraph as in the echo transition above, while the other propels the article in *new* directions:

> Jones advises caution when interpreting brain research that purports to measure qualities like intellect, as do other respected neuroanatomists. Even though technical advances are enabling researchers to assign the responsibility for certain brain functions to finer and finer subdivisions of the brain, the tendency, says Jones, is to think that intelligence is related to things like the number of nerve connections or the efficiency of brain chemistry—and to processes that can't be documented by counting cells.
> If science with its present knowledge can learn nothing of real value from Einstein's brain, then why is the organ being preserved? Whose idea was it, anyway, to study the brain, and why did it wind up with the obscure Thomas Harvey, an M.D. with no particular reputation as a neuroscientist?

Springboard Devices. Poolside springboards are launching pads speeding divers and jumpers in fairly predictable directions.

Transitional springboards are triggering devices that allow you to jump smoothly and rapidly from the present to the past or from one situation to another because there is some *object common to both* the here and now and the then and there. For example, the object might be a Pacific Islands coconut, now a varnished pencil holder on the doctor's desk, which serves as a war memento and springboard in an interview to the ways war has influenced medical treatment in the last thirty years. Remember, though, a good transition doesn't draw attention to itself—it's strictly a means of moving the story along.

As for "meanwhile back at the ranch," can you ever use these in good conscience? Of course. Once you know the rules, you're free to manipulate them. In "Haute Goes Healthy," Carol Kramer's *Cuisine* article on chic restaurants featuring tasty nutritional meals, "meanwhile back at . . ." appears with no apologies to transitional chic. But then ranches and Texas are Lone Star State staples. At this point in her article she is discussing adjustments in recipes for calorie- and salt-conscious dieters. Chef Renggli is with Four Seasons restaurant in New York City; Houston's Chez Eddie is run by the Institute of Preventive Medicine of the Methodist Hospital.

> And Renggli grimaces at the very mention of the word *margarine.* "Margarine doesn't taste right to me," he says. "When my wife and two daughters went on a diet, they wanted to use it. We had a big fight. I said, 'Use less butter'."
>
> Meanwhile, back at the ranch, Chez Eddie has been educating Texans to the possibility that "eating wisely and well" is not necessarily a contradiction in terms. . . .

Visuals. Not all transitions are "bonding" ones. Sometimes the best way to tie a piece together is to break it up into *easier*-to-read segments. Flip through any magazine, and you're sure to find at least one article in which a large first letter or *initial cap* heads a new paragraph, separating it with extra white space from the preceding one. Perhaps the art department has embellished this first letter or word; sometimes, the whole first line is set in caps.

Like shorthand signals, these visuals alert readers to change— time's a-passing, the story scene is moving backward or forward, the article is about to take off in a new direction. This is important, you're telling readers, and at times like this you need to think like editor *and* graphics director.

Now's the time to go back and look at your sample copies of the magazine you're writing for. How have such transitions been handled before? How can you show off your piece to best advantage? Most likely, you won't have a say in the artwork, but you can type a line in full caps, separate paragraphs by extra white space, use italics (sparingly, please,) or three-dot journalism (the ellipsis . . .) for special effects like fade-ins and fade-outs.

See how effectively Robert W. Stock has used ellipses and italics to distinguish his daydream of sports glory from reality in "Daring to Greatness," a *New York Times Magazine* opinion piece on men's fantasies.

> At 10:30 A.M. of a summer Saturday, the sunshine dazzling, the temperatures kept in the 70's by a playful breeze, I stood on the center court at the Newport Casino, racquet to hand, and dreamed a dream of another me. . . .
>
> *The clamor from the bleachers fills my ears. The smell of new-mown grass fills my nose. Tilden and Budge rose to glory here; Laver and Rosewall paused for a triumph or two on their way up. Now it's my turn.*
>
> *Sure I'm old for the tournament—nobody thought a 53-year-old could even qualify—but here I am in the finals, and McEnroe looks worried. No wonder. He can't get a racquet on my warm-up serves.*
>
> *Now it begins. The crowd is still. I show McEnroe the new balls, and then I toss one into the air, a white globe against the soft blue sky. It rises higher and higher and higher. . . .*
>
> "Watch out!" My wife's warning reached me just as her serve— uncharacteristically hard and straight—bounced off my forehead. The offending ball was of that white variety made specially for use on grass, and the green carpet at my feet had been freshly cut. Otherwise, dream and reality weren't close. As usual.
>
> And the next few minutes widened the gap.

ATTUNED TO TONE

Editors can tell within a paragraph or two if you've hit the right tone for the topic you're writing about and the publication you've sent it to. Some magazines go for the "soft-sell"—writing that's chatty, friendly, reassuring, maybe humorous, and frequently conversational in tone. Other editors look for hard-hitting, fast-paced, crisp prose that almost commands the reader's attention. The tone you take in your manuscript tells the editor at a glance whether you've studied the publication and *know* the market you're trying to sell to.

"Tone," says Connie Emerson in *Write on Target*, "determines whether a piece will be academic, formal, straightforward, instructive, reportorial, conversationally chatty or breezy; whether it will be serious, lighthearted, or humorous."

But how do you achieve the right tone when you're not used to writing for popular media?

First, think of yourself as *talking* to *someone* you want to have remember what you're talking about. A colleague, for example, might want you to cut the small talk and get on with the facts. A piece written for this person most likely would be more formal. No need or time for breezy anecdotes here. This person wants you to get to the point and have data to back it up. You'd want your tone to be convincing, authoritative, straightforward, and, in some cases, instructional.

In talking to your neighbor, on the other hand, you might start off with a question, tell a story or two, repeat a comment or some news you'd heard that would lead to further discussion of the subject at hand. Without even realizing it, you'd have spontaneously built into that neighborly chitchat four typical editorial leads: the *question*, the *anecdote*, the *news peg*, and the *quote*. In writing for this reader (who has just as much right to information as your colleague), your tone most likely would be conversational, informal even when informative or reportorial, and maybe even witty—if you're the neighborhood Erma Bombeck or Art Buchwald.

Fine Tuning Your Manuscript

Once you've put your *first words* on paper, you've overcome a writer's biggest problem—getting started. Keep writing. Don't break the flow of words by stopping midstream to edit what you've already written. It breaks your concentration and makes it that much harder to pick up where you left off. Some authors, in fact, always stop writing for the day at a point in the story where the action is on-going or a link to the next paragraph is so obvious that they'll have no trouble starting up again the next day.

If, however, your writing comes to a halt, check to see if you've done all the *research* you need at that point. (I used to think I'd run into writer's block, when in reality I was merely missing the right quote, or fact, or anecdote that would move the article along. Going back to my notes or doing one more interview was often all it took to get the creative juices flowing again.)

If your deadline allows, take a break. After you've completed a first draft, put the pages aside for a day or two. With fresh eyes, you'll be able to see what you missed earlier in that first rush of brainstorm writing.

Now's the time to look critically at structure: is there a discernible beginning, middle, end? Are transitions smooth? Have you made your point clearly, without excess words, dangling participles, rambling sentences? Such perfection is rare in a first draft, so be prepared to excise precious words, move paragraphs around for greater emphasis and clarity, rework, rewrite, and yes, reread—but this time, read your writing *out loud*.

Clear writing takes both time and energy. In reading your own writing, you'll find yourself stumbling verbally over unwieldy sentences, four- or five-syllable words. Those are important warning signs—if you can't say it aloud easily, no one else will be able to read it easily. Words don't have to be long to be first-rate; short words, remember, are not only easier to read but stronger to boot.

ENERGIZE YOUR WORDS

You may be so familiar with health-related jargon that you don't spot it in your own writing. A reading of your manuscript by someone who doesn't work in the same field can quickly point up lingo outsiders will have trouble with. (See chapter 10 for pointers on eliminating troublesome jargon.)

Frank Grazian, executive editor of the monthly *Communication Briefings,* believes the key to making your prose vigorous is to weed out weak verbs and verb forms. These not only slow the pace of a sentence, they rob it of life as well. Here's his "Verb Power Index℠" which can help you measure the verb power of your writing. (For a free copy, send your name, address, and SASE to Frank Grazian, 806 Westminster Blvd., Blackwood, NJ 08012.)

Take a 100-word sample of your writing and circle every verb. Then:

1. *Count the total number* of verbs including infinitives. Do not count verbs used as nouns (swimming, running) or verbs used as adjectives (the *finished* product).

2. *Go back and count* the verbs of one or two syllables in the sample. Don't consider the word *to* when counting infinitives and don't consider helping verbs, such as *have,* as in "I have given." Just note the main part of the verb. Also, count verbs made into three syllables by adding -es or -ed.

    However, exclude all verbs that are part of the verb *to be* (*is, am, was, were,* etc.) Example: "John *was* an officer." Add this number to the total number of verbs in the sample.

3. *Count the number of punchy verbs* in the sample. Examples: pry, snare, strike, banish. Examples of nonpunchy verbs: give, get, look, walk, write. If in doubt, don't count the verb. Score two (2) points for each punchy verb and add this number to the total in No. 2.

4. *Count the number of verbs* in the passive voice. The passive voice occurs when the subject of the verb is acted upon. Passive voice: "The book *was written* by Mary." Active voice: "Mary *wrote* the book." *Subtract* one point for each verb in the passive voice. This is your "Verb Power Index."

What does your score indicate? Here's the rule of thumb Grazian has devised for his college students and writing seminar participants:

- High verb power: *28 or more*
- Moderate verb power: *20-27*
- Low verb power: *under 20*

He arrived at these figures, he says, after analyzing hundreds of writing samples. He concluded that effective writers tend to use between 13 and 16 verbs in a 100-word sample. Of these, about 9 to 11 are countable short verbs, two to four are punchy verbs, and none to three are in the passive voice.

Certainly other yardsticks for evaluating the readability of your writing, such as Robert Gunning and Douglas Mueller's *Fog Index*, have been around longer. But I decided to include Grazian's new formula because it zeros in on *verbs*. Since professional-journal manuscripts are almost always couched in passive voice, it's a problem for many health-care professionals who consider themselves "writers" to turn around and put those same verbs in the *active voice* when writing for the public. They're used to writing the other way—and it doesn't feel "right" to use the active voice, to say nothing of contractions in verbs and pronouns.

Yet use of *it's, here's, haven't, you're,* and *I'm* is the number-one style device of modern professional writing, according to Rudolf Flesch, one of the foremost authorities in the field and author of *How to Write, Speak and Think More Effectively.* Don't forget that the number-one stylebook used today in nonfiction writing for the public is the *Associated Press Stylebook and Libel Manual* mentioned in chapter 3.

While you're checking your writing sample, be on the lookout for the *shoulds, woulds,* and *coulds* that indicate you're hedging your bets and undermining your position. For example, "it would seem that this conclusion could be drawn from that example which should serve as a warning." In other words, watch out—this example leads to that conclusion!

If the muses have really been kind to you, you will know someone you can ask to read your manuscript who understands two things: *nonfiction editorial needs* and *how to help you meet them.* Your mother and husband may like your writing because they love you, not because it's publishable. Your friends or colleagues who say, "You really ought to send that in, it's great," may be doing you a great disservice if they're not familiar with what editors look for, buy, and want.

One way to help someone help you editorially is to give that person guidelines for critiquing your manuscript—guidelines that will give you an idea of where your strengths are as a writer and specific aspects of your article that need reworking. Here are the guidelines that work well for my writing students. Don't forget, "I like it" is not critiquing a manuscript. If your outside reader likes your work, ask her to tell you why. If she feels it needs strengthening, ask her to tell you why in a positive way, based on one or more of the following points:

GUIDELINES FOR CRITIQUING A MANUSCRIPT

1. TITLE
Is it appropriate?
Is its meaning clear?
Does it catch your interest?
Is the length appropriate for intended publication?
Could it be made stronger, more catchy? How?

2. LEAD
Does it grab your attention?
Does it sound fresh?
Does it make you want to keep reading?
Does it contain a "billboard" sentence?
Would another type of lead work better? What kind?
Does it set the tone for the article?
Does it promise more than the article can deliver?

3. STYLE
Is the article well paced?
Are transitions smooth?
Are sentences varied in length?
Is the article tightly written? (No extra words?)
Is the tone (light, formal, chatty, scholarly, etc.) appropriate for the subject and the publication?
Are verbs phrased in active rather than passive voice?
Is the pronoun I used judiciously? How about You?
Have all scientific words been adequately explained?
Has all "medicalese/dentalese" been eliminated?

4. CLOSING
Is it satisfying to the reader?

Is it appropriate for what's gone before?
Does it drag on—or is it a quick, efficient, effective exit?
Are there any questions left unanswered?
Does it "tell 'em what you told 'em" or leave readers with a takeaway thought?

5. GENERAL COMMENTS
   Is the theme consistent throughout the piece?
   Does the piece digress, get sidetracked, or bog down? Where?
   Is the article "fleshed out" with appropriate quotes, examples, anecdotes, etc.?
   Is the length of the article appropriate for the topic and publication?
   Is the type of article and style appropriate for the intended publication?
   Does the material presented hold your attention throughout?

The purpose of getting outside, *informed* opinions is to learn what works, what doesn't, and why. Too many opinions can be confusing—especially if they all differ. Ultimately, it's your manuscript and your choice. So listen to the comments. Accept those that make sense to you emotionally and intellectually. Reject the rest. Rewrite.

Send off your piece and let an editor give you the opinion that really matters. You won't go wrong if you take to heart Dr. William J. Mayo's advice: "Begin with an arresting sentence; close with a strong summary; in between speak simply, clearly and always to the point; and above all be brief."

THE FINAL PRODUCT—
DON'T NEGLECT EYE APPEAL

Manuscript mechanics can seem like a major comedown after the creative high of receiving an editor's go-ahead and actually writing the article or book. And, of course, many authors write sample chapters or even the entire book before submitting the manuscript for consideration. But the job's not over until you've put together a package that not only looks professional but *is* in every sense of the word.

Start with your paper. It should be white and it must be standard sized (8½ by 11 inches). Editors wince at tissue-thin paper, flashy colors, floral or gimmicky borders. Never use erasable typing paper—it not only smears, it's hard on the eyes. So, too, are letters produced by worn-out typewriter ribbon. Always use a dark *black* (not colored) typewriter ribbon. If the enclosures in the letters *a*, *b*, *d*, *e*, *p*, etc. are inked-in, clean your keys.

Some editors accept computer printout submissions, but all who do prefer letter-quality printers to dot-matrix. They *dislike* (and often refuse to look at) hard-to-read or unusual type faces, such as script, italic, all-capital, etc. After working so diligently writing your manuscript, don't blow your chances of selling by ignoring these editor preferences.

On a page-by-page basis, book and article manuscripts are similar. However, most book manuscripts contain a cover page which includes the title and sometimes a blurb, by-line(s), and name, address, telephone number (*with* area code) of the author or coauthors. You don't need a cover page, however, for an article manuscript. Simply place your name, address, and telephone number in the upper left corner of the first page, then center your title and by-line two to three inches below it. Your telephone number is important because an editor may not want to wait for the mail to get in touch with you quickly to clarify a point of information or ask for a sidebar to run with the piece.

Editors will expect to see an approximate word count in the upper right-hand corner of your manuscript. (The easiest way is simply to average the number of words per line, count the number of lines per page, multiply, and round out the total to the nearest ten.) Consult *Writer's Market* for detailed information on manuscript preparation and packaging.

Be sure that you put your name on each page along with an identifying word or *slug*. *Slugline* is a newspaper term for an abbreviated title or the like, which the reporter chooses to show at a glance what the story is about. For example, I used *Child's Doctor* for a piece called "How to Talk to Your Child's Doctor"; *Tranquilizers* for an article titled "What You Should Know about Tranquilizers." In preparing a book manuscript, substitute your chapter title or an abbreviated version of it for the slugline. (Caution: avoid using single words like *what* or *how* which might apply to more than one manuscript the editor could be working on at the same time.)

Generous margins are a plus. Many writer's instruction guides suggest 1¼-inch margins on all sides of each full page of typewritten manuscript. Some editors like 1½-inch margins even better. The purpose is to give editors enough white space so that it's easy for them to read, edit, and mark copy for typesetters.

Avoid hyphenated words at the end of a line. It makes more sense to stop short of a margin, or run over just a bit, than it does to split a word in an awkward spot. Don't worry. No editor will hold it against you if margins aren't ruler perfect. If, however, your word processor or electronic typewriter has the function to turn out justified (even) right margins, don't use it. In estimating the number of pages or columns your manuscript will fill, editors start with the assumption they're dealing with unjustified copy.

After you've typed the final word, move down three or four spaces and use some end mark or symbol to indicate that there is no more to come. You can do this in a variety of ways, such as writing The End (the traditional stop-sign of book authors); centering and spacing a series of three asterisks or the numeral sign #, or using -30-, which is newspaper code for the end of a news story.

MAILING MATTERS

Unless you are working on direct assignment from a magazine, enclose with your manuscript a self-addressed, stamped envelope (SASE) with correct postage. (A word to the wise: in sending your manuscript out of the country, avoid sending commemorative stamps as return postage, since these are collector's items and occasionally end up in someone's album instead of on your return envelope. Some free-lancers who send personal checks to cover return postage from foreign publications say they are rarely cashed.)

Never staple or paper-clip your pages together. Says one editor at Ticknor & Fields, "You can do it, but we'll just take them out." Do make a copy of your manuscript, covering letter, and invoice for expenses (if your editor has agreed to reimburse you).

HOW LONG SHOULD YOU WAIT FOR A REPLY?

Each day, book and magazine editors are deluged with query letters and manuscripts sent in hopes of quick sale or go-ahead. Some editors are extremely slow in responding; others, quite prompt—even if the reply is only a form rejection saying, "Sorry, your material doesn't meet our editorial needs."

However, what if six to eight weeks have passed and you haven't heard a word? Will inquiring about your proposal or manuscript cost you a possible sale? Is the editor still considering it? Is your manuscript sitting at the bottom of the slush pile awaiting its first reading? Worse yet, was it lost in the mail?

You may never know unless you requery an editor about your letter or manuscript. But there is an acceptable waiting period. After all, many editors are short-staffed, and the slush pile can grow mountainous overnight. As a guide to the writer who wants to know when it's safe to inquire about a query or submission, *Writer's Digest* lists the average time publishers and agents take to report back to the author:

Average Reporting Time

Magazine	Six weeks to two months
Book publisher	Two to three months
Literary agent	Three weeks to two months

If you decide to inquire about your manuscript, make your letter short and to the point. Include the title and a brief description of the idea or article. If you're trying to learn the status of a query or proposal, it makes more sense to photocopy the original and send it with a brief note and self-addressed, stamped envelope.

If you still have not heard from the editor or publisher in four to six weeks, you or your agent may wish to send a letter advising the editor you are withdrawing the manuscript from consideration at that publication, to submit it elsewhere.

FOR THE RECORD—AND THE IRS

Before you turn to your next writing project, complete the record-keeping chores related to this one. Be sure copies of your manuscript, query and covering letters, invoice for expenses and/or services rendered, and any other relevant notes, correspondence, and research material are filed together in an easily identified folder. If an editor calls you three weeks later to check on a point of information, it will be much simpler to find the answer if your records and data are all in one place.

Even part-time writers need efficient bookkeeping procedures that will hold up to Internal Revenue Service scrutiny in the event of an audit. All writing-related income and expenses must be recorded.

Some authors use standard accounting ledgers or computerized accounting systems, making journal entries on the date money comes in or expenses occur. Other free-lancers prefer log books, in which they note mileage, telephone calls, appointments, query and manuscript submissions, etc., with receipts attached to appropriate pages.

Still other writers find all they need is a large manila envelope in which to store receipts until tax time, plus a notebook or recipe file box to keep track of query and manuscript submissions, rejections, sales, and other writing income.

One writer I know keeps writing receipts, statements, etc., in an accordion-style file with twelve compartments labeled Postage, Office Supplies, Research Materials, Travel, Gasoline, Photography, Telephone, Admission Fees, Lodging, Dining, Photocopies, and Income Receipts. At the end of each year, she adds up the income, subtracts the expenses and tax-deductible items, and places all the receipts in a manila envelope on which she's written the appropriate tax year. Her accordion file is then ready for reuse in the current tax year.

Whatever record-keeping system you choose, make sure it's suited to your needs and you're comfortable using it. If in doubt about what is tax-deductible, consult your accountant. A book you might find helpful in answering business-related questions is Kay Cassill's *The Complete Handbook for Freelance Writers.* Cassill discusses various roles free-lancers play, including those of bookkeeper, cost accountant, and bill collector.

RECYCLING TURNDOWNS

"Never let rejections hold you back," the late actress Mary Pickford once said. "It's not the being down that's harmful, it's the staying down." Professional writers agree. Rejection may be painful, but it's never fatal.

Frequently, the rejection stems, not from the writing, but from the fact you sent your material to the wrong market. One way to find out is to send the rejected manuscript (or a query describing it) to another appropriate market. But be sure you reread the piece first.

A fresh look may show you some minor details that need editing to fit the new market. If the manuscript has fingerprints, wrinkled pages, or a coffee stain or two, retype or command your computer printer to do it for you. Don't give up easily. It may take several round trips before the piece is sold.

If, however, you draw fifteen to twenty rejection slips without any editorial encouragement, you might want to consider the possibility it's not the market that's wrong, it's the manuscript. This could mean anything from wrong slant to heavy-handed writing with no reader takeaway value.

Chances are you won't sell every manuscript the first time around. But if you want to be on the money for fast-track success, take to heart one free-lancer's motto: "There is no good medical writing—just good rewriting."

8 □ WRITING TO INFORM

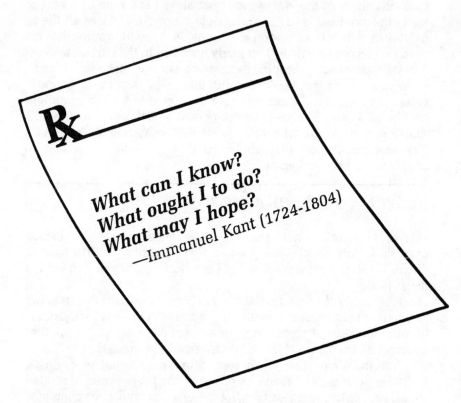

Rx

What can I know?
What ought I to do?
What may I hope?
—Immanuel Kant (1724-1804)

Knowledge, wrote Samuel Johnson, is of two kinds: we know a subject ourselves, or we know where we can find information on it. For many Americans today, the newspaper or magazine is where they find the *health* information they can understand and use.

"One indication that medical science has become ineffective in communicating health information is that patients increasingly turn to popular newspaper columnists for answers to medical and sex problems," scientific communications expert Lois DeBakey is quoted as saying in a *Los Angeles Times* article. The same article notes an open letter to doctors with which Ann Landers began a 1974 column: "Dear Doctor, Ann Landers has a problem. She receives almost 1,000 letters a day and in every mailbag, there are at least 100 letters that should have been sent to you."

Today health- and fitness-related columns and factual articles are the backbone of almost every publication. Without them, many consumer, trade, and technical journals would be out of business. Whether it's a woman's magazine, newspaper supplement, house organ, regional or specialty publication, giving readers health information is one of the major facts of editorial life.

Who's reading these health publications, and what do they want from them?

"This is an audience that really wants *information*," *Health* managing editor Joan L. Lippert said at a national writers' conference. "When *Health* magazine (formerly *Family Health*) started, its purpose was to tell mothers and fathers how to care for their children; wives, how to care for husbands; couples, how to care for aging parents. Now *each* family member wants this information in more depth," she explained, "and they're *not* hypochondriacs. Rather, these people have a healthy interest in the subject of health and fitness, and are interested for themselves and the people they love."

"There's no *end* to what they're interested in," agrees Dianne Partie, health director of *Self*. "The medical pieces run consistently high [with readers]. Nothing seems to be too technical for them. . . . The question is: What can this do for the reader?" she says, adding, "You really have to make it practical."

TAKING THE AUTHORITATIVE APPROACH

In addition to stressing consumer-related aspects of medical topics, a major editorial change at many magazines is a much more *authoritative* approach to health subjects.

"One of the things I've instituted at *Parade*," says health editor Earl Ubell, "is to try to make the articles that we run on health and science have a very strong underpinning of science. Once we give an assignment, we will pay for a computerized literature search so we know you have gone through the material, and gotten everything about the subject you possibly can, and have gone through what's up-to-date and what isn't."

Before going to press, major magazines check out medical facts appearing in articles and review quotes with the experts interviewed for the piece.

At *Self*, for instance, any article containing health information is reviewed first by health director Dianne Partie, who is a registered nurse. "There's also a research department," Partie says, "which does all the fact-checking for every sentence that appears in the magazine. Writers are asked to submit all their backup material, and every fact has to be checked with an authority in that field."

"*Self*'s philosophy," she explains, "is to try and present a balanced view—both sides of an issue. We don't feel we should be telling women what to do. We try in each article to give them enough information so they will be able to make an informed decision for themselves."

This philosophy will serve you well, too. As a writer, you are not in the practice of medicine. Your role is not to advise but to inform and clarify.

Traditionalists will say that giving information as a part of the decision-making process is the physician's role—whether verbally or in print. But today, more and more physicians are coming to realize the value of the well-written, informative book, article, and pamphlet in supplementing the doctor-patient communication.

"The more intelligent the patient, the more extensive is his or her need for information," says Dr. Ernest L. Mazzaferri, chairman of the department of medicine at Ohio State University College of Medicine. A noted endocrinologist and author of several professional texts, Mazzaferri says in the twenty-three years he's been practicing, two major changes in medicine have become irrefutable.

One is that the *nature* of what physicians see in their offices is changing. ("No longer," he says, "do we see many diseases in their full horrendous manifestations because patients are so well informed and seek treatment earlier.") The other change is that patients now demand extensive, detailed explanations of everything—which translates into more *time* spent with a patient. ("If somebody comes into your office with a serious problem, you may have to spend an hour explaining it to him—and no doctor has an hour per patient.")

"That's where public writing comes in," says Mazzaferri. In his practice, for instance, he uses a number of publications written by scholarly people and directed to patients to help them understand more about their medical problem or condition. He estimates that just one publication on thyroid disease has saved him 100 patient-hours. Mazzaferri believes, however, that *only physicians* should write about medicine for the public.

You will meet physicians who side with Mazzaferri; you will meet others who disagree. Yet the public's need for accurate, up-to-date information continues to grow, and there is no way doctors alone can meet that need. No doubt about it, the responsible writer who can take complex material and explain it accurately and clearly for the nonprofessional person—whether through mass media or medical media—makes a vital contribution to medicine and to the nation's health.

MEDICAL NEWS IN QUICK TAKES

Many editors report that among the most popular sections of their magazines are those containing medical newsbriefs, updates, or breakthroughs.

McCall's, for example, runs an eight-page section, "Vital Signs," which is one of the five most-read sections in the magazine. Health uses about fifteen of these short newsbriefs every month—on subjects ranging from artificial corneas to how your kidneys affect blood pressure. Breakthrough pieces at Self pay about seventy-five dollars. Bruce Jenner's Guide to Better Health & Living, a new bimonthly, pays about fifty dollars for hard-news items on health, fitness, and medicine for its column. And the call for short news items and newsy reports continues to go out from publications like Ladies' Home Journal, Aerobics & Fitness, American Health, Celebrate Health, and Science Digest, which has recently started two new sections—"Medicine" and "Behavior."

Although writing fillers and brief 50- to 350-word pieces is an easy way to get started free-lancing in many other fields, it's not necessarily so in health and medicine. One reason is the tight writing required; another, the fact that many publications assign staff writers to these sections or turn them over to regular contributors who are experts in various medical specialties.

Good Housekeeping, for instance, has a regular medical column by Alan E. Nourse, M.D., who covers the medical field for the magazine to see what's new. "The Better Way" is a section open to free-lancers, but in rather a limited way, says GH's articles editor Joan Thursh.

"Requirements are very specialized," she explains, "and they pack a lot of information into a very small amount of space. Unless one is truly proficient and knowledgeable in the field, one would have to spend as much time doing an article for 'The Better Way' section—to compress it into their pages for generally lower fees—as one would in writing a major article for us for a substantial amount of money."

If you have an idea for a medical brief or filler, the best way to approach an editor is with a query briefly describing what you have in mind and the source of this information.

FOR YOUR INFORMATION—THE TOP FOUR

The most popular types of factual articles that appear regularly in newspapers and magazines are: the health service piece; quiz plus answers; the myths-or-fallacies-dispelled article; and the granddaddy of them all—straight facts, and lots of them, reported objectively with information attributed to experts and dispensed in quick, easy-to-take doses.

Titles range from the prosaic to the exotic—yet all have important information to convey to the public, whatever its age. "Surgery under Glass," for example, is a sophisticated *Health* piece by William A. Check, Ph.D., on how doctors reattach severed limbs and substitute toes for fingers while peering through microscopes at the tiniest nerve endings and blood vessels. "Facts about Homosexuality," a *Seventeen* article; "Wellness in the Workplace" (*Signature*); "New Help for Total Deafness" (*National Retired Teachers Association Journal*); and "Smallpox—the End of a Disease" (*Highlights for Children*) may be short on title pizazz, but all speak directly to the targeted readership of these publications.

Editors of juvenile publications say they're on the lookout for health and science articles well written on the children's level—but they're hard to come by. Catherine Johnson, assistant editor at *Highlights for Children*, is eager to run more articles on health and medicine but says, "Frankly, we have a hard time finding articles on these subjects that are handled well at a child's level. Some of the factors, she says, that help pieces succeed where many fail include:

- *Avoiding a textbookish approach to health*
- *Dealing with topics and concerns that are current and relevant both in youngsters' lives and in the larger world*
- *Respecting the intelligence of the reader*

Johnson's pointers carry over into writing for adults, too. You don't want to talk down to readers, nor do you want to overestimate their knowledge. Even the brightest people need introductions to entirely new subjects. For instance, most readers have heard of a *gene*, but try getting a description of what a gene is or what it does. The same for antibodies or cloning or bioethics. That's why you have to provide the information clearly, simply, and without editorial putdowns like "*Of course, a gene is . . . .*"

Regardless of the age of the audience or the length of the piece, the informational article has one main job—to convey knowledge. This can be done either formally or informally. To be effective, the story must leave readers feeling they learned something new or received reinforcement for something already known, though perhaps known only in part.

Nothing says, however, that factual writing can't be lighthearted or entertaining. In fact, some of the best learning occurs when information is presented this way. Purists among medical free-lancers may find this hard to swallow, but listen to what Joan Lippert of *Health* had to say at a writer's workshop: "Our readers want to be entertained. As writers, there's room for your creativity as well as your accuracy, your thoroughness and your good reporting."

AT YOUR SERVICE

Service pieces and their first cousins, the *roundup* articles, deal with consumer topics, such as health-care products, consumer services, or common problems to avoid. Acting as middleman between expert and reader, the writer rounds up the facts so that readers can make fair and accurate comparisons in selecting something in a given category or evaluating it for themselves.

A travel publication might be interested in an overview of health and fitness programs offered at spas or resorts in your area. Your newspaper might welcome a comparative piece on services provided by child-care or extended-care facilities in your city. You might check on what to look for in, and prices of, hearing aids, eyeglasses, or home fitness equipment at locales ranging from doctors' offices to discount outlets and specialty shops. But whatever the category, the aim of the service piece is always to keep readers from making mistakes and enable them to get the best deal the first time around. Unlike the "how-to" article, however, the service piece does not provide specific step-by-step instructions. Rather, it contains general guidelines, usually backed by quotes from experts. For example, in "Celebrity Workouts: Will They Work for You?" *Self* magazine asked three experts to give guidelines for selecting books on fitness and to evaluate six workout programs endorsed by superstar-authors like cover-model Christie Brinkley, comic-coach Richard Simmons, and *Dynasty* actress Linda Evans. The end result: readers could rate for themselves their chances of success in hitching their own diet/beauty/fitness routine to a star's.

Editors of city, regional, state, special interest, and consumer publications buy service pieces. Often these include charts or side-bars summarizing data for easy "comparison shopping." Because service and roundup articles require time-consuming research and often legwork as well, many newspaper and magazine staff writers are not enthusiastic about doing them—which makes these good entrees to editors for free-lancers.

Your best bets are in sticking with local or regional markets for your service piece, as you can't compete successfully with *Consumer Reports* on the national scene. There's even an added bonus—researching consumer topics in your own backyard gives you the kinds of personal insights that make the facts truly informative for your audience.

Occasionally, however, you can combine hometown research with the national picture. Consider how many times you've driven past or stopped at a McDonald's, Burger King, Pizza Hut, or Long John Silver's seafood restaurant. Prevention senior editor Kerry Pechter decided to take a look at "The Best (and Worst) at Famous Restaurant Chains." In researching the article, which appeared in the July, 1983, issue, Pechter talked to several restaurant chain executives and American Heart Association program associate/nutritionist Anna Marie Shaw. She received nutritional data supplied by the Frances Stern Nutrition Center, a part of the New England Medical Center in Boston, plus menus by the dozen.

Her conclusion: There's still plenty of grease and salt on the menu, but your chances of finding healthy food at the big chains are better than ever since many include options for the calorie or sodium watcher. And because of her legwork, readers know where to go for an inexpensive, convenient, and nutritious meal—and what to watch for in hidden salt, fat, and cholesterol. It's a service piece any free-lancer could have researched and written from home with a few telephone interviews, a tank of gas, and enough willpower to pass up a quarter-pounder or two—with onions, lettuce, tomatoes, side order of french fries and a soft drink or chocolate shake.

TESTING YOUR QUIZ QUOTIENT

Most of us dreaded quizzes in school even after we'd spent half the night boning up on the subject matter. But quizzes in magazines— aaah, that's another matter. Few of us can resist testing our wits against the experts or finding out more about ourselves.

This kind of minitest, for example, allows us—in the privacy of our own reading space—to check up on our stress levels or ability to think creatively, learn how compatible we are with the boss, or what we really are seeking in a spouse, roommate, or pet. A Woman's Day cover line, for example, reads, "What Kind of Mother Are You? Rate Yourself in Our Revealing Quiz." One from Self points readers toward "The You Others See—Do You?" (a test to spot and correct your self-image blind spots). A Glamour quiz, "Are You Scared of Rejection?" is taken from The Love Exam, by Rita Aero and Elliot Weiner, Ph.D.

Basically, there are four quiz forms editors find appealing:

1. True/False and Yes/No. After a paragraph or two introducing the topic come eight to twenty consecutively numbered or

lettered questions or statements to be answered with a T or F; yea or nay.

2. Multiple choice. A brief umbrella statement usually introduces this quiz, then come directions for checking responses and totaling your score. Generally, the reader is offered three or four choices for each question or statement.

3. Mix and match. Typical is the quiz with a lettered column on one side and a matching numbered column on the other. The idea is to cross the gulf of white space between them and match right answer to correct item, name, place, or category.

4. Fill in the blanks. Less commonly seen in magazines, these quizzes are always test-your-knowledge types. To complete the quiz, the reader must write the answer in a blank space appearing somewhere on the page—often at the end or in the middle of the question.

Answers to quizzes may appear in the back of the book, printed upside down somewhere on the page (editors know it's more fun to peek), or listed right side up beneath the quiz itself. According to writing instructor Connie Emerson, author of *How to Make Money Writing Fillers*, free-lancers who want to cash in on the quiz market have chosen a winner. "The field," she says, "is open and unexplored by most writers."

To be salable, quizzes must meet certain criteria, among them: Questions must be clear and concise; the subject must appeal to a wide range of readers; the theme must be appropriate for a publication and play on the reader's curiosity; the quiz must have a "game" or challenge factor to it, and finally, the quiz must be suited to the reader's level of skills.

"Often in creating these quizzes," Emerson says, "you don't even have to make up the questions. Just find authorities willing to share research findings and little tests they have devised, write a few words introducing the subject, and put the scoring information from those experts into prose form."

One writer who has built this type of quiz into a highly successful form is John E. Gibson. His nationally syndicated quiz column appears in more than 300 newspapers with 30 million readers. Questions in his quizzes play on the reader's curiosity to know more about himself or herself, and answers come from studies and surveys conducted by health-care professionals and sociologists in major research centers and universities.

You'll frequently see short quizzes inserted as sidebars within factual articles. Florence Isaacs, for example, included a ten-question, true-false quiz ("How Does Your Marriage Rate?") in an original article she wrote for *Reader's Digest* titled, "Long-Term Marriages: What Keeps Them Going?" Isaacs worked out the quiz and how to score it with Roberta Wool, Ph.D., a New York psychoanalyst and sociologist.

DEBUNKING THE MYTHS

In the ancient world, myths represented the collective wisdom of a particular group of people. Passed from generation to generation in the form of legends, these myths were attempts to explain natural phenomena, belief systems, institutions, or particular practices that had become so imbedded in the culture that no one could really remember their origins. Myths were sacred; questioning them was indeed risky business.

"Myths" are still with us—but today *not* questioning them can be risky business.

The kind of "myth" we're talking about is the *misinformation* that can circulate in the form of stereotypes, superstitions, popular notions, and health "facts" about everything from feeding a cold and starving a fever to "male menopause" or the "unfemininity" of female athletes. The free-lancer who can dispel such myths with facts to the contrary not only provides a service to readers but has the satisfaction of banking an editor's check as well.

This is one time the writer doesn't have to struggle to find a lead. The "myth" is it. Notice how well it works for Dr. Jane Patterson in her *Shape* article "The Myths of Menopause."

> Whenever I hear another bit of misinformation about menopause, I think of my Aunt Mary. When I was young, Aunt Mary was admitted to a mental institution, where she remained until she died. My mother always told me that Aunt Mary's menopause had made her crazy, and for a long time after I believed that there was a big risk to women when they reached that stage of their lives.
>
> A lot of other myths about menopause are still floating around. I hear them all the time from my patients. The truth about menopause isn't all good news, but it's nothing to be horribly worried about either.

Patterson, coauthor of *Womancare: A Gynecological Guide to Your Body*, explains what menopause is and examines the reasons why it has developed such a bad reputation in many quarters. In the process, she provides data from various studies and dispels the myth of "craziness" long attributed to the female "change of life."

When several "myths" are related to a single subject, such as mental illness, infertility, or middle age, the article frequently follows a simple one-two/myth-rebuttal pattern. First the "myth" is stated, sometimes in boldface, in a simple declarative sentence. Then the record is set straight in one or more paragraphs (usually no more than three) packed with facts, research findings, quotes from experts, and perhaps an anecdote or two that reinforce the point the writer is trying to make.

In a *Woman's Day* article, "Anxious about Infertility? New Hope for Troubled Couples," Robin Marantz Henig looks at five popular beliefs in a sidebar titled "Myths that Plague Infertile Couples" and counters them with findings from various sources, among them a government report and a national organization for infertile couples. Here's how Henig treated two of these myths:

> *If you've been pregnant once, you can get pregnant again.* Not necessarily. A government report found that 60 percent of infertile couples who want a child are suffering from "secondary infertility"; they have given birth to one or more babies but seem unable to conceive another.
>
> *Infertility is usually the woman's problem.* According to RESOLVE, a national counseling and support organization for infertile couples, 40 percent of infertility can be traced to a problem in the wife, 40 percent to a problem in the husband, 10 percent to a combination of male and female problems, and 10 percent to no diagnosable condition.

Folklore is another rich source of health-related information. But if you're writing about folk medicine cures or remedies, be careful. It's illegal to practice medicine without a license.

For example, *American Health* magazine, which has a section called "Folk Medicine," makes it clear that the feature "explores the scientific evidence for (or against) some popular medical beliefs. It is not medical advice, which is available only from your own physician." In looking at the science behind a few superstitions, here's how *American Health* correspondent Carol Ann Rinzler handled the castor oil cure for warts:

> A reader reports that she cured her plantar wart by rubbing castor oil on it, and she has recommended the treatment to friends with great success. Alas, when we investigated the healing power of castor oil, we discovered that the FDA has ruled that there is no evidence of castor oil's safety or effectiveness as a wart treatment and has banned it from over-the-counter remedies.
>
> That's not to say that we doubt it worked for our correspondent. Warts sometimes disappear spontaneously because our bodies have activated an immunity to the virus that causes them. Sometimes they disappear for no apparent reason. That's why there are so many popular (and sometimes effective) folk remedies for them.

FOCUS ON FACTS

A fact can be defined as "something that actually exists or has actually occurred; something known by observation or experience to be true or real: a scientific fact." Therein lies the expository writing tale.

Scientific and medical facts can be fascinating—or excruciatingly dull, depending on who's reading what and why. (Gray's Anatomy, for instance, may be intriguing to the anatomist whose bible it is or to the teenager concentrating on the pages of reproductive organs, but it can be difficult reading for the medical student who's trying to learn the twelve cranial nerves.) In the leg-bone-connected-to-the-ankle-bone department, a little goes a long way without some relief—editorial or otherwise.

Factual articles strive to explain a topic in an objective and, often, detailed manner. If there is a difference of opinion about the facts, both sides (or three or four) are presented. But even when the topic is controversial, such as attendance at school by children who've developed AIDS following blood transfusion or metering water usage because of a city's dropping water table, the primary purpose of the factual article is not to persuade but to inform readers. (That's not to say, however, that the chips won't fly once the facts are out.)

The most common types of factual articles are list stories, straight news accounts, disease articles, reports, and features like Good Housekeeping's "50 Fascinating Facts about Mother's Milk," and "Your Heart: Hard Facts about Longevity and Health" in Science Digest.

In an Atlantic report on "Nutrition: Sweetness and Health," Boston-based free-lance science and medical technology writer Ellen Ruppel Shell presents evidence that no link between sugar and disease has been substantiated, whereas sugar substitutes—while low in calories—may actually stimulate the appetite. A heavy barrage of facts laced with statistics on the manufacture and consumption of sugar substitutes opens the piece. "Paradoxically," writes Shell, "the success of artificial sweeteners has not diminished demand for natural ones"—which leads to more facts on sugar itself.

Shell then examines the safety record of various artificial sweeteners like saccharin and aspartame, and concludes that at present it's not clear that either of these two controversial products poses a threat to health. She discusses popular criticisms of sugar, alleged links between sugar and various conditions or diseases like acne, cancer, diabetes, and behavioral problems in children. In the final analysis, she concludes, the real threat to health may not be a "sweet tooth" at all. Shell winds up her conclusion with a summarizing quote from a medical expert as follows:

Research suggests that controlling weight has far more to do with curtailing fat than with curtailing sugar and that obese people are more likely to have a "fat tooth" than a sweet one. Rena Wing, an assistant professor of psychiatry and epidemiology at the University of Pittsburgh School of Medicine and a specialist in weight control, says, "The facts are simple: fats have more than twice as many calories as carbohydrates, and it is fat that contributes to weight problems." Many foods that people identify as sweet, such as ice cream, chocolate, pie, and doughnuts, are actually high-fat foods flavored with sugar. "Let's face it," Wing says. "No one gets fat from Life Savers, which derive virtually all their calories from sugar. What we really need is a fat substitute, not a sugar substitute."

PERSONALIZING THE IMPERSONAL REPORT

Nothing brings a report to life as quickly as putting yourself in the position of testing its hypotheses and conclusions. That's what Kate White did in a *Glamour* piece titled "Eye Power," in which she personally tested research findings by experts on the effects of eye contact and staring.

In "Storms—Are They Sexier than Sunshine?" meteorologist Gordon Barnes introduces us to his role as an investigator in a two-year study of young married couples carried out by doctors at an unnamed northeastern university. Purpose of the project was to determine the time of the year in which the greatest frequency of sexual relations occurred. He opens his *San Francisco Chronicle* article with a play on words, and one of the love-making advantages in knowing results of the study and being able to read a barometer:

> When I'm introduced socially as a meteorologist, there's almost always some self-styled wit who has to say it: "Ah, that means you can look into a girl's eyes and tell 'weather' or not."
> I desperately try to look as though he said something original.
> But, to tell you the truth, all I have to do is look at my wristwatch (I've got a barometer in it) to determine whether or not a woman is in the mood.
> There is a close correlation between barometer readings and people's inclination toward sex, which was disclosed during a project I once worked on.

The study attempted to correlate weather patterns with reported dates on which a group of married couples said they had sexual relations with each other. Results of the study indicated that the highest rate of sexual intercourse is in December and January. Long, cold winter nights seemed the logical explanation for all the activity—until Barnes discovered that barometer readings at the same time were always below 29.90.

LINING UP A LIST

In list articles, like Felicia Lee's *USA Today* report of findings from a study on sexual child abuse, one or two introductory paragraphs set the stage for the numbered or bulleted list of data that follows.

> Most men who were sexually molested in childhood never reported it and refuse to label the experience as abuse, a new study reveals.
>
> The 3½-year study of 122 men by Knoxville, Tenn., social workers will be presented at a two-day national symposium on child sexual abuse that opens today in Burlington, Vt.
>
> The study suggests that we vastly underestimate the incidence and impact of male sexual abuse, says Charles Gentry of Knoxville's Child and Family Services.
>
> Among the findings:
>
> ● Only three of the 122 men told anyone of the abuse before they reached age 18.
>
> ● 75 percent of the abusers were female—often family friends or relatives.
>
> ● 20 percent reported the abuse had a negative impact on their sexual performance.
>
> ● 75 percent reported fear, confusion, anger, and resentment over the incidents.
>
> ● 20 percent had fantasies about sex with children.

News stories focus on the who, what, where, when, how, and why of an event or situation. These accounts traditionally are written in the so-called *inverted-pyramid* form. In this form, the most vital material appears in the lead paragraph (the wide top of the inverted pyramid). Subsequent paragraphs contain less-important facts in descending order of priority, with the least significant one tapering down to the tip of the pyramid, the end of the story.

In these accounts, there are no surprise endings, no suspense. The first paragraph tells all, though the original reason for writing this way has long since passed. During the Civil War, correspondents wrote stories *chronologically* and transmitted them back home via telegraph. But the telegraph system was not always reliable, and enemy action along the lines was. All too often, the "hot news" or latest developments at the front were lost in transit, never making it to page one. The inverted-pyramid style insured against such loss—if *anything* was transmitted to the home newspaper, vital facts would be first.

If you want to brush up on journalistic style, learn how to cover meetings or speeches, write fast-breaking news reports, or produce in-depth news features, see William Metz's highly readable *Newswriting: From Lead to "30."* A former newspaper editor and retired journalism professor, Metz says his goal is to talk about writing and reporting "in much the same way as a city editor would discuss those things with a cub reporter on his staff." Here's a book where you can find out much you always wanted to know about press hospital codes, hospital reporting, or the right to privacy in disaster stories—but didn't know who to ask.

INVESTIGATIVE REPORTING— THE STORY BEHIND THE STORY

Investigative pieces focus on the why and how aspects of a topic—ultimately seeking out who's responsible and asking what can be done about it, what should be done. They explore pros and cons of such controversial issues as the use of animals in medical research, hospitals that dump patients who can't pay, why there's a shortage of certain vaccines, or how credible children are as witnesses in sexual-child-abuse cases.

They may also tackle subjects like faith healing, use of laetrile in treating cancers, chelation therapy in vascular disease, or megavitamins to improve the intellectual potential of the retarded person.

Exposés, on the other hand, ferret out the facts behind bad judgments, misdeeds, and other acts that are not in the public interest.

Investigative writers must guard against being carried away with what they perceive or believe to be the facts and crossing over into the realm of irresponsible reporting—and libel suits. As an investigative reporter, you must combine excellent research techniques with skill in interviewing. Critical factors include finding the right sources, asking the right questions, understanding how to interpret responses correctly, and knowing where to locate experts who can help put your findings in the right perspective.

Sometimes writers stumble on the investigative angle in the course of researching something else. One free-lancer who specializes in investigative writing about medical topics says of herself, "I'm a very analytical person—behind every story that's told, there's another one that I'm always looking and listening for."

Famous in this tradition were turn-of-the-century muckrakers like Ida Tarbell and Upton Sinclair. In his novel *The Jungle*, Sinclair tackled the meat-packing industry, ostensibly to arouse public empathy for the working conditions of packinghouse employees. Instead, he succeeded in provoking a nationwide furor over unsanitary practices and adulteration in the meat-packing industry, resulting in passage of the first U.S. Pure Food and Drug Act in 1906.

DISSECTING THE DISEASE ARTICLE

In the mid seventeenth century, John Mayow observed that "as a rule, disease can scarcely keep up with the itch to write about it." What would he say today—when the morning newspaper is as likely to carry two or three disease articles as the major league baseball scores, and newsstand cover lines are a hypochondriac's delight?

Everyday coverage keeps us informed about emphysema, osteoporosis, arthritis, herpes, mononucleosis—plus a whole host of diseases whose names read like a celebrities' *Who's Who*—baseball great Lou Gehrig's disease (amyotrophic lateral sclerosis) for example, or that of folksinger Woody Guthrie (Huntington's chorea).

Not surprisingly, the itch to write about disease is still spreading, only the volume is even greater than before. More people want to read about the "retribution of outraged Nature." We're not *yet* down to editorial disease-of-the-month features, but when an *Esquire* cover highlights "10 Diseases That (honestly) You'll Wish You'd Never Heard About," one wonders, uneasily, what the *eleventh* will be.

Although these popular "disease" articles often contain highly sophisticated information for the layperson, the article structure itself is plain and simple. See how free-lancer Kathy Crump, who specializes in health and behavior subjects, treats systemic lupus erythematosus in her *Family Weekly* piece titled, "The Disease Doctors Don't Understand":

> Systemic lupus erythematosus. It's an appropriately strange name for a strange but all too common disease, one that has more than half a million people in this country in agony. Lupus can strike anyone, but most sufferers are women of child-bearing age. Fifty thousand new victims are hit each year.
>
> Basically, lupus is a disorder of the body's immune systems. Explains Dr. Peter Schur, professor of medicine at Harvard Medical School, "Antibodies normally protect us against viruses and bacteria. But in a lupus patient, the antibodies attack the body itself, rather than protect it from outside elements."
>
> The disease has no known cause (though overexposure to sunlight, stress and drugs can trigger flare-ups), no cure and no predictable series of symptoms. For some victims, lupus begins as arthritic swelling or joint pain. Others develop a skin rash or hair loss. Many experience overwhelming fatigue or high fevers. And in its more severe form, lupus can attack the kidneys, lungs, blood vessels or brain. Ten percent of the cases are fatal.
>
> The difficulty in diagnosing lupus adds to its reputation as an odd ailment. Not only is there a wide array of symptoms associated with lupus, but they mimic the warning signs of many other il-

lnesses, including arthritis, diabetes, and even mental disorders.

According to Dr. Schur, a typical patient recites a laundry list of symptoms, and then when the doctor is baffled, she seeks help from another—or several others. "The problem is that the physician often doesn't consider lupus," says Dr. Schur. "The trick is to educate doctors—and patients—to think of the disease as a possibility so they'll order the appropriate blood tests." Even then, such tests are unfortunately far from foolproof.

Like other lupus patients, Henrietta Aladjem, author of *Lupus: Hope through Understanding*, met with a variety of symptoms during the time her doctor attempted to come up with a proper diagnosis. Sudden exhaustion gave way to increasing weakness to collapse to phlebitis to life-threatening kidney disease, which is a frequent by-product of the illness.

"It was just one thing after another," says Aladjem, "almost as if the organs in my body were taking turns to show which could do more harm.

"But at least I had a doctor who wouldn't quit looking for the cause. Some patients begin to believe that the disease is in their minds." This feeling of "I must be crazy" is just one of many psychological pressures that a lupus patient must face.

"The struggle of getting a diagnosis may cause anger or frustration," points out Dr. Malcolm Rogers, assistant director of psychiatry at Brigham and Women's Hospital in Boston. Another hardship is "the obscurity of the disease, which makes it difficult to explain to friends what is wrong."

Patients must also contend with the changes in physical appearance: skin rashes and lesions. Female sufferers may have to reconsider their feelings about having children. Not only can pregnancy exacerbate the illness, but, says Dr. Rogers, "If a woman chooses to have a baby, she may not have the energy to provide initial care."

Still, there is hope. In the last 10 years, a rapidly expanding knowledge of the immune system has led to new treatments—for example, separating blood cells in order to remove the defective plasma that may be contributing to the disease. There are also therapies designed to suppress symptoms and lessen discomfort, such as the administering of aspirin-type drugs, or cortisone treatments for skin lesions and rashes. In addition, doctors have also found antimalarial drugs very useful for treating those who have drug-reaction or skin problems. One of the more basic recommendations made by physicians is the use of sunscreens to help protect a person from ultraviolet light. And finally, for those with arthritis-like symptoms, they are prescribing anti-inflammatory agents.

In addition, doctors and researchers are learning more about the important role that genetics and nutrition play in triggering flare-ups of the disease.

Years ago lupus was automatically considered fatal. But with new knowledge and drug therapy, 90 percent of all patients will live 10

or more years after the onset of the disease.
For information, contact the Lupus Foundation of America at
11921 A Olive Boulevard, St. Louis, Mo. 63141.

YOUR STYLE IN HOUSE STYLE

The idea for Crump's piece on lupus originated with a *Family Weekly* editor who called the Montana writer and asked her to write a 1,000-word article. Suppose, however, you received a go-ahead on speculation from *Family Weekly* (now *USA Weekend*) to write a short piece on some other disease, such as Hodgkin's disease or glaucoma. With the lupus piece in front of you, it would be simple to put together your article using the same format as a guide.

For starters, you might consider the different questions the author has answered in the article. These are basic questions your readers would want answered, too:

1. *Who gets this disease? What are the statistics?*
2. *What is the disease? What part of the body does it affect?*
3. *What causes it?*
4. *What are its symptoms?*
5. *Is diagnosis difficult? Why?*
6. *What are the stages of the disease?*
7. *What advances have been made in diagnosing/treating the disease?*
8. *What is the focus of research efforts now?*
9. *What resources/sources of information are available to patients and their families?*

Notice that the article contains few numbers or statistics, but Crump has placed them in the all-important lead and closing paragraphs. A check of other *Family Weekly* disease-oriented articles could tell you if this is typical or atypical—a clue to where you might want to place your statistics and how many to incorporate in the piece.

Note, too, that the author has quoted two medical experts on the subject (both from the Boston area) and a patient who has written a book on disease—a book with an upbeat title. By quoting these authorities, a writer can impart some of the article's information in quotes rather than in visually heavy blocks of expository writing.

The article closes on a hopeful but realistic note and provides readers with a source for additional information on the disease.

Through tight writing and carefully chosen quotes, Crump has covered the topic in less than 650 words. You can too.

But there are some caveats that Crump feels any health and medical writer should be aware of.

Family Weekly had requested 1,000 words, and Crump's original manuscript was in the 900-plus range. The editor, she says, called her for clarification on a few points in the article and also said he wanted an even shorter piece. However, when he read the new version to her over the phone, Crump says, the reality of this complex disease had been distorted in the editing. She objected. Then the editor called one of the experts to discuss changes in his quotes. The physician backed Crump, saying she was right in the first place.

"You have to really be careful that an editor, who has done none of the research for the article and is trying to shorten it by a couple of hundred words, doesn't shorten it to the extent that the meaning is distorted," cautions Crump. "Ask the editor to send galleys or, at least, call and read the edited piece to you over the phone. I have no objection to being edited whatsoever," she continues, "as long as it remains true and accurate to what my sources have told me—especially regarding quotes from people—because those people not only give their time to you, it's their reputation, too."

SIDEBAR SAVVY

Good articles contain lots of good information. But sometimes there's still more that would round out the piece or help readers find additional sources of information. Sidebars are showcases for these extra facts, insights, resources, glossaries, or opinions that are important to the reader's understanding of the subject but wouldn't fit well elsewhere.

Set apart visually from the rest of the article, the sidebar highlights data and other information in easy-to-read segments. For example, an article on the instant multimillion-dollar business created by new AIDS screening tests might include a sidebar giving the chronology of developments involving AIDS and blood transfusions. A sidebar with warning signs of teenage depression would add much to a piece on helping young people handle pressure. An article I wrote for Odyssey on traveling with sick children included a boxed list of must-take-with-you medical items.

Sidebars featuring secondary stories with eyewitness accounts or comments from rescue workers and survivors almost always accompany news accounts of major tragedies or natural disasters. Magazines, too, will frequently place charts or "cameo" stories in sidebars with decorative borders, contrasting color, or a different typeface and give them titles of their own.

Package the article and sidebars attractively on a page and voila! The sum is greater than the parts. What about the sum paid the author? Should a free-lancer expect to be paid extra for doing a sidebar?

It depends on the agreed-upon assignment and the variables that turn up as the writing takes shape. If a free-lancer promises a sidebar in the query and gets a go-ahead, there's no extra pay. When an editor requests a sidebar *after* giving the assignment, a fee is certainly negotiable.

Once when I was doing a piece on women and tranquilizers for *Ladycom*, I felt a sidebar would be more effective in getting across information on the top "problem" drugs—information which then-editor Anne Taubeneck and I had agreed would be *in the article.* Clearly this sidebar was not "extra," and I didn't expect additional pay. However, I did send a note explaining why I thought a sidebar would work better and asking her approval of the change.

"Go with the box," she wrote back. Headlined "America's Top Five Problem Drugs," the sidebar gave generic names, indications, side effects, and warnings for Valium, Librium, Miltown, Darvon, and Dalmane.

One final word on sidebar surplus. *Save* whatever material you haven't used this time around. With a fresh slant, a return trip to the library, more computer modem time, or quotes from additional experts, you're on your way to a new market, new article, new sale.

9 □ HOW-TO KNOW-HOW

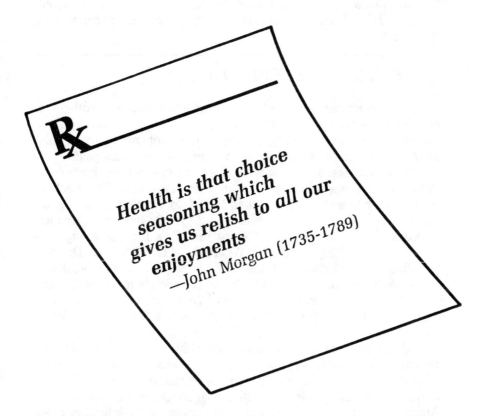

Health is that choice
seasoning which
gives us relish to all our
enjoyments
—John Morgan (1735-1789)

Back when life was simpler, people could be divided into two types: those who thought about their health only when they were afraid of losing it and those who worked so hard at staying healthy that they barely had time to relax and enjoy life. Quick to avoid the sick ones and eager to dismiss the others as health nuts or touchy-feelies, most of us were happy if our allergies were at bay and our calorie-filled plates were carrotless. While we savored health like a choice seasoning perking up everything we did, we didn't see it as something to work at daily.

That was back then. Before *prevention* had become the watchword of the decade—and looking good was tied to wellness.

Spurred on by books like Norman Cousins's *Anatomy of an Illness* and *The Healing Heart*, both of which promote the patient's taking an active role in the healing process, Americans increasingly have caught the do-it-yourself fever with fervor. "Illness," says noted medical ethicist Daniel Callahan, "was [once] something that happened to you. Maybe a person could try to avoid physical injury, but germs—like fate—were out of your hands. Now, we know a lot more about health and there's good evidence to show that what you *do* can make a difference."

NONFICTION'S BEST SELLERS

The writer who can produce helpful how-to's not only lets others in on what he or she knows but sees a surge in query go-aheads and article sales. Anyone who doubts the staying power of how-to's need only skim the morning newspaper lifestyle, health, or fitness pages.

A quick check of one month's magazine cover-lines shows how-to's outnumbering others two to one. Among them: "The Back-to-Basics Guide to Better Sex"; "Wham! Pow! Coping with Kids' Aggressions"; "Face Up to Your Phobias—They Can Be Beaten"; "Tips for Avoiding Workout Injuries"; "Surprising Tips for Achieving Success"; "How to Bring Yourself Up Where Your Parents Let You Down"; "Dealing with an Impossible Boss"; "Eight Steps to Prevent Strokes"; "Nine Ways to Prevent Wrinkles"; "12 New Ways to Prevent Headaches"; "25 Unfattening Ways to Spend Your Lunch Hour"; "26 Keys to Super-Fitness"; and "If Your Guy's Feeling Blue, Here's What to Do."

Skim the titles next time you're in the library or bookstore. On the shelves under Health, Psychology, and Medicine, you'll find dozens of topics including parenting; grandparenting; pregnancy; dieting; child rearing; communicating with teenagers; dealing with stress and fitness at work; eliminating backache; coping with migraine headaches; overcoming chocolate, caffeine, and other addictions; living with heart problems, high blood pressure, diabetes, cancer, asthma, and hot flashes; dealing with biomedical dilemmas; handling the young cerebral palsied child; and how to change your voice to change your life.

Cross over to the sports section and you'll find how-to's on improving performance, eating to excel, and workouts to work by, to name but a few.

All these topics call for *new* how-to treatment as people find better ways to raise children, lose weight, look younger, enjoy intimate relationships; as medical experts discover new causes, new treatments, new strategies, and ways of coping with disease, emotional problems, sports injuries—and *preventing* them in the first place.

Clearly, the outlook is bright for the writer who can combine information and advice with tidbits of experience and lessons to be learned in coping with a problem. Americans are an enterprising people. They may be discouraged over the general health of the nation's economy, environment, or institutions, but basically they are a practical people convinced there's a better way—whether it's self-improvement or getting more out of life, more for their money, or simply less hassle along the way.

Shouldn't you be one of the free-lancers cashing in on the insatiable demand for how-to's?

BASIC ELEMENTS

Good how-to books and articles embody three essential qualities: a topic of interest, expert knowledge of the subject at hand, and an ability to put that expertise on paper in *practical* terms. Theory alone won't do the trick here. How-to writing is process oriented, clear, and to the point.

If you're not a health expert yourself, consider teaming up with one to coauthor a how-to article or book. With my husband, who's a pediatrician, for example, I've written how-to articles on traveling with grandparents, talking to your child's doctor, and dealing with child abuse. Based on my own experiences, I've sold how-to pieces on everything from the craft of paper quilling to the ABC's of returning to school successfully as a mature woman.

The back-to-school piece, which appeared in 1974 in *Marriage and Family Living*, taught me an important lesson about writing how-to's based on one's own experiences. Unless you are an authority on the subject you're writing about (in this case, continuing education, family interactions, and counseling), editors will expect you to round out the piece with quotes, facts, and advice from those who *are* experts.

Even though I'd managed to juggle family, studies, and free-lancing for four years while pursuing a master's degree in journalism (before going back to school was commonplace), my experience was at best a launching pad for the article. For credibility, I needed backup. To get it, I interviewed Dr. William Davies of Purdue University and three others: a registered nurse and mother of eleven children who had just earned a master's degree in counseling and guidance; a teacher who was working part-time in research while studying for her doctorate; and the director of Nevada's Employment Security Department, a woman attuned to the problems of the mature woman in the highly competitive job market.

The article followed a typical how-to format, with a short introduction followed by eight steps to consider in making "sending mom
back to school" a family affair. Summing up what the whole piece was
about were these three paragraphs which appeared in the lead:

> Mature women can compete, can study effectively, can contribute
> to an enrichment of the whole class. First, however, they must over-
> come fear of the unknown on campus and a lack of self-confidence
> in their abilities.
>
> Can I do it? Am I too old? Will younger students accept me? Can I
> get back into a routine of studying, writing themes, taking—and
> passing—tests? What will it do to my family? And, finally, do I
> have a right to spend so much money on myself?
>
> To all these questions, those who have successfully resumed stu-
> dies in traditional campus settings, as well as the emerging "schools
> without walls," reply "yes." Age has nothing to do with qualifying
> for admission; neither does being a woman. What counts is mobiliz-
> ing enough courage to write to, or personally visit, the school and
> find out what's available and where you fit in; then applying for ad-
> mission, and learning from the experiences of mature women who
> have already succeeded. What do they suggest?

SIX POPULAR HOW-TO'S

It's the suggestions, tips, hints, pointers, advice, and step-by-step directions or instructions that characterize the how-to-do-it book or article. As you analyze the publications you want to write for, you'll find
that six kinds of health-related how-to's appear over and over. These
are the reportorial how-to; the steps-to-take article; various "ways-
to"; checklist and questions to ask; pitfalls to avoid; and the dos-and-
don'ts piece.

Reportorial

A journalist's stock-in-trade, this how-to is one of the easier types to
write. The lead typically sets up the problem. The body of the article
provides a reportorial account of the matter at hand. The how-to ends
with advice on what to do to achieve certain results, and may include
pointers on how other people, groups, and organizations can use the
same methods or system.

A trade article, for example, might tell how a hospital instituted a
cost-effective satellite-clinic program, then wind up with pointers
other hospital administrators might find helpful in developing a similar system. An article in a woman's magazine might highlight latest
findings on treating breast cancer by lumpectomy (surgery that re-

moves the malignant lump but saves the breast) and conclude with advice on how to seek a second medical opinion or find a surgeon willing to consider this option.

As you might expect, reportorials are the how-to of choice in covering certain types of professional-meeting reports or panels. Notice how effectively this format works in "How to Avoid Traveler's Diarrhea" by Don Kirkman of Scripps-Howard News Service, who was reporting on findings of a National Institutes of Health panel.

> *Washington*—Americans traveling to Mexico and certain parts of Africa, Asia and the Caribbean are being warned to use care in what they eat and drink and to take along a supply of over-the-counter and prescription drugs to combat diarrhea.
>
> This advice was offered last week by a National Institutes of Health panel which said more than 1 million Americans usually experience painful and embarrassing bouts of bacterial and viral-caused diarrhea while on vacations or business trips overseas.
>
> Though the illness isn't life-threatening, victims normally suffer three to five days with fever, cramps, vomiting and frequent trips to lavatories. Those who don't take precautions sometimes suffer repeated attacks.
>
> Approximately one-third of the Americans who travel to Mexico are hit by the illness, which also is epidemic in Tunisia, Morocco, Kenya, Thailand, Sri Lanka, Haiti and Honduras, the panel said.
>
> "If you can't cook it, boil it or peel it, forget it," said panel chairman Dr. Sherwood Gorback of Tufts University School of Medicine, Boston.
>
> Especially risky are raw vegetables, raw meat, raw seafood, tap water, ice, unpasteurized milk, dairy products and unpeeled fruit.
>
> A single dietary lapse can unleash an attack. Wise travelers, Gorbach said, have drugs with them that can cure mild or severe diarrhea in 30 hours.
>
> The best-known treatment for mild diarrhea is Pepto-Bismol, an inexpensive over-the-counter remedy, Gorbach said. Faster relief for mild attacks are provided by the prescription drug Lomotil and Imodium. For serious attacks, the panel recommends the prescription-only antibiotics Bactrim or Septra.

Full-length treatment of a topic in a book chapter or article, of course, allows the author to go into much more detail, fleshing out advice with examples, quotes, case histories, or additional facts that make the point.

Steps to Take

This type comes closest to fulfilling what's promised in the how-to title. For instance, "How to Complain and Get Results," "Publish in a

Medical Journal? Any Doctor Can," or "Potty Training the Easy Way" leave no doubt about what's going to be covered in the article—or what the reader should get from it.

A classic example of the steps-to-take article is this *San Francisco Chronicle* piece, "Toothaches on a Vacation," by Timothy C. Gogan, D.D.S. It's the kind of article the wise traveler packs along with airline tickets and passport. See if you agree after reading the steps to take for the two dental emergencies described:

BROKEN FILLING

1. *Rinse mouth with lukewarm water to remove food or debris.*

2. *Avoid very hot or very cold substances.*

3. *Avoid eating on that side and avoid chewing anything sticky, i.e., caramels, gum, etc.*

4. *If your tooth is sensitive to the air, cover the tooth with a wad of sugarless gum, beeswax, or sticky adhesive cream.*

5. *Buy some oil of cloves at a pharmacy. Dip some cotton into the clove oil and cover up the hole in the tooth with the cotton.*

TOOTHACHES OR SWELLING

1. *Use some ice packs to reduce the swelling. Cold will reduce swelling. Heat will bring infection to the surface.*

2. *Try to get a prescription for some pain pills from a dentist or a physician so you can get some sleep.*

3. *Do not put aspirin tablet near the tooth. The aspirin can burn the gum tissues or the cheeks.*

In similar style, the rest of the article covers what to do if you have broken dentures, a lost cap, or periodontal problems, and concludes with additional advice on travel preparations and how to locate emergency dental care overseas. Most important, Gogan is careful to protect himself from any potential liability he might incur if a reader were to suffer harm or develop additional dental problems in following his suggestions. Early in the piece, he includes the basic warning: "Remember, at the most you should wait 24-48 hours for dental care. Do not wait more than two days if you have one of the following emergencies."

Gogan's "toothaches" piece contains all the critical elements of the steps-to-take how-to: first, the lead is short and to the point, setting up the situation or problem to be solved. Next, the body of the article gives advice, rules, directions—either numbered or bulleted for easy reference. The article stops when all the points have been covered.

As readers we feel confident in following Dr. Gogan's advice. It's presented logically, makes sense, and comes from a dental authority. There's no promise of instant relief or success. There is, however, the reassurance that we'll feel better knowing what to do, how to do it, and where to go for help and more information. In a nutshell, that's what every good how-to strives to accomplish.

Various Ways-to

There may be only one way to build the perfect sandbox or whisk egg whites into a souffle. But when it comes to health, you can bet there's more than one way to do just about anything—and the experts are there to tell you how to do it their way.

The "various ways-to" piece presents diverse ways of dealing with the *same* problem. Opposing groups of people, for example, may have come up with equally good solutions. Various experts may suggest complementary methods or even totally opposite ways to achieve a goal or solve a problem. Although such treatment of a subject lacks depth in any one area, its strong point is in presenting readers with *options* they may not have known about before.

Each way is described in a few paragraphs—all *equally* weighted. When you're writing this type of how-to, be sure you stick to one problem or facet of the problem. Don't make the mistake of mixing apples and oranges. It's a mix that won't make it past the editor's blue pencil—and may even get a query rejection before you've gotten *that* far.

In writing how-to's, however, you can mix *formats*. Janet Weiner's article, "Why Compliments Are So Hard to Take," mixes and matches the "reasons why" with a "right way/wrong way" format to come up with an explanation of why some people react to compliments with feelings of uneasiness, defensiveness, and cynicism, and what they can do about it. First, she gives brief summaries of six reasons, three of which follow:

> *Reciprocity.* A compliment seems to imply a certain felt need to return it, usually as quickly as possible.
>
> *Modesty.* You feel you must neutralize the compliment so that you don't appear conceited. You say, "I can't take all the credit. I had lots of help." Witness the Academy Award speeches. Or you can credit luck or circumstances.
>
> *Ulterior Motive.* Some compliments are devised to manipulate you. Sometimes you can see through a person's veneer. But when you're unable to detect an ulterior motive you begin to feel uneasy, mistrustful.

Following these "reasons why," she closes her article with tips from experts on the right and wrong ways to give and accept compliments:

- *Acknowledge a compliment with a simple "thank you."*
- *Put it into perspective for yourself. Make no more nor less of it than it is.*
- *Don't prolong a compliment. To dwell on it results in embarrassment for both of you.*
- *Be specific. Instead of "You look wonderful," say, "You look wonderful in that dress."*
- *Don't constantly compliment someone. Habitual praise can eventually become meaningless.*
- *Give nonverbal compliments. You can show approval by a smile or a pat on the back.*

An interesting variation of the "right way/wrong way" how-to is the *right reason/wrong reason* format. As used by Robert E. Gould, M.D., in a *New York Times Magazine* article, "The Wrong Reasons to Have Children," its structure closely resembles the "myth" format for a factual article. Gould, an associate professor of psychiatry at New York University Medical Center, examines eleven reasons people advance for having children.

In his article, he argues it's time "we recognized these reasons so that we can stop having babies who seem to be wanted, but are in fact only expected." Following a brief lead, Gould boldfaces each *wrong* reason and comments on it in one to four paragraphs. In some cases, he offers suggestions for dealing with some of the pressures couples put on themselves to have a baby—or allow to be put on them from well-meaning friends and relatives.

Some of these wrong reasons, he says, are: "we thought it would help our marriage"; "a child is my only claim to immortality"; and "our parents want grandchildren." Here is how Gould treats *Wrong Reason #2: "We can afford to have a baby":*

> Traditionally, the young couple scarcely clears the economic hurdle of "Do we earn enough to get married?" before rushing to the next one: "Can we afford to have a baby?" To convince neighbors and friends—and sometimes each other—a couple will scrimp to produce an heir. Keeping up with the Joneses' birth rate, however, is hardly a sensible motive for having children.

Checklist

This how-to is made up primarily of a series of items, questions to ask, or points to consider—sometimes up to a dozen or more. Because of this and the fact that the length of the checklist rarely allows for much explanation or elaboration on any one item or aspect, this type of how-to is generally considered weaker than the others. Don't let that scare you off, however. There are times when the checklist is the most effective way to make a point or create an impression on a large scale.

In his book *The Peter Pan Syndrome*, psychologist Dan Kiley provides readers with a checklist of twenty behaviors he says men with this affliction (PPS) typically display (four of which follow). Purpose of the checklist is to help women decide whether the men in their lives are victims of the man-child syndrome, as was the legendary Peter Pan who relied on Wendy for mothering.

Kiley prefaces his checklist with a warning, and you should too if you use this format. Kiley cautions that just because an adult male exhibits a rich imagination and yearning to stay young, it doesn't necessarily mean he is a victim of PPS, and the reader must be careful in labeling someone as such on the basis of only a few attributes. Here is the checklist:

> A simple test will help you decide whether or not the man in your life is a victim of the PPS. Read each behavioral description and rate the degree to which it applies to the person under consideration. A rating of 0 signifies that this behavior never occurs; 1 signifies that this behavior occurs sometimes (for instance, that it has happened once or twice but not very often); 2 signifies always (or you can barely remember it not happening).
>
> ● When he makes a mistake, he overreacts, either exaggerating his guilt or searching for excuses to absolve himself of any blame.
>
> ● He forgets dates such as anniversary, birthday.
>
> ● At a party he ignores you but does his best to impress other people, especially women.
>
> ● He finds it almost impossible to say "I'm sorry."

Remember, these are only four of the twenty behaviors on the checklist. At the end of the list, Kiley provides readers with a rating system so they can judge for themselves the extent of the problem.

> Now add up the numbers you have selected for each behavioral description. Use the following guide to judge the degree of affliction.
>
> 0 to 10: Not a PPS victim. His problems tend to be isolated and are not very serious. If there is a bothersome situation, talk with him about it. Most likely it can be resolved in a spirit of love and cooperation.
>
> 11 to 25: The PPS is definitely a threat. There are steps you can take to improve the situation, but the higher the score within this category, the harder you must be willing to work.
>
> 26 to 40: The Peter Pan Syndrome is functioning. If the man

won't seek help for his problems, you should probably talk with a professional about what you can do to cope with the situation.

Subsequent chapters, naturally, deal with these behaviors in more detail and suggest ways of helping these men deal with their immaturity and grow up—*before* life turns sour.

POP PSYCHOLOGY—MORE HURT OR REAL HELP?

Psychology forms the basis of many more free-lance articles today than in the past. In recent years, however, psychological self-help and health-related how-to articles and books have come in for serious criticism. Some health-care professionals claim that, at best, the information and advice are superficial. At worst, the contents are misleading, contradictory, and in error.

"The self-improvement industry raises expectations by playing on fear, loneliness, shame, and discontent," writes well-known essayist Harriet Van Horne in a *Family Weekly* column headlined, "Help Yourself: Self-Help Books Won't Do It for You."

In an April, 1984, *APA Monitor* article, "Self-Help Authors Lack 'How-to' Manual," staff writer Kathleen Fisher reports on a talk at the 1983 annual convention by a former chairperson of the American Psychological Association ethics committee. "Patricia Keith-Speigel of California State University—Northridge," writes Fisher, "suggested in a talk on 'Hot Ethical Issues' . . . that 'cold economic times' may provoke even more psychologists to concoct what she calls the '$3.95 fix.' "

And free-lance writer Susan Crain Bakos in an *American Way* article titled "Mom and Pop Psychology," quotes New York City therapist Aileen Murray, who says, "No professional, even a very competent one, can provide all the answers a patient needs in a few hundred written words or a 60-second span of airtime. A book may not provide enough space."

(However, any trade book that *completely* covered a topic would most likely exhaust the average reader by its size, weight, and meticulous detail. That's what professional textbooks are for—complete coverage, documentation, and illustration.)

And there is another way to look at pop psychology, as clinical psychologist Jaqueline Hornor Plumez points out. "From the positive sense, I never knock anything popular," she says. "If a book *sells*, it has to really *affect* people. Just because a pop psychology book doesn't speak to me as a professional, doesn't mean it can't help my clients."

As a professional psychologist, she's had clients come and tell her that a certain book has really affected and helped them, she says, citing as one example Dr. Wayne Dyer's *Pulling Your Own Strings.* "However, what I get very upset about," Plumez explains, "is people—whether doctors or psychologists—who write about their own opinions which aren't based on hard research. I think that's offensive and I think this happens, especially in child guidance and child-rearing books."

Plumez contrasts self-help information and advice aimed at *adults* and based on the writer's professional and personal experience in successfully treating patients, with that of the professional person writing a how-to who doesn't want to do accurate backup research first. What this person wants, she says, is to see his or her ideas and theories *in print.* (The latter, she believes, occurs quite commonly in the child-care/child-behavior field.)

In writing self-help articles and books, it's essential that you provide practical, down-to-earth information based on sound principles which recognize that people are individuals with different responses, needs, reactions. No self-help formula will work for all; no steps-to-take book or article can ensure success in every situation. Buyers should beware; writers, even more so. Quick "fixes" ultimately fix little, if anything, and can undermine a writer's reputation as a professional.

"Bad self-help is presumptuous," *Family Circle* special features editor Ellen Stoianoff said at a national writers' conference. "It speaks condescendingly to the poor, ignorant slob of a reader. It's loaded with hype and it's not very helpful. I'm not saying that it doesn't sell well— some of it does."

Criteria for self-help articles at *Family Circle,* she says, are: appealing subject matter, credibility, good ideas, good organization of material, and a friendly tone of voice. "Good self-help," Stoianoff explains, "proffers fresh ideas, makes sound suggestions, shares experiences, points out options and actions that people may not have thought of for themselves, and serves the reader every bit as well as any other nonfiction form."

So choose your topics and the professional experts you interview with care. You can be an important link between the practitioner and the general public, encouraging do-it-yourself problem solving where posssible and greater enjoyment of life. But helping readers recognize when they need to seek professional counseling and medical care is still one of the most valuable contributions the self-help writer can make.

Pitfalls to Avoid. There's a bright side to looking at the bad, and free-lancers who can come up with enough pitfalls, traps, or other watch-out-for's to fill an article will find the negatives of life have silver linings. Editors know these articles can be highly effective—simply because they aren't seen as often as other types of how-to's. Their titles beg to be read: "10 Mistakes People Make in Choosing a Dentist," for instance, or "How to Be Your Best During the Worst." (I consider myself an optimist, yet I couldn't resist reading the latter in *Self* to learn the "five specific moves to put you in control of disaster days, weeks, months.")

In his article, "How to Tell if Your Doctor Is Giving You Good Care," Leonard Sandler puts the pitfalls in the guise of ten telltale signs everyone should be on the alert for. Information comes from a highly credible source, Dr. John Kelly, then-president of the Academy of Family Physicians. Effectively using the bulleted statement/direct quote format, Sandler manages quickly to give us the clues we should look for and, in Doctor Kelly's words, the reasons why.

> Is your doctor giving you proper health care? A leading expert offers some simple suggestions that will enable you to tell.
>
> "The consumer has a right to expect adequate health care, but most Americans don't understand how their doctor works," declared Dr. John Kelly, president of the American Academy of Family Physicians.
>
> Here are ten telltale signs of the doctor who isn't doing his job:
>
> ● He doesn't spend much time with you. "It takes time for the physician to obtain all the information he needs for a diagnosis," says Dr. Kelly. "An office visit with your family physician should last about 15 minutes, but appointments with specialists can take an hour or more.
>
> "Your doctor needs a complete health profile on you, and should ask you to either complete a written form or answer extensive questions."
>
> ● He fails to give you an appropriate physical examination, or only covers the areas where you have symptoms.
>
> "Your physician should give you a basic screening examination, including pulse, blood pressure, weight and temperature, and check your eyes, ears, nose, throat, chest and abdomen. This is in addition to examining the areas affected by your symptoms."
>
> ● He doesn't educate you about your illness, or explain why the prescribed treatment or medication is necessary. "If your doctor fails to give you all the information you need to understand your illness, he isn't doing his job properly."

In writing about the negative side of things, you want to avoid a few pitfalls yourself. Basically, these articles have a don't-do-this or negative tone. Too much can be a downer for *both* editor and reader. So be sure to include some positive tips or guidelines that show readers there's a way out—or at least a way to cope.

Also, magazine-length treatment of such topics usually calls for examples, anecdotes, quotes. Finding people willing to go public and admit they've been taken in by medical quackery, or have goofed in solving a problem—and maybe lost their savings to boot—can add hours and even days to research legwork.

Ideally, your article tells the story through these examples. In other words, the reader "gets smart" as he or she learns the different ways these pitfalls have trapped other unsuspecting people, businesses, or groups in the past. The message, loud and clear, is: Whatever else you do, don't do or think as these unwary individuals did. Backed up by quotes from experts, you've got a potent tale to tell and sell.

A final drawback to the pitfalls format is that some editors have a bias against the negative approach to a topic. If you run into that kind of editorial rejection, think positive. Turn your pitfalls around and restructure your article in one of the other how-to styles.

Dos and Don'ts

For a minilesson in how to write an all encompassing dos-and-don'ts piece, study this Swedish proverb: Fear less, hope more; eat less, chew more; whine less, breathe more; hate less, love more; and all good things are yours.

The global approach, of course, doesn't work for today's magazines. But the specifics do—which means zeroing in on a topic, providing basic information in a "do this/don't do that" format, and backing it up with expertise.

To get the data and quotes you need, go to primary resources. Get your facts from people who are tops in the health-care field. And when you consult these experts, try to get them to answer your questions in a way that lends itself to "do/don't do" quotes. (The person you're interviewing may not phrase the responses that way, may not even realize that the very thing he or she considers trivial is exactly what you need as an example or quote, so be prepared to guide the interview along the lines you need.) That means asking questions that bring out the how-to answer.

What questions would help in getting the right answers? To get down-to-earth advice, I often find it helpful to present a hypothetical situation or simply say, "Suppose I am the person with such and such problem:"

- What do I do first? Next? After that?
- What should I be aware of? Are there any musts? Anything I should be careful to avoid?

- *What should I do if I run into such a situation or problem? Who can I go to for help? What kind of help could I expect?*

- *What's happened to other people in this situation? What did they do? What should they have done?*

By grouping these questions chronologically—first, next, after that, and sources of help—it's easier to recall them in an interview. By moving from "my" situation to someone else's, you're more likely to get some examples, anecdotes, or case histories which help in building reader identity and involvement in the topic.

One question I've always found to be a winner in interviewing an expert is, "What would you do if you or someone in your family were in a similar situation?" If that doesn't work, I say, "Tell me, what is the one thing you *wouldn't* want someone you loved to do in this situation?"

If this line of questioning doesn't elicit more than enough dos and don'ts, practical advice, and helpful suggestions, your best bet is to find another expert to interview. Some people may know their field inside out, but they are not articulate at a practical level. Before you say goodbye, however, ask one more question:" Who *else* would you suggest I talk to about this subject?"

In writing a "questions-to-ask" how-to, you need to list the various questions readers need answers to and explain *why* it's so important to ask them. What could happen, for instance, if you *don't* ask them? What answers should you expect? No one is left wondering about these matters after reading Maxine Abrams's *Harper's Bazaar* article, "How to Interview Your Plastic Surgeon." In it, she gives some leading questions plus tipoffs in evaluating which physician is the right one for you.

By providing key questions, comments, and responses from experts, this type of article allows readers to work toward solving a problem for themselves. That the topic is complex and wide ranging and includes many variables is implicit in this approach. In effect, the author is saying, "If you're aware of these questions, you have a better chance of coming out ahead." And who wouldn't want to know, for instance, "The 10 Questions You Should Ask Your Anesthesiologist *before* Your Operation" or "Five Questions You Want Answered before Giving Your Baby DPT Shots."

WRITING FOR THE DIET AND FITNESS MARKET

You may agree with workout guru Jane Fonda ("Not being hard on the eye—that's a neighborly gesture. It's socially considerate. Just like keeping a clean house, looking after yourself is pleasing.") Or perhaps you prefer Thomas A. Edison's holistic approach to health and life-style ("The doctor of the future will give no medicine but will interest his patients in the care of the human frame, in diet, and in the cause and prevention of disease.")

Whatever your personal stance, one thing is certain: diet and fit-ness are extremely popular topics and among the top health concerns of the public today. In growing numbers, people are assuming greater responsibility for maintaining their own health. They know that life-style, nutrition, and exercise are important aspects in looking good, feeling good, and staying healthy. What they want to know is how to diet painlessly; how to exercise without knocking themselves out.

The editorial temptation, of course, is to think that a book or arti-cle on your own novel exercise or weight-loss program is the godsend editors have been waiting for. Unless you're a celebrity or unique in some way, you'll have to offer more than "How I Lost 10 Pounds in 2 Weeks Plus 5-Minute Fail-proof Recipes" or your answer to "Firm-ups and Fat-offs for Computer Literate Flabbies."

True, there's a healthy market for books, articles, and columns on diet, exercise, and the mind-body link. And each year new publica-tions targeted to these topics make their debut. Among diet and fit-ness magazines which use free-lance material, you'll find *Bruce Jen-ner's Better Health & Living; New Body Magazine; Body in Motion; Total Fitness; Running & Fitness; Muscle & Fitness; Slimmer, Health and Beauty for the Total Woman; Total Health; Whole Life Times; Weight Watchers Magazine; American Health;* and *Bestways.*

However, many book editors, among them Simon & Schuster's Bob Bender, believe the fitness market has now peaked. "Simon & Schuster was one of the leading publishers in that field," he said at a national writers' conference, "[but] we're not looking for any fitness books right now. There's no question that that's a market which has died—it's been saturated."

Whether you're writing from a consumer's point of view, from personal experience, or from professional expertise (as a dietitian, physician, athletic trainer, sports psychologist, to name but a few), you can't ignore marketing realities. Before dashing off a query to your favorite publication, take a tip from writing instructor and author Duane Newcomb, who says, "The more crowded a field gets, the thin-ner your angle has to become."

Study the market carefully. Review newspaper health-and-fit-ness supplements, magazine-cover blurbs, and book titles to see how successful writers slant diet and fitness topics for targeted audiences. A quick check of a local bookstore and newsstand will reveal count-less fit-or-fat psychological angles; superstar secrets; food/allergy/illness links; "proven program" and "new hope" treatises; as well as gimmicks to make it easier for calorie counters and those who detest exercise in any form.

A few examples make the point: healing foods and recipes; dieter's deficiencies and how to remedy them; a low blood-sugar diet, another one for people with arthritis; new hope for binge eaters; "thinking thin" to be thin; at-home fitness and health programs from famous spas; exercises that keep six superstars super shapely; how much exercise your child really needs; food-awareness training; and even a "blackmail diet." (The blurb on the latter, outlined in a Ten Speed Press book by John Bear, promises psychologically valid techniques for setting up a self-blackmail diet plan that works.)

Yes, But Is It Nutritionally Sound . . . Anatomically Correct? Who says what and by what authority is an ever-increasing problem, according to Sachiko St. Jeor, Ph.D., associate professor of clinical nutrition and director of the Nutrition Education Research Program at the University of Nevada School of Medicine. "There's a lot of dietary misinformation floating around," says the registered dietitian, "and the fallout from crash diets and other nutritionally unsound dietary behavior can be costly—not only nutritionally and medically, but emotionally and economically as well."

Noting that even *doctors* have come out with some extremely controversial diets, one editor comments: "This combination of amateur appeal and specific health-related advice means the writer has to be especially careful that the advice he offers is not only well researched, but is backed by some *nonquirky* medical authority. The potential is too great for real harm to result from following bad advice on diet and exercise."

A real need exists for good writing on nutrition and fitness, claims St. Jeor, who recently received a federal grant of nearly $1 million to study weight fluctuation and its impact on cardiovascular disease. Her advice to writers: "Anyone writing about nutrition and health should be familiar with the 1985 *Dietary Guidelines for Americans* from the U.S. Departments of Agriculture and Health and Human Services; the American Heart Association's *Eating for a Healthy Heart*, revised in 1984; and the 1982 "Interim Dietary Guidelines" put out by the National Research Council's Committee on Diet, Nutrition and Cancer." (For a free copy of the first brochure, write Dietary Guidelines, Dept. 622 N, Consumer Information Center, Pueblo, CO 81009. The second, *Eating for a Healthy Heart* is published by the Alameda County Chapter of the American Heart Association, 11200 Golf Links Road, Oakland, CA 94605. "Interim Dietary Guidelines" are found in *Diet, Nutrition, and Cancer* available from National

Academy Press, Constitution Ave. NW, Washington, DC 20418. Most likely, you can find these publications in any life-sciences, medical, or university library as well.)

In making assignments and buying manuscripts dealing with fitness and nutrition, most editors place heavy emphasis on the author's credentials, expertise, and sources of information. For example, Simon & Schuster's Bob Bender cites a book in the diet and health field which he signed up. The book is based on a five-year, federally funded $5 million study. "It's being written by the director of the study," explains Bender, "by a doctor out in Oregon who's got a seasoned writer working with him. And that's a book I think we can convince people to buy—we convince booksellers, anyway, to buy."

Magazine editors, too, are looking for *authoritative* articles. Writers' guidelines for *Bestways*, for instance, state that the magazine, which emphasizes holistic health, is "interested in original, well-researched, informative, clearly written articles on the positive values of vitamin and mineral supplements as well as other factors in natural, prevention-oriented health care." Popular subjects include exercise, diet programs, natural beauty treatments, and negative effects of food additives, drugs, caffeine, etc.

Explains editor and publisher Barbara Bassett, "We want articles that are authoritative and fresh, with a positive, upbeat approach." All manuscripts must be accompanied by a separate page with bibliography and reference notes.

Weight Watchers Magazine buys general health and medical pieces; nutrition articles supportive of Weight Watchers International Food Plan and based on documented research results; fitness pieces on types of exercise that don't require special skills or extensive financial costs, and weight-loss stories with an interesting angle. Editors look for detailed query letters outlining the idea, your qualifications for writing the piece, and, if possible, a list of *sources* you plan to use.

"If an article is not written by someone in the field," says senior editor Cheryl Solimini, "then [it must be] by a writer who's consulted experts—*everything* is documented." The magazine has its own medical consultants, she adds, "and someone in the legal department of Weight Watchers International reads *all* of our articles."

Let's Live Magazine accepts 750-word "My Story" or thoughtful "The Last Word" features if exceptionally well crafted, but the mainstays of the publication are articles by qualified professionals (M.D.'s, Ph.D.'s or persons with equivalent degrees) in preventive medicine, nutrition, or other sciences devoted to good health (of both mind and body), physical conditioning, and proper diet. The publication also considers articles by nonprofessionals if thoroughly researched and accurately documented, or if developed around question-and-answer interviews with recognized and/or highly accredited doctors or authorities in the field.

But magazines don't survive on editorial content alone, and associate editor Bill Reinshagen makes a point free-lancers should keep in mind. "Be aware," he notes, "that the main function of many magazines is to sell advertising—professional as well as consumer—and often, articles support the advertising."

Not all publications, of course, have a direct advertising/editorial tie-in. But in querying an editor or submitting a manuscript unsolicited, remember this editorial rule of thumb: *Don't offend or alienate advertisers.* If a publication runs ads for body-building equipment, for instance, you won't score many points with a piece on "10 Rip-Offs the Body Building Industry Doesn't Want You to Know About." When the bulk of a magazine's ads depict vitamin supplements and health foods, you won't make much headway with an article on "How the Health Food Scam Hurts Your Pocketbook" or "Vitamin Supplements You'll Feel Better Without."

That's not to say you shouldn't write these articles. Rather, you must select a different *forum* for your ideas. Consult *Writer's Market* for other publications that use articles on life-style, health, diet, and exercise, such as general interest, women's, or specialty publications, plus newspaper life-style sections and supplements on health and fitness.

DISCLAIMERS YOU CAN'T DO WITHOUT

Cautions and guidelines are important protectors, not only for readers, but for writers and publishers who don't want to run the risk of liability for injuries, illness, or other problems a reader might incur following the author's advice. Typically, disclaimers urge readers to get clearance from their physicians before beginning an exercise or diet program and absolve the publisher from responsibility for ideas/opinions/advice contained in the book, magazine, or other printed material. Some typical disclaimers:

● Before you begin *any* exercise program, consult your physician.

● Individual dietary needs vary and no one diet will meet everyone's daily requirements. Before starting the X-Y-Z Diet, check with your doctor or nutritionist.

● If you are pregnant, over 35, have any old injuries or doubts about starting a workout routine, get approval from your doctor first.

● If you have any doubts, questions, or persistent symptoms, see your doctor at once. [This type of warning frequently accompanies articles on topics like breast or testicle self-examination, fitness, high blood pressure, etc.]

● If your condition requires you to be on a special diet, consult with the doctor or nutritionist before beginning this "Healthier-You" program.

● Don't forget, all work and no play are unwise physically and psychologically—whether you're training for the Olympics or working out at the local gym. Consult with a doctor, trainer, coach, or sports psychologist about your own needs for a change of pace.

Magazine publishers protect themselves with disclaimers like the following one, which appears in *Prevention*'s letters-to-the-editor section: "Mailbag is an exchange of ideas on health-care issues and experiences among interested readers. Letters should not be construed as scientific information or as substitutes for professional medical advice." In its "Nutritional Q & A" feature, *Bestways* includes a disclaimer which reads in part: "Answers are not intended to substitute for your physician, who should be consulted in cases of doubt or persistent symptoms."

Disclaimers, explains Theodore Berland, who's written several diet books, including *The Dieter's Almanac* and *Rating the Diets*, say in essence: Reader beware: follow this advice, diet, exercise regimen, or whatever at your own risk. "As an author," warns Berland, a former president of the American Medical Writers Association, "be sure you put your disclaimer on the copyright page where everyone can see it, then repeat it a number of times in the text itself."

Berland stresses that writers must tell people that before starting the diet or exercise program, they should check with their personal physician. (Even if you're a doctor or other health professional, you still must include a disclaimer in what you write for the public. For example, *San Francisco Chronicle* columnist Karl Neumann italicizes this disclaimer, which appears between the column's title and his by-line: "Dr. Karl Neumann's health tips for travelers are meant as general advice. Before you travel, please consult your personal physician for your specific travel needs.")

"What you're doing," Berland says, "is protecting yourself from claims you're practicing medicine without a license or giving *medical advice*. You're not giving medical advice—you're giving *medical information* that is available. Specific medical advice," explains Berland, "can only be given to an individual by a qualified professional who knows the patient's history, diagnosis, prognosis, and anything else relevant to the case."

Here's the disclaimer in the form of a "Publisher's Note" which appears on the back of the title page of Ada P. Kahn's book *Diabetes Control and the Kosher Diet:*

> The suggestions for medical treatment, diet, and specific foods in this book are not intended as a substitute for consultation with your physician. All matters regarding your health require medical supervision. The use of specific products in this book is for product identification only and does not constitute an endorsement by the author, physician, rabbi, dietitian, or publisher.

One of her first steps in writing the book was to hire a registered dietitian to develop and test recipes and servings. A rabbi approved the religious content; a physician, the medical content. Both wrote forewords for the book, which was illustrated by a professional artist.

Based on her experience, Kahn offers food for thought to anyone considering self-publishing a diet book. "Try to find a publisher first; think twice before self-publishing. If you decide to do it yourself, you must think through two questions: (1) How will you advertise your book and who will pay for it? and (2) How will you distribute your book—are you willing to become a shipping agent?"

FINAL WORD ABOUT LIABILITY

In addition to prepublication review of health/diet/fitness material by legal and medical consultants and prominent display of disclaimers in print, many magazine and almost all book publishers seek to protect themselves through specific clauses in author contracts.

A magazine, for example, may require writers to sign a contract that specifically absolves the publisher from responsibility in libel suits or from liability for injury or harm a reader might incur from following health-related advice in the publication. Here's what one *Weight Watchers Magazine* editor says about such liability: "Our contract with writers says we're not liable for something that's in an article—if they misquote someone or whatever. In order to get paid, writers have to sign a contract that we are not held responsible for any resulting litigation."

You'd never know that, however, from reading the editorial guidelines *Weight Watchers Magazine* sends to writers. Reference to "responsibility" is made only once: "The publisher assumes no responsibility for unsolicited manuscripts."

SELLING POINTS

How-to's rarely run more than 1,500 words, and are more likely to be between 650 and 1,200 words. Check *Writer's Market* for the preferred length in the magazine you hope to sell to, or review three or four back issues of the publication itself. (If you can't write the how-to in the stated length, either you don't have all the information you need or the angle you've chosen isn't *suited* to how-to treatment.)

Check your publication for style. What kind of title and lead appear most often? Are the experts quoted in these articles all from *one medical specialty* or one area of the country? Sometimes scattering your experts geographically or choosing authorities from several disciplines makes for a stronger piece.

But it depends on the subject—and the pool of experts available. If you're talking about informed consent in cases of transplants from animals to humans, as in the unique Baby Fae case, you are more limited in choosing experts than if you are writing an article about human-to-human kidney transplants, since many of these procedures have been done in every major medical center in the country.

It goes without saying that not all how-to's deal with bioethical heavyweights as these two transplant issues do. But the good writer (regardless of subject) is an ethical and responsible person who does his or her best to provide readers with the most accurate and up-to-date information possible.

Remember, whether you're writing the self-improvement how-to which is psychologically oriented or the informational how-to with its direct problem/solution approach, readers want specific and practical advice plus insights into the problem drawn from everyday life. You must get the facts, but you must also dig for the *lessons* to be learned from those facts.

Don't forget, your job in writing the how-to is to convey information *and* confidence. But in writing for the general public, be sure to protect yourself from potential liability or claims that you are giving specific medical advice or practicing medicine without a license. Always include a disclaimer or warning to readers that they must get approval from their personal physician, dentist, or other health-care professional before starting the diet, fitness, or other health-related program or regimen you're writing about. If the how-to is based on your own experience, the message is: If *I* can do it, you can, too, and here's how. It's this spirit of confidence backed by expert opinion, data, advice, and common bits of experience that make how-to's the best sellers of the nonfiction field.

10 □ TELL ME, DOCTOR

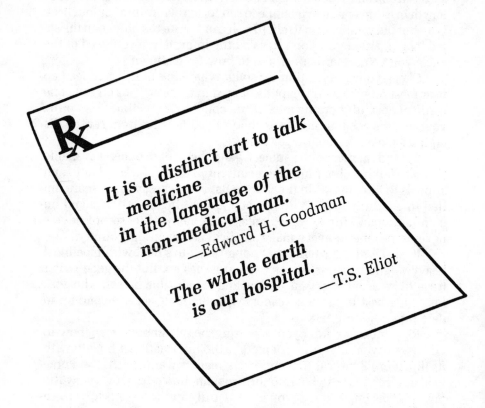

It is a distinct art to talk medicine in the language of the non-medical man.
—Edward H. Goodman

The whole earth is our hospital.
—T.S. Eliot

Whether you have two minutes, two hours, or two days to complete a health-related interview, your goal is the same: to get information, opinions, and feelings that can *only* be obtained by talking to a certain person who, for whatever reason, is the *expert* you need for your story. To achieve your goal, you must know what you want, how to line up the interview, what questions to ask when, and—on occasion—how to turn a potential fiasco into a plus.

How you do this will depend as much on your personality—and what you're comfortable doing—as it does on the assignment.

For example, early in the 1970s when the link between psyche and obesity was a hot topic, California-based author-psychologists Lillian Dangott and Leonard Pearson conducted a workshop in Reno on the psychology of overeating. For them, my interview was the last of a long afternoon of meetings with various radio, newspaper, and television reporters. I knew my questions would be covering the same ground—and Len Pearson already looked exhausted and wary of yet one more journalist. I sensed he wanted to call it quits for the day. Taking a risk they might cancel the interview altogether, I said, "If you'd like ten minutes to catch your breath, I'd certainly understand."

Pearson perked up. "Five minutes would be plenty," he said, quickly leaving the room to fix himself a thick chocolate milk shake (which later launched us into a discussion of energy, chocolate, and food cravings). Feeling better, he returned to give me a meaty hour-long interview.

I never told Dangott and Pearson, who had been featured in *Woman's Day* and other national publications, that theirs was only my *third* interview or that butterflies had taken over my stomach just before I asked my first question: What's the secret to success in weight control? Their answer, "Food liberation," became the article's lead.

THE LIBERATED INTERVIEWER

Delete the references to eating, and the concept of *liberation* applies to successful interviewing techniques as well. The right way to eat, claimed Pearson and Dangott, is based on the freedom to choose (what and when to eat or *not* eat) rather than on slavish adherence to written and unwritten eating commandments. For this method to work, say these experts, you must have the freedom to know yourself, know your body's needs—and accept both.

Attend any writer's workshop and you'll find interviewing also has its written and unwritten commandments and formulas for success. Several of these dos and don'ts are included in this chapter because they work well for many free-lancers. But you'll also discover a strong "liberating" message coming through: Once you know the ground rules, *be flexible.* Trust your instincts, your curiosity, and what you know is right for you, your assignment, and your subject.

As John Brady puts it in his splendid primer, *The Craft of Interviewing:* "The interviewer seeks the truth—but his work does not require the creative surges of art, nor does it possess the certitude of science. And, unlike the scientist, the interviewer has no 'rules' that aren't broken daily by fine writers getting great quotes."

INTERVIEWING'S GUISES, SIZES, AND SURPRISES

There are *one-to-one* interviews; *group* interviews; *composite* interviews, typically seen in the *New Yorker* and *Playboy* (here is a portrait of "X" based on interviews with the subject as well as friends, enemies, family, co-workers, etc.). Even in generally staid medical and health writing, you'll sometimes come across offbeat interviews, such as the historical *interview of place* (generally a series of interview/vignettes in the "if these walls could talk" vein) or the *noninterview/interview*—what to do when you're not allowed access to the interviewee but your editor won't take no for an answer.

(For example, in 1976, a California writer assigned a piece on then President Ford—whom she could not get clearance to see—interviewed everyone blocking her way. The resulting article written in the present tense gave a sense of person, place, and urgency which said much about an American leader who had just experienced an attempt on his life in Sacramento.)

Frequently, an editor takes all the guesswork out of interviewing. She knows exactly what she wants, lines up a writer, assigns the topic and format, and even suggests the expert to interview and questions to ask. This is especially true when a newspaper or magazine has a regular interview feature such as *Mademoiselle*'s Ask the Expert series. New York free-lancer Florence Isaacs, for example, accepted an assignment from the magazine to interview Dr. Charles S. Hollander, professor of medicine and chief of the division of endocrinology at New York University Medical Center, for an Ask the Expert piece titled, "Hormones: Can They Give You Beauty Problems?"

Writers, however, interview experts not only after they've been assigned articles but also *before* querying an editor with an idea for a piece. "A number of professional writers, experienced writers, do *exploratory* interviews," says *Ladies' Home Journal* executive editor Jan Goodwin. "This gives them a good quote to pitch to me—it also makes sure the story exists. Sometimes writers will sell a story. We'll give them an assignment because it's a fabulous story, and then they'll have to come slinking back some weeks later and say they can't get it. For example, [take] Princess Diana. It's not a given that someone [like her] is going to share the secrets of a happy marriage—you have to find out [first] whether she will."

Because of some preliminary interviews in 1983 with doctors working on new ways to treat headaches, Montana-based free-lancer Kathy Crump knew she had a fresh angle for a much-worked topic. She sent a query for a general piece on headaches to *McCall's*, which, unknown to her, was planning to launch an Ask the Specialist series. Editors soon contacted her about doing an interview in question-and-answer form for the new feature. Crump's article, "Heading Off Trouble: What You Should Know about Headaches" was the second in the series; the expert was noted neurologist Seymour Diamond, founder and director of the Diamond Headache Clinic and the National Migraine Foundation, both in Chicago.

In keeping up with what's happening in medicine and science, background interviews are important to Montreal Gazette science and medicine feature writer Nicholas Regush, who doesn't hesitate to ask experts the open-ended questions, such as What's new in AIDS? or What's the latest in cancer? "It breaks every rule," notes Regush, whose mandate at the newspaper is to produce stories of potential national impact in Canada. But then his expertise, education, and credibility as a journalist who's prepared, knows what he's looking for, and is open in dealing with his sources, allow him to ask experts the open-ended question—usually considered an interviewing no-no.

Focus group interviews—a type of data-gathering discussion popular with advertising marketing experts—works well for many authors, including Norman Lobsenz, who specializes in writing about marriage, divorce, and family matters. In a group setting, the interviewer poses questions to a number of people (three to six is average) who share a common interest in a given topic.

There's no guarantee, of course, that the advance interview will pay off in a go-ahead from an editor. "But," explains award-winning medical writer Gloria Hochman, "it's an investment that we all have to make on the front end, or we can never get the assignment to begin with—it's one of the facts of the business."

INTERVIEW GAME PLAN—
DON'T LEAVE IT TO CHANCE

Every interview is a human encounter—however fleeting. In it is the potential for all manner of human dynamics, from development of genuine trust between you and your subject to power plays like keeping you waiting or how the chairs are lined up.

"I try to be incredibly honest and up front, and not play games with people," explains Montreal Gazette's Regush. "Two reasons: I've decided, for better or worse, I'm not going to be loved by most people and experience has proved it true and, secondly, medicine to me is an area of extraordinary controversy and nothing is correct [if it comes] from only one person. I want to know if this expert is on top of things or if he has an axe to grind." The focus you take, adds Regush, "largely depends on what you're after—but personality plays a big part in the kinds of strategies you develop."

Basics of interviewing are covered in many writers' guides, but for the most comprehensive and entertaining approach, consult Brady's The Craft of Interviewing. The purpose of this chapter is to share with you strategies successful health and medical writers use to obtain authoritative information, jargon-free quotes, and specific examples which give their writing the reader-takeaway editors insist upon.

LINING UP THE INTERVIEW

Write, telephone, telegram, buttonhole your expert on the run, advertise for interviews. Contact professional societies and associations; hospital, pharmaceutical company, and medical-school public-information directors. Go to media resource services, such as the free referral network of about 15,000 science, technology, and health experts, which is operated by the Scientists' Institute for Public Information (SIPI). (Addresses, toll-free telephone numbers, and additional suggestions for finding experts are listed in chapter 5.)

Ask neighbors, co-workers, your manicurist, your mentor, friends of patients, colleagues of experts to help you—in short, do what you have to do to get the interview you need. But remember, in setting up your interview, the approach professional writers use will get you further, faster:

Try to Enlist the Aid of the Expert's Secretary. Once in a while, you will run into a hostile secretary who's trying to *protect* the doctor from the outside world, but in general, a secretary is an interviewer's best friend. Most are extremely courteous and helpful.

When you call, identify yourself and your publication, if you already have an assignment. Tell why you need to interview the doctor and what *deadline* you're working against. If you're working on a breaking story, for example, you may need to interview the expert within the next few hours. Better to know at the outset that the expert in liver transplants will be tied up in surgery all morning or that the neurologist lecturing to medical students has a fifteen-minute break at two o'clock when he can return your call.

Access to experts, of course, can also come through family members. Stevan Allen, who writes for the *Washington Post*, needed to get an interview with world-famous forensic anthropologist Ellis Kerley, Ph.D., a professor at the University of Maryland. In 1985, Kerley represented a team of American scientists sent to Brazil to examine the alleged remains of the infamous Auschwitz doctor and Nazi war criminal Josef Mengele.

But Kerley, apparently, had not been entirely satisfied with an earlier newspaper article resulting from that case. When Allen telephoned to discuss a possible interview for the *Post's* regular Sunday feature "The Outlook Interview," he talked first to Mrs. Kerley. He expained that the Q & A format would be straightforward. Basically, recalls Allen, "I told her this was a chance for her husband to speak about what he does—and have it printed verbatim. It was a mild sort of screening process," he says, "but the point is, you have to know *why* you're doing an interview because you may have to explain it first to someone else." The interview, published October 6, 1985, was titled: "Mengele, Like Other Dead Men, Had Tales to Tell."

Be Patient but Persistent. "You have to be willing to call many times—sometimes as many as fifteen times," says Florence Isaacs, "not because doctors are avoiding you but because they are so busy. So if you want to get hold of them, especially if they are well-known experts, you have to be persistent and keep calling day after day to catch them at a free moment."

Kathy Crump uses a three-step telephone approach. First, she telephones the physician's office to introduce herself and set a convenient time when the expert will be free to talk about an interview. During the second call, Crump discusses the assignment, the purpose of the interview and what she wants to ask the expert about. Then a time for the actual interview is agreed upon.

This approach, she says, ensures that the subject has scheduled enough time for the interview and is prepared for the questions. When she begins the interview, Crump asks if the doctor would object to her tape recording it for accuracy. She concludes by asking, "If I run into problems, need to verify what I've got or find that I need more information, may I call you back?" So far, the answer has always been yes.

Try Name Dropping if an Expert Refuses to Be Interviewed. Occasionally, you'll find the expert whose input you really need to complete your article or chapter says no when you request an interview. Take a tip from noted endocrinologist Ernest Mazzaferri, M.D., chairman of Ohio State University College of Medicine's department of medicine, who tells this story about himself.

Patient Care, a professional publication for physicians, requested some telephone interviews for a series of articles on thyroid disorders. "My answer was no, I won't do that," recalls the noted endocrinologist-author. "They said, 'that's too bad' and then they named the two top thyroid guys in the country, and I said, 'Oh, well, okay.' I wonder to this day if they didn't do this same trick on all three of us."

Eventually, Mazzaferri says, four physicians were involved in the project, which lasted several months. "The writer would bounce [ideas and information] off each of us—Physician A said such and such; Physician B, this and that." After finding out the points of controversy or differences of opinion, he says, the author then turned in four articles that were "beautifully written in terms of clarity and understanding."

TRANSLATING "MEDSPEAK" AND OTHER TECHNICAL TERMS

Plato was one of the first on record to note "they do certainly give very strange and new-fangled names to diseases." Medicalese (dentists have their own version) is not only elitist but a technique many practitioners find useful in keeping professional distance and, in some cases, withholding information from patients. While giving lip service to the need for good communication, many doctors have forgotten the knack of speaking plain English.

"Medicalese is most pervasive in terms of abbreviations (IV, COPD, GI, MI, etc.)" explains Peter MacGarr Rabinowitz, M.D., author of *Talking Medicine: America's Doctors Tell Their Stories.* "I changed many of these in my book to full words but in retrospect feel the American public, after years of "Marcus Welby, M.D.," "Emergency," "M*A*S*H," daytime soaps, and now "St. Elsewhere," can follow most medical jargon."

(While I recognized IV, GI (gastrointestinal) and MI (myocardial infarcts, the damage to the heart muscle following blockage of the coronary arteries), I must admit, Dr. Rabinowitz, that I had to check on COPD, which turns out to be chronic obstructive pulmonary disease. Nor are laypeople the only ones in the dark sometimes. More than a few doctors confess to using the term *CAT scan* in talking to patients without really knowing what *CAT* stands for. (Answer: computerized axial tomography.)

Unless you're searching in a reference work like *Abbreviations in Medicine* or *Acronyms, Initialisms & Abbreviations Dictionary,* you won't find *CAT* or many other jargon words or phrases in a standard medical dictionary. As for everyday words like *elegant* or *exquisite* (as in "an elegant experiment" or "you are having exquisite pain"), which take on special meanings in a medical or scientific context, all you can do is ask someone who knows.

Eliminating Jargon
The problem becomes acute when the writer must translate jargon for a lay audience and make sure that direct quotes will be both accurate and clear—yet not boring to readers. Here are pointers from several successful medical free-lancers and authors:

Ask "What do you mean by that?" and ask for examples. "If a physician says a term I don't understand," says Florence Isaacs. "I always ask him to please explain it to me, and I'm persistent that way. Sometimes it's difficult because doctors and scientists are so used to speaking in technical terms, it's hard to get them to talk as though they were talking to a layman. I always say, 'Explain this to me as if you're talking to your mother'."

Anticipate problem spots and help the reader out. If the spelling of a name or medical term is markedly different from the way it is pronounced, give the reader a clue to the correct meaning or pronunciation (e.g., "... said Dr. Comet [pronounced 'co-may']"). In using initials, such as PPOs or DRGs, give the meaning in parentheses (preferred provider organizations; diagnosis-related groups).

You'll find it's better to err on the side of being too informative rather than less. The person who's just suffered an MI, signed up with an HMO (Health Maintenance Organization), or volunteered to help raise funds for MS (multiple sclerosis) will be up on the latest jargon. But give your reader the benefit of the doubt. Explain somewhere in the text what unusual medical terms mean, what initials and acronyms stand for. For instance, in the award-winning 1984 *Annual Report* of the Children's Hospital of Philadelphia, Shirley Bonnem, vice-president for public relations and development, includes on nearly every page a short *glossary* of terms, ranging from R.R.T. (registered respiratory therapist) to invasive monitoring (procedures that involve insertion of catheters or other devices into blood vessels or other tissues to obtain essential physiologic information).

Personalize technical material. People don't like to read about abstract concepts—too dry, they say. To bring technical data down to a level people can identify with, sandwich the dry facts between the fascinating story of how one person, company, or industry is affected by the technology. "That's what the *Wall Street Journal* does in its blockbuster articles," says writing instructor and author Connie Emerson. "People like human interest; they want to read about other people—so don't forget that you can get even the driest facts off to an appealing start with dialogue, a quote, or an anecdote."

Take a conversational approach. "Pretend you're talking to someone who is in the first year of college or last year of high school," advises Denis Waitley, best-selling author and motivational psychologist. "In writing the piece, try to explain what you want that person to believe or understand using a conversational approach. Just talk to him or her. Don't try to be clever or use gimmick words—it sounds contrived."

Go back to your sources and check it out. "In medical writing, there's no room for a mistake," says one Boston free-lancer, adding, "I rarely ever send the copy to my sources, but I always call them back when I have the article written and ready to be sent out, and read back the quotes. Because I'm not doing the kind of article where I'm trying to expose corruption in the police department or something similar. I want to get the facts and quotes and I want them to be accurate."

MEDICAL INTERVIEWS

If you're assigned an article for a professional audience or a story that deals with the latest in drug research, clinical trials, or new treatment methods, you're going to need facts, figures, results, and opinions from medical experts. "The more eminent they are," says one medical journalist, "the more eager they are to talk to you—especially if they're surgeons."

Fran Lowry, for example, is a staff writer for the *Medical Post*, a newspaper for physicians in all specialties. Staffers are sent to large medical meetings, where they must write a story a day, often buttonholing researchers and clinicians to get an interview as they step down from the speaker's podium. Under pressure to produce accurate copy on tight deadline, Lowry relies heavily on the following questions which, she says, practically write the story for her. She begins by asking the doctor for his or her name (and correct spelling), title, and academic affiliation, then goes down her list:

1. *Why did you decide to study this?*

2. *How common is this disorder, this problem?*

3. *What has been the traditional treatment?*

4. *How much better is this treatment than other treatments currently in use? Are there alternatives that are just as good? What are the advantages of this treatment?*

5. *Is this being used in human beings? How soon will it be available on the market? Has the drug been approved by the FDA? What are the advantages of this treatment?*

6. *How many patients took part in the study? Did any drop out? How did you select your study population? Criteria for entry?*

7. *Describe the protocol. [A protocol is a document which specifies in detail how patients will be selected for research projects and how the procedure(s) will be carried out.]*

8. *How did you get on to this? What gave you the idea?*

9. *How much does it cost?*

10. *Is anybody else doing this?*

11. *Are there any adverse or dangerous or any other kind of side effects? [Most drugs have some side effects.]*

12. Are there any pictures to illustrate the article?

13. What are the indications and contraindications for treatment? Who will benefit most?

14. Did you find anything unexpected, or were you surprised by any of your findings?

15. Have I gotten the main point, or is there something more you would like to add?

16. What's the bottom line? A summing up sentence? Main message for colleagues?

17. Is there a phone number where I can reach you for any future questions?

Lowry finds that a doctor's answers to questions 2 (how common the problem is) and 16 (main message or summing-up statement) frequently provide her with the article's lead. Summing up her own approach to medical interviewing, she says, "Be prepared, know your subject well, research what you will ask—if a doctor agrees to be interviewed, you've already got an ally. But don't ask questions that can be answered with a simple yes or no. For instance, ask: *What are the best drugs?* rather than, Is this the best one?"

An additional question I frequently ask, not only of researchers but also of impassioned supporters of various health-related "causes," is: "Who's funding your research? Who's paying for all this?"

FOILED BY INGELFINGER

Most clinicians and basic scientists are willing to share what they know with a writer who's professional, reliable, and competent. However, you may run into experts who refuse to discuss their current work with you, citing the *Ingelfinger Rule.*

Ingelfinger is not a household name, but it is a powerful one in professional publishing circles. Instituted in 1969 by Franz J. Ingelfinger, a former editor of the *New England Journal of Medicine,* the "rule" supposedly denies publication to any scientific or medical article whose essence already has been revealed in the popular press. To put it another way, the lay press cannot have access to the basic information before the research has been accepted by a peer review panel and the article published in the *Journal.* "However, many doctors are misinformed about the Ingelfinger Rule," explains Fran Lowry. "They can talk to you *informally,* as long as they don't give you data in graphs and charts and the like."

For the record, here is what *NEJM* editor Arnold S. Relman, M.D., said about the Ingelfinger Rule in an October 1, 1981, *Journal* article:

> In 1969, after *Medical World News* had published a summary of a
> report scheduled for publication in the *Journal*, our editor, Franz In-
> gelfinger, formulated a policy which we have followed ever since.
> As stated in the form letter we currently use to acknowledge receipt
> of new manuscripts: ". . . the *Journal* undertakes review with the
> understanding that neither the substance of the article nor any of its
> pictures or tables have been published or will be submitted for pub-
> lication elsewhere. . . . This restriction does not apply to abstracts
> published in connection with scientific meetings, or to news reports
> based *solely* on formal and public oral presentations at such meet-
> ings, but press conferences at these meetings are discouraged."

Later in the article, Relman states that although would-be *Journal*
authors are cautioned against holding press conferences, "unfortunately, that admonition has led to the misapprehension that *any* conversation with reporters to clarify what was said at a meeting will dis-
qualify a manuscript." Relman notes that although the unreviewed
and unpublished work presented at a meeting is often not a reliable
source of information for the public, it is important that reporters covering such meetings get their facts straight. The *Journal*, he adds,
"does not object if authors help them, provided that this does not result in the prior publication of the essential substance of a manuscript
submitted to us."

The "rule" works because researchers obey it. They know the scientific journal will reject their manuscript—and they won't risk that
for a news story. Some claim the policy of "first publication only" was
in effect at good scientific journals long before Ingelfinger. Supporters
maintain it keeps medical researchers from making unsubstantiated
claims; quacks and charlatans from promoting "magic pills" and tout-
ing "discoveries" in the popular media.

Opponents argue the "rule" is self-serving, allowing journals to
build not only prestige but power as the gatekeepers and
newsbreakers. Critics claim doctors and researchers who accept federal funds are legally no different from other citizens in business—
whether they're building contractors or aerospace computer program-
mers. The public has *allowed* the scientists receiving public monies
to make their disclosures through medical journals and scientific
meetings—but, say the critics, it isn't a *right* to which researchers are
entitled.

Be that as it may, you can find your story blocked by Ingelfinger's
"rule." When that happens, you can wait for the doctors to publish
their findings in a professional journal, which can take a long time, or
find someone else to interview. But sometimes, explains one free-lancer, "the doctor you're talking to says the research is 'hot' when you

know it's 'old hat.' Then you can try to point out that this particular work is not likely to be published by the *NEJM,* and most other journals don't care about prepublication press coverage."

Says New York free-lancer Alice Fleming, "Usually, the kind of stories I write don't depend on just one expert. But if I've run into someone saving the findings for the *New England Journal of Medicine,* they've usually written somewhere else so I've been able to quote from an already published book or article. I really can't think of anyone who is world famous—and the *only* one who can say something intelligent on a subject."

Ingelfinger from an Editor's Viewpoint
Unless you're writing a breaking story, most trade editors are looking for information that's *useful* to readers.

"To some extent," *Self* senior editor Jennifer Kintzing explained at a writers' conference, "we don't necessarily want the news before it's come out in some of the [professional] journals because a doctor working on his own may think: This is the best thing since sliced bread. But once it comes out in a journal, it's been exposed to peer review by other doctors in the field who pass judgment on it. Since we as editors can't be experts in every area, I like the reassurance of having something come out in a journal where it's been subject to [such] review."

Another reason, Kintzing points out, is that many so-called breakthroughs never pan out, and those published in the prestigious journals often are the ones that do merit further attention. Additionally, she says, "it's only after something has been out not once, not twice, but five times in these big journals, that they [the findings] actually become useful to the reader. And that's the point often when we're going to [want to] learn about it—not when something is in second-stage clinical trials that nobody's going to be able to get for twenty years."

CHECKING FACTS AND QUOTES

If you use an article from a medical journal in researching an article for *Self* or many other consumer publications, you will be asked for a copy of the article or at least the citation so fact checkers can refer to it if necessary. You'll also be asked to supply a list of phone numbers of everyone you interviewed so that quotes from these experts can be verified for accuracy.

When real controversy surrounds a topic, *Self*'s health director Dianne Partie says, the expert's quote or facts in the article may also be cross-checked with more than one authority in the field—to avoid the possibility that biased or incorrect information may be passed on to readers. Says another major women's magazine editor, "If we have quotes from a medical person, we want to know the medical quotes have been verified by the source. If doctors are mentioned by name, they *must* have the opportunity of checking their material to make sure that it's accurate."

How Do You Know What You're Reporting Is True?

This question came up at a recent American Medical Writers Association meeting. The answer? Medicine is an extremely complex subject. Conflicting opinions are common, and what is "true" today may have changed by tomorrow as researchers come up with new findings.

As a writer, of course, you *knowingly* will never mislead or misinform your readers. Nor will you rely on only one source for your information. But you can't be held responsible for what individual medical experts say or claim is true.

Your responsibility is to report what is said *accurately* and *clearly* in words your audience can understand. Putting it in the context of *who* that person is—title, expertise, and academic or other affiliation—allows readers to evaluate the merits of the quotes and information for themselves.

There are four types of accuracy that free-lancers in the health and medical fields must be aware of:

1. *Is the material scientifically factual?* Literally, the only way you can personally verify the *validity* of what is presented at a professional meeting or what you read in a journal is to reproduce the study—which is, in fact, what peers, competitors, and other scientists do. They try to determine if the study design was sound, if data were adequately collected and properly analyzed, and if conclusions reported follow from that sampling and analysis.

If you have the time and ability to dig through the original research—as do many health professionals, such as "ABC News" medical editor and *Harvard Medical School Health Letter* coeditor G. Timothy Johnson, M.D.—you can judge the material's validity for yourself. With an informed skepticism, you can look at what the medical data will or won't support. If you are a layperson, don't be scared off from researching materials in professional journals, but be selective in the journals you choose. (For pointers on reading and evaluating articles in medical and scientific journals, see Dr. David Bergman's comments in chapter 5.)

2. *Are you accurately reporting what is truly a trend in your field?*

The crucial point here is whether you're assessing the situation, consensus, thrust, or whatever correctly. For example, when it's clear that there is confusion or conflict regarding diagnosis and medical treatment, the cause of a disease or condition, a study and its findings, report this in your article. Present a round-up of current theories or treatment options. Interview a number of scientists and doctors. Add their opinions to your piece for a well-rounded picture of what's happening in the field and what the latest thinking is on the topic.

3. *Are you quoting what was said correctly?* The quickest way to verify quotes is to telephone your source and review the quote with him or her. But sending the expert the page on which his quote appears, or even the entire piece, allows checking for context as well. If your publication's policy doesn't permit review of quotes, go over your notes carefully and listen one more time to the tape recording of the interview. (Before you accept another assignment from a publication with such restrictions, however, think twice. You *could* lose much more than you gain in clips and credits.)

4. *Are you reporting what the person said or what he or she really "meant" to say?* In other words, are you faithful to the *intent* of what was said? One free-lancer interviewing a noted immunologist was surprised to hear him state, "It's fortunate that the AIDS epidemic is occurring right now."

"I could see the headlines: Noted Researcher Says AIDS Epidemic Comes At Right Time," the writer says, "so I asked the doctor if he *really* wanted to say that. He gave me an odd look—the interview wasn't 'off the record'—and said, "Oh my God, no. You know what I *meant* to say—that the field of immunology is at a stage now where we have a good chance of finding the cause and thus a drug to treat the disease.' "

The published article contained the doctor's second quote. "I wasn't out to crucify the guy," says the free-lancer, adding, "he's a reliable source of information and I'll need to interview him again some time. Going for the sensational quote would have been self-defeating and actually, not true to the *sense* of what the doctor really wanted to say."

ON AND OFF THE RECORD

"Off the record," "not for attribution," and "background only" are protective terms that can mean different things to different people—even writers and reporters. The only safe way to handle potential bad feelings or the loss of a valued source is to get the terms straight *before* the interview takes place. Usually, this frankness gets the interview off to a positive start.

Some journalists, however, feel such discussions put a damper on the interview before it even begins. They make the assumption that the subject has agreed to talk for the record and, as long as nothing is said to the contrary, what's said is printed on the record.

This approach may be valid for public officials, public persons, experts, and others who are aware of how the media operate. But, says one hospital public-information director, "it doesn't seem right when the interviewee is a patient, for example, or a family member who's *unaware* that he can't say something one minute, then turn right around and say, 'Wait, that's off the record, that's not what I wanted to say'—and expect the reporter to honor it."

I always begin an interview with a brief review of why I'm doing it; the publication that has assigned it or, if it's a book, who the publisher is. If it's appropriate, I talk about disguising the person's name, occupation, and geographical location—for example, in the case of a patient who wishes to remain anonymous. When I'm interviewing a person who is not likely to be familiar with terms like *on* and *off the record*, I discuss what they mean—so that there will be no misunderstanding later. I think it's important in building rapport and trust. Moreover, since my work does not involve investigative reporting, I'm not out to trap anyone into saying something they don't want to say for the record.

On the Record. Whatever is said during the interview can be used and attributed to the source.

Off the Record. Before answering a given question, the subject requests the interviewer to accept her response as being off the record; if the interviewer accepts the information under those terms, he is ethically bound not to publish it. (If you will not accept answers that way, make it clear from the start that *nothing* is off the record.) However, nothing says you can't try to get your subject to rephrase the answer or rethink her "off-the-record" stance. Sometimes, pointing out that you've already heard the same thing from another source makes your interviewee realize there's no need to speak confidentially.

Not for Attribution. The person can be quoted, but not identified by *name.* You see this often when a quote is linked to "a close observer of the medical industry"; "a spokesperson for the hospital"; "a representative of such and such committee," or "a long-time faculty member."

Background Only. No quoting whatsoever.

Writing in the Summer, 1975, issue of *Perspectives in Biology* and *Medicine*, two noted professors of scientific communication, Lois and Selma DeBakey, sum up the ethical responsibilities of the medical and science reporter:

> Like other forms of social behavior, ethics and etiquette in biomedical communication change with time. Their basis, however, remains the same—honesty, integrity, humanity, courtesy, and consideration. . . .
>
> The science writer, who is an important link between science and society, including government, should obtain scientific information by ethical means and should use every resource to validate that information before reporting it publicly, so as to avoid premature, inaccurate, or sensational stories that ill serve society or science. For everyone involved in the communication of biomedical information, the Golden Rule is a useful guide to ethics and etiquette.

PRIVACY, CONFIDENTIALITY, AND INTERVIEWING PATIENTS

When the crash of a Galaxy Airlines charter flight in Reno in 1984 left seventy dead and one seventeen-year-old survivor—all from the Minneapolis-St. Paul area—St. Mary's Hospital and Washoe Medical Center were besieged with calls from friends, relatives, and 169 media representatives, among them local TV crews and those from the Twin Cities, NBC, ABC, CBS, and the "Today Show."

"Media were clamoring for personal interviews and photographs of George Lamson, Jr. [the sole survivor], his mother, or both, or anything that would make a good story," says Jack Bulavsky, Washoe's Community Affairs Director, adding that within minutes of the crash, a hospital media crisis team had been called into action. "Its responsibility," he explains, "was to communicate to the public, through the media, the most complete and accurate information available and to successfully balance the patient's right to privacy with the public's right to know."

MEDIA CODES AND GUIDELINES

In more than thirty states, media codes or guidelines have been worked out between hospitals and the press. The Connecticut Hospital Association's "Release of Information" guide is a good example. The first part makes the distinction between "cases of public record" and other cases that are private. The opening statement reads:

> While hospitals have a duty to protect the privacy of their patients and in general not to release any information without the patient's

consent, routine information may be released in some cases of public record (fires, accidents, police cases, etc.) Such information may include:

1. **Acknowledgment of a patient's admission.**
2. **The patient's name, address, marital status, sex, age and, if verified by police, occupation, and employer.**
3. **A statement on the patient's general condition, using the following American Hospital Association-approved terms. Copies of these terms should be given to the media.**

>   GOOD *Vital signs are stable and within normal limits. Patient is conscious and comfortable. Indicators are excellent.*
>
>   FAIR *Vital signs are stable and within normal limits. Patient is conscious, but may be uncomfortable. Indicators are favorable.*
>
>   SERIOUS *Vital signs are unstable and not within normal limits. Patient is acutely ill and may not be conscious. Indicators are questionable.*
>
>   CRITICAL *Vital signs are unstable and not within normal limits. Patient may not be conscious. Indicators are unfavorable.*

Spokespersons are advised not to use terms such as "guarded" or "stable" since they are meaningless to the layperson. However, in police and accident cases, a statement may be made regarding the general nature of the accident (i.e., an auto crash, shooting, fire, etc.) but no statement should be made concerning the circumstances (victim's car hit another, children started the fire, etc.). With regard to injuries, the following information can be released:

1. *BURNS: Statement that patient was burned, degrees and the areas of the body involved.*
2. *FRACTURE: (except head injuries) body member involved and whether simple or compound.*
3. *HEAD INJURIES: Only a simple statement that there is a head injury.*
4. *UNCONSCIOUSNESS: Only a statement that the patient was unconscious upon arrival.*
5. *SHOOTING, STABBING: Only a statement that there is a penetrating wound and its location.*
6. *SUICIDE OR ATTEMPTED SUICIDE: No statement should be made using the term "suicide" or "attempted suicide" or making reference to such actions.*

7. *INTOXICATION:* No statement as to whether patient was intoxicated.

8. *POISONING:* No statement may be made concerning either the motivation or circumstances surrounding a patient's poisoning unless it is clear and verifiable that the poisoning was accidental.

9. *RAPE, CHILD ABUSE, MORALS CRIMES:* No statement may be made concerning the nature of the incident or injuries. Condition of the patient may be given.

10. *DRUG AND ALCOHOL ABUSE:* No information of any nature may be released with respect to patients KNOWN to have been admitted for treatment of drug or alcohol abuse.

11. *BIRTHS:* Provided written consent is given by the mother, the name, sex, weight and time of birth of a child may be released, together with the names and addresses of the parents. No newspaper or TV photograph should be allowed without the written consent of the mother or father.

12. *DEATHS:* Because deaths are a matter of public record, hospitals usually release information after notification of next of kin. Information which may be released includes name of the deceased, time of death and cause, if determined by a physician and/or medical examiner. In cases involving prominent persons, the hospital may take the initiative to notify the media once the family's permission has been received. The name of the mortician receiving a body may also be released to the press.

Press law distinguishes between the *public* person (for example, the actor, celebrity, musician, politician, expert, or author who submits his or her work for public approval) and the *private* person who for whatever reason seeks medical care. Since the days of Hippocrates, physicians have respected the patient's right to privacy and maintain confidentiality in almost all circumstances. There are times, however, when the private citizen—like the teenager who survived the Galaxy plane disaster—becomes, at least temporarily, a *public* figure by virtue of some newsworthy activity, event, crime, or accident that propels him or her into the public eye.

"Rules governing the release of information on private (nonaccident) cases vary," writes William Metz in *Newswriting: From Lead to "30."* "Generally, however, the rule is to release all 'nonconfidential' information, such as name, address, sex, race, general condition, and admission and discharge dates. 'Confidential' information commonly is given to the press only with the permission of the patient and the attending physician."

Of course, when it comes to famous persons, public dignitaries, and local celebrities, explains one hospital community-relations director, "we know the press is going to be interested and try to point out that by entering the hospital they've voluntarily placed themselves in the public domain and it's to their advantage to have information coming from us—rather than from rumor mills."

LINING UP PATIENT INTERVIEWS

Many patients and their families *want* to talk, want to tell their story, want to feel some *good* can come from what may have been a painful, sad, disturbing experience. Others need the help of the media in obtaining a transplant organ, for example, or funds to help pay for a child's medical costs. Often patients are flattered that someone considers their experience significant enough to want to interview them.

In researching their book *All About Hysterectomy*, for example, Dr. Harry Huneycutt and Judith Davis interviewed more than 150 women who had had hysterectomies about a year before. The authors began by sending these women, who were Huneycutt's patients, a three-page questionnaire which included questions such as: Is your relationship with your family better, worse, or the same? What effect has the hysterectomy had on your ability to enjoy sex? Do you get tired as easily as before, or more easily? Do you still experience premenstrual tension or "blues" at regular intervals?

"We also asked about their experiences in the hospital, both before and after surgery," says Huneycutt, adding that coauthor Davis also visited approximately fifty other patients in the hospital a few days after he had performed their hysterectomies. "She asked them what experiences they were having with gas and postsurgical depression, how they were coping with catheters and hurting and hospital life. She asked them what questions they'd had about the surgery before the actual experience and what they wanted to know about the future. Naturally, the names and personal data used throughout the book were changed so that these patients' privacy is protected."

If you are coauthoring a book or article with a health professional, you may find access to patients easy, as did Judith Davis. But that's not always the case.

"The biggest problem in getting patient interviews," says one free-lancer, "is getting *beyond* the doctor who's trying to protect the patient's privacy—but hasn't checked to see how the *patient* feels about being interviewed. Many people want to talk—they're just leery of talking to someone who's not a responsible writer. If you can just persuade the doctor to *ask* the patient if he'd be willing to talk to you,

you'll find many doctors are surprised when their patients say yes."

(Don't forget, however, that even if the patient consents to be interviewed and the doctor gives you the go-ahead to talk to the patient, you may not automatically have access to the patient's *room*. And don't count on getting "lost" in hospital corridors as a way of circumventing hospital clearance procedures. In the Galaxy case, for instance, Washoe Medical Center limited media to a specified "interview area" and posted a security guard outside the room of George Lamson, Jr. "Security," says Bulavsky, "also guarded public elevators and stairwells to make sure unauthorized personnel or 'lost' media did not find their way to his room.")

Before your interview, ask the hospital's public-information officer/media coordinator about any special clearance or permission you need to be in a certain part of the hospital or in the patient's room. One problem that occasionally arises in interviewing a hospital patient is that someone from the public-relations department will insist on sitting in on the interview.

Sometimes you have no choice, but in general, third parties— merely by their presence—tend to inhibit what's said. Whether the interview takes place in a hospital, pharmaceutical firm, private home, park, or any other place, try to interview your subject, if at all possible, *without* "chaperones."

HOW ONE AUTHOR HIT
THE PATIENT-INTERVIEW JACKPOT

When Nancy Yanes Hoffman needed to talk with former heart bypass patients for her book *Change of Heart: The Bypass Experience* (Harcourt Brace Jovanovich), she decided to advertise for them. Her notices in various high-circulation commercial and labor-union publications brought nothing. Then, she says, "lightning struck and I went to the *Fortune 500* list and asked them to publish a call for bypassers in their corporate newsletters—that doesn't mean just CEO's, it means workers on the line as well." She was so successful with the first *Fortune 500* that she wrote to the second 500. Ultimately, 1,100 former bypass patients filled out a lengthy questionnaire; from their responses, Hoffman selected 300 people for face-to-face, two-hour-long interviews. (The *Fortune 500* lists appear annually in special issues of *Fortune* magazine. For example, a listing of the 500 largest U.S. industrial corporations, ranked by sales, appears in late April/early May; in June, another list gives the 500 largest U.S. nonindustrial (service) corporations, ranked by sales and types, i.e., retailing, banking, insurance, utilities, etc.).

Many times, Hoffman's subjects shared intimate and emotionally painful information with her in these interviews. Some wept. In such situations, she advises, "just keep going—it's *good* for them to talk." Many people, she says, are grateful to talk and thankful that someone will listen. Most important, it's a relief to know that what they are experiencing is *not* some terrible thing. Often they feel this way because nobody has talked to them *after* their operation. In researching *Change of Heart*, Hoffman found that many fomer bypass patients were grateful to know that "yes, indeed, other people have memory loss, get depressed, are confused and yes, it passes off and you shouldn't let it get the best of you."

CONSIDERATION, RESPECT, SENSITIVITY . . . AND KLEENEX

You won't find it mentioned in other treatises on interviewing, but I've found in talking to patients, their families, and even health professionals who've cared for them, it pays to have extra minipackets of Kleenex tucked away in my pocket, purse, or briefcase. During an interview I did with a nurse who'd cared for a dying child, for example, tears suddenly spilled down her cheeks. Another time, while I was talking to parents of an infant born with multiple defects, both the mother and father unexpectedly choked up. With tissues on hand and a minute or two to grieve together, we could continue the interview without disrupting the flow of their thoughts.

(It's all right to shed a tear along with your subject. Some writers are afraid this shows a lack of professionalism or objectivity; what it really shows is that you are a human being who cares. Your professionalism shouldn't rule out empathy.)

If your subject is seriously ill, you must be attuned to nonverbal signals that he or she may be getting overtired, needs a break before continuing or perhaps a drink of water or some other liquid to soothe a dry throat. One free-lancer told me her longest interview was with an artist who had terminal cancer. He wanted to tell his story, but shortness of breath allowed him to talk only a few minutes at a time. "He felt frustrated and so did I," says the writer, "because he was such a sensitive person, and I knew what an effort it was for him to talk. It took several days to complete the interview, but some stories are worth huge chunks of time and emotion."

Such interviews can take a toll on *your* health and emotions as well. Jo Imlay, for instance, won a prestigious award in the 1982 J. C. Penney-University of Missouri Newspaper Awards for her feature story, "Farewell to Phyllis." Judges cited the article, which detailed the final months of a hospice nurse struggling to accept her impending death, as a "shining example of good objective reporting and clean simple writing." Commenting on her award and article in the May, 1983, issue of *Press Woman*, Imlay says she started out "wanting to report the facts, not get personally involved. I was naive."

Among problems she and photographer Tim Jewett encountered early were the need to establish open communication with Phyllis, negotiate with balky family members protective of her privacy, and work around the periods in which she was simply too ill to see them. Though the twosome worked on other newspaper projects, the hospice was their first priority; they were on call twenty-four hours a day. Each buoyed the other's spirits and took turns dealing with crises in relationships with various family members. Though Imlay says she grew as a writer and as a person, she's not sure she'd ever do a similar story again.

> I envied Tim after Phyllis' death. His work was essentially done. For me, the hardest part remained: condensing 22 sets of transcribed notes into a story encompassing five drama-filled months. Those nine days of writing were the hardest I've ever spent, in part because of the bulk of the story and in part because of my own emotions about watching Phyllis die.
>
> But it's foolish to think that stories that tell real-life dramas in detail shouldn't affect us. When we care, it's conveyed to readers. And our readers responded, more than on any previous story I've done. Most mentioned the story's universal appeal: that in describing one person's death, we'd dealt with the fears and questions everyone experiences when faced with death.

In interviewing a person who is disabled, take into account the nature of the disability, tailor your space and mode of communication accordingly, then ask your questions as you would of any other interviewee. One of my most challenging interviews took place in a factory, where the decibels would have ruled out any ordinary interview. But Dolores Follette, who is deaf and blind and who then was breaking all records for assembling label-marker parts, simply plunked her TellaTouch machine on a desk and said, "Talk to me." (The TellaTouch resembles an ordinary typewriter, with a braille key in the back. As a message or question is typed on the keyboard, Dolores' finger picks up the corresponding braille symbol and she gives her response.) On the spot, my typing skills deteriorated.

Afraid that I was confusing her with "typos," I tried to X out whole questions. But Doris had dealt with poor typists before, and she was good at second-guessing what I was trying to ask. Right away she put me at ease. The interview, which appeared in a local paper, accomplished its purpose: exposure in the media so that she could garner enough name recognition and support to attend a mid-1970s White House Conference on Handicapped Individuals. The news peg: the 4,800 to 5,500 parts a day she could assemble—well above normal production quotas for any other worker in her plant.

In writing about people who are disabled, take to heart the suggestions that the United Cerebral Palsy Association and National Easter Seal Society provide in their free brochures for writers. Summed up by author-speaker Bonnie G. Wheeler, the main point is that "personhood should always be recognized above any qualifying labels."

Stereotypical images of dependency and helplessness, for example, are reinforced when a person is described as a *victim* of a disease, a *cripple*, a *deaf-mute*, or *afflicted* with such and such condition. Words like *disabled* or *handicapped* and specific disabilities, e.g., polio, cerebral palsy, multiple sclerosis, shouldn't be used as labeling adjectives or nouns. For instance, don't write, "Mary, a teenage epileptic" or "John, the blind downhill-skiing champ. . . ." If a person's disability is important to your story, say, "Ted Kennedy, Jr., who lost a leg to cancer. . . ." or "FDR, who had polio. . . ."

For a copy of the brochures that offer general advice and guidelines in writing about handicaps, write: The National Easter Seal Society, "Portraying Persons with Disabilities in Print" (NESS Guidelines, 2023 W. Ogden Ave., Chicago, IL 60612) and the United Cerebral Palsy Association, Inc., "Four Letter Words in the Dictionary of the Disabled" (UCPA Public Relations, 66 E. 34th St., New York, NY 10016).

HANDLING A HOSTILE INTERVIEW

"Medicine and journalism need each other—journalists are explainers of complex issues," says former CBS News president Fred W. Friendly. But not all health professionals agree that the media *can* do the job. You may run into doctors or scientists who have a low opinion of the press, feel they've been stung before, and aren't about to take that chance again.

"Journalists by nature are lightweights," one Yale University medical expert says in commenting on the tension that exists between medicine and the media. "I don't see how they can possibly grasp the depth of issues, like medical ethics for example, and without that [depth] they can't be helpful to the public. You try to help the media and get stung every damn time."

True, some physicians believe they've been treated unfairly by the media. They don't want to talk to writers, reporters, Mike Wallace, Barbara Walters, or anybody else. Why bother, they think. The press will just get it wrong again, quote me out of context again. Suppose the expert you must interview takes that stance. How do you handle the hostile interviewee? Here are some tips from writers who've dealt with the problem successfully:

Keep clearly in mind what you want to get out of the interview.

Keep your cool so you can recall the questions you've thought out in advance and your game plan for asking them. "I've found what works best," award-winning free-lancer Bonnie Remsberg says, "is to go very slowly, very carefully. Absolutely essential," she adds, "is to know what you're talking about." For a *Ladies' Home Journal* worldwide exclusive story on America's first test-tube baby, Remsberg went twice to England where she interviewed Dr. Patrick Steptoe, who developed the in vitro fertilization procedure. Steptoe, she says, was cooperative but quite guarded in his replies to her questions, partly, she thinks, because the term *test-tube baby* was itself a press creation.

Be sensitive to what's happening during the interview. If you feel you'll be cut off abruptly, ask your most important questions up front. Remember that many physicians are coached in media relations by experts who emphasize the point that although the interviewer asks the questions, it's the interviewee who controls the answers.

According to Gordon Shea, author of *Managing a Difficult or Hostile Audience*, the key strategy the interviewee should employ is to concentrate on getting beyond that "human filter" (you as reporter/interviewer) to reach the desired print, TV, or radio audience. That calls for strategies to influence the content, tone, and viewpoint of the reporting. For example, Shea suggests experts can try to divert questions they feel are biased by talking about other things they value or consider more important. Your job, of course, is to be aware of such manipulation and keep the interview on track.

(Little grandmothers can be manipulators, too, as I found out in interviewing a woman who'd agreed to talk about problems she was having relating to her grandchildren—but who kept talking about a religious institute she and her husband had founded many years before. When I told her there was no point in continuing our interview since she refused to discuss children, she confessed she had agreed to the interview only because she hoped to interest me in writing her church's history.)

THE BIG TEN

Free-lancers and journalists agree that certain basic rules apply to interviewing. "Apply them," says one writer, "and you'll have a hard time going wrong." The ten rules are as follows:

1. *Always be up front about the thrust of your article and intended*

publication. For instance, if you're interviewing an expert at the National Institutes of Health about the use of fiber in the diet to prevent colon cancer, don't mislead the person by saying you're writing an article on the value of high-fiber cereals in treating chronic constipation. Your chances of getting the most candid quotes escalate when you level with your interviewee—and it's helpful in obtaining interviews with doctors if you're *not* writing for tabloids like the *National Enquirer, Star, Globe,* or *Sun.*

2. *Reconfirm the time and place of your interview.* Ask about any special arrangements you must make, e.g., security, hospital, pressroom, or other clearance or visitor parking permit. If weather is a factor, plan an alternate way of getting to your destination—and check on bus, train, or metro schedules.

3. *Make sure all equipment is working properly.* If you'll be taking your own photographs, check camera for film and ASA setting; flash attachment for batteries. Have handy extra pens, ballpoint fillers, batteries for tape recorders, etc. Some free-lancers take no chances that a tape recorder will malfunction or a tape will end just as the interviewee makes a crucial point. They use two recorders and double-tape the interview.

4. *Know what you need and plan your questions accordingly.* What's the purpose of the interview? Who's your audience? Keep your readers in mind as you interview—what data, results, feelings, or opinions will they be looking for in your article? Although there's no substitute for being prepared to do an interview, circumstances sometimes force you to "wing it." A *generic* list of questions (like the one *Medical Post* staffer Fran Lowry shares earlier in this chapter) is helpful if you write a certain type of article often.

In a pinch or panic, structure your questions around the time-honored *GLOSS* formula: *goals,* objectives or what the person hopes to find or accomplish; *length* (how long will project take/has it taken?); *obstacles* to achieving the goals; *solutions* proposed; how he got his *start* (what triggered interest?) and *satisfaction* (what makes it all worthwhile?). Finally, ask the person to sum it up briefly with a final thought or message. Two encore questions: Is there *anything else* I should know that I haven't asked you about? Is there *someone else* I should talk to?

5. *Be persistent.* You may not get the answer the first time around. Try rephrasing the question. Use a word bridge, talking around the controversial issue. Come back to your original question later in the interview. "The key to a good interview," says *Washington Post* writer Stevan Allen, "is establishing a bit of trust, then really letting the person you're talking to, talk."

6. *Don't hesitate to ask for clarification.* What do you mean by that? Can you give me an example? An anecdote? How would you explain this to your own mother? "If I can understand it, I can explain it to readers," says one New York free-lancer who passes on another tip: "One picture can be worth a thousand words of jargon, so ask the doctor to give you a photo or draw a diagram on paper for you. Try to interview your expert near a blackboard. Most doctors like to teach. Given chalk and a willing listener, the expert often forgets the interview was only supposed to last fifteen minutes."

7. *Beware of hidden agendas.* Most experts are straightforward and ethical. But, warns an East Coast hospital public-relations director, "so many doctors now have to worry about money and increasing competition, that *ethics* can go out the window fast. They know if Dr. 'X' gets a story on TV or in the newspaper, everybody goes to him for the next two months—it's a good way to increase their practice.

"They also learn quickly that if they have a 'first,' they tend to get a lot of media coverage," she adds, "so they tend to make up a lot of firsts. As a reporter, you have to be careful you're not taken in by someone who's just looking for a quick way to get his name before the public."

8. *Make accuracy a paramount concern.* One way to ensure you've quoted experts correctly is to allow them to proofread the pages on which their quotes appear prior to publication. Another is to telephone the interviewee and read the quotes back for verification. Some free-lancers send the complete article so the expert can see his or her quotes in context.

Says Barbara Chapman, who frequently conducts interviewing workshops for medical writers, "Newspapers have a fit if you suggest it and many don't allow it at all; but I always tell writers, if you work for an organization or publication that will permit you to extend this protection and courtesy to your sources, you've made a friend for life of that resource person." When a dispute arises over wording of quotes or what to include/exclude in the article, talk it over with your editor.

9. *Obtain signed releases for all photos and, if your publisher requires it, for interviews as well.* In tape recording an interview over the telephone, be sure to inform your subject and get his or her permission on the tape. In most states, it's illegal *not* to inform the interviewee he's being taped. Save your notes and transcripts; store your tapes (hard-drive and floppy disks, too) in appropriate covers and containers away from dust, heat, leaky ceilings, and other destructive elements.

10. *Send a copy of the published article or interview to your subject*

for his or her files. Be sure to attach your business card even if you write a brief note. You may want to interview this doctor again; he or she may be looking for a coauthor in the future. Keep your own Rolodex or card file up to date, adding names of experts who give good interviews. Stay in touch with a telephone call from time to time. It's a painless way to stay abreast of what's happening in the field and generate additional article ideas.

"Remember," says *Montreal Gazette*'s Nicholas Regush, "there's more than one way to do interviews and some people are saying, 'Throw away the rule book and learn who you are in relation to this expert and this subject. Understand your motivations and how good you can become in the process of doing the job.' Personality is the starting point, but if you feel you can't compete . . . or be at the top of things, you're in the wrong business."

If that sounds intimidating, don't forget the good interview breaks down to about 90 percent research; 9 percent skill and observation; 1 percent, luck. True, interviewing is *both* a skill and an art, but no one inherits either one. You can learn how to interview and how to compete just as every other writer has had to do. Starting points are personality and preparation. Then, *listen* to what your subject is saying and take it from there.

11 □ PERSONAL EXPERIENCE (YOURS OR THEIRS)

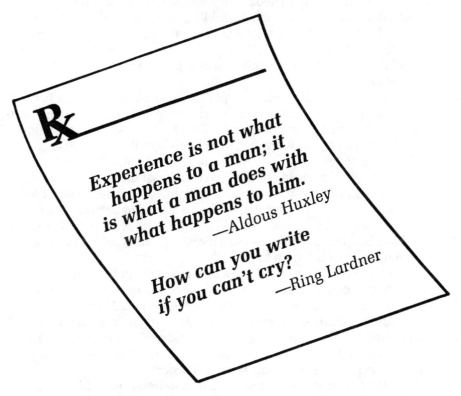

Experience is not what happens to a man; it is what a man does with what happens to him.
—Aldous Huxley

How can you write if you can't cry?
—Ring Lardner

"How most of us make it through the sawblades and steamrollers of life is statistically miraculous," comments David Hon in his book *Trade-offs*. Knowing, however, that you can communicate what you have been through, felt, and found out about yourself, can take some of the sting out of those unpleasant and trying experiences.

"Yet writing the first-person story is the hardest story to do categorically," *American Health* managing editor Hara Estroff Marano said at a writers' conference, "and in health, it's even harder."

What makes writing the personal experience so difficult is twofold: the amount of research involved if it's *not* your own story, and the old problem of not being able to see the forest for the trees if it *is* yours: as *Good Housekeeping* articles editor Joan Thursh puts it, "being able to see what is and isn't relevant to the story" when you're at the heart of it.

A MATTER OF INVOLVEMENT

Many people try to write about their health-related experience because they figure they know all about it. After all, they've had the illness or operation—or someone they know has had it. They've survived a disaster, come through a disabling condition or difficult situation with sanity and spirit intact. They've learned something that cries out to be shared.

While this experience is a starting point, sad to say, it's not enough to guarantee a sale.

Is this callous? Not really, explains *Good Housekeeping's* Joan Thursh. So many people have an experience that is very important to them—it's overwhelming; it's tragic. Yet, she notes somewhat apologetically, "so *many* are submitted to us for publication that we can get 'jaded' with them.

"We get hundreds of queries a week, a great many of which are amateurish and totally unsuitable, and returned. Very few make it to the top," she says, "but some do. The most interesting personal stories are plucked out of the mail," she adds, "because they are experiences that have happened to people—and there's no way you can manufacture those or call them up to order."

Certain major themes surface again and again in the personal experience and drama-in-real-life stories: *survival* against all odds; *rescues,* such as the child pulled from icy waters or the SOS received just in time; *adaptation* and *acceptance,* i.e. learning to live with a problem or finding a solution unexpectedly; and perhaps that most difficult theme of all to convey, *grace under pressure*—that special ability to draw on inner resources hitherto unknown.

Finding such stories is second nature to free-lancers like Elaine Fein, who specialize in human-interest articles. Fein says she is a prolific reader, and even at a party she's on the alert for potential personal-experience leads. "You have to be able to smell out a story," she says, "then be prepared to do a tremendous amount of investigative reporting to track it down."

For example, a two- or three-line *New York Times* or wire-service story may catch her attention as grist for a wonderful true-life drama. Locating the people and health professionals involved—especially if it's an out-of-town story—may require calling the newspaper, the AP or UPI bureau, the hospital or clinic where the physicians named in the news story cared for the patient. Even at that, she says, she's not always successful. "I can spend a lot of time and money on the telephone to track down a story and then get nowhere."

How does she break the ice if the people she's tracking down haven't given thought to telling their story to the public? "When I get hold of them," she says, "I tell them who I am, what I am, and what I do. I ask if they'd be interested in having their story in one of the women's magazines because it would be very helpful to other people to know what happened, how they reacted, and how they recouped—the courage with which they faced the ordeal." If they agree, Fein then arranges for a preliminary interview before querying an editor.

THE WRITE-IT-YOURSELF EXPERIENCE

Basically, there are two approaches you can take in writing up the personal experience story: the *factual*, which reports mainly action, and the *emotional*, which focuses on character development, for example, in facing a tragedy or struggling to regain confidence in oneself after a serious blow to one's ego.

In assigning the personal experience article, editors look for a story that transcends one person's experience and taps into a universal one that readers can identify with or find meaningful. Don't forget, however, that if you recount your experience in first person, the "I" has no place to hide. While this is a strong point of that approach, it can also be its pain. Early in the 1970s, for example, I offered to help a young U.S. State Department wife, whose husband was one of the first diplomats kidnapped by Central American guerrillas, write her experience for a *Redbook* Young Mother's Story. She had already completed a first draft of what she wanted to say, but in it, there was no *personal* story.

It was as though she had written one long thank-you note to several people who had helped her and her children during the three-day crisis—a time in which rebel demands had tied her husband's return to the release of guerrilla prisoners being held in a Mexican jail and some of these people could not be located. We started over.

"Forget about writing," I suggested, "and tell me in your own words what happened, how you felt at the time, and what gave you the strength to carry on."

The tale that emerged rivaled the best in spy thrillers and today's best-selling novels. Yet this young mother's real story was never submitted to *any* publication. It was too painful for her to reveal in print that her marriage was failing and that the husband the media had portrayed as something of a hero was in fact a man with feet of clay whose release would further complicate life at home. Down deep she was a very private person. To let others know what she had learned about herself and how this experience had changed her as a person was simply *too* personal to share.

On the other hand, some writers find it helpful to write about their strong feelings and troublesome personal experiences.

One of these is New Rochelle, New York, writer Paul Levine, who says that writing about "the things I've been through is a good way for me to get at my feelings, too. By putting thoughts down on paper and seeing them reduced to the printed word, I am more effectively able to deal with them. When I write about something that is bothering me (I have written articles about surviving a job, dealing with a teenage daughter, dealing with death, commuting, being single, facing a fortieth birthday, etc.) I am forced to think about a topic in as orderly a fashion as possible."

A rehabilitation counselor with the Westchester Association for Retarded Children, Levine writes about life in a family and general living setting to which, he says, other people can relate. His by-line has appeared in *Newsday* and *The New York Times*, which published "Letting Go when Adolescence Claims a Daughter" and "Sprinting to the Ends of a Bell-Shaped Curve." Here are the opening lines of this masterfully crafted piece contrasting the world of the retarded person with that of the gifted—and showing, in the telling, how both lend a special quality to Levine's own life.

> Sometimes I feel as if I'm sitting on top of a bell-shaped curve looking through binoculars. Toward one end is my work as a counselor with retarded adults in White Plains. Toward the other end is my life with my two daughters, both of whom have been in talented and gifted programs in New Rochelle.
>
> I often wonder why I am so comfortable as I go from one world to the other. But there I am walking out into the far reaches of the skews they represent. Toward one end are "thinking exercises," independent research, and Iowa test results that nudge the upper limits of the graph paper.
>
> Toward the other end is my job in a vocational-rehabilitation center, where the floors are color coded so the clients will know where to go. Where the labels of "backward" and "retarded" are worn as obviously as sandwich board signs, and where touring visitors whisper, "There but for the grace of God go I."
>
> I guess I need each world so that the specialness of the other can be put in perspective. I need my daughters' world of trips to Stratford, Conn., and the New York City Opera so I can deal with grown men who carry Partridge Family lunch boxes.

The strength of Levine's article doesn't flow from high drama. Nor does it come from an exceptional experience. Rather its appeal lies in Levine's ability to see a connection where normally we would find none and to help us see, despite the extremes of the bell-shaped curve, that there is a common thread of humanity and desire to learn running from end to end. Levine builds his case with an exquisite point/counterpoint as follows:

> So there is my eighth-grade daughter in the Izod blouse telling me she wants to go to Princeton and asking me what Columbia was really like. I need her asking me for help with polynomials and factoring so I can deal with a 45-year-old man who sleeps in his clothes every night. I need her asking me for hints in remembering formulas for tangents and cosines so I can deal with a client who bangs his head with his fist every time he feels tense. I need to attend her All County Choir concert for yet another year and visit the library where her painting of a Japanese maiden is on display, so it will be easier for me to deal with a young man who keeps jumping because he can't concentrate on his work.
>
> And then I am listening to my sixth-grade daughter tell me she was appointed to the school newspaper. She is in a program where "is willing to take risks: and "displays growth in problem solving" are graded on her report card. I need her asking me whether her independent-research report should be on Greek architecture or Greek literature, so I can deal with adults who are unable to tell the difference between a nickel and a dime.
>
> And then I need to see clients who struggle to reach the point where they can be placed in a regular job outside the workshop so I can realize that reading scores four grades ahead are not the greatest achievement in life. I need to see the happiness of someone who learns to ride the public bus so I can accept the idea that going to the best schools and earning multiple degrees are not the most important goals.
>
> Oh, it's easy for me to sit at school meetings and listen to such topics as, the future of the talented and gifted program should be graded or nongraded. Not like the parents of the retarded who come in for conferences. You can see them listen and feel them listen for something positive. Sometimes you can hear how hard they listen by their silence.

Levine's exit is economic, clean, and from the heart. He pulls the story's threads together, and us along with them.

> In my spare time I write, and I visited my younger daughter's school some months back and gave a talk on creative writing. Although only in the fifth and sixth grades, many of the children had already started writing stories and poetry.
>
> At work I also share my writing. I run a poetry group. It's strange, I guess, running a poetry group for retarded individuals. But they love it. And they come each week without being reminded. Most of them listen as I read a poem or a short story. But a few clients try to write some lines and there's one woman who brings in the copied words of songs she has heard. That's poetry to her. They want to learn, just as my daughters want to learn. They need what I give,

just as my daughters need what I give.

So there I am. Sliding down and sprinting to the ends of the bell-shaped curve. Oh, so easily. First in one direction. And then the other. To one a counselor. To the other a father. Embracing the specialness they have. Each in their own way.

"I carry a small notebook with me and write down ideas for stories or articles," explains Levine who says his ideas for fiction often come out of the blue but his articles are drawn from areas of concern or experiences he's gone through. "Once I have my topic, I write my thoughts out on paper as quickly as I can. Then I go back and add to it. To me that's the easy part.

"The hard part," he says, "is writing an article fit for publication. This involves rewriting and cutting. It usually takes me seven to nine drafts before I am willing to send something out. My advice to other writers is to do as many drafts as necessary to make the article sound right."

VARIETIES OF EXPERIENCE

Personal-experience articles (and books) come in various forms, ranging from opinion pieces, personal reminiscences, and how-to's (all covered in other chapters in this book) to "drama in real life" and direct "first-person" experiences—which may be written by the individual involved or another author *as told to.*

For example, in researching a story for *McCall's* on the parents' movement against drugs and how to form such a parents' group, freelancer Elizabeth Tener explained at a writers' workshop, she interviewed several parents, including a mother in California with a lively, articulate daughter named Debby. Later, when *Young Miss* approached Tener about a story on drugs, she instantly recalled Debby and went back to talk to her. The article, *by* Debby Jensen *as told to* Elizabeth Tener was titled, "The Drug Trap: A Young Woman's Story of Her Battle with Addiction." (All names except Debby's were changed.)

When well written, someone else's experience enables us to escape the humdrum of everyday living or look within ourselves more deeply. Vicariously, we explore new vistas of mind, body, and spirit we would otherwise not think of. We can compare our own situation with that of another person. What would we have done in similar circumstances? What can we learn *now* from this person's experience? Some of these experiences are the "thank God it didn't happen to me" type; others, the "why can't I be that lucky" kind. But whatever the type, the personal experience must have one essential element: Other people must be able to relate to it and find it meaningful.

"People care more about people than about anything else in the world," explains Lois Duncan in her book *How to Write and Sell Your Personal Experiences*. Duncan has written twenty-two books and sold more than 300 articles and stories, yet claims, "None of the material of my stories and articles is particularly exciting or sensational. It is as available to you as it is to me. People find it interesting because they can relate to it."

SEEING THROUGH THE NARRATOR'S "I"

First-hand, direct-experience stories tell simply and sincerely about an event or experience in your life that was important to your development as a person. While that may sound easy—after all, the experience *is* the story—beginning writers often make the mistake of literally transcribing the experience chronologically just as it happened. In the process, they not only overwrite, but they also miss the crucial reader-identification link.

There's no missing that link, though, or its reader takeaway-value in James Comer's *Los Angeles Times* piece titled "Food for Thought." Comer had agreed to host the main course for a church progressive dinner. But after forty-five guests had eaten and gone on to the next house for dessert, there was still enough *arroz con pollo* to feed thirty more.

> As with most hosts, my greatest concern had been running out of food. God forbid that one Presbyterian should be denied a third helping. As a result, I was now faced with mounds of yellow rice, pineapple, olives, and marinated chicken. Two enormous serving bowls could barely contain the overflow from my culinary insecurity.
>
> That food was not going to waste. And it was not going to my waist. I decided to give it away.
>
> Because I'm on a mailing list shared by every charity, humanitarian effort, and liberal cause in the country, I knew about a local mission for the homeless. On Sunday morning, I called them to ask if I could donate the food. They gave me directions and seemed genuinely enthusiastic about the prospect of having my cooking grace their tables, which was all the encouragement that I needed. I drove downtown feeling good, as only a do-gooder can.

We're hooked. Who among us hasn't known the good feeling that comes with the generous impulse that's acted upon? And who hasn't shared the dilemma of what to do with leftovers *en masse*? (If, however, you're feeling a little uneasy at this point, it's not purely by chance. *Do-gooder* is a loaded word.)

Comer leaves the freeway and enters a landscape totally alien from the Los Angeles he knows. That scene, however, could just as easily be in New York City or Washington, D.C., or the Tenderloin district of San Francisco. We've seen it before—rags, filth, explains Comer, the "kind of stereotypical despair that one associates with grainy news film from Third World shantytowns."

He stops twice to ask for directions. The mission, when he finds it, is not only as seedy as the street people who frequent it, but closed.

> I'd expected a warm welcome from the staff. Now I couldn't even get into the place.
>
> My chicken and I were on the street, but soon we had lots of company. Within 30 seconds I was at the center of 15 men and women who wanted something to eat. They didn't have to tell me that they were hungry. It showed.
>
> I explained that I'd brought the food for the mission to distribute.
>
> "You don't understand, man. They don't serve food on Sunday morning. And I'm hungry now. What have you got in there?
>
> "Chicken. A lot of chicken. But it's real messy. You need a fork or spoon."

Hungry people, of course, don't *need* forks and spoons. Within minutes, most of the food is gone. Comer looks over the scene. What started out as doing good while getting rid of leftovers is now awkward. Deftly incorporating a "full-circle" ending, Comer brings us back to the progressive dinner party the night before. Now, however, we're ready to see such dinners in a new light. Here are his closing lines:

> As I watched them scramble for a taste of the leftover rice, I tried to imagine how they felt. I knew how I felt. I was embarrassed for all of us. That they should be hungry and I should be trying to lose weight. That stomachs should be empty when warehouses are full of surplus food.
>
> As the platters rapidly emptied, I recalled the gaunt Ethiopian faces that I turned away from on network news. And I looked back on the church dinner of the previous night and wondered how "progressive" it had been. Real progress would have been to feed the hungry.

It's the rare reader with enough food on the table and a church supper or two under the belt who can't relate to his experience. This is writing that truly *shows* rather than tells. Nowhere, for example, does Comer tell us he feels "guilty." He paints a word picture that leaves no doubt about his true feelings over weight watching when others are starving.

Nor does he hit us over the head with his "moment of truth." It evolves naturally from all that has gone before. And the call to action for him—and for us—is clear: real "progress" *is* (and always has been) feeding the person who's *hungry.*

PROBLEMS AND DILEMMAS—THE BIG THREE

"Life," George Santayana wrote, "is not a spectacle or a feast: it is a predicament." With no shortage of predicaments, selling the my-problem-and-how-I-resolved-it article becomes a matter of targeting the right publication and shaping your problem/solution so that the reader can profit from your experience. The big three in the predicament-and-what-I-did-about-it category are: physical problems, emotional trauma, and medically related ethical dilemmas.

To benefit from your experience, however, the reader must understand: (1) what the problem or dilemma is; (2) what the complications or conflicts were all about and how they affected you; (3) what you did about the problems and (4) what happened *then.* To really care enough to benefit from your experience, the reader has to "walk in your shoes"—if not the proverbial mile, at least a few paragraphs.

Some of these problems stem directly from physical causes, diseases, or disabling conditions. Titles that reflect such health problems/experiences include Roger Ressmeyer's personal account of "The Day-to-Day Struggle of a Diabetic" in *California Living;* "I died at 10:53 A.M.," Victor D. Solow's *Reader's Digest* First Person Award article about a close call in the emergency room; and "Toxic Shock," former *New York Times* reporter Nan Robertson's Pulitzer Prize-winning story of her miraculous recovery from this devastating, lengthy illness which required amputation of her fingertips because of gangrene.

Personal experiences that deal with family or job problems—e.g., how you handled the empty nest syndrome or coped with a difficult patient—focus heavily on mental and emotional well-being and emphasize *psychological* aspects of human relations. Typical titles in this category are: "My Boss Wanted More than a Secretary," a *Good Housekeeping* My Problem and How I Solved It article dealing with sexual harrassment on the job; "I Always Knew I Had a Double," a *Redbook* Mother's Story describing the emotional void that led one woman in the United States to search for a twin sister adopted in Germany as a toddler; and, from *Medical Economics,* "I Didn't Go to Med School to Let Patients Play Doctor" by general practitioner Stephen M. Del Giudice, M.D.

Most unsettling of all is the third type of problem-experience, which is becoming more common as science and technology outstrip the art of medicine. If you write a bioethical dilemma/resolution article, be prepared for the strong reader reaction it will provoke. That's because biomedical issues are complex; there are no easy answers, and feelings run strong about life, death, suffering, and "playing God."

Titles of health-related ethical-dilemma articles tend to be straightforward. A 1984 article by Rayna Rapp in Ms. magazine, for instance, was titled, "The Ethics of Choice: After My Amniocentesis, Mike and I Faced the Toughest Decision of Our Lives."

One which has become a classic case history in the limits and excesses of modern medicine is Robert and Peggy Stinson's article "On the Death of a Baby," which the Atlantic Monthly ran in 1979. Later published by Little, Brown as The Long Dying of Baby Andrew, the story told of the short, cruel, institutional life their baby underwent as a result of "heroic" medical efforts to save him.

THREE STEPS TO BETTER PROBLEM SELLING

Several years ago, award-winning author Jerome E. Kelley set out to sell a First Person Award story to Reader's Digest, which offers $3,000 for such pieces. As he thumbed through the magazine, he noticed something that up to that point had escaped his eye. The pattern of these First Person stories never deviated from a simple format, which he quickly jotted down on a scrap of paper.

The formula, which then was a winner, is still the same:

1. A problem exists.
2. The problem intensifies.
3. The problem is solved—or at least ameliorated to the point where the individual or persons involved can live with it. Problem and solution are then wrapped up with a satisfying conclusion.

Kelley wasted no time in putting on paper an outline of a personal experience he'd had in the Canadian Army after the American Marine Corps had turned him down for being flat-footed, underweight, and underage early in World War II. His story, "The Pied Piper of 'A' Company" had a double payoff. Not only did the Digest run it as a First Person Award story, he also received an extra $200 for a Humor in Uniform paragraph which had triggered his thinking about "A" Company in the first place.

Kelley's approach will work well for any free-lancer. Study the publication you want to sell to for style. Analyze the structure of the personal-experience pieces appearing in the magazine. And finally, think in terms of a problem that gets worse before it gets solved.

A March, 1978, Good Housekeeping piece, "The Face Lift that Flopped," could serve as a my-problem-and-how-I-solved-it primer. There was no by-line, but the writer told what happened when she felt compelled to rescue her marriage and try to rekindle love through plastic surgery—despite one doctor's advice not to undergo cosmetic surgery. (A problem exists: A marriage is in trouble, a wife wants to believe that worry lines and crow's-feet are to blame and that a face lift will work a miracle.)

When a highly recommended plastic surgeon refuses to give her a face lift ("It's an operation to improve slack skin, not slack lives"), she finds someone who will operate—for a hefty fee. Next, the problem intensifies: The botched surgery needs fixing, the woman refuses to leave the house or have friends in until healing is complete, and a fascinating "other woman"—one of the husband's graduate students—becomes an invisible guest each night at dinner as the husband praises the abilities of his top student and enthuses over her excitement about life.

The problem is not solved, but it is ameliorated when the husband suggests his wife meet the femme fatale she has dreamed up and judge for herself what really is at stake.

Meg—the dreaded "other woman"—turns out to be in her mid-fifties, with graying hair and a lined face. She is so charming and reassuring that the wife forgets her initial embarrassment and awkwardness. The two women have much in common, but one has filled her empty nest with new interests, including graduate work.

The author winds up her personal experience with a new attitude toward beauty, a resolve to seek out new directions in her life (as Meg has), and the courage to be honest with herself for the first time. Her husband, delighted to have a wife who's no longer "moaning about her face" all day long, is as enthusiastic about her future as he was over Meg's.

Look at this story as an editor might. Medical facts about cosmetic surgery are unobtrusively woven into the personal experience. Skillfully handled dialogue moves the action along quickly. The story transcends one woman's experience and holds an important message for all women, namely, the folly of disregarding sound medical advice and the toll that inventing "the other woman" can take on a marriage. Problem and resolution are tied together in a satisfying conclusion: "It took a botched job that needed fixing—and a fascinating 'other woman'—to show me what my marriage really needed."

BEHIND THE SCENES OF THE TRUE-LIFE DRAMA

"There are only two or three human stories," Willa Cather once said, "and they go on repeating themselves as fiercely as if they had never happened before." However, many people who experience life's most compelling dramatic events lack the skills to structure their story and put it on paper. The writer who can internalize other people's experiences and tell the story from that person's viewpoint has a handle on the elusive editorial pot of gold.

True-life drama stories are in demand by almost every editor—from general-interest publications like *Reader's Digest* to specialty, teenage, and women's magazines like *Ladies' Home Journal* and *Family Circle*. Sometimes real-life drama stories are ghostwritten, in which case the reader is led to believe the subject of the story is the author. In other cases, the by-line reads "as told to" or simply credits the free-lancer who researched and wrote the piece.

For example, in her *Family Circle* article "The Boy Who Cheated Death," Elaine Fein tells the dramatic story of Brian Hancock's agonizing fight for survival following a 1982 drowning accident when he was four years old. Deftly, Fein details the forty-eight critical hours in the hospital and weaves into the story information on the latest medical techniques used in Brian's case, plus quotes from physicians caring for him.

Fein opens Brian's story in the present (two years after the boy was pulled from icy waters on a Kentucky army base), then flashes back to the accident. This technique allows Brian's mother, Maureen, to tell what happened through dialogue with her other children who were at the scene and with rescuers, doctors, nurses, and others summoned to help her son, who by nearly every medical definition had already died. Fein then brings readers back to the present as she follows the case through months of slow recovery to Brian's clean bill of health a year later when neither his doctors nor his teachers could detect any sign to indicate he'd ever had an accident.

Real-life drama writers, like Fein, are skilled storytellers. They're masters in using fictional devices, such as scene setting, flashback, dialogue, conflict or crisis, suspense (will he or won't he survive?), and often, compression of time. (The shorter the time period, the greater the story's impact on the reader.) Action verbs, brief punchy sentences, and rapid rhythm of dialogue help project the dramatic quality and urgency of the situation.

The secret of writing successful real-life stories lies in accurately conveying the emotions associated with the drama. As in the best of stage plays, such emotion must be imparted—not directly by the author—but rather *indirectly* through the action, dialogue, and characterization of the person whose story is being told.

Getting inside the mind and heart of your subject so you can reveal his or her story requires skillful interviewing techniques and good "people skills." You need empathy, patience, intuition, and a sense of confidentiality akin to a psychiatrist's. Sensitivity to what's being said and what's behind the words helps in knowing when to probe further and when to call a halt. Drawing people out—especially those who aren't naturally talkative or accustomed to talking about their feelings—may require hours of your time and emotional energy.

To get the specific details that give a picture of the person or family she's interviewing, Elaine Fein says she visits the people personally, spends a lot of time with them, and talks to them as though they were *friends*.

"I'm very low-key because I'm really interested in how this happened and what they did about it. I'm very involved in every story I write—I really get into it completely in depth. I sort of immerse myself emotionally and yes, sometimes I cry," she says, adding, "I guess it just happens, but maybe that's why they come out so well."

12 □ MIND OVER MATTER

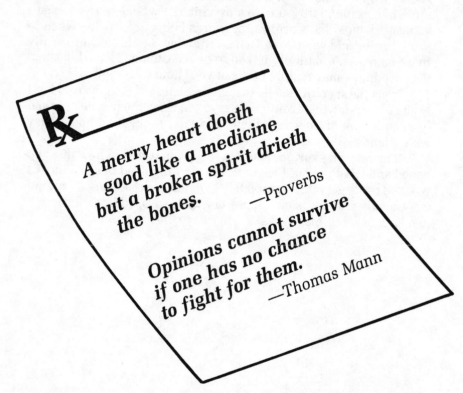

Rx

A merry heart doeth good like a medicine but a broken spirit drieth the bones. —Proverbs

Opinions cannot survive if one has no chance to fight for them. —Thomas Mann

Opinion, like variety, is the spice of life. While it's one thing to hold an opinion, it's even more satisfying to get paid while you present your strong feelings and argue your case in print. If you read *USA Today*, *Newsday*, the *Washington Post*, or other large-city newspapers, you already know the "op-ed" market. (Op-ed simply stands for the page where free-lance opinion pieces usually appear—opposite the editorials.)

Many magazines run *viewpoint* or *commentary* pages as well—publications like *American Way*, *Glamour*, *California Living*. *McCall's*, for example, pays $1,000 for 1,000-word Back Talk essays "in which the writer makes a firm statement of opinion, often taking an unexpected or unpopular point of view." *Woman's Day* calls its section "Reflections." Opinion pieces of 1,000 words here are worth $2,000. Topics can be controversial, but they must be convincing, say the editors. "We look for significant issues—medical ethics and honesty in marriage rather than the slight and trivial issues." Recent health and medically oriented essays have included Eda Le Shan's "Why Johnny Can't Sleep" and Martha Weinman Lear's "Down with High-Handed Health Care!"

Essays, of course, can be traced as far back as classical Greece and Rome. But it's Michael de Montaigne, who first paired words to the form as we know it around 1580, who's generally credited as "father of the essay." Once a thriving popular tradition, it lives today in various disguises—ranging from New Journalism and political or travel writing to op-eds and scientific meditations, like those of Dr. Lewis Thomas.

Among professional publications that use opinion pieces on medically related topics are *Private Practice* (Reader Forum); *American Medical News* (My Opinion); *New England Journal of Medicine* (Sounding Board); and *Journal of the American Medical Association* (A Piece of My Mind).

Ideal markets for beginning writers, op-ed pages offer writers a chance to speak up on pet peeves or causes; American customs, foibles, habits; politics, policy, education, law, language, life-styles—you name it, and most likely you can sell your point of view somewhere. Your point may be backed by quotes, statistics, and information from authorities, but the article must be *commentary*; subject, *topical*; and viewpoint, *yours*.

However, as in other markets, there are requirements for submissions, editorial needs, and, in some cases, seasonal lead times and taboos. *American Way*, for example, pays $200 for articles in its Seems to Me section. Nearly any topic is fair game—except religion, politics, or sex. Some publications want humor, others don't. Explicit sex and violence are taboos at *The New York Times*, while the *Christian Science Monitor* wants no op-eds on medical or psychological topics.

CONVINCING OPINIONS

Opinion pieces come in three forms: critiques/reviews, such as book reviews; essays/commentary; and satire or humor. Few writers ever master the last form, however; and no matter how hilarious your friends think you are when you *talk*, remember being funny *on paper* is extremely hard to pull off—even for the most talented free-lancers.

Beginning writers often find local issues and items are fertile topics for op-eds in community newspapers.

So the first rule, as with any other type of writing, is *study your market*. Review several local-issue op-ed articles your paper has already published. Check the word length, how articles are put together, what kinds of subjects have been covered, and from what point of view. (If you disagree with an op-ed piece already run, for instance, your first writing effort might take the form of a rebuttal.)

Once you've got your market targeted, *pick your topic*. It should be one you feel strongly about—and one you know enough about to be able to support or attack with *convincing* evidence to back up your opinion. In other words, readers will want to know why you feel as you do, what facts support your position, and why it behooves them to change their opinion to match yours. While you've got carte blanche to present your side, editors do want *informed* authors. If you merely want to sound off about a topic, write a letter to the editor and don't expect to be paid for it.

Although there are variations, opinion pieces basically follow a three-step pattern: they lead with a statement of opinion, move on to supporting examples and/or arguments pro or con, then wind up with a summary of major points covered in the piece and a restatement of the author's opinion. As you read Long Island, New York, college student Elizabeth Donovan's article, which appeared in *Glamour*, July, 1984, note how well this three-step format works to sell her "Viewpoint: As a Disabled Person, I May Never Exercise the Right to Die."

> I believe that a person who is severely sick or handicapped but mentally sound should have the right to die. Denying the right to refuse artificial or superhuman lifesaving treatment cruelly strips the sick of their most fundamental and, too often, their last measure of control.
>
> I was born with cystic fibrosis, a fatal disease primarily affecting the lungs and digestive system. Half of the people with CF die before they reach twenty-one—my age now. In addition, I've developed rheumatoid arthritis, a painfully crippling and degenerative disease of the joints. I have experienced firsthand what disease steals from life.
>
> Poor health has deprived me of both big and little pleasures that most people take for granted. Such routine tasks as shopping and getting dressed are now incredibly difficult or impossible. I walk slowly and can't stand for long periods of time. Even hugging someone is now painful for me.
>
> I also have to contend with looking ill. Sometimes I hardly recognize myself in the mirror, and I want to weep with longing for the way I once was. Over the years I have lost thirty pounds, and I'm unable to gain them back. My fingers and knees often swell from the arthritis.
>
> Socializing, too, is hard to manage. My best-laid plans for a night out can be ruined by an unexpected staircase or heavy door. Some friends have become scarce because they can't cope with their own

frightening feelings about illness. Able-bodied people often assume that if you're disabled, you're also asexual and mentally deficient. Our society makes life unnecessarily difficult and discouraging for people with disabilities by denying them the equality, respect and chance to make a living that able-bodied people take for granted. Some are understandably driven to despair.

A tragic example is Elizabeth Bouvia, the twenty-six-year-old Californian with cerebral palsy, who wanted to starve herself to death. She's a quadriplegic, dependent on other people for her survival. Bouvia, who holds a degree in social work, lost her will to live after learning that because of her handicaps she would probably never find work in her field. Her case is complicated because she needed a hospital's cooperation in order to die. The courts upheld the hospital's refusal to help Bouvia die, and I understand its difficult position. But I believe that Bouvia should be allowed to die if she wishes. She's the only one who can decide whether her life is worth living.

We'd like to believe that family and medical personnel always have a patient's best interests at heart. But those close to a sick person are often so preoccupied with their own needs that they ignore—or don't even perceive—the patient's wishes.

Several times a year I develop a respiratory infection that requires hospitalization for at least two weeks at a time. In the hospital, I receive oxygen, intravenous antibiotics and physical therapy. If one day I refused to be hospitalized again, it's certain I wouldn't live much longer. It's also certain that my family and doctors would protest vehemently. Whenever I've expressed doubts about wanting to continue my treatments, I've been told, "Don't be a quitter" or "You don't really feel that way."

Choosing to take my treatments gives me a sense of control over my life and helps me look toward the future hopefully. My life is worth living because the joy I experience outweights the hardship. But if I reach the point where I no longer wish to fight off death, I don't want to be forced to continue.

I want the same right to make life's major decisions as a person who is healthy. I may never exercise the right to die, but for my peace of mind, I need to know that I could.

This was not an easy article for Donovan to write. When I talked to her several months later, she said she had written several lengthy first drafts, then a final long one which she sent to *Glamour*. Editors, however, wanted 1,200 words and a more personal "I" approach, which they wrote into the piece for her. When Donovan saw the extensively edited and much shorter version of her viewpoint, she couldn't accept it. "They had given out the wrong message—it was almost exactly the *opposite* of what I wanted to say and I was very upset."

The idea for the Viewpoint piece had been suggested originally by the editors, she says, after her sister who is a free-lancer had queried *Glamour* about an article on dealing with family illness, describing her family background and Elizabeth's problems with cystic fibrosis. Editors turned down that article but later invited Elizabeth herself to submit an opinion piece from the viewpoint of a seriously ill person. It was her first attempt at writing for a magazine.

Had editors misunderstood her point of view in the original version of her manuscript? "I think it went through so many editors," says Donovan, adding, "I saw everybody's initials on it. I think they made assumptions about me and about illness and about the disabled which weren't true." But, she adds, "when I called to talk to them, they said, we want to work with you" and did. After her Viewpoint was published, Donovan says, *Glamour* received many letters to the editor. A few were supportive of her position. Sadly, "most people," she says, "*didn't* understand."

SHOULD YOU QUERY FIRST?

At publications where op-ed articles are assigned, queries are essential. One of these, for example, is the *St. Petersburg Times*, which runs authoritative articles on current political, economic, and social issues. However, most editors don't require queries, and accept articles "over the transom." *Newsweek*, for instance, accepts unsolicited manuscripts up to 1,100 words for its prestigious My Turn opinion column, which has run articles like Texas author Deborah Fallows's "What Day Care Can't Do" and New York philosophy professor Michael Levin's "The Case for Torture."

Since most op-ed articles run less than 1,200 words and may require relatively little research, many free-lancers simply write the piece, submit the manuscript on speculation—and skip the query altogether. (Does it make much sense, they ask, to write a 350- to 450-word letter about a 850-word article?) Free-lancer Paul Levine, whose op-eds have appeared in *Newsweek* and *The New York Times*, speaks for many other writers when he says, "I do not clear the idea for my articles with editors first for I feel this would place my writing under constraints I do not want to have."

In cases where you are a recognized author or have already established a relationship with an editor, a phone call outlining your idea is often enough to get a go-ahead. This is especially true if you have special expertise, experience, or other qualifications for writing such an op-ed piece.

Be sure, however, to include a covering letter with your opinion piece. Briefly describe it and give any particular qualifications you have for writing it. Enclose a self-addressed, stamped envelope for return of your submission. To keep track of their op-eds, some writers also enclose a self-addressed, stamped postcard. On it, they type the title of the article and name of the publication to which it's been sent, requesting that the editor indicate whether the piece has been accepted for publication.

Keep a separate file folder for each submitted manuscript (even those that don't sell). When your article is published, add the tearsheet and make extra photocopies. Then, if an editor asks for clippings of your work along with your next query, include one of your best op-eds.

RIGHTING THE RECORD

"What if" is the breeding ground of many a fiction writer's most creative plots. But *what if* can also turn into an op-ed writer's nightmare. What if, for example, you later come to feel that what you wrote the first time around not only needs updating, but worse yet, is potentially harmful to the public health? That's what happened to Frank A. Oski, M.D., a highly respected author, professor and chairman of pediatrics at the Johns Hopkins University School of Medicine.

In 1979 *The New York Times* had published his op-ed piece on the pluses of smoking. "I wrote the first article in the *Times* on a whim. I did not contact the *Times*—I merely wrote the article and sent it in. I did not contact the editor about the second article either. I just felt compelled to write it after the experience I had." Oski's "what if" was a heart attack. Here's the follow-up, titled "Doctor Stops Smoking Quickly."

"I smoke for my health," I proclaimed on *The New York Times* op-ed page in 1979.

Since I am a physician, this medical advice attracted amused attention. I reasoned that smoking made me cough and thus prevented pneumonia. Smoking made my heart go faster and eliminated need for additional exercise. Smoking curbed my appetite and kept me from getting fat. I no longer smoke for my health.

My health can't stand the help. At 51, I had a heart attack. I squandered my inheritance. Risk factors for early heart attacks include hypertension, diabetes, a family history of heart disease, abnormal blood lipid patterns, and smoking. All the risk factors that I had no control over were in my favor. I chose to smoke. Strange how the evidence that linked smoking to heart disease appeared equivocal to me last month, and now the same data appear overwhelmingly convincing.

Why stop now? Smokers who stop after their first heart attack have an 80 percent chance of living 10 more years—if they don't, a 60 percent chance.

As a smoker, I always resented the fact that we, as a group, received no gratitude, only scorn, from non-smokers. How could non-smokers know that smoking was bad for health if there were no smokers to prove it? Being a member of the experimental group, rather than the control group, deserves a certain measure of societal appreciation. I've done my time—I'm now ready to be a control.

Will I miss the late-night trips to find a store still open and selling cigarettes? Will I miss rummaging through ashtrays to find the longest butt that is still smokeable? Only time will tell. Not smoking may give me the time to find out.

Was it easy to stop? Sure. Here is all you have to do. First, experience a severe crushing pain under your breastbone as you finish a cigarette. Next, have yourself admitted to a coronary-care unit and stripped of your clothing and other belongings. Finally, remain in the unit at absolute bed rest for four days while smoking is prohibited. This broke my habit. See if it works for you.

LAUGHTER—GOOD HUMORS FOR BODY AND SPIRIT

"The arrival of a good clown," wrote Thomas Sydenham three centuries ago, "exercises a more beneficial influence upon the health of a town than of twenty asses laden with drugs." Called by some the "English Hippocrates," Sydenham is noted for his clinical observation and studies of the epidemic diseases, gout (from which he suffered), and hysteria—which today we call psychosomatic disease.

Many experts now give credence to theories that there's healing power in old-fashioned fun and smile-yourself-back-to-health humor. However, whether you can conquer certain diseases, like advanced cancers, or even hold them at bay with a positive attitude and good sense of humor is under debate.

Most famous of the medicine-of-mirth authors, of course, is former *Saturday Review* editor Norman Cousins. In his book *Anatomy of an Illness* he details the battle plan he devised with his doctor to counter the "negative effects of negative emotions" on body chemistry and speed his recuperation from a supposedly crippling, incurable disease. "Is it possible," he asked himself and his doctor, "that love, hope, laughter, and the will to live have therapeutic value?" His amazing recuperation may hold the answer—though some critics writing in the *New England Journal of Medicine* take issue with the theory of self-healing through positive thinking and the negative pressures that can accompany it. (A sense of humor, positive mental attitude, good social contacts, and happy life aren't enough to halt cancer's spread or prevent relapses, they say, and no one whose condition worsens should feel that somehow he or she failed in the psyche department.) Nevertheless, relaxation is a worthy goal in itself and laughter, indeed, good medicine.

Not only that, authors who can write truly humorous articles are in short supply. Be warned, though, that humor pieces face tough competition from regular columnists and syndicated writers such as Erma Bombeck and Art Buchwald. Every writer has a funny story to tell, but few sell. That's because what tickles one person's funnybone can leave another's untouched.

"Humor" said Mark Twain, "is the good-natured side of truth." The truth is, you can learn how to write almost any other kind of article, but no one can teach you how to be funny in print. However, there are techniques you can use to build reader identification and bring out a chuckle:

Put Yourself Down—Gently. Readers like to laugh *with* you as well as *at* you. Tell your story in *first person*—and shine at being a bumbler, goof-off, or health nut gone bananas with natural food, natural childbirth, or natural teenagers feeling their oats. Remember the father who at the end of a graduation ceremony rose to say a few special words: "My daughter has asked me not to talk too long, not to talk about her, and not to talk about the way things were when I was her age. So in conclusion. . . ." and former president Gerald Ford had made his point.

Make It Relate to Your Audience. Humor may be lighthearted, but never underestimate its potency as a device to help readers remember your message and *retain* complex material. Humor that's subtle has its charm. For maximum effect, though, make your message relevant to your audience—and make it *pointed.* For example, writes George Banks, M.D., in the August, 1983, issue of *Private Practice,* if your audience is physicians and your point is that this is a time of great medical progress and doctors must keep up, what better way to zero in on the need for continuing physician education than through a story like this:

> A medical school dean was asked, "Doesn't it bother you that your department heads continue to use the same examination questions over and over?"
>
> The dean answered, "No, not really. You see, we keep changing the answers."

Keep It in Good Taste. It may be obvious, but "sick" humor isn't healthy humor. Ribald humor may work for selected specialty magazines, but in general, most newspaper editors echo the sentiments of Robert Ramaker, commentary-page editor of the *Providence Journal*, who doesn't want anything unfit for family reading.

Keep It Short. It's hard to sustain humor for long, so aim for about 1,000 to 1,500 words at most. "If you use too many words, you lose *power*," explains Rob Dwyer, an Illinois community-art-center director who teaches humor writing and has written one-liners for professional comediennes including Joan Rivers and Phyllis Diller. Take a short, out-of-the-ordinary news item, give it a twist or humorous tag line, and you've created the kind of quip that the *New Yorker* buys.

You can sell short shorts—those smile-inducing fillers, jokes, or one-liners—to many tabloids and publications, among them *Modern Maturity, American Legion Magazine,* and *Reader's Digest.* The *Digest,* for example, pays $300 for up to 300-word, true, unpublished personal-experience stories with a humorous or appealing Americana slant. For items used in Laughter, the Best Medicine, minimum payment is $50. *American Health* offers $40 for humorous quotes and anecdotes on medicine or fitness—80 words or less.

Listen, Look, Learn to Recognize Funny Things—then Exaggerate. Everything you do has in it the seeds of humor. Particularly ripe are the everyday bits and pieces of living that usually go unnoticed. In "Country Air for Country Folks," James Gorman pokes good-natured fun at the preventive-health inconsistencies the average city-dweller exercises during summer vacation living. The serious undercurrents of his message, however, are ignored at one's peril. Here are the opening lines from the article, which appeared in the June, 1984, issue of *American Health:*

> Last summer in upstate New York, where the skies are clear and the mountains are high, I was standing in the yard of our summer cabin, breathing the healing country air . . . when I realized that I was actually breathing charcoal lighter fluid. My thoughts, which had been running in the pastoral mode, came to a dead halt.
>
> I also realized that earlier in the day I had breathed deeply of gasoline when I filled the mower to do the lawn. And the night before I had been so liberal with the hornet spray while attacking the yellow-hornet nest that I could still taste synthetic pyrethrins mingled with the beer I was drinking.
>
> The next day, in the garden, I would be inhaling powdered chicken manure, and polyurethane fumes when I finished varnishing the floor in our cabin's back room. Then I would go fishing, with a cigar, after having painted every visible patch of skin with an insect

repellent proven in Vietnam.

Paul had his road to Damascus, I had my charcoal lighter fluid. I realized that something had happened to me. In Manhattan I had always taken good care, some might have said obsessively good care, of my health. I never painted anything. I wore a mask to breathe. And here I was, having some sort of rural seizure that made me expose myself willingly to chemicals and sharp tools.

I put together a tally sheet to see how bad it was.

Gorman uses his tally sheet to compare four categories of city-versus-country activities: eating, breathing, drinking, and risk-taking activities. Here's how his country eating habits stack up:

City: Bok choy, chicory, arugula, shallots, shiitake mushrooms, some tofu, pasta, sole (broiled), yogurt, whole grains, vitamins.

Now that, I thought, is the kind of diet that will get you into the "Living" section of the New York Times. Unfortunately, it looked not only fashionable, but suspiciously healthy. And what did I really eat in the country? I looked with dread at the grill in front of me—barbecue.

Country: Pork—sausages, ribs, chops, roasts, usually barbecued; chicken (barbecued); steak (barbecued); venison; hamburgers (barbecued); eggs (fried); pancakes and waffles, with butter and maple syrup; potato chips; corn doodles (when fishing); fish (from local streams with PCBs); Twinkies; Reese's Peanut-Butter Cups and fudge (when hiking); garden vegetables the bugs didn't get (mostly zucchini.)

This diet could also get me into the newspaper—the obituary page. Not only were vegetables lacking from my fresh air fare, but I had fallen into thinking that as long as I was hiking and swimming and cutting wood, I was entitled to Twinkies and candy bars and those spicy little sausage sticks made of processed pork pieces and neurotoxins. They go so well with beer. . . .

After leading us down the Love-Canal-path, Gorman exits with a surprising twist.

Obviously the city was the healthier place to be, at least in the summer. And I hadn't even put acid rain on the tally. If I cared about my health, I had to do something to save me from country vacations, and I did. I moved out of the city.

During the winter, out here in the country, there's no bug spray, no barbecue, no lawn. There's no fishing and no canoeing. I don't paint anything.

Come August, when the country gets unhealthy, we're going on vacation. Where?

New York, here I come.

Gorman, who's also written a book, *First Aid for Hypochon-driacs*, lets us in on his sense of humor by the way he structures and develops his basic idea—unhealthy things we do on vacation we'd never be caught dead doing the rest of the year—or would we? You, too, can learn to structure and develop your writing more effectively so that it appeals to an editor's sense of humor.

Don't Take Being Funny Lightly. Humor writers are serious professionals when it comes to reliability, manuscript packaging, and craftsmanship. So meet your deadline, complete the nitty-gritty follow-up correspondence and record keeping. As for rewriting and reworking your funniest lines, grin and bear it—then laugh your way to the bank.

Collect and Dissect Examples of Good Humor Writing. Keep a file of humor articles that appeal to you. Make a photocopy you can mark up or cut apart. Note the main theme. Check the anecdotes and placement of examples which build on the basic idea. What's the tone of the dialogue (if any), and where does the author fit into the story? Try to pin down what it is in the article that most appeals to your sense of humor. Notice the pacing, rhythm, word order. Experiment. Take the paragraphs apart and move them around. Is something lost in the telling? Something gained?

Next time you have an idea that lends itself to a similar humor format, use these examples as structural models. Rest assured, you won't stifle your own brand of humor. Sound structure and craftsmanship only *enhance* it.

Lead with a Grabber and Leave 'Em Laughing. No matter what your style, you must set up the *expectation* of humor at the outset. Don't wait. And don't promise readers, "Stick with me, folks, it'll be funny in a minute." Set the tone for humor, and launch into it. Add a visual dimension with vivid writing, and your readers will hit the humor jackpot—words *plus* mental images to chuckle over.

Do this with a catchy title, like "Getting in Touch with My Male-ness," and you're off to a fast start in the fun-mental-pictures department. With tongue in cheek, *San Francisco Chronicle* columnist Jon Carroll sets out on this gender-laden quest. In the opening lines, he tells us why. (Hector, by the way, was the bravest of the Trojans, but his name is forever linked to bullying and torment by words.)

> Lately, it seems, the popular press has been filled with hectoring articles encouraging men persons to get in touch with their male-ness. Such contact, it is alleged, will lead to deeper self-understand-ing, a more positive self-image, and a greater ability to deal with household appliances.

I have always been a bit dubious about the advantages of increased self-understanding—most of the true villains of the world seem to excel in self-understanding—but the overwhelming critical tone of the articles finally got to me. I was forced to confess that I had not yet gotten in touch with my maleness; I was compelled to promise that I would make the attempt.

Easier said, of course, than done. My maleness doesn't just hang around the house waiting for me to engage it in conversation. . . .

We know Carroll is in for trouble. Here's an elusive "maleness" out on the town and out in the world. In the next three sentences, we've sighted Macho himself at work and at play. Getting in touch is not going to be a piece of cake:

Sometimes it [his maleness] travels to Alaska on a whim, to pick up a few dollars working on the pipeline, and it leaves no forwarding address. It pretends occasionally that it goes on mountain-climbing expeditions in South America, although I suspect that it just checks into a cheap motel in Manhattan Beach and spends the daylight hours watching ESPN. Often, it's at the track, talking out of the side of its mouth and making arcane calculations in the margins of the Racing Form.

Poking fun at himself, Carroll describes the humiliation of having to call poker-playing friends, like Bobbo, to ask if they know where his "maleness" might be at the moment. Bobbo, who works in television, adds insult to injury. "It's 11 o'clock; do you know where your maleness is?" And so it goes, a frustrating chase from bar to bar. Carroll gives up, but not without salvaging his male ego.

So that was that. Not very successful. Still, it was better than the time I tried to get in touch with the feminine side of my nature.

That was a real disaster.

But you know women.

Humor may come to you spontaneously, but the resulting article will still have to meet publication guidelines to sell. Satire, for example, will have a better chance at the New Yorker or Esquire than it will at Family Weekly or Reader's Digest. Paradies and spoofs require an audience thoroughly acquainted with what's being spoofed, and irony (the stock-in-trade of many a columnist) becomes tedious under the wrong pen.

The biggest humor market is for light humor—those gentle pokes at human nature that all of us can identify with. But you must select your market with care. If you can identify it before you write, you're that much further ahead.

WRITING TO INSPIRE

Some critics might say it's splitting hairs to distinguish certain types of mind-over-matter stories from personal-experience pieces. Yet there is a difference, if only a subtle one. Not all personal-experience stories, interesting as they may be, *inspire* or *encourage* others.

Health-related mind-over-matter books or articles not only convince us we've come in contact with a truly unusual human being, they nudge us to reevaluate our own attitudes, values, beliefs—and to rethink what's important to us. Writing that inspires gives us a lift, reaffirms meaning where once things seemed meaningless. Perhaps the singular gift of such writing is that it can restore *hope*—which French novelist Honore de Balzac once described as "a light diet, but very stimulating."

Take, for example, the story of Patty Wilson, which was first told in *Family Weekly* by Sheila Cragg in 1977. Titled "Patty Wilson's Magnificent Marathon," the article recounted how Patty, then a fifteen year old who had epilepsy, had run 1,300 miles and set a distance record for women—long before distance running was commonplace for women, much less for anyone with epilepsy, a disorder marked by recurrent convulsions.

Overnight Patty had become a national inspiration, as detailed in a *FW* follow-up story a year later. For weeks after the original article first appeared, the Wilsons received letters and telephone calls from all over the United States. A young man in prison wrote to say Patty had inspired him to do something positive with his life.

A film producer took the article to Universal Studios, which developed plans for a two-hour movie on Patty in conjunction with ABC television. A Harper & Row editor asked Cragg (whose son also has epilepsy) to write a book on Patty. *Reader's Digest* reprinted the story in its April issue, and a textbook company condensed it for fourth and seventh grade readers as well as into braille and recordings for the blind.

"Pied Piper" Patty continued to run. She set a goal of raising $2 million in an attempt to increase the public's awareness of epilepsy and reduce the stigma faced by people having the disorder. Her courage and determination had touched others, and she continued to receive letters from people with epilepsy and other handicaps. Her story was a challenge to others. Her motto: "I haven't been stopped because of epilepsy. I never will."

Another case in point is that of Agnes de Mille. One of America's most dynamic dance artists, she almost died in her mid-sixties when she suffered a massive stroke just as she was about to go onstage for one of her famous lecture-demonstrations. A heart attack followed. Her right side was totally paralyzed. Only Herculean effort of body and will allowed de Mille to perform the most mundane of movements.

"I was once able easily to do 144 reves, 64 fouette pirouettes and hold prolonged balances on full point," she says in her book Reprieve: A Memoir. "But that trip to the bathroom, which, of course, became my habitual path, was as big an achievement. And it involved terror, which the ballet stunts did not."

Why did she write the book? "Well, because I survived," she said in a 1981 interview with San Francisco Examiner dance critic Allan Ulrich, "and came through to a better way of living, even though there was no body to support it."

Psychologists tell us that in order to succeed at whatever they're doing, people need to develop skills and a strong belief in their capabilities. New studies, which show self-confidence improves health, also indicate people are more likely to quit smoking or recover quickly from heart attacks if they believe they can do it. Such research brings new respectability to the link between mind and body.

Is it too far-fetched to imagine a day when a doctor's prescription for medication or treatment might also read: "Take three mind-over-matter articles twice a day, swallow their message, and believe in your own inner strengths." What kinds of articles would do the trick?

Stories of success in the face of incredible obstacles, like those of Agnes de Mille and Patty Wilson, are one type. In the same class are "tributes" to people who surmount tragedy or disaster and help others to live in a creative way. In a tribute to his wife, Mary, which appeared in Good Housekeeping, April, 1985, Lee Iacocca tells of his first wife's lifelong struggle with diabetes and of her inner strength which supported the whole family in times of crisis—one of which was his being fired by Ford Motor Company. But there are three other kinds of inspirationals which lend themselves to health-related themes: art-of-living, lessons-to-live-by, and slice-of-life articles.

State of the Art of Living

Art-of-living articles usually are personal experiences which fall into two categories: one is an upbeat sharing of the joy of living—e.g., finding renewal in nature or new strength in family or friendship. The other type depicts a personal problem in the psychological area and tells how the writer found ways to overcome it. Low-key self-help is the heart of these motivational articles which, some say, double as the poor man's psychiatrist.

Suzanne Massie, for example, in her Family Circle piece "Getting to Know You," opens with the global scene—"Every living thing needs space to breathe and grow"—then zeroes in on the need each of us has "to preserve within ourselves, a space for breathing and growing that is nourished and fed in our own individual way." Her message: developing the inner self is a creative effort. When life is busiest, one must make time to smell the daisies and concentrate on one's own individuality.

In a *Reader's Digest* piece titled "Lessons from Aunt Grace," Nardi Reeder Campion describes how six surprisingly simple steps to happiness revealed in a Victorian woman's diary helped her to become more involved with others, and, hence, less "buried" in herself. The opening lines read so smoothly, it's easy to overlook how much they convey in four sentences.

> The day we moved away I hit bottom. Saying good-by to my friends and to the house I had loved made me feel as though my mooring had been ripped loose. Now, in what my husband kept calling "our new home" (it wasn't new and it wasn't home), I was so awash in self-pity that I almost ignored the white-leather book I found while unpacking an old trunk. But something prompted me to examine it.

Opening her great-aunt's diary, Campion stumbles onto six rules of living which helped her Aunt Grace always look on the bright side of life. Unmarried, unemployed, forced to live with relatives, and grieving over the death of her sweetheart in the Spanish-American War, Aunt Grace seemed to have all the cards stacked against her. Yet Campion tells us what she remembers most about this plain and frail woman was her unfailing cheerfulness.

That her aunt forced herself to map out a plan for conquering the gloom which engulfed her comes as a shock. Campion quotes from the diary:

> My unhappiness is a bottomless cup. I know I must be cheerful, living in this large family upon whom I am dependent, yet gloom haunts me. . . . Something has to change or I shall be sick. Clearly my situation is not going to change; therefore, I shall have to change. But *how?*

Campion's personal awakening occurs when she reads Grace's solution.

> The simplicity of Aunt Grace's rules-to-live-by took my breath away. She resolved every day to:
> 1. Do something for someone else.
> 2. Do something for myself.
> 3. Do something I don't want to do that needs doing.

4. Do a physical exercise.
5. Do a mental exercise.
6. Do an original prayer that always includes counting my blessings.

What distinguishes the art of living article from other how-to's is its highly personal, philosophical—and sometimes faith-oriented—underpinnings.

(For religious markets, faith, of course, plays a much greater role—but even then, religion must be integral to the piece. "When faith does play a part in your story, don't hesitate to present it," advises Dina Donahue in *Writing to Inspire*. "But never drag religion in simply to justify yourself as a Christian writer. Spirituality should be evident in your caring, your feelings, your awareness of others. An inspirational story should be as well written as a secular one.")

Sources of Inspiration
Without three vital elements, no story will inspire anyone else: The reader must care enough to become involved; she must have a stake in the outcome; there must be takeaway value—an added dimension *beyond* entertainment or information. It's this twist, this final warm note of positive encouragement or insight, which inspires the reader to work on her own problem, see the wonder in nature, believe in herself or try harder.

Ideas for inspirational articles often come from people you know, conversations overheard, or problems you've struggled to resolve. Another tack is to take abstract concepts, such as truth, honesty, gratitude, or guilt, which pose psychological dilemmas and look at either the positive or negative side. (The truth *doesn't* set you free, for example, is a negative; honesty is the best policy, a positive approach.)

Books of printed sermons for ministers can help those who write "devotionals" separate the inspirational wheat from the chaff. In her book, *Writing Articles that Sell*, writing instructor and author Louise Boggess says, "other suitable subjects are: never say never, "thank you" is a good habit, the helpful hand, the forgiving heart, the contented mind, self-pity, the best you have. A good way to find these subjects is to think of the personality traits of your friends and acquaintances. Are they grasping, self-centered, generous, positive thinkers?"

Lessons to Live By
If you've got friends in high places, celebrity inspirationals make highly salable articles, In 1983, for example, *Guideposts* magazine told how four prominent Americans discovered the enduring value of

some simple "lessons to live by." Arlene Francis talked about learning to listen; actor Pat O'Brien discussed doing something with all your might, even if the task seems thankless; television's Willard Scott and Walter Cronkite told about problems they'd encountered in the media and how they solved them. Cronkite's theme was "watch for the gray areas" and dealt with the vigilance honesty requires of anyone who's going to stay clear of ambiguity.

Each of these authors opened the "lesson" by relating an experience any reader could identify with—an experience that, in fact, conveyed the opposite trait (or wrong image) of the main theme of the article. Cronkite's tale dealt with a one-dollar watch in a local drugstore he'd wanted as a youngster. With no money to pay for it and no clear way of earning any, he had nonetheless talked the druggist into letting him have it while paying on time. When Cronkite's mother learned of the deal, however, she made him return it. In her eyes, her son had taken advantage of another person's trust. Though no dishonesty had been involved, she saw it as one of life's tricky "gray areas" to be aware of, and so warned him—a lesson that had stood him in good stead all these years.

This lead is typical of many art-of-living pieces. After setting up the *wrong* image, the writer then proceeds to show the changes that took place in his thinking or actions and what brought them about. The message may be implied or explicit, but it's always clear: you the reader can profit by the writer's experience.

Slice of Life
One of the most popular types of mind-over-matter articles is the "slice-of-life" piece. Its success depends on the writer's ability to sense the germ of a *story* idea in everyday happenings or casual remarks that others miss or downplay.

This column by the Reverend John V. Ryan of Las Vegas ran in the *Las Vegas Sun*. Although it was written during the Christmas holidays, Harrah's hotels and Casinos (which owns the Las Vegas Holiday Inn/Holiday Casino) reprinted "A Brighter Vision" a few months later in its in-house publication *Harrah*scope*.

> Perhaps it's the Christmas spirit, but during the past few days I've witnessed such shining manifestations of good will.
> Standing in line briefly for the Holiday Inn buffet, I was finally seated. An elderly woman was at the next table quite close to mine, (why do the tables at buffets have to be pressed together?) and she was eating very little. A busy waitress approached her.
> "You're Mabel, aren't you?"
> "Yes."

"I've waited on you many times. Thought I remembered your name. What's the matter, deary, you're hardly touching your food?"

"I thought I could eat something, but I'm not hungry. I have to go to the hospital. The doctor said they're going to try to do something to my heart." Tears clouded the aged eyes. "It's hard. My husband's at home. He's blind."

"Now you listen to me," the waitress said, "I don't want you to try to get there by yourself. Here, I'll write my name and phone number on the check slip. You just call me when you need a ride to the hospital, and I'll pick you up." The waitress, indeed a beautiful person, smiled and hurried to wait on another table.

Short and sweet, the piece speaks for itself. Adding to its punch is the fact that the incident occurred in *Las Vegas*—the gaming mecca hardly known for its compassionate image. Father Ryan sets the scene with his presence, then bows out, knowing the dialogue will enable us to "see" the two women in a way no description ever could. The structure here, as in many inspirational articles, is basically factual, but the "feel" of the piece stems from fictional devices, i.e., dialogue, staging, complications, and resolution. The "slice of life" unfolds through real-life emotion, concern, and action.

MAKING THE POINT WITH PUNCH

For dynamic writing, keep "inspirational" adjectives to a minimum. In other words, stay out of the way of the story. Descriptives like *courageous, awe-inspiring, heroic, noble,* or *selfless* are much more effective if they come from quotes of witnesses, co-workers, family, or teammates. See if you don't agree after reading this sports story from the *Reno Gazette-Journal:*

Kevin Leneker was born with no right arm and with little muscle development on the right side of his body, but that doesn't stop the 11-year-old youngster from being second baseman.

When he's in the field, he catches the ball with a gloved left hand, and almost in one motion he tucks the glove under his right arm, extracts the ball and makes a defensive play.

When he's at the plate, he guides the bat with his artificial right arm while he applies the power with the left.

Leneker, who plays for the Napavine, Wash., Little League Minor Team, is in his third year of Little League baseball. He played a year of T-ball and one year in the minors before missing a year with an injury. But he got back into the swing of things this season.

Because of his style, Leneker's teammates awarded him a trophy, inscribed, "Mr. Inspirational Award."

"He does everything he wants to do and he does not quit," his mother Diana said. "He looks ahead to new challenges, new things to accomplish. I'm really proud of him."

THE ULTIMATE CHALLENGE

Being able to write so that your words help people to "see" events, situations, experiences, or handicaps, illness, even death in a different light is the first step in *selling* such pieces. The second is convincing readers the effort is worthwhile.

But there's more to it than meets the eye. To be genuine, the message of hope cannot be *canned*. This is no place for tacked-on morals, sermonettes, preachiness, or Pollyannas. Embellishing the truth to the point where your article loses its reader-payoff value will not only cost you a sale, but bore an editor along the way.

The mind-over-matter challenge is no small one. Once you as a writer have met it, your task is to inspire the reader to go and do likewise. The enticement? At its best, such writing can inspire one to rise above a problem through hope and positive thinking—a personal renaissance. But at the least, inspirational writing can lead to renewed awareness of the wonders of planet Earth—and the finer qualities of those who share it.

13 □ PROPOSING AND PROMOTING YOUR BOOK

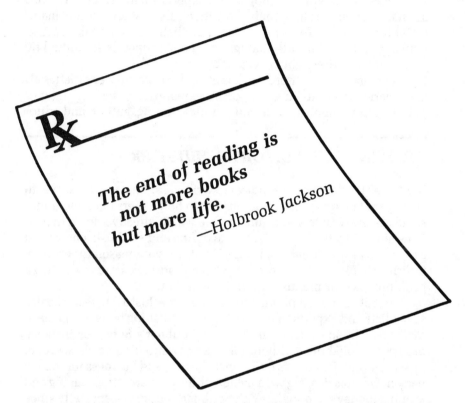

The end of reading is not more books but more life.
—Holbrook Jackson

Early in spring, 1985, a California literary agency polled editors of both hard- and soft-cover books to find out about their interest in various categories of books and to determine which were the most and least popular. Responses from 118 editors revealed the least popular category is parapsychology (only 25 percent showed any interest at all). The *most* popular—with 72 percent of editors indicating interest—is general health and healing.

It's not surprising when you consider that "health" is targeted as one of "10 Forces Reshaping America" by *U.S. News & World Report* and other nation-watchers. However, an idea for a book in this category is only the beginning. Editors also take a good hard look at the writer—and most often what they want is an author or coauthor who's an *expert* on the topic or *specialist* in the field.

"In the book market today," Bantam Books executive editor Toni

Burbank said at a national writers' conference, "the phenomenon of the expert main authors—the M.D's, the Ph.D.'s with the collaborators who are now getting full credit—is an increasingly important phenomenon. We're looking for the expert credentials."

If health is a winning subject and experts are in demand, why do so many health professionals find themselves stuck with a manuscript that bounces from publisher to publisher with no takers? And why are so many carefully thought out book proposals submitted by independent writers going begging?

Each book and author is different, and no one answer satisfies all the vagaries of publishing today. But no manuscript sees the light of publication without the right mix of idea, timing, author, and editor.

APPLYING THE EDITOR'S YARDSTICK

Most health-related books today are written for four main reasons: to share personal experience and insight; to help others help and understand themselves; to add to and update what's already known in medicine and allied health fields; and to define and establish a new field as a viable professional discipline. Whatever your reason for wanting to write a book, you need to know what editors look for in evaluating a book proposal or manuscript and the author.

First of all, not all publishers are the same. Just as there are health specialists and experts in certain fields, publishing houses, too, have their areas of specialization. (Charles Scribner's Sons, for instance, has been publishing self-help for nearly twenty-five years, with emphasis on practical books on science, health, and business for the layperson. Queries dealing with babies, children, parenting, making and keeping money are popular with Scribner's editors—especially since there's renewed nationwide interest in having children.)

Go to the bookstore and your library. Look at publishers' catalogs and book review sections. Take a look at *Publishers Weekly, The New York Times Book Review*, and *Books in Print*. Find out who the publishers are in the subject areas you're interested in. (For specifics, consult the discussion in chapter 3.)

In evaluating proposals, editors consider where the book might fit in their overall marketing plan. Basically, publishing houses have four types of lists: the *best-seller, frontlist, midlist, and backlist*. The frontlist is made up of the publisher's new releases, the books making their debut this season. Every publisher dreams of coming out with a best-seller; but at the very least, a book is expected to earn a profit or attract favorable attention before being remaindered. The mainstays of publishing, however, are the backlist books which keep on selling months and years after they've first been published. In other words, they've got *staying power.* Their authors make good money—and so does the publisher. (The midlist is an author's limbo—books that were published but perished, books that didn't stay around long enough to make it to the backlist.)

Editorial success lies in identifying the backlist book. (There are also books that fit neatly in no list—one-shot topics that do well because they meet the needs of a specific market at a given time.) Occasionally, an editor will pinpoint a subject ripe for the backlist or a given market, get approval to commission a book on it, then approach a literary agent or go directly to a writer and try to interest him or her in writing it. More often, though, the idea for a book is submitted through an agent or directly by the author.

What does it take to *sell* the editor on the idea? "Nonfiction books need to answer a question to something that fills a need," explains Viking Penguin Inc. editor Amanda Vaill. "Books are marketed—not to readers' interest and desire to know—but to their *need to know* and/ or *need to be entertained.*" (It's a subtle distinction, but one that can mean the difference between an advance on your book and a pile of rejection slips filed with a book proposal or manuscript.)

At the time, I was trying to convince Vaill that there was indeed a market for a book on grandparenting in the new extended his-hers-and-theirs family. I offered statistics on first-time grandparents and pointed out that many who baby-sit on a regular basis for career mothers or single parents are basically parenting the second time around—with less energy, often less enthusiasm, and more headache as child-rearing practices have changed and children themselves are subject to greater stress.

Vaill, however, was not convinced this was a market of roughly 20,000 buyers "willing to shell out about $17.95 for such a book." Her point was this: the proposal did not speak to a *crisis/grabber situation* which would make a person say, "I've got to know more about that; I've got to *have* that book." Grandparents, especially, she thought, would feel secure enough after raising their own families to "wing it" the second time around. Frankly, I still believe there's a market for a book targeted to the "new" grandparents, but Vaill has convinced me that a revised proposal must address a crisis/situation that grandparents *haven't* faced before and are having difficulty coping with now. One idea: grandparent visitation rights.

MATCHING BOOK IDEA AND EDITOR

Approaching an editor through an agent is easier because agents know what certain houses are looking for or what a specific editor's interests are, have access to publishers and can make the intitial contact—which often is the hardest part. But whether you submit a proposal on your own or go through an agent, you'll have to convince an editor that:

- *there's a market for the book,* and it's big enough to make publishing your book worthwhile.
- *this book reaches that market and you're the person to write on the subject.* Perhaps you're an authority in the field, you've teamed up with someone who is, or you know whom to talk to and how to reach the experts who have the information your audience wants.
- *you have the skills* to write a popular book (or professional book, if that's your audience).
- *you can cover the subject,* do the research, organize the material, and turn in the manuscript on time.

We're talking about a major selling job—but that's the nature of the publishing business. "It's a selling process all the way down the line," Simon & Schuster senior editor Bob Bender explained at a New York writers' conference. "The bookseller has to sell the book buyer—the reader who walks in the store. We have a sales rep who has to sell the book to the bookseller. The editor within the house has to sell the book to the sales rep, and you've got to sell the book to the editor."

If you're Norman Cousins, Jane Fonda, Benjamin Spock, or another author with a track record of successful books, the welcome mat is out at publishing houses for any and all ideas you may come up with. But if you've never written a nonfiction book before, you must give serious thought to the selling process and how you'll go about it.

PROPOSING TO AN EDITOR

A book proposal begins with a letter, similar to the query letters described in chapter 4. Some editors want to see this letter first. If interested in your book, they'll ask to see a more detailed proposal including a table of contents, a sample chapter or two, and "sales ammunition" which can be used in selling the book to senior editors and staff marketing specialists. Don't propose your book idea over the telephone or drop into an editor's office to discuss it uninvited.

"What I want is a good letter," says one New York editor. "Tell me about the book you propose to write, why you think the book should be written, and what you've got to say about the subject that no one else has said. It doesn't hurt to say these are the only books on the subject—here's what they don't do and what *mine does.*"

"The covering letter is really crucial," explains Simon & Schuster's Bob Bender. "You have to be able to get your point across quickly in one or two pages, because everybody in the publishing house has to do the same thing." Simply put, to sell your book, you have to get to the *essence* of it rapidly, because everyone—from the editor who takes your book before an editorial board to the publisher's rep who persuades a bookseller to give it window display—must also get to the heart of its selling points quickly.

For example, if a book rep has a list of, perhaps, 100 titles, he's doing well if he has the bookstore owner or manager's ear for *two or three minutes per book.* Says one Little Professor bookseller, "If a title piques my interest, I may spend a bit more time, but in general, I make up my mind to take a book or not in less than three minutes—add it up for yourself, and you'll see the total time spent on just one publisher's list."

Here are some guidelines for putting together a complete and effective proposal. They can help you organize your material and alert you to those items editors consider important. Only you, of course, can decide how best to present the *total* package so that it becomes an effective selling tool for the book you want to write.

● *Choose your book title carefully.* Don't underestimate the selling value of a catchy title that sums up what the book is all about. "Nobody believes a title is absolutely vital to the success of a proposal," says one editor, "But that doesn't mean it's not important. It helps the author focus his material and it gives our promotion and ad people something to get their arms around."

● *Show how you expect to organize the book's contents.* Be sure there's an internal logic to the way you arrange your material—a natural flow in how the theme is developed. Many writers find it works best to go through their research and other materials; sort them into related groupings; then label and file each group in a separate folder, and work from these to come up with chapter headings.

By reviewing the folder's contents, you can also provide brief chapter descriptions which will meet the editor's requirements for chapter outlines. Sometimes I write a paragraph or two detailing the chapter's contents; other times, I simply separate phrases using the three-dot-method.

● *Talk about your primary sources of information and how you plan to gather it.* (Will you be interviewing patients? Talking to families? Mailing questionnaires? Which experts will you consult? How much data have you already collected? How much more do you need?)

● *Give your credentials as well as those of your coauthor if you have one.* Include any expertise in medicine or allied health fields, your publishing credits, and any personal experience or education that makes you the person best qualified to write the book.

● *Don't dwell on competing books but mention obvious ones.* The editor will find out anyway, and this gives you a chance to point out how your book differs, why it needs to be written at this time and which audiences your book will appeal to. "More and more writers," says one editor, "are doing their own market surveys and telling editors what the competition is and what specific books are out there and why the other books aren't as good as this particular one will be."

● *Enclose a sample chapter but don't send artwork.* (You can mention availability of graphics, photos, or illustrations in your covering letter and proposal, but don't send the originals.) Select a chapter of about twenty to twenty-five pages (or excerpts from a couple of chapters) which shows off your style to advantage and accurately represents the tone and approach you'll take in the book as a whole.

● *Refine the message of your book to the point where you can state it succinctly in a sentence or two.* If you have a quote, anecdote, or statistic that illustrates the point you're trying to make, use it in the lead of your proposal. Remember, you want to hook the editor so she'll keep reading.

● *Let your enthusiasm for the project come through your words.* If you're not excited about it, who will be?

Here's a draft of the cover and first pages Ann Giudici Fettner and William A. Check submitted in their proposal for a book on immune-suppressant diseases. Published in 1984 by Holt, Rinehart and Winston, the award-winning book ultimately was titled: *The Truth about AIDS: Evolution of an Epidemic.*

Cover Page

PROPOSAL FOR A BOOK

Aids: Homosexual Killer Diseases

Ann Giudici Fettner and William A. Check, Ph.D.

This proposal includes the following:
   A. *Description of the subject*
   Method of structuring the book
   Use of consultants/interviewees
   Length and time-frame

B. Outline of chapters and sections
The Introduction

First Page

PROPOSAL FOR A BOOK
Aids: Homosexual Killer Diseases
Ann Giudici Fettner and William A. Check, Ph.D.

a full-length medical/health book for the lay reader dealing with a mysterious, increasingly prevalent and deadly group of viral and other infections

Subject
The proposed book concerns a newly identified disease which over the past two years has caused more than 300 deaths, principally among young homosexual men. The cause of acquired immune deficiency is not known and there is much speculation concerning its origin. While hope exists that science will soon resolve the numerous problems presently obscuring possible prevention and treatment, the complex and novel nature of the illness holds out little hope for a speedy solution.

Of those dying, one-third have contracted Kaposi's sarcoma, a rare type of cancer. *This is the first human cancer ever to have occurred in epidemic form.*

Sixty percent of AIDS patients suffer from *pneumocyctitis carinii,* a rare, usually fatal form of pneumonia. These . . .

A major selling point in dealing with such a timely topic comes on page four of the proposal: the authors estimate the book will be approximately 300 pages, or 130,000 words including illustrations, glossary, and index. They state that they expect to deliver a first draft within four months of contractual agreement with the publisher, with a final draft forthcoming two months later. "Everyone said the book wouldn't even get into print before 'the doctors' solved it (the illness)," comments Fettner. "But my gut feeling was quite the opposite: I'd seen too much strange illness in Africa during the years I worked there."

MULTIPLE SUBMISSIONS

In their book *How to Get Happily Published,* Judith Appelbaum and Nancy Evans take up the question of multiple submissions of the same proposal. Innovative literary agents, they note, have been catalysts in changing the way manuscripts and proposals are submitted to publishers. (For example, literary auctioning of manuscripts, inaugurated by New York megabuck agent Scott Meredith in 1952, still is limited primarily to celebrity and name authors.)

But even a first-time author can submit a manuscript or proposal to more than one publisher or agent simultaneously—the so-called "multiple submission"—as long as he or she is up front about it. If you decide on this route, take a tip from professional editors Appelbaum and Evans: Tell each editor and/or agent what you're doing.

"Don't use the words 'multiple submission,' " they say in their book. "They act as a red flag to many editors, who resent being asked to spend time considering a manuscript that they may have to compete for if they decide they want it. Formulations like 'Several publishers have expressed interest' or 'I'm exploring publication possibilities with a number of houses' should serve to keep editorial dispositions relatively unruffled."

Remember, the editor you send your material to may indeed like your idea and want to publish your book. But decisions at most publishing houses are made by committees of senior editors, with input from the sales manager and chief of marketing. If you receive a phone call with the good news that everybody likes your idea for a book, the next step is agreeing on money, a deadline, a contract.

If you receive a negative response, keep circulating your proposal. What makes one editor's eyes glaze over in boredom may make the next editor's pupils dilate with excitement. And it only takes one publisher to say yes to get your book published. You may also want to consider the self-publishing option or query a small press that specializes in your type of book and subject area.

A BOOK BY ANY OTHER NAME . . .

In discussing your book, an editor may use terms like: "We see this book coming out as a *trade book* and then possibly a *quality paperback*, but it's highly unlikely it will go to a *mass-market paperback*."

The term *trade* refers to books—both fiction and nonfiction—that are sold to a general audience. Paperback is a division of trade publishing. The mass-market paperback is the typical four-by-seven-inch paperback you see in supermarkets, airports, bookstores, and the like. Quality paperbacks are often larger than the standard newsstand paperback and sometimes printed more carefully on better quality stock with a more durable cover. Scholarly books, textbooks, and special interest books may be hardcover or paperback. Although, according to my friends who are medical librarians, *all books*, regardless of type and size, are officially termed *monographs*, general usage of the term confines it to a particular type of publication.

HEALTH AND MEDICAL MONOGRAPHS

Mention monographs, and the image that most often pops to mind is the thin, scholarly treatise that fills a need between two extremes—the longer scientific article and skimpy minibook. "Although they vary in nature, monographs are generally a type of scholarly publication," says University of Nevada—Reno journalism professor and author Myrick E. Land. "For the most part, they tend to be an intensive look at a very tightly defined subject matter."

The American Academy of Pediatrics (AAP), for instance, publishes supplements or monographs of 100 to 150 pages, frequently consisting of a group of articles on a specific topic or area of interest, e.g., the legal rights of adolescents or a handbook on poisonings in children.

While "informative but dull" reading might once have characterized such publications, today's monograph is just as likely to make news and rate headlines of its own. In fact, it was through an intriguing *San Francisco Chronicle* article that I first learned of Dr. V. W. Greene's fascinating monograph, "Cleanliness and the Health Revolution." The sixty-eight-page report was commissioned by the Soap and Detergent Association.

Greene, a microbiologist and noted environmental scientist from the University of Minnesota, debunks the nostalgia of the "good old days" of "healthy living" and discusses the health revolution; he supplies tables on everything from mortality figures to health-hygiene characteristics of developing nations and speculates about some of the factors that brought these health changes about.

His conclusion: People who credit breakthroughs in medicine and surgical techniques for health improvements may be overlooking a vital ingredient in the modern world's march toward longer life: soap. Says the expert on infection control, "There are millions of people alive today who owe their sight, their health and their very lives to such trivial things as soap and water and laundry detergent and plumbing."

Monographs are often published following medical symposia or meetings. They're also put out by university presses, the federal government, medical associations, centers, foundations, and research institutes. Monographs on medical topics and health-related products are often commissioned by advertising agencies, medical publishing houses, pharmaceutical houses and trade associations, such as the Soap and Detergent Association which underwrote Greene's report.

To some people, however, the fact that a publication is sponsored or underwritten makes it instantly suspect. "As soon as somebody is paying to get the story told," explains Land, "people wonder if the entire story is told."

In the health and medical field, the fact that such publications are sponsored doesn't rule out their value to practicing physicians and others, who can judge for themselves the worth of the drug product, sponsored message, or courting of good-will. (CIBA Pharmaceutical Company, for example, for years has published *Clinical Symposia*—monographs on a variety of medical subjects—which are highly valued by physicians all over the world, not only for their data but also for medical artist Frank Netter's superb illustrations.)

"The facts, research data, and clinical findings reported in such monographs are often extremely helpful," says one medical school professor, adding, "No one else is going to have the time to put all that information together in readable form. However," he cautions, "you need to be aware that conclusions drawn from that data will most likely point favorably to the use of the sponsor's drug or product in treating certain medical conditions."

Monograph Proposals

To get such assignments, a writer must be knowledgeable about medical topics and medical writing. Usually, writing a monograph pays well on a fee basis. But in some cases, the author is offered a contract and royalty arrangements.

For instance, medical librarian Laurie Conway, a registered nurse, has been asked by the Medical Library Association (MLA) to submit a proposal for a monograph of 100-150 pages for a new series of short, soft-cover books designed to provide treatment of timely topics. (These monographs will be contracted on a royalty basis.) Emphasis is on services and sources librarians will find useful. One book for which the MLA has identified a broad market is "A Practical Guide on How to Provide Consumer Health Information."

In its "Call for Proposals," the MLA asks authors to submit the following information:

1. A narrative in several pages which clearly explains:
    a. *need for the book*
    b. *purpose of the book*
    c. *scope of the book*
    d. *audience for the book*
    e. *benefits and unique features of the book*

2. A carefully structured outline which includes:
    a. *a descriptive narrative of the contents of each chapter*
    b. *a detailed phrase outline of each chapter*

3. **A curriculum vitae which includes publications and/or writing and publishing experience**

With modifications to fit your topic or project, you could use the MLA model to develop a proposal for almost any monograph on a health-related subject.

PERILS OF "PUBLISH OR PERISH"

"Publish or perish" is no joke in academic and scientific circles. But according to a number of health professionals, publishing in the lay press carries little weight academically and doesn't help the author in being considered for promotion or tenure. The scientific community considers books and articles in the lay press as little more than the author's opinion.

"It's literally looked on with disdain," says Dr. Ernest Mazzaferri, head of internal medicine at Ohio State University College of Medicine. The reason, he explains, is that when one publishes in a professional journal, such as the *New England Journal of Medicine* or *Journal of Clinical Investigation*, the paper is reviewed first by a panel of peers. If a paper can't withstand that kind of scrutiny, then it's rejected. But, of course, there's no such review in the lay press. "Writing textbooks, or writing books of any kind," he says, "simply isn't given the same weight—although they take an enormous amount of time."

It's important that a free-lance writer understand why a medical expert may not be interested in taking time out from his or her medical practice or scientific work to coauthor a trade book or article. If a book for the layperson is a liability in terms of an academic career, then there had better be some other pluses that make it worthwhile.

Many health professionals, of course, do find the effort pays off in service, satisfaction, *and* royalties.

Harry Huneycutt, for example, is a successful Reno obstetrician and gynecologist and a clinical assistant professor at the University of Nevada School of Medicine. With the late Judith Davis, he coauthored *All about Hysterectomy*, published by Reader's Digest Press, which had compiled exciting sales projections for it. But then Reader's Digest Press was sold, Huneycutt says, and the book essentially became an "orphan book"—one the new owners didn't promote as their own or promote effectively. Sales fell off. Huneycutt eventually bought back all rights to the book. Although he says that initially he had hoped the book would sell well, in the long run he gained out of it what he wanted.

"My original goal was I wanted something I could give my patients. Basically, all the physicians in our office use the book. All patients who are going to have a hysterectomy are given a copy of the book, so they can read it before they have the procedure. The majority do read it, and that gives them an opportunity to ask specific questions. It's entered into their medical record that they read the book, so it becomes part of the Informed Consent, too."

Health professionals who teach in medical centers or universities often feel there's a "book" in their lecture notes. What does it take to write a popular trade book from your notes?

When I asked that question of Dr. Isadore Rosenfeld, a New York City physician and medical-school professor who's written three bestselling medical-advice books, he replied, "First of all, the person's got to have something to say—you can't just want to write a book because you want to write—and that message should be unique. And second, if he can't write himself (and very few doctors know how to write so people can understand), then he's got to be able to explain it to someone who can."

The problem is finding the right person to collaborate with and then developing a smooth working relationship.

COLLABORATING—LIKE A MARRIAGE, ONLY . . .

"For better or worse" could just as easily apply to the writing partnership as the marital one. As one writer put it, "Collaborating on a book is just like a marriage—minus the sexual relationship. You've got all the same reasons for conflict, like who's contributing more or who should have the final say. By the same token, all the issues that make for a successful marriage also go into coauthorship."

In talking to successful ghostwriters and coauthors (plus a few authors who swear they would never collaborate again), I found the following factors mentioned over and over as being crucial to a good writing partnership:

● *A shared vision of what the final product should be and do and who's doing what.* "A tug of war gets you nowhere in writing a manuscript," says one author who's had enough of collaborating with doctors. "It's exhausting, counterproductive, and in the long run doesn't sell books. The physician should be the medical authority; the author, the expert writer who shapes the editorial product. You get into trouble when you've got a doctor who wants to write, who says he doesn't have enough time to write—but then is forever fussing with the final draft."

● *A common "word sense" and respect for ability.* To collaborate successfully, two people must be on the same wavelength when it comes to words on paper and competence in their respective fields. Some health professionals "audition" writers first, asking to see clips or other samples from free-lancers they're considering working with as coauthor.

One clinical psychologist looking for a ghostwriter told me she gave some of her research to the two or three writers she was thinking of hiring. She paid them to write a draft of several pages so she could see the different ways in which they would organize her material and rewrite it. From those writing samples, she selected the ghostwriter she knew she could work with and whose style and approach would meet her needs.

When *both* authors will be contributing chapters, it's more difficult to tell ahead of time whether writing styles will mesh. Gary Kreps and Barbara Thornton, coauthors of *Health Communication*, divided the chapters of their book according to each professor's expertise. Each wrote a first draft on one of a pair of compatible word processors, then mailed the chapter on disk to the other partner for comments, expansion, and revision. After exchanging the revised draft, both authors would agree on a third rewrite. "We each took primary editorial responsibility for the content of certain chapters," explains Kreps, but at the same time, we each maintained editorial responsibility for the *whole* book. I think this is why our book has a meaningful flow to it that's so often missing in others which sound as if each chapter has been written by a different author."

● *A sense of dependability and integrity.* Your coauthor must not only be willing to stick to the work schedule you both decide upon, he or she also must be dependable in keeping appointments and being on time for interviews, for which thorough preparation has been done. If you're doing a chapter on quality of life for handicapped infants and your collaborator is the one set to interview U.S. Surgeon General C. Everett Koop, you must feel confident that your partner will do the job in a competent and ethical manner—since any nonprofessional attitude or behavior on your partner's part will reflect badly on you as well.

● *The ability to talk things out and compromise.* "A rule of thumb, as in any marriage," says Bonnie Remsberg, who coauthored *The Stress-Proof Child*, "is that it's important not to allow the little glitches on the radar screen to become big ones—whether it's a personal problem or something as simple as 'I'd prefer to work at my place rather than yours.' " Most writing partners spend hours of time together, so it helps if you have personalities that complement each other. "In medicine, a strong ego is often a professional trait," says one writer, "but it can be a millstone in a two-party operation. Potential coauthors must be willing to think in terms of 'we,' not just 'me'."

● *Realistic expectations.* Writers are often faced with unrealistic expectations on the part of health professionals who think the piece should be right the first time around. "Convince him or her," advises one ghostwriter, "that it *won't* be right in the first draft—maybe, not in the second one either. That to do a good job, it will need rewriting in most cases. Offer a sliding scale. Say, 'If it's right the first time, the fee will be this, but if I have to do a lot of rewriting or redo the manuscript a number of times, it could be up to this much'—and name your new figure."

In a good writing partnership, two pens are better than one. You can have an off day in writing and know there's someone equally concerned with producing a good book who'll polish your words. When my husband and I work together on health-related books and articles, I have the last word on writing, marketing, and style. He has the final say on content as it relates to health and medicine. But he looks over every first draft and reviews every final one for *both* content and readability. He invariably suggests changes that clarify and strengthen what I'm trying to say.

But I also call on two friends for writing advice—one a journalism professor and the other a free-lance writer.

There are times when every writer needs a friendly critic—someone who's knowledgeable about writing, who can read the manuscript with a fresh eye and put the writer back on track before she's strayed too far in the wrong direction. If you've yet to meet the right "critic" for your work, consider joining a writer's group or auditing a nonfiction class. Listen to class comments or presentations at the writers' sessions. Usually, there's at least one person in the group whose opinion you respect and whose experience would serve you well.

If you're looking for a writing partner or ghostwriter, you can't go wrong starting in the places where writers hang out—conferences, writers' associations, nonfiction classes, and workshops. Tell people you're looking for a collaborator. Advertise, but be sure to mention any special qualifications you require of a coauthor or can offer to someone else looking for a writing partner. Talk to people in public relations—especially those who work in health and medical settings. They frequently take on free-lance writing assignments or know others who do.

Eventually, publishers may come to see you as a collaboration specialist and expert in writing certain *kinds* of books. Whenever one of their authors needs a coauthor, you will be their first choice. And certainly, your credits as second author will boost your chances of obtaining a book contract on one of your own projects.

LITERARY AGENTS— CAN YOU GET ONE, DO YOU NEED ONE?

Do you need an agent? The answer depends on whom you talk to and whether that author has had a good or bad experience with an agent. It also depends on how successful the author was in negotiating a contract on his or her own.

Isadore Rosenfeld, M.D., for example, has had an agent for two books and negotiated a contract for another by himself. ("I had an agent whom I called and said, 'I've just sold my book to Simon & Schuster, negotiate a contract for me.' Then my second book I didn't even have an agent—I negotiated the contract myself which was a mistake. Now my third book, I have an agent who got me a fantastic contract.")

Good advice I've followed comes from Alden Todd, author of *Finding Facts Fast* and a member of the American Society of Journalists and Authors. "I urge you to get a literary agent, given the fact that you live in Reno. To heck with the agent's fee. What you need is someone close to the buying editors' ears and eyes, who can present your book proposals to more buying editors in three months than you could in a year." Todd says his agent sent *Finding Facts Fast* to ten publishers before it found a taker. "He could do it much faster and better than I could."

Of course, there are hundreds of authors who are not represented by agents. They submit all their own manuscripts, negotiate the contracts, keep track of royalty statements, and generally are satisfied they're better off without a literary agent. (It's still a good idea, however, never to sign a contract until you have it reviewed by an agent or attorney who's knowledgeable about the pitfalls of agreeing to certain clauses that appear in publisher's contracts. Although you hear about *standard* publishing contracts, the fact is no two are identical. And negotiating which clauses stay and which are eliminated is a task the novice should approach with counsel and care. (For a clearheaded look at the whole business of understanding terms and negotiating with editors or publishers, see Richard Balkin's *How to Understand and Negotiate a Book Contract or Magazine Agreement*.)

Many of the major publishing houses accept proposals and manuscripts *only* when submitted by literary agents. Manuscripts mailed in by unrepresented authors are lumped together in the "slush pile." Modest estimates are that a publisher receives as many as 5,000 of these each year, and the screening process that takes your book to the top of the editorial decision-making process is time consuming and costly.

"For this reason," writes Richard Curtis in *How to Be Your Own Literary Agent*, "it can be stated with some accuracy that a publisher will read the most dismal piece of junk submitted by a literary agent faster and maybe even more attentively than he will a good book that comes in on the slush pile." The problem is you may need an agent, but an agent may not need you.

For one thing, your book may not be a blockbuster or best seller, and some agents handle only that kind of material. Other agents may see a conflict of interest in handling manuscripts from clients in the same profession. For example, literary agent Margaret McBride, who had handled the contract for *Quantum Fitness* by Irving Dardik, M.D. and Denis Waitley, Ph.D., refused to represent another sports psychologist author whose book proposal Waitley recommended to her, citing potential "conflict of interest" as the reason.

You can find literary agents listed in *Writer's Market, The Literary Market Place*, and *Literary Agents of North America Marketplace*, usually located in the reference section of most college, university, and public libraries. *Literary Agents*, for example, is an annual guide to more than 650 literary agents in the United States and Canada. It specifies each agency's reading policies, special areas of interest, commission charges, types of manuscripts considered, and recently placed titles, as well as names to contact and submission requirements. A special introductory essay explains dos and don'ts of dealing with agents and describes the current literary climate. (For your own copy at $16.95 plus $2.00 for shipping/handling, write Author Aid/Research Associates International, 340 East 52 St., New York, NY 10022.)

Another way to find a literary agent is to consult the current edition of the *American Society of Journalists and Authors' Directory* which lists agents used by ASJA members. Many university and public libraries purchase the *Directory* and keep it on reserve at the reference desk, but you may also be able to borrow a copy from a friend who's a member. (Copies may be purchased directly from the American Society of Journalists and Authors, Inc., 1501 Broadway, Suite 1907, New York, NY 10036; $50.) Frequently, authors will mention their agent on the acknowledgments page of their book—and you can always ask writers you know if they have an agent they'd recommend.

You will be working closely with an agent and paying anywhere from 10 to 15 percent commission for his or her services, so don't pick one at random. (An agent that's not right for you will be worse than none.) Some authors interview agents first, checking on everything from personal compatibility to the list of clients they represent. Ask around and ask why an author does or doesn't recommend a certain agent.

Remember, few authors these days are in the $50,000-$100,000 advance payment category, or even in the $25,000-$35,000 range. (One recent survey revealed most writers receive advances of less than $10,000.) Differences in advances for a book stem from a publisher's decision that one writer's reputation and the potential value of his or her book is worth more than another author's reputation and book's potential value. An agent will work to get you the biggest advance possible; it's money in his pocket as well. But an agent can't work miracles with a so-so proposal, or one from an author with no previous track record—something to consider in talking with dissatisfied authors.

What should you do if you feel you need an agent but can't get one right now? Or if you've heard so many horror stories about agents from dissatisfied authors that you'd rather go it alone? Read Curtis's book. As a former author turned literary agent he knows both sides of the business. See "Selling Books: Prevailing and Recommended Practices" (chapter five) in *The ASJA Handbook: A Writers' Guide to Ethical and Economical Issues.* In addition to explaining book-contract issues, the handbook also offers suggestions on how to negotiate favorable contract arrangements. Filled with information on writing books and magazine articles, as well as writing for business, this booklet is a bargain at $3.50 to ASJA members, $5.95 to the public. It can be ordered directly from the American Society of Journalists and Authors, Inc., 1501 Broadway, Suite 1907, New York, NY 10036.

PROMOTING YOUR OWN BOOK

In an ideal world, the author's main task would be to write the best book he or she could—and then rake in the royalties. But in today's publishing world, authors are expected to take more and more responsibility for promoting their own books to the audiences most likely to buy them. The key is identifying and reaching that audience, then seeing to it that the publisher is doing everything to ensure that the book and reader will catch up with each other.

This can be done in three ways that may overlap: (1) promotion by the publishing house; (2) the efforts of the author working on her own, or (3) the implementation of a plan devised by an independent outside agency that specializes in book promotions for a fee.

That a publisher would come out with a book and then let it languish for lack of promotion can come as a shock to the author. That a publisher would promote your book but not follow through on *distribution* is even more upsetting. But forewarned is forearmed. And as James Ennes points out in "Give Your Book a Promotion," (*Writer's Digest*, September 1982,) there are at least twenty ways you can increase sales and the shelf life of your book.

Let's look at a few methods successful authors use to make sure the word about their book gets out to those with the most influence—the sales representatives, the booksellers and reviewers, the potential reader and the media.

• *Carefully fill out the "Author's Promotion Questionnaire" your publisher sends you.* Here's your chance to name reviewers, experts in the field, authors (and celebrities if you know them personally) who might endorse your book or give it their blessing. Editors also want to know your network of contacts. Do you belong to an organization, or know of one, that will help promote the book? Which radio or television personalities might be willing to interview you? (Be sure you keep a copy of the completed questionnaire and any other information you send for your files.)

• *Assist in writing promotion copy.* No one knows your book better than you. If you're adept at copywriting, you can highlight your book's selling points better than the staff publicist can: "The first book that lets you in on . . . the only book that shows you how to . . . with the approval of the National Council for . . . simple, easy-to-follow diagrams . . . checklists for up-to-the-minute . . . sold to 'X Network' for a miniseries. . . ."

Some authors write their own dust-jacket blurbs and provide copy for news releases and press packets. But even if your forte isn't writing promotion copy, put your ideas on paper and offer them to your editor, staff publicists, and other key people at your publishing house. Ask to see and approve dust-jacket blurbs, press releases, promotion and advertising copy before they're printed.

• *Make sure your dust-jacket photo reflects the image you want to project.* Will your lab coat with a stethoscope hanging from your neck do the trick? Does it project the doctor "always on duty and ready to help" or the health professional "too busy to *listen?*" For their book *The Stress-Proof Child*, Bonnie Remsberg and clinical psychologist Antoinette Saunders chose to be photographed in the dining room of Bonnie's house. "We wanted to convey the maximum amount of warmth," she says, adding, "we wanted people to feel we're the kind of people you could talk things over with and we'd understand."

Give the same kind of thought to the image you want to convey, and discuss your ideas with the photographer and your editor.

- *Work to get media exposure for your book.* Media representatives are swamped with phone calls, review copies of books, and press kits from publishing houses around the country. Your book may sit in the growing stack of unread, unreviewed, and unappreciated materials unless you take time to write or telephone local and regional book reviewers, newspaper reporters and columnists, radio and television talk-show personalities.

  A little soft sell from a local author can go a long way if you sum up what your book is all about and why it will appeal to their audiences.

- *Talk about the book.* Health professionals are frequently asked to speak at conferences, talk to community groups, and serve as panelists in a variety of media and community settings. Universities, medical schools, and research centers often have speakers' bureaus whose services are advertised as part of an on-going public-information program. Volunteer to be a speaker.

  Offer to discuss writing a first book (or whatever) at a writers' conference. You'll meet not only editors and agents, but also writers looking for speakers for other groups back home. The conference publicity director can also help in arranging additional radio and newspaper coverage.

- *Print up giveaway cards.* When people ask, "What's the name of your book again?" give them a card and tell them where they can buy the book. One author hands out his business card on the back of which he's rubber-stamped the publisher's name and the title of the book. Nancy Yanes Hoffman not only wants people to know about her book *Change of Heart: The Bypass Experience,* she wants to alert them to risk factors they shouldn't ignore. So she gives out a small card listing the title and publisher and her own name, address, and message-tape phone number on one side. On the other, as a service to potential readers, she lists nine risk factors that can lead to heart disease.

  Another writer prints up postcards with a photograph of the cover of her book on one side and publishing information on the other. These are mailed with a personal note to friends and targeted audiences who might be interested in the subject and the approach she's taken in her book. "Postcards also come in handy," she says, "when you're invited to give a talk on your topic. You don't have to scribble the title on tiny scraps of paper for each person who asks, and the photo makes it easy to identify the *right* book on the supermarket or bookstore shelf."

- *Consider signing up with a professional book-promotion agency.* This tactic works best for the midlist book and mid-range author, who doesn't have a potential best seller on her hands but who does have an important work that deserves more attention than it's getting. And many of these books fall into the health-related category—the book on grandparenting, for example, or one on coping with a retarded child.

Some of these agencies specialize in arranging radio and television appearances. For instance, the Frank Promotion Corporation (60 E. 42nd St., New York, NY 10017; [212] 687-3383) tailors professional publicity programs for clients, many of whom are health professionals who have written books they wish to promote.

Sensible Solutions (14 E. 75th St., Suite 5C, New York, NY 10021; [212] 861-3693) was founded by Judith Appelbaum and Nancy Evans, who's now head of the Book of the Month Club. For a fee that generally does not exceed $1,500, Appelbaum and her current partner, Florence Janovic, will develop an action plan for promoting your book and consult with you on how to carry it out. Recently, Janovic successfully put Sensible Solutions' strategies to work in promoting her own Berkley Publishing Group book *The Hospital Experience*—now in its third printing.

● *Make the most of your public appearances.* Once in the spotlight, you have three goals: to let the audience know the title of your book, what it's about, and why they should buy a copy. "The secret is do one's homework," says Samm Sinclair Baker, in *Writing Nonfiction That Sells.*

In promoting his own books, among them *The Complete Scarsdale Medical Diet*, couthored with Dr. Herman Tarnower, Baker prepares extensively and uses the book as his main prop. Inside the cover, he tapes notes on important points he wants to get across and attaches small tabs to pages with a chart or picture he may want to refer to later. "Speak truth only, no deception, no double-talk," advises Baker. "If you're asked a question, and don't know the answer, say 'I don't know.' That eliminates any tension from faking and being found out. It's blissfully liberating. People understand and appreciate honesty."

Always bring an extra copy of your book with you and autograph it for the interviewer before you leave the station. Ask for a tape of the program so you can listen to yourself later and work on improving your delivery the next time around. Follow up with a thank you note. You may want to appear again, and you can't go wrong with simple courtesies and a complimentary copy of your book.

One final word of advice. Nothing is more frustrating to the touring author and audience excited about your book than to discover later that it isn't available locally. (You may be interviewed on New York City radio and television talk shows or speak at a city university, for example, but many of your listeners and viewers will want to buy your book at bookstores and shopping centers where they live—in the suburbs of Westchester, Long Island, or New Jersey.)

Some authors find it pays to call or visit area booksellers a few weeks before a media or speaking engagement to make sure their books are on hand or have been ordered. They introduce themselves to the manager of each store, tell him about the book and describe its special features, give him a copy if he hasn't seen it, highlight its selling points, and persuade him to order a copy from the publisher's sales distributor or representative.

Others contact the publisher's sales representative for their area directly. (You can get name, address, and telephone number from your local bookseller.) Publisher's reps handle sales for several companies simultaneously and push a list with hundreds of titles. What you want to know is, Is your book on that list? If not, forward favorable review comments and urge the rep to read the book for himself. You can also make yourself available for book fairs and author parties.

Will it make a difference?

Here's what Richard Curtis says in his book *How to Be Your Own Literary Agent*: "I have seen authors charm store managers into ordering copies, displaying books more prominently, stacking copies in store windows, or even throwing impromptu book-signing parties." These authors start close to home where they're known and fan out (as money and opportunity allow) to proven book-buying cities like New York, Boston, Los Angeles, and Chicago.

Book-industry watchers agree that the era of the publisher-sponsored, twelve-city author publicity tour is ending. But that doesn't mean the author must sit back and watch his or her book's sales do poorly. *Creative self-promotion is the name of the game.* Your options are growing, and they range from sending out flyers to taped interviews sent by satellite to 650 TV stations nationwide. They're time consuming and costly. But as royalties pile up and sales projection figures soar, you will know your time, effort, and money have been well spent

14 □ SPECIALIZED HEALTH COMMUNICATIONS

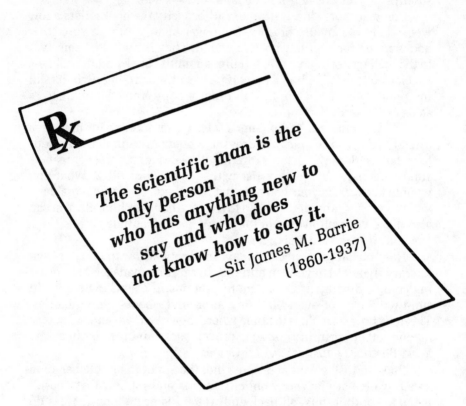

The scientific man is the only person who has anything new to say and who does not know how to say it.
—Sir James M. Barrie (1860-1937)

Communications guru Marshall McLuhan once described media as "the extensions of man." In a personnel-intensive industry such as health care, it comes as no surprise that a large percentage of communication involves media of various kinds. And predictions are that the use of mass media and in-house and specialized media in health-care communications will continue to expand in the future.

MEDICAL MEDIA AND SERVICES

In general, the term *popular media* refers to books, magazines, newspapers, films, and radio and television programs aimed at the general public. The term *medical media* usually covers the wide variety of health communications, including, but not limited to, clinical and re-

search papers, abstracts, monographs, scientific exhibits and brochures, doctors' brochures, pamphlets, flyers, patient-instruction
sheets and educational aids, manuals and guides, medical and dental
film strips, textbooks and study guides, continuing-education materials, pharmaceutical package inserts and advertisements, as well as
speech writing, book reviews, and special reports or overview articles
on health and medical topics.

Assignments come from many sources, among them journal advertising, professional free-lance directory listings, referrals from satisfied clients and fellow writers. In writing for medical media, the
ideal combination, of course, is the person who has scientific or medical background who can also write for the public. But the combination
is rare.

"There is a dichotomy that makes this unlikely," explained Amy
Selwyn at a writers' conference. "That's because most people who decided to be writers were liberal arts, English, or communication ma-
jors—or majored in other nonscientific fields," said Selwyn, assistant
editorial director of *Hospital Practice*, a monthly which goes to nearly
200,000 physicians in hospitals, family practice, general surgery, and
internal medicine.

It may also explain why so few free-lancers know how *vast* the
medical media are—or what their best bets are for breaking into this
kind of health communication. In fact, I didn't either until I saw an
American Medical Writers Association listing of medical media and
related services.

Look over the two lists that follow. Remember, you can't make a
sale to a market you don't know exists. And matching ideas to markets
and services to potential clients is the crux of successful free-lancing.

MEDIA _____

Abstracts	Direct mail
Advertising	Encyclopedias
Annual reports	Exhibits
Audio tapes	Films
Audiovisual material	Flyers
Books	Grant applications
Brochures	INDs/NDAs*
Case histories	Journals
Catalogs	Magazines

*IND—Investigational New Drug; NDA—New Drug Application

Manuals	*Proceedings*
Monographs	*Proposals*
Newsletters	*Protocols*
Newspapers	*Radio*
News releases	*Reports*
News services	*Television*

SERVICES

Abstracting	Photography
Audiocassette preparation	Proofreading
Audiovisual production	Publication design
Author's editing	Public relations
Bibliography	Reporting
Cinematography	Research
Consulting	Review/criticism
Copy editing	Scriptwriting
Exhibit preparation	Surveying
Ghost writing	Teaching/training
Graphics	Translation
Indexing	Typing/word processing
Literary agentry	Writing
Marketing/promotion	

In one chapter, of course, it's not possible to cover fully all the free-lance opportunities that fall under the heading of medical media or specialized health communications. And certainly, a large percentage of health communications are staff written. However, the wide-reaching medical market is open to you as a serious free-lancer if you have underlying journalistic skill, interest in the field and subject of medicine and public health, and respect for the audience you're writing for—whether it's the health-care consumer, provider, educator, student, or salesperson.

To succeed, you'll need sufficient knowledge of the language of medicine and the courage to use it. Formal training in science is a help—but it is not always necessary. "What's more important," said *Hospital Practice* assistant editor Amy Selwyn at a writers' conference, "is to be able to talk to scientists and physicians and other health-care professionals, to ask questions about what they do, and to be a *communicator.*"

Determine your interests, study the field, develop your skills through workshops and networking in professional medical and science writers' groups. Consult *Freelance Jobs for Writers* (edited by Kirk Polking) for information on indexing, convention free-lancing, fund raising, grant proposal writing, programmed instruction materials, speech writing, and advertising copywriting.

What follows is a look at the major areas in medical communications open to free-lancers.

AUDIOVISUAL MARKETS

For the free-lancer with the skills and discipline to meet the demands of this fast-growing area, the audiovisual field is a wide-open market. And the medical field, underwritten by the pharmaceutical industry, is where the *money* is right now.

Although major ethical pharmaceutical advertising agencies have audiovisual divisions that produce medical education films, there are exciting opportunities in the audiovisual marketplace for free-lancers, especially in the rapidly expanding field of continuing education for physicians and other health-care workers. (Used in this context, the word *ethical* refers to divisions of major pharmaceutical companies that develop, test, and manufacture prescription drugs rather than proprietary medications sold over the counter. Originally, the word was used to distinguish "ethical" companies from "unethical" patent-medicine men who peddled their wares along with exorbitant claims for cures, relief of symptoms, and so forth.)

Where do you start if you haven't used your electronic pen before?

Basically, good programming starts with a good script. And a good script is based on a logical approach to a good idea, which has been broken down into segments of manageable and useful proportions.

The idea may be one you've come up with yourself, written a proposal for, and sold to a medical association or audiovisual company that produces such material. Or just the opposite—a medical society, hospital, or professional group may want to produce a package that might include a film or film strip; tape recordings and/or monograph produced from a medical conference or lecture series; a study guide; and possibly, self-evaluation materials. You are awarded the contract, but don't expect a by-line, too.

The next step in getting started is to check the film library or audiovisual department in a medical or health-sciences library. You can get valuable information from existing films and pick up pointers on writing scripts, study materials, or monographs by reviewing those already on file. Medical journals, with their extensive coverage of disease, diagnosis, and treatment options, are a good source of new ideas suited to audiovisual presentation.

"The market is there, just keep poking around," medical freelancer William Kitay said at an audiovisuals workshop during a New York City writers' conference. A specialist in writing audiovisual cassettes in continuing education for physicians, Kitay told of a woman he knew who "read a couple of pieces on transplants, thought to herself, 'That's a honey of an idea, who'll be interested?', presented it in a proposal (the same way you do a magazine query) and after a year got a go-ahead on the project from a major company."

THINK BACKWARD TO COME OUT AHEAD

"One of the first things to think about in designing a production is the *last* thing that will happen to it," advises author and AV producer Don Sutherland in a January, 1985, *IABC Communication World* article. "How the audience will watch it, under what circumstances, and through which medium, are fundamental to the design of the production. This is true for most of the audio-visual media we use: slide and multi-image programs, movies (yes, 16mm is alive and well, Panavision tells me), filmstrips, even overhead projection to a degree."

Since nothing is as dull as listening to someone drone on about disease or technology for thirty minutes, make your film or slide show as interesting as you can. Write in a conversational manner. Try to be spontaneous about it. And be prepared for numerous *rewrites*.

In addition to continuing education for health-care professionals, two other areas are opening up in the audiovisual field. One is self-help/self-improvement audio- and video-cassette tapes; the other is patient information.

Self-help and self-improvement cassettes are becoming much more popular as celebrities like Jane Fonda and motivational specialists like Denis Waitley have produced best-selling cassettes for the general public. Patient-information audiovisuals, which focus on common health problems and patient-instruction needs, are being supported by a large number of institutions such as Blue Cross/Blue Shield and nonprofit groups like Consumer Health Education, Inc., of Washington, D.C.

One big advantage of being the *writer* hired to do the job is that you can leave filming, production, funding, and distribution worries to the pros in that arena. You should be aware, however, that these projects are rarely *pure educational efforts.* Pharmaceutical companies that make audiovisual materials available free to physicians have a vested interest—a product or drug on the market or simply goodwill they hope to accrue.

Among audiovisual companies seeking free-lancers are:

- *Audio Visual Medical Marketing, Inc.,* 404 Park Ave. S., New York, NY 10016. (212)532-9400. Jan Robinson, President
- *BMA Audio Cassettes,* 200 Park Ave. S., New York, NY 10003. (212) 674-1900. Peter Wengert, Director, Continuing Education Program
- *Health Projects International Inc. (HPI),* 24 E. 21st St., New York, NY 10010. (212) 460-5900; (800) 221-2207. Patricia Coleine, President

(According to Theodore E. Moore, HPI's vice-president of operations, the company prefers to see ideas from free-lancers submitted by letter.)

You'll find additonal audiovisual markets listed in *Audio Video Market Place (AVMP.)* A multimedia guide published annually, this directory covers everything from distributors and dealers to awards, production companies, software producers, reference books, and associations. Another directory highly recommended by medical AV free-lancers is *Jeffrey Norton Audio Forum/Video Forum.* (Jeffrey Norton Publishers, Inc., 96 Broad St., Guilford, CT 06437. (203)453-9794; (800)243-1234.) This publication lists about 650 audiovisual companies by subject and type of work they do. A third publication, *Pharmaceutical Marketing Directory,* has one section that lists audiovisual companies, types of work that interest them, and who heads the company.

Other helpful reference books in the audiovisual field include two published by Knowledge Industry Publications, Inc., of White Plains, N.Y. One is *Video in Health,* edited by L. George Van Son, a practical and thorough examination of how to use video in the health field; the other, *A Practical Guide to Interactive Video Design,* by Nicholas V. Iuppa. Section 7 provides a selected list of major audiovisual reference materials that deal with such topics as AV production techniques, multimedia education, and AV hardware, software, and review sources.

Introduction to Reference Sources in the Health Sciences, edited by F. W. Roper and J. A. Boorkman, is intended as a text for health-science library students but contains one chapter on "Audiovisual Reference Sources." The Medical Library Association publishes *Index to*

Audiovisual Serials in the Health Sciences—a listing of titles, including cassettes such as the *Audio Digest Series*, which come out periodically on "hot topics" in medicine.

Many of these audiovisual reference guides and directories are located in the reference sections of university, college, and public libraries. However, to consult highly specialized indexes and selected directories designed for health professionals and medical librarians, you may have to go to a hospital, medical school, or health-sciences library. Before you go, check to see if the library is open to the public. In some cases, special arrangements must be made ahead of time for use of medical or health-related library facilities.

PHARMACEUTICAL MARKETS

Pharmaceutical companies in general are in the business of developing, testing, and manufacturing pharmaceuticals. Writers prepare summaries of new drug research conducted in hospital and clinical settings, edit and rewrite special reports and manuscripts, and write abstracts for published and unpublished studies. They also prepare drug fact sheets, produce marketing monographs, and develop sales training and educational materials.

These tasks may be performed by either a free-lancer or an in-house medical writer. (Outside writers, however, usually have less input in the planning aspects, as they are given assignments with definite marketing goals and themes.)

All new drugs, of course, must be approved by the Food and Drug Administration (FDA). This involves a written submission of documentation to the FDA—the New Drug Application (NDA)—which is time consuming and requires much original writing and a great deal of editing. Included, for example, are the writing of interim and final reports of clinical research studies, investigator's brochures (covering both clinical and preclinical experience with the drug), and volumes of paperwork supporting the efficacy, safety, and manufacture of the new drugs.

In completing an assignment, a writer may work with as many as a dozen different experts, among them data processors, regulatory affairs personnel, biometricians, chemists, pharmacologists, photographers, printers, and MD/Ph.D. directors of various departments, such as that of clinical research. The audience ultimately is the FDA reviewer.

In pharmaceutical advertising and marketing departments, writers are often called upon to assist in the development of sales bulletins and training materials for sales representatives and the creation of promotional brochures and journal advertisements for company products. They write copy and make suggestions regarding illustrations, and they interact with advertising and/or public-relations agencies for graphics and promotional themes.

Writers may also evaluate current medical literature for suitable quotations to support copy, and they often work closely with staff in preparing material, e.g., proofreading galleys and approving layout of graphics and copy to be sure the literature meets company standards, industry codes, and government regulations. In addition, free-lancers may be asked to write speeches and assist in preparing poster displays.

Audiences for both print and audiovisual media may include physicians, patients, company personnel, or salespersons in the field.

"Wearing my marketing hat," says one free-lancer, "I work with the individual drug product managers on assignments that include the full range of advertising services, e.g., patient-information brochures and inserts, promotional items, journal advertisements, fact sheets, direct mail, and 'dear doctor' letters. In some cases, the product manager approaches me with an idea; in others, the idea for a project comes from me."

Another free-lancer, for example, says she creates and regularly publishes an eight-page newspaper for the sales force plus weekly bulletins filled with business information (background data on new products, new uses for existing products, and newsworthy information about competitive products) for the sales force and field sales management.

A third writer involved in creative health-care communications says she prepares manuscripts, medical summaries or abstracts, brochures, competitive briefs and monographs for health-care professionals. In addition, she reports summarizing papers presented at professional meetings or appearing in the current literature—often following through from idea concept to layout and production.

HELP WANTED—SCIENTISTS WHO CAN WRITE

This is one market where it's a definite asset to have a science background. "I've found it's easier to train someone to write than it is to teach someone all the science needed," says Elizabeth A. Ashraf, Ph.D., director of medical communications and New York-based medical writer who has been with Ives Laboratories, Inc., since 1977. (The company is an ethical division of the Fortune 100 American Home Products Corp.)

Ashraf, who holds a B.A. in biology and graduate degrees in pharmacology, lectures on medical writing in the pharmaceutical field at medical writers' conferences. She has put together a list of ideal skills for a medical writer as follows: accuracy, technical knowledge, medical knowledge, inquisitiveness, creativity, writing ability, audiovisual talent, dependability, productivity, and interpersonal skills.

"Interpersonal skills are important in the pharmaceutical industry especially," she explains, "because the writer functions as *liaison* between the medical and marketing staffs." However, in-house writing courses, says Ashraf, who over the years has hired a number of writers, "are an inadequate way of learning to write because a writer can only perfect his skills through 'hands-on' experience under the guidance and direction of a seasoned professional."

What does it take to break into this field as a free-lancer? It doesn't hurt to show some initiative.

By joining a professional association such as the American Medical Writers Association (AMWA) and attending its functions, freelance writers meet pharmaceutical and other health industry executives and staff who know of, or are in a position to hire, outside support personnel. (For information on AMWA and other science/health-related professional communicators' groups, see Appendix C.) Follow-up, says Ashraf, is a must. "A resume, writing samples, and a covering letter are a good idea," she says, adding that "on numerous occasions, colleagues call and ask if I know of a good free-lancer for a particular project."

PUBLIC RELATIONS

Edward L. Bernays, widely considered the father of public relations, once defined public relations as "an art applied to a science, which advises a unit—profit or nonprofit—on how best to achieve his or her social goals." A nephew of Sigmund Freud, Bernays (now close to ninety-five) has integrated many of his uncle's precepts into his public-relations work, which goes way beyond getting the client's name in (or keeping it out of) the newspaper—for years the number one rule guiding many a PR practitioner, past and present.

"Publicity," agrees Lou Joseph, senior health communications specialist at Hill and Knowlton, Chicago, "is one of the facets of the overall PR operation, getting word of newsworthy events to the news media. But PR goes beyond that—getting support for your organization, counseling senior management on how to communicate or not communicate with various target audiences, and serving the public interest. Medical PR," adds Joseph, a former American Dental Association public-relations director, "is a catch word often used as a synonym for goodwill."

As such, health-related public relations today covers everything from community and media relations to certain aspects of governmental affairs; speech writing; employee communications and newsletters; annual reports; house organs, physicians' bulletins plus external communications with specific publics. It can also include communication audits; initiating special events and evaluating results; fund-raising and promotional efforts; and educating the public as well as legislators, health-care decision makers, consumers, and news media about good health.

Crisis communications—as in the Tylenol-drug tampering incidents and the Three Mile Island nuclear reactor accident—present a special public-relations challenge. Counseling senior management on how to handle these and other crises has become a major function for health PR practitioners—whether in-house or from an outside PR firm or free-lance employment.

But pharmaceutical companies, government and private agencies, hospitals and medical centers of every size must be prepared for the potential crisis—whether it comes as an epidemic of E. Coli diarrhea in the newborn nursery, a rash of malpractice suits against the chief of surgery, charges of fiscal incompetence leveled against the chief executive officer—or a community accident that focuses attention not only on the company but also on the hospital caring for those injured.

Virtually every hospital in the United States today has a public-relations/public-information office. But cost-saving measures and personnel layoffs enacted by many hospitals have reduced some PR departments to one-person operations, explains Constance A. Arkus of the American Society for Hospital Marketing and Public Relations, which has about 2,500 members. These small PR departments, she says, rely heavily on advertising agencies to produce the brochures, publications, or other marketing materials they need.

In addition, public-relations people work in medical schools and centers, research institutes, medical-supply houses, medical-specialty associations, pharmaceutical firms. The nation's largest public-relations firms have special departments servicing the needs of health-care clients.

Local medical and dental societies, certain specialty clinics, health-maintenance/wellness programs, or physicians' groups use public relations consultants from time to time to help promote objectives, increase visibility, or enhance their image and strengthen ties with various audiences whose support they seek. At the same time, an effective public-relations program can help to neutralize or minimize the negative impact of groups opposed to specific health-care policies or practices.

Often, public-relations free-lancers are just what the doctor ordered for these groups whose volume of business does not warrant a full-time PR office, or to help out with specific projects when full-time staff is already overextended.

A good way to get into medical public relations, says award-winning public-relations practitioner Lou Joseph, is to have a degree in journalism, "because much of your work in PR is media relations. You need to have good oral and written communication skills, and it's helpful if you have a scientific background, too. But, he says, very few people in this world combine both. "You also need good contacts for stimulating stories and placing them—locally and nationally, but," adds Joseph, "you don't do it overnight."

It helps to cultivate the acquaintance of key public-relations agency directors, public-information officers; and publicity directors in your area. Prepare a succinct resume and attractive portfolio of your health-related work, articles, brochures, etc. Make an appointment to see these key people personally. Let them know you're available for free-lance assignment and what areas, if any, you specialize in.

You'll find public-relations agencies listed under that category (and also under *publicity*) in the Yellow Pages of your telephone directory. For the national picture, consult the membership directory of the Public Relations Society of America (PRSA). A copy is generally available at college and university libraries, especially at schools which have a program in public relations.

TECHNICAL WRITING

Although we tend to think of technical communications in terms of reports, manuals, proposals, and spec sheets in such "high-tech" industries as aerospace, computers, and heavy machinery, there's no denying high technology has radically changed the way medicine is practiced today. In view of this, it's not surprising that many medical writers are members of the Society for Technical Communication (See Appendix C).

Basically, the technical writer and the science writer cover the same general subject matter, but each focuses on a different *audience*. The technical writer, says the society's executive director, William C. Stolgitis, bridges the gap between technical-information producers and consumers. "In this context," he explains, "technical information is defined as having to do with the practical, industrial, or mechanical arts or applied sciences."

The technical writer deals with scientific and technical developments mainly for professionals in the field. Hence, the emphasis is on detailed specifics and technical language. Technical writers who specialize in health sciences and medicine are employed by hospitals, universities, foundations, federal agencies, organizations with research programs, manufacturers, and other businesses with health-related interests, as well as scientific and medical publishers. Some of these writers are free-lancers.

According to the Bureau of Labor Statistics, 25,000 technical writers were employed in 1980, the last year in which that category was tallied apart from writers and editors as a whole. It's not known how many technical writers were active in biomedical communications. However, Susan Toronto, director of communications for the Society of Technical Communications, says that in 1984, an unscientific survey of its 9,000 members indicated only 37 out of 1,250 who responded were medical/biological writers. (Perhaps the others were too busy writing to fill out the questionnaire.)

A look at some of the winning entries in the society's 1984 International Technical Publications Competition shows medical topics in the categories of audiovisual communications, annual reports, newsletters, news articles, training manuals, brochures, and bulletins. Some titles: "How Does Your Child Hear and Talk?/ Que Tal Habla Oye su Nino?" (brochure); "FDA Drug Bulletin" (bulletin); "Self-Help: Your Strategy for Living with COPD" (training manual); "Donors Are Red Cross Lifeblood" (news article); "Drug Abuse in the Third World" (periodical article); "The Methodist Hospital Journal" (complete periodical); "Roanoke Memorial Hospital—Annual Report."

Katherine Haworth of Burroughs Welcome Company received one of the top ten awards for her writing and editing of a series of newsletters for gout patients, titled "Getting Along with Gout." And in the audiovisual division, three special categories are directed to medical topics, i.e., safety instruction, medical instruction for a general audience, and medical instruction for a professional audience. Again, titles give a clue to the wide scope of technical writing—"The Diagnosis of Brain Death," "External Ventricular Pacemakers," "Autonomic Nervous System Drugs," "Alcohol and You," "Child Abuse: The Silent Epidemic," and "Placement of the Hickman Catheter via Subclavian Vein."

Best background for a career or free-lancing in technical communications is a science or engineering degree plus skill in communication.

SCIENTIFIC EDITING

Editors are paid to take sows' ears and turn them into silk purses. Among the ultimate editorial challenges are medical and scientific manuscripts.

Editors of such prestigious professional journals as the *New England Journal of Medicine* or the *Journal of the American Medical Association (JAMA)* hold M.D. degrees. Editors of many other major professional publications hold degrees in those specialties, e.g., nursing, dentistry, veterinary medicine. But not all do.

For example, the physician-editor or nurse-editor whose name appears at the top of the masthead works closely with the journal's editorial board of health professionals to set editorial policies and select the articles to be published. The actual day-to-day work of editing manuscripts and preparing the journal for publication is usually carried out by other editors (sometimes free-lancers) who need not have a professional health degree.

"Degrees may or may not be critical to the work at hand," says Philadelphia-based free-lance medical writer and editor-consultant Bernice Heller, "depending upon whether or not you're working in a highly specialized area." Heller, whose background is music, is a former senior book editor with twenty-five years' experience in medical editing and frequently gives editing workshops to writers' groups.

Editors, she notes in a workshop handout, work both in-house and free-lance. The in-house groups are located in hospitals; schools of medicine, nursing, and allied health sciences; professional journals; publishing houses; private agencies; and other health-related institutions. Free-lancers often work on specific projects for publishing houses, as author's editors, and as editorial consultants.

Basically, there are three types of editors: manuscript or copy editors, development editors, and sponsoring or acquisitions editors. (Production editors are more involved with type, traffic, and scheduling.)

Acquisitions Editors

Heller says acquisitions editors are the heart of the publishing operation—hunting up people to write, negotiating with those people to write books that will fill gaps in the publisher's list, negotiating contracts—not only staying within budget, but estimating profit margins and return on investment. If the group of authors is well known, you're competing with other publishers for these prestigious names.

"In addition to being an excellent speaker, good listener, always calm in the face of disaster, and having a splendid sense of humor, acquisitions editors must have a keen sense of markets and trends and be able to leap tall conventions and fly like a bird from author to author, from school to school," she says. "Often the deciding factor [in signing an author] is that the author feels more comfortable with you and that gets the contract."

Development Editors
According to Heller, development editors are heavily involved with the author throughout the process of substantive editing and rewriting of the manuscript. Such editors need a secure sense of self-worth and must be intuitive and extremely sensitive to the author. Diplomacy is a big asset as the editor pushes, pulls, and shoves the author toward the mutually agreed-upon goal—all the while maintaining a warm professional author-editor relationship. Development editors must be able to envision the final product and shape it to audience needs and market requirements. Like authors' editors, they also must be able to rewrite "sloppy, turgid, dull, confused manuscripts."

Manuscript/Copy Editors
On the other hand, manuscript editors usually have minimal author contact. Their job primarily is to review grammar, spelling, syntax, and often minor styling. In some cases, they proofread and code the manuscript, tying up loose ends and checking to see if anything has been overlooked. These editors may be on the staff of the journal or publishing house or may be free-lancers. The latter often feel they do better in an unstructured situation, working in their own environment at home—which makes it appealing free-lance work.

Successful copy editors, says Heller, have some distinct qualifications, including, "a 'look it up' mentality, keen mind for detail, devotion to fine written expression, and devotion to correct grammar."

How can you get into the field? "Other things being equal," she says, "be persistent. If you're turned down the first time [by a publishing house], go back a month later. It shows you really care about the job and are motivated in pursuing your goal." Heller says fees for editorial work vary according to the type of work that has to be done. Fee range for free-lance development editing, rewriting, editorial consulting, and similar professional activities is approximately forty to fifty dollars an hour. Long-range projects are usually negotiated on a project basis, rather than hourly basis. A highly experienced editorial consultant may charge considerably more than fifty dollars per hour, for instance, for presenting a workshop for less experienced editors or for some other activity requiring a high degree of skill. Copy editors, in most instances, earn much less than forty dollars per hour, as copy-editing is regarded as a lesser skill than development editing, to give but one example. Free-lance copy editors generally earn from ten to twenty dollars per hour—but, assuming copy editing is all they're asked to do, fees closer to the ten-dollar range are more common.

Heller says she usually tries to come up with a fee for the entire project rather than charge piecemeal. Always, she gets the agreement in *writing* to protect both the group that has hired her *and* herself. (For additional pointers on setting fees for projects, see chapter 15.)

PROFESSIONAL JOURNALS

In 1985, the National Library of Medicine received more than 23,000 serial titles which included professional journals from all over the world. That same year, under the heading "Medical Sciences," *Ulrich's International Periodicals Directory* listed 7,906 titles.

How many medical/scientific and allied health journals are published worldwide? According to a 1978 article in *The Quill,* Dr. Arnold S. Relman, editor of the *New England Journal of Medicine,* said that there is no accurate tabulation of the number of medical publications worldwide. All that's known is that it's impossible to keep up with the volume of professional journals, and their number is *increasing* each year.

Most are aimed at the academic community and professional health-care provider—physicians, nurses, dentists, nutritionists, rehabilitation specialists, psychologists, etc. The wide focus and range of interests is reflected in such titles as *Journal of Bone and Joint Disease, Nursing 86, Journal of the American Dental Association, Cancer, Journal of Philosophy in Medicine* (ethics), and *Medical Heritage,* a new journal highlighting medical history, as well as medicine and art, literature, and anthropology.

Major national medical journals have full-time staff. Many state, county, and highly specialized journals operate on smaller budgets. They often rely on part-time staff or free-lancers for editing, production, and other services. Such services may include, for example, editing accepted papers; preparing retypes for author and printer; reading galley and page proofs; checking illustrations, photographs, captions; working closely with the editor-in-chief, editorial board, printer, and advertising sales agency.

Other free-lancers function as author's editors—editing content and copy of a physician's manuscript *before* it's sent to a professional journal. "Writing is considered particularly credible for the researcher," explains heath-communications expert and author Barbara

Thornton, "because the written document allows scrutiny by one's peers."

Since the "publish or perish" syndrome is real in academic and professional circles, and since physicians, scientists, and other health-care professionals concentrate on developing scientific rather than literary skills, help with writing and editing can be crucial to publication.

Ghostwriters can find a market at some professional journals. One editor of a well-known health publication told free-lancers attending a national writers' conference that it's their practice to have the major articles by-lined by medical-school professors whose names lend authority to the presentation. "We find this successful," the editor said, "but it means, of course, the writer functions as a ghostwriter. In addition to good remuneration, there is the satisfaction of doing it well. But to be candid," concluded the editor, "the opportunity would be *greater* to do reporting at medical meetings, events at medical teaching centers, and so forth."

At another company, PW Communications, associate editorial director Lucy Kavaler says, "we use some free-lancers, but only those with medical-journal experience." Kavaler, who is in charge of five publications (*The Female Patient, Primary Cardiology, Hospital Physician, Physician Assistant,* and *Group Practice Journal*) says most work is in editing, rewriting, copy editing. "A free-lancer with some experience might break in by suggesting an interview with a physician known to him or her on a topic of interest to the particular journal. Interviews," she adds, "are the only free-lance work given out."

These journals definitely are *not* interested in "my operation" stories or encounters with physicians—whether good or bad. Articles reflect scholarly research in various scientific and medical disciplines, and many of these are subscription publications. The market for free-lance writers is almost nil in these *refereed journals*—so-called because clinical and basic-research manuscripts are always submitted to a panel of peers for review.

Another category of professional publications falls under the umbrella of unsolicited—those underwritten by drug companies or other health entities and sent to doctors *free* of charge. Don't underestimate, though, the quality of articles that appear in some of these journals—many of which are included in the Brandon List of respected journals (see chapter 5). Among these free journals are *Hospital Practice* and *Postgraduate Medicine*—both of which are known for good, clear review articles and being up-to-date on what's going on in medicine.

(There are other free publications, however, that doctors refer to as "throwaway journals" because they are of relatively little value to the health-care professional.)

Authors generally are not paid for their contributions to professional journals—though there are exceptions. The usual practice is payment in tearsheets, reprints, offprints, or complimentary copies of the issue in which the article appears. But for the professional, being published in a prestigious journal such as the *Lancet* or the *New England Journal of Medicine* is itself high reward.

Publication guidelines are usually printed in the journals themselves. However, the *Directory of Publishing Opportunities in Journals and Periodicals* contains detailed information on scope of topics, audience, and manuscript requirements for about four thousand publications. Included are medical journals, whose "specs" (specifications) are often difficult to obtain in other market lists. You should be aware, however, that the *Directory* was last published in 1981 (the 5th edition). Until an updated edition comes out, don't rely solely on this source for publication guidelines. Go directly to the journals you're interested in and look up current manuscript specifications and editorial requirements. Since editors change, too, check the masthead and guidelines for correct name, title, and spelling.

Other marketing directories are listed in an excellent guide to publishing in this field—Edward J. Huth's *How to Write and Publish Papers in the Medical Sciences.* Huth speaks with authority. He's editor of the highly respected *Annals of Internal Medicine.* This gem of a book can be found in most university and health-sciences libraries and some public libraries as well. It covers everything from finding the right journal to researching, writing (and revising) the research paper, editorial, case report, book review, and letter to the editor—all of which are types of medical communications that appear in scientific journals.

TRADE PUBLICATIONS AND IN-HOUSE MAGAZINES

Every industry has its specialty press covering news, names in the news, new products and services, trends, updates, case histories, conferences or meetings. Being a good reporter is vital to writing for these markets, and especially so for the free-lancer who wants to sell to health-industry news tabloids, newsletters, and trade magazines. In some publications, the focus is on *medicine;* in others, on health-care facilities *management* and *marketing/selling* health-related products and services.

"Trade publications are among the most stable and steady freelance markets," says one medical writer who estimates about 70 percent of his writing business comes from this well-paying "hidden market." With rates that range from five cents a word to $1,200 for up to 3,000 words, trade-publication fees are competitive with many mid-range consumer magazines.

Health-related trade publications can be divided into the following categories:

Medical News Tabloids

Written in newspaper style, medical news tabloids feature factual reports of medical developments, news briefs, updates, interviews with health-care VIPs and often opinion pieces, profiles, and analysis of legal, sociological, and economic factors affecting the medical profession as well. Among the most widely circulated are *Medical World News, Medical News & International Report, Medical Tribune, U.S. Medicine,* and *American Medical News,* a publication of the American Medical Association.

Some typical front-page stories: "New DRGs Would Freeze Base Rates and Shift Pay for Types of Cases"; "Caring for Unreached Patients—the Homeless"; "Letting the Bad Times Roll: The Bike Safety Lag"; and "Bionic Bill's Heart: Critics Say Deficient." Not seen often, however, are page-one stories like this: "Flight from Terror Paved Way to Stardom: Physician's Academy Award-Winning Role Re-enacts Horrors of Cambodian Bloodbath"—an article about refugee-physician Haing S. Ngor.

Health Facilities/Professional Practice Management Journals

Publications aimed at the health-facility administrator focus mainly on personnel, purchasing, financial, legal, ethical, and administrative matters. Those designed for the health-care professional in a private practice, hospital, or clinic setting highlight practice-management strategies and personal/finance advice. Among these trades, you'll find titles like *Nursing Homes, Hospital Gift Shop Management, Dental Management, American Druggist,* and *Hospital Supervisor's Bulletin.*

Podiatry Management, for example, is a national business publication for podiatrists. It pays between $150 and $350 for how-to articles, general-interest pieces, interviews, and profiles related to podiatry and building a bigger and more successful practice. Medical professionals make up the readership of *Private Practice,* where articles on socialized medicine and state or local legislation affecting the medical field earn up to $350; short news pieces on local medical societies, $250. Best paying of all, *Medical Economics,* a biweekly with circulation of 165,000, offers $500-$1,200 for up to 3,000 words for how-to's, factual, and travel articles.

Health-Care Products/Programs/Services Publications

Titles in this category usually are self-explanatory, e.g., *Medical Product Sales, American Clinical Products Review, Medical Electronics & Equipment News, Health Care Computing & Communications,* and *Health Care Marketing Quarterly.*

For example, *Corporate Fitness and Recreation,* read by directors of employee fitness and recreation programs, pays up to $240 for articles on planning, supervising, and evaluating such programs as well as pieces on exercise physiology, sports medicine, and life-style improvement for workers. The bimonthly *Medical Meetings Magazine* is edited for medical-meeting planners. It runs articles on planning medical meetings and travel pieces on American cities and regions as meeting and convention destinations.

Association, Foundation, and Special-Interest Newsletters and Journals

Here you'll find sponsored publications aimed at selected groups of health professionals—e.g., *The New Physician,* published by the American Medical Student Association, and *Medical Student,* put out by Pfizer Pharmaceuticals. So-called disease organizations keep patients and supporters abreast of the latest medical news, consumer issues, and fund-raising projects through such tabloids as *Asthma and Allergy Advance* (Asthma and Allergy Foundation of America); *Commitment* (Cystic Fibrosis Foundation); *National Spokesman* (Epilepsy Foundation of America); and *National Arthritis News,* a twelve-page membership publication of the Arthritis Foundation.

On a smaller scale, newsletters provide information to targeted groups and membership. The Scarsdale Family Counseling Service, for instance, produces "Grandparents . . .," a four-page newsletter for grandparents in divided families. Wellness and self-help groups around the country produce hundreds more—ranging from community committees to aid abused women to the "People's Medical Society Newsletter," which pays $35-$125 for up to 1,500 words. A bimonthly newsletter for Society members, it covers grass-roots health actions, medical politics, health and medical issues from a preventive and consumer-oriented viewpoint.

House Organs

Company newspapers, magazines, and other publications are produced by pharmaceutical companies, hospitals, individual businesses, medical schools, and other health-related institutions. Their basic purpose is to help management communicate its purpose, philosophy, goals, news, and important and useful information to selected audiences.

When designed for employees, sales personnel, and professional staff, for example, they are called *internal* publications. *External* house organs are those distributed to stockholders, legislators, community decision makers, clients, and potential customers.

It's not unusual for free-lancers to work on special writing or editing assignments in whole or in part—especially when such publications are produced in-house. In recent years, however, many hospitals and health-care consortia have joined together in cooperative purchasing of support services, including magazines, from such publishing giants as the Webb Company of St. Paul, Minnesota (producers of several in-flight publications), and the Meredith Corporation of Des Moines, Iowa, which also publishes *Better Homes & Gardens.*

To get an idea of the hundreds of trade publications and house organs in the health/medical field, consult volumes three and four of *Working Press of the Nation,* which some libraries keep on reserve in the reference section. However, since house organs and many trade journals are limited-circulation publications, you'll have to send for sample copies or check with a health-products supplier, university, or medical school library. You'll also find copies of some publications in the doctors' reading room at a community hospital or regional medical center.

Some editors send sample copies to medical writers only. This is the policy, for example, of the *Medical Post,* a Canadian biweekly, which pays eighteen cents a word for newsy, factual, 300-800-word reports of medical developments, and *Oncology Times,* a monthly tabloid covering cancer research with a clinical emphasis for oncologists and allied health personnel.

However, free sample copies and writers' guidelines are available to free-lancers from many others, among them *Orthopedics Today,* the *Surgical Technologist,* the *Canadian Doctor,* and *Patient Magazine.* A marketing tool for hospitals, the last is an annual magazine for hospitalized patients and covers equipment, care, treatment, and facilities. Rates are negotiable for 500-700-word articles that inform, educate, and entertain the patient/consumer.

Another publication, *Celebrate Health,* began as an in-house publication at Bergan Mercy Hospital in Omaha, Nebraska, and today is a quarterly, consumer-oriented magazine which pays up to $500 for 2,500 words on upbeat news and features in the health/medical field.

The key element in selling to the trade and in-house magazines, of course, is understanding the publication's editorial style, readership, and article needs. But keep in mind that the lifeblood of these publications is advertising and sponsorship. If you're trying to sell an article that would antagonize a sponsor or advertiser, you're ignoring the first rule of free-lancing—know your market.

Breaking into that market starts with a well-worded query on a business-related or medical topic. Be sure to mention where and how you will research it, what approach you'll take, your expertise or qualifications for doing the assignment, and the availability of photos (taken by either you or others). Some editors pay extra for them; others do not.

According to many trade editors, one of the biggest problems they have in working with free-lancers is that they submit general articles rather than the more sophisticated type that health-care specialists in a given field expect. Here's where the medical writer has a distinct advantage over other free-lancers. In addition, medical free-lancers who specialize in *business* aspects of health care usually make it their business to keep tabs on the *Wall Street Journal*, *Business Week*, and the business section of *The New York Times*.

PUBLIC EDUCATION AND PATIENT INFORMATION AIDS

When *North Carolina Medical Journal* editor Eugene A. Stead, Jr., M.D., heard from a friend about to undergo surgery that a booklet produced by Duke University Medical Center was "the single most helpful piece of paper ever given to her by a doctor," he decided to publish the complete document in the *Journal*'s May, 1985, issue. Titled "So You Are Going to Have a . . . Total Hip Replacement," the sixteen-page booklet was written and edited by Ann Kirk, B.S.N. It falls into a special category of printed materials known as patient education or information aids.

If you've had a tooth extracted, periodontal surgery, special X rays, gynecological tests, or a host of other medical or dental procedures, you're already familiar with the brochures or fact sheets handed to patients which include pre-op and post-op instructions and other information. (In a special category is the informed consent form, which must be signed prior to any surgical procedure. While most of these consent forms are fairly standardized, those that deal with experimental surgery or research procedures are quite complex and detailed; a prime example is the one used by Dr. William DeVries and the Humana Hospital for artificial heart implants.)

Because of medical malpractice suits and court decisions nationwide, doctors are recognizing the importance of properly obtained informed consent—the first step of which is providing the patient with adequate information. Physicians provide this information in a number of ways, verbally and in writing. Often brochures, articles, and fly-ers detailing the disease, disorder, or disability and its treatment op-tions, risks, and benefits open up the dialogue, which then allows the patient to ask questions and clarify concerns or fears—*before* giving consent.

But there are at least four other reasons for developing public-ed-ucation and patient-information aids.

First, and basic to maintaining the "wellness life-style," is pre-vention of disease and disability. Then, there are *altruistic concerns*, e.g., donating body organs or blood or taking part in a research study. Next is *consciousness raising* regarding potential health problems, and finally, *how to cope* with health problems once you've got them. To this end, there is an enormous flow of printed materials from dis-ease-related organizations and special-interest groups; medical asso-ciations; the U.S. Government Printing Office; the Centers for Disease Control; public-health entities; medical centers and hospitals; medi-cal and dental clinics; and the offices of private doctors, dentists, chi-ropractors, and podiatrists.

For example, the American Academy of Pediatrics produces doz-ens of pamphlets, flyers, and handouts which doctors can buy in bulk to give to patients and their families—covering everything from im-munizations and allergies to breast feeding, adoption, and how to help your dying child. Similarly, the American Medical Association, American Dental Association, American Hospital Association, and American Public Health Association, to name just a few, publish hun-dreds of informational brochures, handouts, and the like.

Local, county, and state medical societies frequently develop their own materials or adapt those of national groups to fit needs clos-er to home. It's here that free-lancers frequently find opportunities to rewrite existing educational and informational materials or create new ones. Special-interest groups such as New York City's Friends and Relatives of Institutionalized Aged, Inc., and DES Action, a com-mittee of the San Francisco-based Coalition for the Medical Rights of Women, produce informational pamphlets, flyers, booklets, and guides as well.

"A Consumer's Guide to Nursing Home Care in New York City" is a comprehensive sixty-eight-page guide first issued in 1982 by the Friends and Relatives of Institutionalized Aged, Inc., a private, non-profit consumer group. Researched and written by a third-year law student, it is a step-by-step guide to placing a relative in a nursing home, with particular emphasis on a nursing-home resident's rights and New York rules and regulations. The booklet, which begins with an explanation of alternatives to nursing-home care for less seriously impaired relatives, also lists all public and private nursing homes in

New York City, their size, and the level of care provided.

According to a *New York Times* article that quoted administrators in the field, "A Consumer's Guide" is one of the few booklets of its kind in the country and the only one dealing specifically with the New York region. The guide grew out of experience with a nursing-home placement and complaint service, which for the most part is telephone service, Jeffrey Ambers, executive director of Friends and Relatives of Institutionalized Aged told the *Times*.

"We get about 1,000 to 1,500 calls a year, and most people who call, whether they're Ph.D.'s or postal workers, know nothing about nursing homes," he said, adding that it was becoming almost impossible to explain all the details over the telephone. Yet callers desperately need complex information quickly, for unless relatives have made a decision regarding nursing-home care, a hospital will make it for them—placing a patient in a nursing home on its own as soon as he or she is ready to leave.

Necessity may be the mother of invention, but wise free-lancers know there's no need to reinvent the wheel. If there's a need in New York City for a guide that covers social resources and medical and legal information, undoubtedly there's a similar need for such booklets in other states or regions. The same is true of many other health-related publications, which—with some modification—can generate new free-lance ideas. The goal is not to copy. Rather, it's to spark your own thinking so you can tailor-make an effective proposal based on what's worked elsewhere.

Such assignments are frequently given to writers who are *health-information specialists*. Generally, minimum educational requirement for this field is a bachelor's degree in communications or journalism, with supplementary science and life-science courses as well. However, many health-information specialists hold graduate degrees in nursing, science, or public health as well. Employed by hospitals, clinics, health organizations, and some businesses, their job is to make authoritative and readily understood health information available to the public in an appealing form.

To do this, all possible channels of communication are used—from mass media to small-group workshops.

RADIO AND TELEVISION

People Weekly says energy-charged Dr. Ruth Westheimer "dispenses clinical chicken soup" par excellence on her top-rated, nationally syndicated phone-in sex talk show over WYNY-FM in New York. Timothy Johnson, M.D., has been described as "doctordom's Walter

Cronkite." A syndicated newspaper columnist and regular medical commentator on ABC's "Good Morning America," Johnson is star of the nationally syndicated "Healthbeat" series and provides on-air analysis of medical news for "World News Tonight," "Nightline," and "20/20" in his position with ABC-TV.

Westheimer and Johnson are but two of several highly visible health professionals who've made a hit taking medicine and psychology to the airwaves. No doubt about it, the public wants health information, and broadcast consultants know it. What do they recommend when network and station ratings are dropping? "More health news and features," says Joel Lanphear, Ph.D., an associate dean at the University of Nevada School of Medicine.

Providing the medical perspective is often the job of the radio or television station's consulting health-care professional. But hundreds of science and medical editors, reporters, and contributors are writing the scripts, news items, documentaries, and features that hold those audiences.

For example, Cleveland-based independent writer Jean McCann, president of Medical News, Inc., is an international correspondent for Physicians Radio Network. Her specialty is coverage of medical meetings worldwide. Free-lancer Diane Ouding of New York City has written scripts and worked with independent filmmakers for Public Broadcasting Service documentaries such as "Toxic Waste: What Communities Can Do," which aired in 1983.

(Don't forget, the anchor and reporter responsible for the six o'clock news don't have time for in-depth investigation of the medical or science-related story. One person who *has* the skills and time to unearth facts and write scripts for the TV documentary or special health-related series aired during newscasts is the free-lance journalist.)

Few American radio stations assign reporters to medical or health "beats," although the likelihood of such assignments rises in proportion to the amount of time a station commits to "heavy news" coverage and, of course, at "all news" stations. Probability of a television station's serious attention to medical and scientific topics is directly related to its size. However, there are cable television shows that address scientific and medical topics, as well as a cable television network, LIFETIME, whose focus is health and medicine.

Among network, syndicated, or cable TV programs whose focus is medical or science topics, you'll find *Regis Philbin's Health Styles* (cable); *Crisis Counselor* (cable); *News from Medicine* (cable); *Nutrition News* (cable); and *Focal Point* (syndicated), a weekly half-hour program using material from two shorter radio shows dealing with science and health.

For a more extensive picture of radio and television health and medical coverage, consult the latest edition of Larriston Communications' *Guide to U.S. Medical and Science News Correspondents and Contacts*. For complete information on the wide and rapidly expanding opportunities in writing for TV, radio, and film, check the *Complete Book of Scriptwriting*.

COVERING MEDICAL MEETINGS

One of the best-paying free-lance opportunities is covering medical meetings for medical publications. Editors are willing to assign meeting coverage—especially if the writer lives in a city not readily accessible to staff reporters or contributors.

To get such assignments, says Lucy Kavaler, associate editorial director of PW Communications, "you need to be a crackerjack reporter and you need to be knowledgeable enough in that field of medicine to recognize what is new—what is the important story there."

Conference directors and media coordinators can help point you in the right direction. For example, here's how Barbara Chapman, former science writer and public relations manager for the College of American Pathologists, assisted the media before and during the group's two annual scientific meetings.

About a month beforehand, she would mail out a packet which included two or three articles describing presentations to be made at the meeting—some that would have general reader, listener, or viewer appeal. She also sent along a list of between fifteen and twenty additional presentations that she thought would be of interest to general-interest publications or radio and television.

Then, if one or more writers informed her of specific interests (say, for instance, a writer would tell her, "I want to know more about this one on increased testing for Pap smears for cervical cancer"), she would make arrangements for an interview with the pathologist presentor of that paper sometime during the meeting.

As a result, for the five days of the meetings, she would be in the pressroom setting up appointments morning, noon, and night for media interviews with pathologists. In addition to arranging interviews for writers attending the meetings, she set up telephone interviews for free-lancers who stayed at home but were writing for medical journals, or lay publications.

Chapman didn't screen media or free-lance requests and says she never had anybody attend a meeting who didn't seem to do a good job. "The one thing I asked for," she told me, "was tear sheets. It wasn't enforced at all, but I would say, 'In case you write for a publication that our clipping service does not pick up, would you send me a tear sheet when the article appears?' " Radio interviewers sent tapes. After making copies of printed materials for office files, she forwarded these and any tapes to the presenting pathologists for their own records.

Says Chapman, who is now media director for the National Center for Missing and Exploited Children, "I always tried to give writers and reporters covering our conferences the opportunity to have a personal interview. I was not reluctant to go to scheduled news conferences, but I think that's not the way most reporters like to work if there's time for the other."

Getting an Assignment

To find out which medical group is meeting where and when, consult the *Journal of the American Medical Association (JAMA)*, which regularly lists medical and health-related meetings and conferences.

Once you've picked a meeting that interests you, write the conference organizer or media director requesting an advance copy of the program and major speakers. With this information, you're ready to contact an editor. Don't start your query with a vague "Would you like me to cover such-and-such meeting for you?" Instead, point out some specific story ideas or potential interviews of interest to publication readers. Mention any special qualifications you have for covering the meeting, but don't promise anything you're not sure you can produce.

An editor generally will decide whether to assign coverage using two criteria: (1) the amount of professional interest (or *public* interest if it's a mass-media publication) in what is likely to be revealed in the papers presented, and (2) the size and significance of the sponsoring organization or society. In your city, for example, a meeting of the state board of medical examiners is likely to produce more news than the monthly meeting of the county medical society; nationwide, the annual meeting of the American Academy of Family Practitioners is generally more newsworthy than the annual meeting of the American Medical Writers Association.

Pressroom Know-how

If you've landed an assignment to cover a medical meeting and it's your *first*, you may find yourself feeling as Barbara Chapman did when she stepped into a major medical conference pressroom for the first time.

In 1971, after working only four months as general-assignment reporter for a Rockford, Illinois, newspaper, she was sent to Chicago to cover her first major medical meeting. It was the first Quality of Life Conference sponsored by the American Medical Association, and reporters from all over the world had converged on McCormick Place, where the historic meeting was being held. Adding to the pressure Chapman felt was the fact that her newspaper had done a large-scale promotion saying she would be filing *daily* stories on the conference from Chicago.

It was bad enough, she says, finding her way around the huge convention center, but the pressroom was just as intimidating. "I got into the pressroom with rows and rows of typewriters, all those reporters sitting there, some of them already working on stories and some conducting interviews and some calling back and forth to one another, 'What are you gong to cover?'—and I just stood there."

A few minutes later, recalls Chapman, Charles-Gene McDaniel, who was then with the Associated Press, introduced himself and asked who she was. "I told him and then confessed, 'I don't have the faintest idea what I'm supposed to do.' "

McDaniel asked where she was from, then led her to a quiet corner and suggested, "Let's look over the program and see what the people of Rockford, Illinois, would be interested in." Says Chapman, "This man, who had been awarded every prize there was to receive over the years, sat down with me and picked out the daily programs for me to report on. I came out of that little session in the corner knowing what I was going to do—when I was really ready moments before to go home a failure."

Guardian angels don't always attend medical meetings, and mere mortals in competition for a lead story are rarely as helpful as Gene McDaniel. Your editor may want you to write everything from reports on speeches and papers presented to interviews with medical experts and, perhaps, even a follow-up story. With large conferences and meetings, which are planned well in advance, it's easier to do your homework ahead of time, collect background material on issues, topics, speakers, and various factions within the organization.

(For a description of various types of meetings, consult the chart below.)

Depending on the assignment, some journalists will cover the conference but wait to write the actual stories until back home. At that point, the reporter submits to the managing editor a story list with one- or two-line descriptions of potential stories. The managing editor meets with the writer, discusses the ideas, decides on what's needed, and then gives some guidelines on story development.

Don't forget, it takes considerable skill to find articles in what the medical profession calls "review papers" and "overview talks." To recognize what's new in the presentation, the writer has to be current in that field and know what's newsworthy. But even when there is no "news," the writer can focus on a specific topic; ask specific questions of the presenter or someone in the audience; do research on the subject, and find experts in the field to interview.

Whether you're writing for mass media or medical media, however, make Gene McDaniel's starting point your own: What do *your* readers want to know about?

TYPES OF MEETINGS DEFINED

Clinic

A training or educational program on one specific subject (for example, house-organ editing or office management), attended by those now working in the field. Instructors present recent knowledge to participants in small groups (ratio of 1:20 or less) and answer questions. Differs from the *workshop* by greater emphasis on instruction. Usually one or two days.

Colloquium

A program (somewhat resembling the *conference*) in which the participants determine the matter to be discussed. For example, in a marketing colloquium, potential registrants would be asked to submit a list of the most pressing marketing problems they face. The colloquium managers would then construct the program around the most frequent problems, bringing in appropriate experts to instruct and lead discussion. Generally a compact group of thirty-five or less participants, with equal emphasis on instruction and discussion. Two to five days.

Conference

A program in which discussion of a subject or related subjects is guided by one or more experts for the purpose of pooling knowledge to solve a problem of common concern. No more than fifteen to twenty participants, with considerable discussion. One to three days.*

Forum

A panel discussion by authorities in a given field with liberal opportunity for audience participation. Usually one-day.

Institute

An intensive program built around several facets of a subject. Primarily a substitute for formal education, and thus instruction-oriented. Likely to have general sessions for an overall view, plus smaller sessions on particular aspects. Usually several days to a week.

Lecture

A formal presentation by an expert. Generally followed by questions and answers. Usually lasts for only part of one day, but several subjects may be handled by different lecturers to make up a day's program.

*In the medical field, a conference may include several hundred participants.

Seminar
A discussion-oriented program in which a group of participants share their experiences in a particular field under the guidance of an expert. Attendance generally thirty or less. As likely to be concerned with identifying and defining problems as with solving them. From one to three days.

Symposium
A panel discussion including the leading authorities in a field, often before audiences of more than 500. Some audience participation, but appreciably less than a *forum.*

Workshop
A program similar to a *clinic,* but differing in its greater emphasis on discussion among the participants. Usually searching for practical solutions to everyday problems. The instructor makes a brief formal presentation designed to identify problems and possible solutions, then participates in the ensuing discussion and summarizes the sense of the meeting. Generally no more than thirty to thirty-five participants. From a half-day to two or three days.

Reprinted from *National Trade and Professional Associations of the United States* published by Columbia Books, Inc., 917 15th Street, NW, Washington, DC 20005.

15 □ Rx FOR A HEALTHIER BANK ACCOUNT

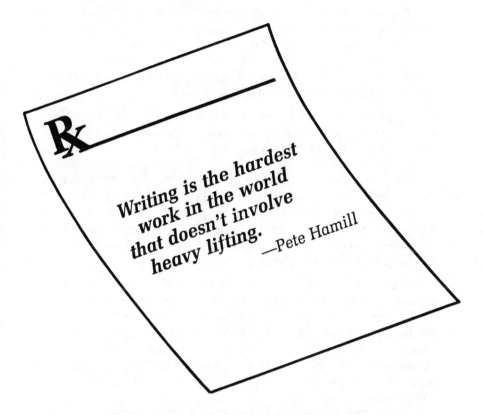

Writing is the hardest work in the world that doesn't involve heavy lifting. —Pete Hamill

Show and sell is the rallying cry of the business world. So are five basics of entrepreneurial success: Know your market, your competition, your product, your client—and yourself. As a free-lance writer, you are a seller in a buyer's market.

To make money, you must sell. To make *more* money, you must take the *free* out of free-lance, recognize that it's a business, think and act like a successful businessperson. Remember, marketing theory holds that a sales opportunity exists when recognized needs are not being met. As a health and medical writer, you have some important factors working in your favor.

First is *timing.* Nearly all free-lancers and editors interviewed for this book agreed it's a good time to be a writer in the health and medical field. Looking good is linked with fitness, and editors like "Thin

Thighs in 30 Days," for example, because it's promotable at the super-market. Health/medical news and features rate extremely high in reader pull, and the trend is upward as populations age and people of all ages become more health conscious.

Growing Health-Care Consumer Movement. Emphasis today is on taking greater responsibility for one's own health. When coupled with escalating costs of medical care and cutbacks in private and public funding, it's essential for people to inform themselves so they can get the best return on their health care dollar. People want health-related information; editors want to provide it.

Legal and Ethical Concerns. It is imperative that patients (and/or families and guardians) have enough information to understand risks and benefits of treatment, surgery, experimental procedures, and drugs. Informed consent is most visible with the patient's signature on an official form, but the process of understanding what's involved and what's at stake begins long before. More and more health-care professionals are coming to appreciate the important role of the well-written, easy-to-comprehend article, book, brochure, information sheet, programmed learning aid, or other audiovisual in this critical communication process.

Marketing. The name of the game in today's health-care industry is marketing. America's health obsession and fitness phenomenon have spawned a wave of new products, corporate programs, special services. At the same time that greater emphasis is being placed on preventive medicine, out-patient care, minisurgery centers, home health care, the hospice movement, and other new forms of delivering health care, hospitals are fighting to keep usage up in an increasingly competitive market.

Public relations and advertising are joint partners in helping industry and health professionals achieve market share, "position," and goals. Whether it's writing ad copy for a new health-care product, producing an in-house publication for a local hospital, writing trade article pieces for health-care facilities, or a marketing prospectus for a health maintenance organization, free-lancers have their work cut out for them—and it starts with *visibility* and *samples* of your work.

Expanding Health and Medical Market. New fitness and health-related specialty publications appear each year, and nearly every magazine of general interest runs a health or science article in each issue. Commenting on the size of the free-lance market, *Parade* health editor Earl Ubell says, "*In the total*, there is a *bonanza* out there as far as magazines are concerned and certainly, the number of science books for the public is increasing each year—though very few become best-sellers."

Ubell predicts the public's interest in health and medical matters will continue to grow as it has for the past forty years. "Health," he says, "is central to human needs—and that need will be reflected in publication and broadcasting."

Do as the Money-Makers Do

Whether your goal is to write a best seller in the health field or make a comfortable living in the behind-the-scenes medical markets, you need to know the facts of free-lancing life.

Free-lancing is no place for the meek.

To tap into the totality of the health and medical market, you need to show, sell, and market your work as the money-makers in the independent writing field do. This means *networking*, creating a *professional image*, setting *realistic fees*, and actively *seeking out* new markets and clients. The ABC's of independent writing are basic to any business:

- *Advertise* and *ask* for assignments in whatever way is most appropriate for you and the market or client you want to sell to.
- *Be competitive* in your skills and your fees.
- *Court* potential clients and, once you've got an assignment, *deliver* work you're proud of *on time.*

Word-of-mouth advertising from satisfied clients is one of a free-lancer's most effective methods of getting more work. But a no-go decision doesn't hurt as much—emotionally or fiscally—if you have several queries in the mail at the same time or have bid on more than one project.

Don't miss an opportunity, advises professional medical writer/editor David L. Raffle, to put your business card in the right hands—those of experts in the scientific or health field, celebrities who might need a ghostwriter or collaborator, and public figures you respect. Seek them out at lectures, seminars, book-signing events, workshops, and public occasions.

It's possible—without being offensive or pushy—to say in effect: "I'm an independent writer who admires your work and your stance. If I can be of help in a writing project, please let me know. Here's my business card."

The Business of Business Cards

Business cards are a *must* for independent writers. If you wear more than one editorial hat, you may need more than one business card. The same holds true for business letterheads. Be consistent in typeface and sparing in color, if you use it. A general rule of thumb for cards and stationery is: Avoid gimmicks and such "cutesy" logos as a quill pen, an old-fashioned typewriter, or oversize pencils tied with ribbon. This is a case where less is more—and more professional, too.

Basic to all letterheads and cards are your name, address, phone number. Not all writers give themselves a title, but a descriptive label or business name helps identify you as an independent writer, scientific editor, indexer, consultant, etc. It's easier for a potential client to think of you first, if your service is clearly spelled out. Reproduced below with the writer's permission is an all-inclusive business card that leaves no doubt about New Jersey free-lancer Tamara Galimidi's wide range of professional services.

Here are some other descriptive titles and labels from business cards of professional writers in health-related areas:

Medical and Scientific Communications

Professional Writer/Editor

Writer/Editor/Researcher

Independent Writer

Writer/Communications Consultant

Editor/Technical Writer

Let me warn you that many writers are contemptuous of the term *free-lance writer*. They feel it sets the writer up as an amateur or one willing to work for less money than a professional writer. Personally, I'm not convinced that's true. I have never lost an assignment that I'm aware of, or been paid less than another writer, because I called myself a free-lance. What matters to the editor or publisher is whether you can get the job done well by deadline—not what you *call yourself* as a writer.

So take your pick of titles, and don't settle for less pay than you're worth.

Don't overlook the fact that when 103 experts helped *Prevention* magazine rank the thirty-nine health and safety factors most important to adults, income as a "health factor" figures in the first fourteen. Simply put, income below poverty level is dangerous to your health. Yet a 1981 survey revealed that only about 5 percent of authors are earning more than $5,000 a year from their writing.

MONEY MATTERS—FLAT FEES AND HOURLY RATES

You can increase your chances of business success—and bank more income from your writing—if you know the going rates for health-re-

Tamara Galimidi
Creative Communications, Medical and Technical

33 Pine Drive, P.O. Box 23
Roosevelt, New Jersey 08555   (609) 443-1888

Creative Communications Specialist (Medical and Technical)

Clinical Programs
Data documentation & submission to FDA (NDAs for drugs, PMAs for devices). Interface with FDA, R&D, marketing, and clinical investigators. Package inserts and other labelling.

Product Concept
Market studies (questionnaires, mailings).

Product Package
- Develop & coordinate advertising, direct mail and other promotional programs, and budgets.

- Professional relations (publicity, medical publications, symposia).
- Advertisements, sales presentations, brochures, and newsletters.
- Audio-visual programs (slides, videotape scripts and production).
- Operation manuals, product information sheets, training kits.
- Trade show exhibit design, management and literature.

Combined with: Technical art and graphic design
(including layouts for visuals and documents, packaging and label design, mechanicals, printing production, and photo editing).

lated free-lance work and how much to charge clients.

Established medical and health writers charge anywhere from twenty-five- to seventy-five dollars an hour. Average is about forty to fifty-five dollars (more or less the same fees charged by free-lance development editors and editorial consultants); copy editors' fees usually range from $10 to $20 per hour. See "Scientific Editing" in chapter 14 for more on fees. However, one medical-school public-information officer says he occasionally free-lances for $25 an hour when the assignment is basically a spinoff from research or other stories he's already done in his full-time job. *His* costs are down, so he passes the savings on to the client. The dividend, he says, is greater volume of such assignments.

While that may work well for the salaried writer, the independent free-lancer has to look out for Number One. How should you construct a fee?

One way is to figure out how much income you would like to earn free-lancing. Let's say $40,000 annually sounds about right. Working on a *full-time* hourly basis (40 hours a week for 50 weeks a year equals 2,000 hours), you would have to *net* $20 per hour. To cover overhead (about 30 percent), expenses, and fringe benefits (another 25 to 30 percent), your *gross* income would have to be approximately 60 percent higher—$64,000—and your hourly rate at least $32.

Another formula for fee setting is to consider what a full-time writer or editor is paid for similar work, then break that down to an hourly rate—and *triple* that. Remember, as a free-lancer, no one else is covering cost-of-living increases or fringe benefits for you, i.e., life and health insurance, paid holidays, vacation, and sick time. (What if you break your arm and can't write for a month or require eye surgery that puts your research on hold for several weeks?)

"That's why you're tripling the fee," explains Ada P. Kahn, MPH, author and health-care communications consultant. If your clients find the price steep, "remind them that 30 percent of your fee is added benefits plus work space you're saving them."

NEGOTIATING AN AGREEMENT

The key to a mutually satisfactory agreement is communication. It is important that you and your client understand each other from the start. Regardless of the type of agreement or contract you ultimately come to, it will be a good one only if you both are honest, fair, reasonable, and clear in stating expectations, needs, and contingency plans.

First, try to find out if there is a budget for the project and what the total amount is. It's easier to deal with a budgeted project because you can always say, "For this amount of money, I can do such and such. I can also do a first draft and one rewrite. However, for additional rewrites, I will have to charge extra."

Kahn also suggests the writer watch out for hidden trouble spots, such as attending meetings, checking references, or doing additional research. "A medical article with numerous references can take a lot of time," warns Kahn, who says that in one such lengthy project she added about 20 percent for documentation. She also lets the client know from the start that if she has to do more extensive research, she will add X dollars more plus travel expenses.

"For example," she says, "you can specify in a letter of agreement that you understand there will be two meetings a week during the project. If you find you have to be in the client's office every day, that will cost extra. Things generally take longer than *you* think they will—or the *client* thinks they will."

By-lines and credit lines spell visibility. What's a by-line worth, then, if you will be ghosting the project? Should you ask for more money? There are no pat answers, but most independent writers agree "invisibility" should be parlayed into more money. At the very least, you should be recognized in some tangible way, especially if you are trying to build up your portfolio of professional credits. One way is to negotiate to have your name listed on the project as a *contributor*. Another is to request a letter for your files. When your client likes your work, ask for a brief note to that effect.

Finally, business negotiations are no place for gentlemen's agreements. Put your free-lance agreement *in writing* so that there will be no misunderstandings later. It doesn't have to be a formal, small-print contract. You can write your understanding of the assignment and your responsibilities, plus those of the client, in a letter of agreement on your stationery. Filling in the blanks to suit your project, you could fashion an agreement like this:

It is my understanding that I am to write [edit, photograph, whatever] an [article, chapter, book, brochure, newsletter, etc.] of [number of words/pages] on [subject/working title] by [date: deadline for final delivery]. I understand I [am selling rights/retaining rights] as follows:

First [draft/outline/layout, etc.] is to be delivered for review by [date].

First payment of the total fee of [$] will be made by you on [date] followed by [other payments as applicable to project].

Included in this fee is one revision of the final [manuscript/report, etc.].

In addition, I understand I will need to attend [number of] meetings per [week/month]during the project. If it becomes necessary to attend additional meetings, the fee will be adjusted as follows [whatever was agreed upon in earlier discussions].

I further understand that you will reimburse me for routine expenses, including long-distance telephone calls, incurred in [researching/writing/ photographing the assignment]. Any other extraordinary expenses, should they be expected, will be discussed with you beforehand. Invoices for these expenses not included in this fee will be submitted for reimbursement within [number of days] of [completion of project or any other payment schedule negotiated].

If this is your understanding, please sign and date the enclosed copy and return it to me.

Sign every agreement before initiating any research, writing, or editing on the assignment. Be sure your client's signature is on it, too. Don't be afraid to voice your concerns during the negotiating period. Many professional writers will tell you what they've learned the hard way: It's better to be safe than sorry—and stuck with an agreement that's not only giving you ulcers but costing you time and money to boot.

Don't forget, free-lancers are traders—merchants of writing in the best sense. While trade-offs are second nature to successful entrepreneurs in other businesses, many independent writers haven't mastered the trade-off balancing act, which often plays an important role in negotiating an agreement. David Hon's book, *Trade-offs for the Person Who Can't Have Everything* orients you in this "savvy" that separates a good trader from an average one.

Hon, the national training manager of the American Heart Association, explains that trade-offs govern your position when power is brought to bear and decisions must be made. Any free-lancer who's ever struggled with three critical conflicts—*quality* versus *cost* versus *time*—will appreciate the solution Hon proposes in chapter 6.

The concept that makes the difference Hon calls "odd trade-off out." Simply put, this means "given the trade-off *you* protect most, and the one the *other* person protects most, then your avenue out of the conflict is the *least* protected trade-off in your interaction."

As shown in the illustration below, cost-quality traders can extend the project's deadline. Quality-time traders should increase the budget. Cost-time traders, where a low-budget project must be completed fast, can lower quality—substituting black-and-white for color photos, for example, or choosing a cheaper grade of paper. (Trade-offs, Hon cautions, are balanced most successfully *before* the final contract is signed, though they are sometimes negotiated during and after— when budget, personnel, or other variables change.)

Remember, cost, quality, and time are at stake in *every* negotiating situation, but you can always say no to a bad trade-off. "You can also increase your basic charge by as much as 50 percent for rush jobs

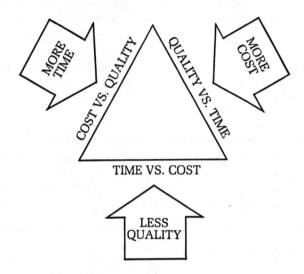

TIME VS. COST

or those that require you to work over weekends," suggests Diana Ben-zaia, a New York City free-lancer who runs her own business, Wordcrafters Unlimited, and consults for pharmaceutical firms, major medical centers, and national health organizations, such as the American Cancer Society and American Diabetes Association.

Similarly, you might consider reducing your fee, perhaps by twenty-five or fifty dollars per day, to obtain a *written* contract from a client specifying a minimum number of days' work per month for a one-year period. Make sure the number of days you're tying up at a reduced rate with one business for a year are worth your while—Benzaia says it should be at least *four* days a month. And her final word of advice? "Just as all businesses increase their prices—for inflation or improved service as they get better at the job—review your rates annually."

MEDIA/NONMEDIA WORK—THE PROS AND CONS

Many independent writers in the health and medical field combine work in mass media with the less-visible, but often better-paying free-lance opportunities in nonmedia. The following chart clearly outlines the advantages and disadvantages of both. It was prepared by Donald Radcliffe, a past president of the American Medical Writers Association who has successfully free-lanced for twenty years.

MEDIA JOBS/CLIENTS	NONMEDIA JOBS/CLIENTS
Magazines Newspapers Radio/television Books/chapters Encyclopedias Field editor/contributor Stringer/correspondent	Advertising agencies Public relations firms Pharmaceutical companies Medical associations Individual clients
Rates are set (not much room for negotiation) Basically, a buyer's market When better-known, a writer can get more $	Fees are negotiable (no one knows exactly what a project is worth) Bids submitted on projects
More competition (but always room for new talent)	Less competition (News of the project/job doesn't get out as easily) Writer can make own contract However, may be competing against one or more writers for same work

Sell your product
   Query/proposal
   Final manuscript
	Sell yourself
	   Product is down the line
	   Talk about the project
	   first with client or committee

Easier to generate (here today, gone tomorrow)	Easier to keep (accounts and clients keep returning to you)
Harder to fulfill (less help from editor, requires good discipline) Writer gets public exposure Research can be fun, stimulating Potential for big impact	More direction from client or committee (sometimes *too much* input!)
In terms of $__, *less* financially rewarding Writer is highly visible Better exposure Enhances writer's professional reputation	In terms of $__, will pay *more* Writer is invisible No exposure Referrals from satisfied clients

Before you decide to make free-lancing a full- or part-time career, take a close look at your budget and financial needs. The bottom line is that you need enough money to live on—whatever that adds up to in your circumstances. To enjoy life, you need a little more.

Don't make the mistake of cutting yourself off from your current livelihood before you have some reliable carryover accounts, clients, or self-generating assignments that will pay the rent and buy the groceries until you can make a name for yourself and build up a viable free-lance business. "If you can establish yourself as an expert in your field," says Radcliffe, "you can start charging bigger rates."

Keep in mind, however, that the $45- or $50-an-hour work is probably no more than 20 percent of your total free-lance time. Most free-lancers neglect to build in time for learning about a project and coming up with creative ideas or approaches. They forget to add in time for business luncheons or entertainment of clients, for bookkeeping (you can spend an hour or more going over old records, billing clients, keeping a daybook up-to-date). Here's how Radcliffe outlines the "Reality of Free-lance Time" at his workshops for medical writers:

Business matters/daily log/tax records	5%
Pro bono work (public service/nonprofit)	5%
Unaccountable time/lost time	5%
Promoting new business (queries, proposals, business lunches, etc.)	20%
Nonproductive (research, telephones, digging in and maintaining files, interviews, editorial correspondence, etc.)	20%
Long-term assignments and sustainer account work (tends to be more efficient and productive work because it's ongoing and familiar)	25%
Writing on new assignments/projects—the $50/hr. work	20%
Acquiring new skills and information	5%

Add them up and Radcliffe's figures total 105 percent because, he claims, "it always seems like there's never enough time. Yet, one of the joys of free-lancing is that *new* assignments are fascinating," he says, adding, "you always have to keep something ahead just for your own mental health."

Emotional health is no small matter to free-lancers. Many are totally unprepared for the isolation of working alone, self-discipline required, or long hours. ("I didn't know what Saturdays and Sundays were," one writer told me. Another put it this way: "If you're not a good boss, it can be the downfall of the employees—especially if you are the *only* employee.")

INCOME BUILDERS AND
STRATEGIES FOR SUCCESS

Most successful free-lancers have many queries and proposals out at one time. Ideas for those queries, says *Parade* health editor Earl Ubell, "come through an *interplay* between what you read in medical and scientific literature, what you hear at scientific meetings, and what you read in popular magazines. And then you'll know, it's possible to make a living—a good amount of money—but you must have a steady base of income."

Here are ten major ways which lead to a healthier bank account and steady base of income whether you choose to free-lance in media or nonmedia:

Networking in Professional Organizations. Many free-lancers find it helpful to join professional organizations, such as the American Medical Writers Association, Society for Technical Writing, National Association of Science Writers, Author's Guild, and American Society of Journalists and Authors. Medical editor and writer Bernice Heller explains why.

> Not only does one receive the stimulation from colleagues that is so important to psychic well-being, this is also a means of staying abreast of developments in the field. Also, true "pros" are generally warm and generous people, and they are happy to give whatever assistance they can to younger and less-experienced persons. Finally, most professional organizations publish internal directories, and this offers members another way to gain the exposure they need.

In business parlance, *networking* refers to third-party introductions to potential clients or VIPs who can help in advancing a career. In some cases, these introductions lead to a "mentor" relationship.

(Kathleen Conaboy, for example, is public relations and development director for the University of Nevada School of Medicine. In choosing a career path, she says, "I had good luck finding a mentor in a woman named Christina Smith who encouraged graduate school and public relations." While in graduate school, Conaboy completed an internship at the National Cancer Institute in Washington, D.C. "There," she says, "I learned everything that I know about medicine in seven months—I got lucky.")

Some professional writers' organizations require sponsorship by a member; others, evidence of sufficient production of quality work within a certain period of time. You can obtain more information and membership requirements by writing to the health-related professional writers' associations described in appendix C.

Free-lance Listing in Professional Association Directories. Members of the American Medical Writers Association (AMWA) are unanimous in saying one of the most important sources of assignments is a listing in the annual AMWA *Freelance Directory.* Cost: Twenty-five dollars a year. The directory, explains executive director Lillian Sablack, is sent to all medical libraries and circulated among selected advertising agencies and pharmaceutical companies which regularly use free-lance writers and editors.

Says Barbara Chapman, media director for the National Center for Missing and Exploited Children, who also free-lances, "I can't tell you the number of assignments I've gotten from being listed in the *AMWA Freelance Directory.*" Chicago-based free-lancer Donald Radcliffe agrees, adding, "I get at least one fairly major assignment each year."

Press Directory Listings. In addition to association directories which include free-lancers, there are other listings such as *Working Press of the Nation* and *Guide to U.S. Medical and Science News Correspondents and Contacts.* The latter includes newspapers, consumer magazines, and radio and TV stations. It pinpoints the names of more than 1,000 persons whose beat includes health and medical reporting, plus about 200 free-lancers in the field—many of whom are available for journalistic and public-relations assignments.

With paid circulation of about 1,000, the annual guide is sent primarily to PR personnel, universities, hospitals, trade associations, and corporations, especially those in the health-care industry. For free listing with a no obligation to buy, independent writers should send a letter describing their work and publication credits to Larriston Communications, P.O. Box 20229, New York, NY 10025. (212) 864-0150.

"We don't pass judgment on the merits of a free-lancer," says Robin Elliott, a partner in Larriston Communications, "but we do ask that they spend a significant portion of their professional time writing science and medical writing for the popular media and general markets."

Advertising in Trade and Professional Society Journals. Dorothy Luckraft, R.N., is an editorial consultant whose quarter-page ad in *Nursing & Health Care* lists her credentials following these four questions: Do you or your colleagues need help preparing a manuscript for publication? Could your staff or faculty benefit from a workshop that emphasizes practical experience in developing a manuscript? Would you want a private, confidential review of your manuscript before submitting it to a journal? Do you have a newsletter or newspaper that you'd like to start or improve?

Many free-lance writers and editors find a $1/16$th-page ad targeted to the professional audience in need of a coauthor or ghostwriter is equally effective in attracting new business. Placed in a local, state, or regional journal, your ad might read: "Do you need help with a journal article, brochure, report, article, monograph, or chapter in a book? I am a professional writer with expertise in medical [or legal or whatever your specialty is] writing [and/or editing]."

Listing in the Yellow Pages. Most free-lancers agree this type of advertising is least productive and tends to lead to low-order and grossly underpaid assignments (one writer reported turning down an offer of $50 for an eight-page brochure). However, if you are going into business for yourself, consider placing a simple, attractive ad plus notice in your local paper's "new business" column and keeping a listing in the Yellow Pages. Although it's not likely to attract many clients, free-lancers say such listings help in obtaining referrals from other writers and for tax purposes, too.

Help Wanted—Writers. Check alphabetized newspaper listings under E (editors); F (free-lance); P (publishing); and W, where I found this listing recently in the *San Francisco Chronicle:*

WRITERS FREELANCE STRINGERS
For HARD NEWS stories, about technology, science, medicine & health-business, political or new development. Clips & resume to: Science News Wire, 236 West 26th St., New York NY 10001.

Similar help-wanted ads for free-lance, full- and part-time positions appear regularly in *The New York Times* and in professional, trade, and journalism publications like *Editor & Publisher, The Quill,* and *Advertising Age.* The *Authors Guild Bulletin,* for example, periodically runs "coauthors wanted" notices—fifty words maximum including brief description of the book and the problem.

Among recent listings in the American Medical Writers Association *Job Market Sheet* have been one for a medical news magazine editor/writer; a writer able to translate scientific and clinical data into lively, informative promotion copy, and a director for a well-known medical center's department of scientific publications. Be sure to check bulletin boards and other message centers at annual meetings of professional organizations, where editors, publishers and others who hire writers frequently post publication fact sheets, "positions available," or "free-lancers wanted" notices.

Credit Sheet/Brochures/Promotional Mailings. Motivational psychologist and best-selling author Denis Waitley sends out an attractive beige folder with a credit sheet (listing books and talks he gives) plus reprints of significant articles from major publications. Printed in darker brown on the folder's cover are his name, address, and telephone number. Since photocopy shops offer many inexpensive options for printing, make your brochure or credit sheet as professional, attractive, and *competitive* as you can.

Credit sheets differ from the typical resume or professional C.V. *(curriculum vitae.)* Generally, the credit sheet lists your achievements as a professional writer, such as books, book chapters, magazine articles, films, documentaries, projects completed—marketing studies, for example, or complete convention coverage. Some writers include their education, but this is optional unless it uniquely qualifies you in some way for special assignments. (Graduate and professional degrees, for instance, are assets in obtaining free-lance assignments in the pharmaceutical industry; an M.P.H. is a plus in community health-care education.)

If you're not sure to whom you should send your packet, brochure, or credit sheet, call the ad agency, PR firm, or pharmaceutical company you hope to sell to and ask for the name of the person who buys their medical writing or makes the editorial decisions. With your packet, include a brief covering letter to introduce yourself briefly. A follow-up call and an offer to send additional samples or come in for a personal interview show you're serious in your efforts to free-lance for that company or medical group.

Letters to Potential Clients. David L. Raffle, a writer/editor from Granada Hills, California, believes mass mailings to physicians pay off in the long run, though you must assume you'll get nothing in the short haul. Raffle, who always staples his business card to the letters as well, sees such mailings as an on-going process—one more thing you must do to discover new clients and promote your writing services.

"Sending letters to physicians en masse is akin to throwing seeds to the wind," Raffle explains. "As is common to most mailings, maybe 1 percent will respond—and then, only 10 percent [of those] will respond affirmatively. The nice part is that while sending out 500 letters to physicians may only result in one response, that *one* more than pays for the time and effort, and your name is now seen by many hundreds of doctors."

Raffle says he's sent countless letters to hospital-based and industrial physicians. In one case, his letter was seen on the desk of a prospective client by another person, and that lucky glance landed him a $2,800 assignment.

In spreading your name around, don't forget the tie-in between law and medicine. Matthew Bender & Company, Inc., for example, is a New York City legal- and tax-book publisher that looks to medical writers in preparing chapters on medical topics for publications marketed to personal-injury and medical-malpractice attorneys.

Writers' Workshops and Communications Seminars. Team up a writing or speech-making workshop for health professionals with a county, state, or regional association meeting to create a strong-appeal program sure to generate specific writing assignments or editorial consulting work.

One county medical society, for instance, offered a Friday/Saturday duo in which a free-lancer presented a "Speaking and Writing Workshop for Physicians" following an American Medical Association workshop on "Marketing Strategies for Private Practice." Among topics that could be covered in a writing workshop are: how to write a patient-information handbook or instruction sheet and how to create publishable articles, including opinion pieces. Another important topic is teaching physicians how to deal with the media.

Nice work if you can get it is giving business writing workshops to physicians on cruise ships. As Internal Revenue Service law now stands, physicians, attorneys, and allied health professionals can get tax benefits in conjunction with continuing education. To write off the cruise, physicians, for example, must attend a minumum of four hours per day for CME (continuing medical education) credit. Your workshop fits into this four-hour period. The rest of the day is free for vacationing in the sun.

Recycling and Secondary Sales. Don't miss out on extra income by neglecting to recycle your original research, idea, slant, *and* even the article itself. Take the same piece, for example, but slant it to a different audience that reads a *noncompeting* publication, and you've made another sale.

When prolific free-lancer Diana Benzaia wrote a piece on twelve ways to cut health-care costs safely, she sold it first for a young female readership to *Self*. Next, she reslanted her information to the over-fifty retirement readership of *Prime Times*, then targeted the piece to family readership and made two more sales—one to *Sunday Woman* and one to *Rx Being Well*.

Selling the *same* article means banking two or more checks *without* having to rewrite. For instance, if you've sold only first North American serial rights to a story, you still have secondary rights to sell. Consult *Writer's Market* for reprint market guidelines and publications that buy second rights, such as *Prime Times* and Eastern Air Lines' *Review Magazine.*

Some editors prefer submission of the original article as it appeared in a noncompeting publication. Others want a clean copy of the manuscript and a covering letter (much like a query) which includes the article's publication history. If you think your article fits the style of *Reader's Digest,* send the published piece with a cover letter saying you are submitting it for reprint consideration. Payment is approximately $900 per printed page, with half the fee going to the author, the other half to the original publication.

International Markets. One of the best global marketeers is Los Angeles-based free-lancer Jim Joseph, whose international salesmanship has brought him up to $20,000 in total sales for a *single* article sold to various publications overseas.

When I asked if there's a global market for science-medical pieces, he told me, "The answer is a resounding 'yes' but it's a very sophisticated market. You need to be a sophisticated marketeer with a highly developed package to do well. And you must write very well and supply first-rate art (almost always color transparencies)."

Joseph, who gives writing seminars in California and sells the tape cassettes, says when he's marketing medical stories to the global market he usually sells only to *weekly* magazines with at least 150,000 circulation. But even at that, "global magazines can fool you," he says, explaining he recently received $800 for Finnish rights sold to a monthly with only 23,000 circulation. Currently, Joseph is developing a package for an article on the intravital microscope, titled, "The Body Eye: New Intravital Microscope Sees inside the Body."

Using syndicates such as Trans World Features can save you time researching overseas markets, but there is less profit in the reprint sale because the syndicate keeps a hefty percentage. A few free-lancers work directly with magazine representatives of foreign markets, such as Australian Consolidated Press in New York City. Some articles are too Americanized to sell abroad, but if such references can be eliminated without undue damage, this is an excellent market for articles on psychological self-help as well as diet, exercise, health, and fitness.

To find information on foreign publications, check *Europa Year Book; Sources of Serials,* which lists by publisher; and *Ulrich's International Periodicals Directory*—all generally available at the reference desk in large libraries. *Ulrich's,* for example, profiles some 110,000 publications from about 65,000 publishers in 181 countries. By using *Ulrich's* database, updated every four to six weeks, you can also learn who's published what by searching for titles using "key word" techniques.

GURNEYSIDE CONSULTS— TO GIVE OR NOT TO GIVE?

Highly paid doctors and dentists don't appreciate cocktail party or curbside consultation from patients or friends. They're used to being paid for their opinion and, in most cases, can't tell what's wrong without *seeing* the patient first. Yet there are health professionals (and their spouses) who think nothing of calling on the phone for a lengthy consultation about a rejected book manuscript or whipping out their latest article or op-ed piece and asking for a quick read from a patient who's a professional writer.

The fact is, it's your skill, experience, and livelihood that are being tapped. It's also your choice whether you want to give them away free. You *can* say no. How you do this—especially if the "politics" of the situation are sticky—is up to you.

One way that works well if you're in the doctor's office is to beg off, saying you'd like to see the manuscript, but find it hard to concentrate on writing when your own physical problems are on your mind. The other is to be more direct. "I'd like to help you but I can't do this for you without charging a fee, since writing and consulting are how I make my living."

Keep in mind that doctors frequently have different financial goals from those of writers. Though medical economics are in flux and the era of six-figure doctor incomes is on the wane, many physicians seek out tax shelters and write-offs to protect their income. In certain free-lance situations, this can pose a problem. One independent writer, for instance, tells of a well-to-do medical expert whose dream was to start his own professional journal—one that would be respected within his specialty. The free-lancer agreed to edit the journal for a set fee. Submissions were invited from the physician's colleagues, an editorial review board was put together, and start-up advertising was solicited.

As paid circulation and advertising revenues increased, the physician decided to renegotiate the contract, offering the free-lancer 10 percent of advertising revenues. Given the rate of advertising growth in the first year, it appeared to be a good deal. But a telephone call to the physician's accountant put the new offer in a different financial light. The doctor, it seemed, had no desire to *make* money on the journal. Simply put, he couldn't afford to. Given his tax bracket, his goal was to keep the publication as a tax *loss*. The real payoff for him was ego gratification.

By assuming the doctor had a profit motive rather than a tax-loss one, the free-lancer almost got himself into a *nonprofit* situation. The moral (with apologies to Dr. Samuel Johnson) is this: No one but a blockhead ever writes for *less* so a doctor can stash away more. So be award of *hidden* agendas.

ENHANCING PRODUCTIVITY

Early to bed and early to rise may once have been the modus operandi of the healthy, wealthy, and wise. But Ben Franklin's sage advice didn't take into account the outside factors, like rejection and writer's block, that impinge on a writer's morale, productivity, and creativity. Time is money to the independent writer, and fresh ideas, the lifeline to by-lines.

Here are some pointers from successful free-lancers that help me—and will help you—put the muses on call, burnout on a back burner, and more editor's checks in the bank.

- *Increase your luck factor.* According to Max Gunther, author of *The Luck Factor,* it's "people luck"—which is largely *self-genera-ted*—that is of the greatest importance in everyday life. Lucky people, he claims, make sure their names, faces, and ideas get around. Lucky people know they can increase their odds greatly by making positive contact with many people. They're ready when "luck" comes their way. The payoff? Exciting ideas, fresh slants, new perspectives, more words to sell, more free-lance opportunities, *and* more money in the bank.

- *Identify the chief decision maker(s) in the project you're work-ing on and ignore the others.* Hours spent in committee meetings are hours you don't have for writing. Establish your working relationship with the decision maker, who may or may not be the head of the com-mittee or project. (I've found this is especially true in working with nonprofit organizations, where the project chairperson may be chief in name only.) Don't let the committee use—or abuse—you.

- *Whittle away small chunks of big projects to make them man-ageable.* If you can't complete a major task in a day, ask yourself what small job you could finish and feel good about.

- *Keep writing while you're hot.* If you're a workaholic, you'll do it anyway. But the secret to keeping production on the fast track is to stop writing in a spot where it will be easy to pick up the flow again the next day. That may mean stopping in the middle of a paragraph where the next sentence flows naturally, rather than completing it.

- *Establish yourself as "the" expert writer on a topic.* But within your specialty be a generalist. Remember, you won't succeed unless you personalize your message and write entertainingly. This means telling the story through people; using examples, quotes, anecdotes: and catching the essence of the piece in a catchy title. Do that, and editors will turn to you first when they need stories on a particular subject.

• *Develop a compatible subspecialty.* Henry Miller once said that our destination is never a place but a new way of looking at things. Editors are always on the lookout for new writers with fresh ideas or different and exciting ways of presenting old ones. Medicine, however, is a demanding specialty—for both practitioner and writer. One way to avoid burnout is to have a second area of writing expertise—whether it be travel writing, collectibles, or food and drink—which you can turn to when business is slow or you feel a need for a change of pace. The extra income is as healthy for the ego as it is for the bank balance.

• *Ask for more money.* If you've written four or more articles for a publication at the same payment schedule, it's time to ask for more money. You won't always get it (especially at low-budget or small-circulation magazines), but it's worth a try, and it definitely pays off at larger publications. Some of the nation's top free-lancers also work out contracts to write a guaranteed number of articles per year for a given publication.

• *Keep your notes and business records.* Don't toss out your notes, tapes, correspondence, manuscript, script, or other project-related materials. Besides being necessary to defend yourself if you're sued over copyright, libel, refusal to reveal sources, or any other legal or editorial hassle, they may be needed to back up your claims if you're audited by the Internal Revenue Service. In some cases, you may be able to donate remaindered books and your notes or other research materials to a library or an educational or scientific organization and receive a tax benefit for a charitable contribution.

Finally, don't forget that you need other people as much as they need you. Free-lancing can be lonely business—so be a joiner, a doer, a goer. Renew yourself with a day on the slopes or beach. Splurge once in a while. Go out for dinner with friends. Stop by a museum; get tickets to a concert or the theater. Volunteer if you can spare a few hours on a regular basis. You'll not only increase your free-lancing network, you'll recharge your spirit and make new friends as well.

SO, HERE'S TO YOUR HEALTH . . .

In these fifteen chapters, we've covered a world of health and medical matters ranging from idea sources to new markets for your work. We've talked about some of the special challenges and opportunities that go hand in hand with health, medical, and health-related writing.

Because of your words, someone else's life and quality of life may be improved. Your article on how to cope or what symptoms to look for, where to go for more information or what to do in an emergency, may make all the difference between early detection of disease and someone's early death. The responsibility is awesome; the chance for positive impact, immense. Words, remember, are the most powerful drug used by mankind. Use them always with care.

Now it's up to you. The opportunities have never been greater to sell what you write on health and medical topics you care deeply about. So, here's to your good health and your success in health writing. May you enjoy both.

APPENDIX A

Honors, Prizes, Awards

Following is a partial list of major prizes, honors, and awards open to journalists and authors in the field of medicine and allied health sciences. Not included are those awards for which membership in a professional society or organization is required, or those prizes given only to health professionals or students.

This list has been compiled from several sources including *Awards, Honors and Prizes*, 5th edition, edited by Paul Wasserman, (Gale Research Co.,) and individual award sponsors. Before entering your work in competition, be sure to check with the sponsoring organization for current deadlines, categories, and eligibility requirements, as these may be subject to change. For prompt response, include a self-addressed, stamped envelope (SASE.)

American Academy of Family Physicians
1740 West 92nd Street
Kansas City, MO 64114

Journalism Awards. In recognition of the most significant and informative writing and reporting on family practice and health care. To a journalist. Monetary prizes of $1,000, $750 and $250. Awarded annually.

American Academy of Nursing
2420 Pershing Road
Kansas City, MO 64108

Media Awards. Entries will be accepted in one or more of the following categories (only one entry per category). Deadline for receipt of entries each year, July 31. (1) To nurses or nonnurses for positive fictional portrayal (novels, magazine articles, television programs, motion pictures) of nurses and nursing. (2) To nurses or nonnurses for positive nonfictional portrayal (books, magazines/newspaper articles, television and radio news commentary, documentaries, talk shows, public service announcements, advertisements, etc.) of nurses and nursing. (3) to a nurse(s) for excellence in presenting health information to the public through the mass media (e.g. newspaper columns, television/radio features, etc.).

American Chiropractic Association
1916 Wilson Blvd.
Arlington, VA 22201

Health Journalism Awards. To recognize journalists whose constructive thoughts suggest solutions to basic health problems, motivate consumers to take care of their health, and contribute to fair and responsible health reporting. To a journalist or team of writers who are responsible for the creation of either a single work, or a series published or produced during the year. Categories include newspapers, consumer magazines, television, radio, trade and professional publications, and audiovisuals. Winner of each category receives $200 and the ACA Distinguished Journalism Award. Special plaques awarded to runners-up. Awarded annually. Established 1976.

American College of Health Care Administrators
Post Office Box 5890
Bethesda, MD 20814

Journalism Award. To recognize an individual or an organization for outstanding journalistic achievement relating to long-term-care administration during the eighteen-month period immediately preceding the convocation. Based on supporting documentation, nominee will be recommended to Board of Governors. Plaque awarded annually. Deadline for nominations: December 31.

American Dental Association
211 E. Chicago Ave.
Chicago, IL 60611

Science Writers Award. For recognition of the best newspaper and magazine article on some topic of dental health and/or research. Monetary prize of $1,000 in each category. Awarded annually. Administered by the Science Writers Award Committee of the association through the support of Lever Brothers Company.

American Heart Association
7320 Greenville Avenue
Dallas, TX 74231

Howard W. Blakeslee Awards. For recognition of the most significant contribution by any medium of mass communication to public understanding of progress in research and in the prevention, care, or treatment of heart and circulatory diseases. Citation and $1,000. Awarded annually. Deadline: February 1.

American Institute of the History of Pharmacy
Pharmacy Building
University of Wisconsin
Madison, WI 53706

Edward Kremers Award. For recognition of an original publication dealing with historical or historicosocial aspects of pharmacy. To a United States citizen. Antique drug jar. Awarded annually. Established 1961.

George Urdang Medal. For an original and distinguished publication or series of interrelated publications in the field of pharmaceutical history. To an author from any country. Bronze medal inscribed with profile of George Urdang. Awarded annually. Established 1952.

American Medical Writers Association
5272 River Road, Suite 370
Bethesda, MD 20016

AMWA Medical Book Awards. Divided into three categories: best book on a medical subject for physicians, best book for allied health professionals, and best trade book for lay readers, To the author for a book published in the previous year. Awarded annually.

AMWA Annual Medical Film Festival Awards. To recognize outstanding examples of medical films, including videotapes. Certificate of Recognition. Awarded every two years (odd number). Established 1973.

William Harvey Award for Writing on Hypertension. For outstanding writing achievement in increasing public awareness and knowledge of high blood pressure and its effect on health. In general-interest publications. Separate awards for newspaper and consumer-magazine writers. First place prize of $1,500; second place, $750; third place, $500. Established 1981. Cosponsored by National High Blood Pressure Education Program and E.R. Squibb and Sons, Inc., Box 4000, Princeton, NJ 08540.

AMWA/College of American Pathologists Award. (See College of American Pathologists.)

Walter C. Alvarez Memorial Award. Bestowed in recognition of excellence in scientific papers, articles, editorials, and other material; for excellence of design, printing, illustrations; and for distinguished service to the medical profession. Awarded annually.

John P. McGovern Medal. Bestowed in recognition of an individual who is a preeminent contributor in any of the various facets of medical communication. Awarded annually.

American Osteopathic Association
212 E. Ohio St.
Chicago, IL 60611

AOA Journalism Awards. To recognize the growing corps of journalists who report and interpret osteopathic medicine to the scientific community and the general public. Awarded on the basis of accepted standards of good journalism and the contribution which the article or broadcast makes toward a fuller understanding of the osteopathic profession. Prize of $1,000 for first place; two supplementary prizes of $500 each. Awarded annually. Established 1956.

American Psychiatric Association
1700 18th Street, NW
Washington, DC 20009

Robert T. Morse Writer's Award. For recognition of outstanding contributions to furthering the public understanding of psychiatry. To a writer outside the field of psychiatry. Plaque and $500. Awarded annually.

American Psychological Foundation
1200 17th Street, NW
Washington, DC 20036

National Psychology Awards for Excellence in the Media. To recognize and encourage outstanding, accurate reporting which increases the public's knowledge and understanding of psychology. To journalists in six categories: newspaper, magazine, book, radio, and two divisions of television/films—TV news-documentary, and TV drama. Prize of $1,000 and trip to American Psychological Association convention last week in August. Awarded annually.

American Society of Abdominal Surgeons
675 Main St.
Melrose, MA 02176

American Society of Abdominal Surgeons Journalism Award. For recognition of a distinguished example of a newspaper or magazine reporter's work, either a single article or a series, relating to the field of abdominal surgery. To a medical writer. Framed, embossed certificate and $250. Awarded annually. Established 1966.

American Society of Anesthesiologists
%Wendy Gross, Senior Vice-President
Golin/Harris Communications
500 N. Michigan Ave.
Chicago, IL 60611

Medical Writers Award. To recognize outstanding effort to educate the public through articles about anesthesiology. To science and health/medical writers. Two prizes: $500, first place; $250, second place. Awarded annually at American Society of Anesthesiologists' convention. Established 1983.

American Speech-Language-Hearing Association
10801 Rockville Pike
Rockville, MD 20852

ASHA National Media Awards. To recognize outstanding contributions to the public's knowledge and understanding of speech-language pathology. Four categories: newspaper, television, radio, and magazine. Award of $1,000 in each category and all-expense paid trip to annual convention for presentation. Established 1978.

Arthritis Foundation
1314 Spring Street, NW
Atlanta, GA 30309

Russell L. Cecil Arthritis Writing Award. To recognize and encourage writing of news stories, articles, and radio and television scripts for general-circulation media (United States) on subject of arthritis. Gold medallion imbedded in Lucite cube. Awarded annually. Established 1956.

Association for Retarded Citizens of the United States
2501 Avenue J
P.O. Box 6109
Arlington, TX 76011

ARC of Excellence Community Media Awards. To honor the outstanding national and community media efforts of the year, as well as individual effort, to create better public understanding of mentally retarded individuals and mental retardation. Certificate. Given annually.

Canadian Science Writers' Association
Awards Committee, Attention: George Truss
%the Wellesley Hospital Public Relations Committee
160 Wellesley Street, E.
Toronto, Ontario M4Y 1J3

Science Journalism Awards. For recognition of outstanding writing in the field of science journalism in Canadian print and electronic media. Four awards (Science and Technology/Industry; Science and Natural Resources; Science and Society, and Ortho Science and Health Journalism Award). Open to any Canadian resident for original material published in Canadian print media or audiovisual media, in French or English, during the calendar year. Print entries must have appeared in Canadian publications aimed at the general public; electronic entries must have been aired on a cable or broadcast system licensed in Canada. Award applicants need not be members of CSWA. Special emphasis placed on the social and economic impact of science and technology in all award categories.

Ortho Science and Health Journalism Award. Two awards in recognition of outstanding writing in the general field of science and health. Scroll and $1,000. Awarded annually. Cosponsored by Ortho Pharmaceutical (Canada) Ltd. Established 1972.

Carnation Company
5045 Wilshire Blvd.
Los Angeles, CA 90036

Golden Carnation Awards for Excellence of Nutrition Coverage by Daily Newspaper Food Editors. To honor outstanding newspaper food editors who are helping to improve the nutrition knowledge and food habits of their readers. Presented in two categories: (1) for newspapers having a daily circulation from 25,000 to 150,000; (2) for newspapers over 150,000 daily circulation. First-place winner in each circulation category receives $500; each of two runners-up receives $250. Awarded annually. Established 1970.

College of American Pathologists
7400 N. Skokie Blvd.
Skokie, IL 60077

CAP/AMWA Journalism Awards. To recognize writing that broadens public awareness and understanding of the specialty of pathology and the contribution of pathologists. To writers of news and feature articles for general interest and magazines. Award of $1,000 and commemorative plaque plus expenses paid to annual fall meeting for recipients of first-place prizes in both newspaper and magazine categories; $500 and plaque for second place in each category. For work published during preceding year. Forward entries to American Medical Writers Association. Established 1984.

Gallaudet College
Office of Alumni and Public Relations
800 Florida Ave. NE
Washington, DC 20002

Gallaudet Journalism Award. To recognize excellence in reporting and writing on topics involving deafness and the lives of deaf people. To nonfiction writer or reporter in two categories: $500 cash award and certificate for best article of 2,000 words or more; $200 award and certificate for best article under 2,000 words, published during preceding year in United States newspaper or magazine.

Health Sciences Communications Association (HeSCA)
6105 Lindell Blvd.
St. Louis, MO 63112

Annual Media Festival Awards. To recognize the best in health-sciences media. Includes film, video, still media, and print formats, among them book/monograph, periodical, brochure/flyers, and campaign formats, i.e., mastheads, logos, booklets, posters, etc.—all part of a "family" of literature entered under one title. All entries must be on a health, medical, or biosciences subject of educational value to health professionals, students, and/or the public. All entries must have been produced, copyrighted, and/or released during the preceding year. Cash awards for first, second, and third-place prizes range from $500 to $100, plus plaques and certificates.

History of Science Society
215 S. 34 Street/D6
Philadelphia, PA 19104
(Contact: Kimberly Pelkey)

Pfizer Award. For distinguished publication by an American or Canadian author on a topic related to the history of science. Monetary prize: $1,000. Awarded annually.

Museum of Science, Boston
Science Park
Boston, MA 02114

Bradford Washburn Award. To recognize an outstanding contribution toward public understanding of science and appreciation of its fascination and of the vital role it plays in all our lives. To an individual anywhere in the world. Gold medal and $5,000 honorarium. Awarded annually. Established in 1964 in honor of Bradford Washburn, museum director from 1938 to 1980.

National Academy of Sciences
2101 Constitution Avenue, NW
Washington, DC 20418

National Academy of Sciences Award for Scientific Reviewing. To recognize excellence in scientific reviewing published anywhere. Monetary prize of $5,000. Awarded annually in a field designated each year by the NAS Council. (Presented in the social and behavioral sciences in 1984; biological sciences, 1985.) Established in 1977 in honor of James Murray Luck. Sponsored jointly by Annual Reviews, Inc., and the Institute for Scientific Information, Inc.

National Association of Science Writers, Inc.
P.O. Box 294
Greenlawn, NY 11740

Science-in-Society Journalism Awards. To provide recognition—without subsidy from any professional or commercial interest—for investigative and interpretive reporting about the sciences and their impact for good and bad. Material may be a single article, a series, or a broadcast script; books and book digests are not eligible. It must be written in English, intended for the layperson, and broadcast or published in a periodical circulated in North America in the previous year. Separate prizes of $1,000, engraved medallions, and certificates. Awarded in three categories: newspapers, magazines, and television/radio. Awarded annually. Established 1972.

National Mental Health Association
1021 Prince Street
Alexandria, VA 22314

Mental Health Media Awards. To honor representatives of the media who have made outstanding contributions in the coverage of mental health issues—through continuous mental-health coverage during the year, a series of mental-health articles or programs, or production of a public-service announcement. Article must have been published, programs or announcements aired, between June 1 of the previous year and May 31 of the year of the awards. Categories include: daily newspaper with circulation over 500,000; daily newspaper, circulation under 500,000; other publications, including nondaily newspapers and magazines: local radio or television stations, for news and entertainment programs; national radio or television networks, or cable systems, for news or entertainment programs; radio/television public-service announcements, and individual reporters. Awarded annually.

National Multiple Sclerosis Foundation
205 E. 42nd St.
New York, NY 10017

MS Public Education Award. To encourage editors, writers, and program directors to learn about and report on multiple sclerosis—the disease itself, efforts to find its cause and cure, and ways patients and their families cope with MS. For articles published or TV and radio programs aired during the year. Two cash prizes ($1,000 each) for best print entry and for best broadcast entry. Awarded annually. Established 1975.

Royal Society of Canada
344 Wellington St.
Ottawa, Ontario K1A 0N4, Canada

Jason A. Hannah Medal. To recognize an important Canadian publication in the history of medicine. To an author for work of high quality published in the ten years preceding the nomination. Bronze medal and $1,500. Awarded annually. Cosponsored by Hannah Institute for the History of Medicine, Associated Medical Services, Inc. Established 1976.

Charles Scribner's Sons
597 Fifth Ave.
New York, NY 10017

Scribner Science Writing Prize. For an unpublished work of nonfiction (full-length treatment or collection of essays) involving natural history, the physical sciences, or the sciences of man. To writers who are American citizens or permanent residents of the United States and who have not previously published a science book for general readers. Award: a $5,000 advance against royalties plus a $5,000 advertising and promotions guarantee. Awarded annually. Submit complete manuscripts with SASE. Established 1984.

Society for Technical Communication
815 15th St., NW
Washington,. DC 20005

International Technical Communications Competition. To recognize excellence in all fields of technical and allied communications, dealing with technology, science, industry, business, government, and medical/health topics for professional and lay audiences. Categories include audiovisuals, photography, and technical publications, among them house organs, brochures, annual reports, periodicals, newsletters, news stories, and feature articles.

APPENDIX B

AMERICAN MEDICAL WRITERS ASSOCIATION

CODE OF ETHICS

Preamble

The American Medical Writers Association (AMWA) has compiled the following principles of conduct for all individuals involved in medical communication to guide them in their relationships with physicians, fellow writers, other health professionals, government agencies, and all others who may be affected by their communications. Writing is a powerful tool that influences the minds of readers in all walks of life. Therefore, medical writers should honor this code of ethics.

Principle 1

A medical writer has the duty to observe the laws and regulations pertaining to the documents he writes, to uphold the dignity and honor of his profession and Association, and to accept their ethical principles. He should not engage in any activity that may bring discredit to his profession or to his Association, such as writing papers or theses for individuals attempting to qualify themselves or preparing other fraudulent documents, and he should promptly expose any illegal or unethical conduct he detects in his profession.

Principle 2

A medical writer should hold accuracy and truth to be primary considerations and he should provide well balanced, unbiased, undistorted information to the fullest extent of his capabilities. He should use authoritative (preferably original) sources as a basis for his writing, and he should give proper credit, including adequate documentation.

Principle 3

A medical writer should never knowingly write or condone the writing of medical information which does not meet high professional standards, whether or not such writing comes under the purview of any regulatory agency. He should always try to prevent the perpetuation of incorrect information, and he should write about a subject only when qualified to do so by training and experience or in collaboration with someone so qualified.

Principle 4

A medical writer should not function under conditions or terms which impair or impede proper application of his judgment and skills, which tend to lower the quality of his services, or which require unethical conduct.

Principle 5

A medical writer should constantly strive to enlarge and perfect his professional knowledge and skills. He should apply these fully, and he should actively participate in organizations that have as their objective the improvement of his profession.

Principle 6
A medical writer should respect the personal and confidential nature of professional records. He should not divulge, without proper authorization, any confidential patient, patent, or other private information to which he has access.

Principle 7
A medical writer may actively seek, through advertisements or other means, ethical professional assignments consistent with his talents and capacity to provide medical communication services. He should accept fair and reasonable remuneration for his services and should honor the terms of contracts he signs.

Principle 8
A medical writer should not exploit his Association financially or otherwise, and he should not use his Association, or its publications, or any activities of his colleagues for his own personal gain.

APPENDIX C

HEALTH-RELATED WRITERS' ASSOCIATIONS

American Medical Writers Association (AMWA)
5272 River Road, Suite 410
Bethesda, MD 20816
(301) 986-9119

The premier medical communicators' group, with a membership of close to 2,700 health professionals and free-lancers, AMWA publishes a *Freelance Directory* and offers members a recognition program, a Core Curriculum continuing-education program in five areas (editing, free-lance, pharmaceutical, public relations, and audiovisual); writing and editing workshops on a regional and individual chapter basis; and a periodic "Job Sheet." Publications include a quarterly journal, *Medical Communications*, bimonthly *AMWA Newsletter*, a membership directory, and local chapter newsletters. Dues are fifty-five dollars a year; membership is open at present.

National Association of Science Writers, Inc. (NASW)
Box 294
Greenlawn, NY 11740
(516) 757-5664

With 1,200 members, NASW holds meetings in conjunction with the American Association for the Advancement of Science, publishes a quarterly newsletter that includes "help-wanted" listings, and sells its membership mailing list to selected clients interested in contacting science writers, e.g., pharmaceutical companies and universities. Write for a free copy of "A Guide to Careers in Science Writing" prepared and distributed in association with the Council for the Advancement of Science Writing, Inc. Sponsorship by two NASW members is required for membership, which is open to writers primarily involved in science writing for at least two years prior to application. Annual dues: forty-five dollars.

Society for Technical Communication
815 Fifteenth St., NW
Suite #516
Washington, DC
(202) 737-0035

High technology today has a major thrust in medicine, and many medical writers work as technical communicators in the field. (See chapter 15, "Technical Writing.") Founded in 1960, the group now numbers nearly 9,000 members, who must be engaged full-time in some phase of technical communication and have been so engaged for at least a year preceding application. The society holds conferences, workshops, meetings, and recognition programs and provides employment referrals, resource information, and publications, including a quarterly newsletter (*Intercom*); journal (*Technical Communication*); and *Proceedings of the Annual Conference*. Membership is currently open; annual dues, fifty dollars.

Health Sciences Communication Association (HeSCA)
6105 Lindell Blvd.
St. Louis, MO 63112
(314) 725-4722

HeSCA is an international professional organization for biocommunicators involved in the instructional design, development, and dissemination of health-related audiovisual materials in human and veterinary medicine. Its 800 members include media managers, medical and allied health professionals, university faculty and industry representatives, biomedical libraries, program producers, and freelance writers. In addition to sponsoring workshops and a media recognition program HeSCA publishes an annual roster; bimonthly (*Feedback*); quarterly (*Journal of Biomedical Communication*); and *The Patient Education Sourcebook*; brochures, monographs, and indexes. Membership is open; annual dues, eighty-five dollars; students and retirees, forty dollars.

Bibliography

I. History/General Information

Ackernecht, Erwin H., M.D. *A Short History of Medicine.* Rev. ed. Baltimore: The Johns Hopkins University Press, 1982.

Cone, Thomas E., Jr. *History of American Pediatrics.* 1st ed. Boston: Little, Brown, 1979.

Fellman, Anita Clair, and Michael Fellman. *Making Sense of Self: Medical Advice Literature in Late Nineteenth Century America.* Philadelphia: University of Pennsylvania Press, 1981.

Garfield, Patricia, Ph.D. *Creative Dreaming.* New York: Ballantine Books, 1974.

Greene, V. W., Ph.D. *Cleanliness and the Health Revolution.* New York: The Soap and Detergent Association, 1985.

Hon. David. *Trade-offs for the Person Who Can't Have Everything.* Austin, TX: Learning Concepts, 1981.

Leys, Wayne, A. R. *Ethics and Social Policy.* New York: Prentice Hall, 1941.

Reich, Warren T., ed. *Encyclopedia of Bioethics.* 4 vols. New York: The Free Press, Macmillan, 1978.

Risse, Guenter B., Ronald L. Numbers, and Judith Walzer Leavitt, eds. *Medicine without Doctors: Home Health Care in American History.* New York: Science History Publications/USA, 1977.

Starr, Paul. *The Social Transformation of American Medicine.* New York: Basic Books, 1982.

———. *Dietary Guidelines for Americans.* 2d ed. Washington, DC: U.S. Departments of Agriculture and Health and Human Services, 1985.

———. *Eating for a Healthy Heart.* Rev. ed. Oakland: American Heart Association, Alameda County Chapter, 1984.

———. "Interim Dietary Guidelines" In *Diet, Nutrition, and Cancer.* Washington, DC: National Academy Press, 1982.

II. Writing/Communications/Research

Angione, Howard, ed. *The Associated Press Stylebook and Libel Manual.* New York: The Associated Press, 1979.

Appelbaum, Judith, and Nancy Evans. *How to Get Happily Published: A Complete and Candid Guide.* New York: Harper & Row, 1978.

Balkin, Richard. *How to Understand and Negotiate a Book Contract or Magazine Agreement.* Cincinnati, Writer's Digest Books, 1985.

Bloom, Murray Teigh, Richard Bode, and Sally Wendkos Olds. *The ASJA Handbook: A Writers' Guide to Ethical and Economic Issues.* New York: American Society of Journalists and Authors, 1985.

Bowen, Catherine Drinker. *Biography: The Craft and the Calling.* Boston: Little, Brown, 1969.

Brady, John. *The Craft of Interviewing.* New York: Random House, 1977.

Clark. Bernadine, ed. *Writer's Resource Guide.* 2d ed. Cincinnati: Writer's Digest Books, 1983.

Curtis, Richard. *How to Be Your Own Literary Agent.* Boston: Houghton Mifflin, 1983.

Deimling, Paula, ed. *1985 Writer's Market.* Cincinnati: Writer's Digest Books, 1984.

Duncan, Lois. *How to Write and Sell Your Personal Experiences.* Cincinnati: Writer's Digest Books, 1979.

Emerson, Connie. *Write on Target: Triple Your Magazine Sales through Magazine Market Analysis.* Cincinnati: Writer's Digest Books, 1981.

Evans, Glen, ed., and American Society of Journalists and Authors, Inc. *The Complete Guide to Writing Non-Fiction.* Cincinnati: Writer's Digest Books, 1983.

Gastel, Barbara, M.D. *Presenting Science to the Public.* Philadelphia: ISI Press, 1983.

Horowitz, Lois. *Knowing Where to Look: The Ultimate Guide to Research.* Cincinnati: Writer's Digest Books, 1984.

Huth, Edward J. *How to Write and Publish Papers in the Medical Sciences.* Philadelphia: ISI Press, 1982.

Kreps, Gary L., and Barbara C. Thornton. *Health Communication.* New York: Longman, 1984.

Leonard, Peggy C. *Building a Medical Vocabulary.* Philadelphia: W. B. Saunders, 1983.

A Manual of Style. 13th ed. Chicago: University of Chicago Press, 1982.

Metz, William. *Newswriting: From Lead to "30".* Rev. ed. Englewood Cliffs, N.J.: Prentice-Hall, 1979.

Polking, Kirk, ed. *Freelance Jobs for Writers.* Cincinnati: Writer's Digest Books, 1980.

Relman, A.S., M.D. "The Ingelfinger Rule." *The New England Journal of Medicine* 305(1981): 824-26.

Strunk, William, Jr., and E.B. White. *The Elements of Style.* 3d ed. New York: Macmillan, 1979.

Todd, Alden. *Finding Facts Fast.* 2d ed. Berkeley: Ten Speed Press, 1979.

Williams, W.P., and Joseph H. Van Zandt. *How to Syndicate Your Own Newspaper Column.* Chicago: Contemporary Books. 1979.

INDEX